Modern Organizations and
Emerging Conundrums

Modern Organizations and Emerging Conundrums

Exploring the Postindustrial
Subculture of the Third Millennium

Edited by Richard A. Goodman

LEXINGTON BOOKS
Lanham • Boulder • New York • Oxford

LEXINGTON BOOKS

Published in the United States of America
by Lexington Books
4720 Boston Way, Lanham, Maryland 20706

12 Hid's Copse Road
Cumnor Hill, Oxford OX2 9JJ, England

British Library Cataloguing in Publication Information Available

Library of Congress Cataloging-in-Publication Data

Modern organizations and emerging conundrums : exploring the postindustrial subculture of the third millennium / edited by Richard A. Goodman.
    p.   cm.
    Includes bibliographical references.
    ISBN 0-7391-0001-7 (cloth : alk. paper)
    1. Corporate culture.   2. Organizational behavior.   3. Management.
  I. Goodman, Richard Alan.
  HD58.7.M627   1999
  302.3'5—dc21   98-38582

Printed in the United States of America

♾ ™ The paper used in this publication meets the minimum requirements of American National Standard for Information Sciences—Permanence of Paper for Printed Library Materials, ANSI Z39.48–1984.

TO—Heather Höpfl, who once said, "This is YOUR conference, you run it!"

TO—Bill Hicks, who once said, "I would really like to be considered as the Publisher of a book from the conference!"

AND

TO—Ann Martin Pollack, whose editorial skills blended so well with my intent and whose long hours and late nights made the book come out on time.

CONTENTS

PREFACE

The history of this book is quite remarkable. It began many years ago when two Ph.D. students asked me to convene a tutorial in organizational culture. They knew I was untrained in the details but they felt I could effectively challenge them and the literature. They even offered to select and bring copies of the material we would discuss. Thus Culture Club was born. Over the course of three years, we met at least once a week—sometimes twice—for two or three hours a session. We talked, argued, and drank innumerable cups of coffee, adopting French roast as a symbol of our bonding. The meetings were incredible and the discussion were exhilarating and eventually served as a model for other engagements. They also proved to have a profound influence on my intellectual pursuits. Sonja Sackmann was the first to finish her studies and moved on—to Switzerland and Germany. Maggi Phillips followed closely behind but remained in the Los Angeles area. Thus, good students became good friends and good colleagues. The first paper of this book represents a later collaboration that occurred over breakfast and was initially written on the place mat at Café Montana.

Maggi and Sonja had learned of the Standing Conference on Organizational Symbolism (SCOS). Their annual conference was scheduled for June in Istanbul and we all decided to submit papers. Our papers were selected and we were placed on the same panel along with a few others. It was an eye opening experience; an intense and simultaneous immersion into the several cultures of Istanbul, European scholarship, SCOS traditions and more. Ironically, the panel we were placed on was entitled "The Future Prospects of Symbolism and Postmodern Research." Suddenly I was on a podium refereeing a discussion among sixty people whom I had only met two days earlier about a subject in which I was a novice. Fortunately, I survived the engagement and so did SCOS. This initial encounter evolved into a long-term involvement with SCOS that eventually led to the book at hand.

Back at UCLA I was later asked to convene an affinity group on "culture." The Director of UCLA's Center for International Business Education and Research

(CIBER) felt that the study of culture was an intrinsic and essential element in International Business Education. The resulting CIBER Cross Cultural Colloquium (C4) began with the meeting of about a dozen UCLA colleagues. The membership now includes forty faculty from twenty-five universities and spans sociology, anthropology, folklore, theater, communications and international business. We meet three times a year for an in-depth seminar setting that is quite unique—though modeled on Culture Club.

Several years later having survived these experiences I was willing to offer the Anderson School as a site for an annual SCOS meeting. Eventually my offer was accepted and in July, 1996 SCOS14 was held in Los Angeles. The initial conference theme was "Medium, Message, and Meaning" and was intended to highlight the idea of cultural diversity and media that are so central to Southern California. The Los Angeles population is arguably one of the most cosmopolitan in the world with some 92 languages spoken and 140 nationalities represented. As the time for the conference neared, the theme was amended to provide SCOS with an opportunity to honor the memory of the late Barry Turner who had been one of the founding forces in SCOS. The new theme "Exploring the Postindustrial Subculture" evolved directly from Barry's early work. This change stimulated me to consider a form of *festschrift* for Barry. And thus, this book was born.

About one hundred papers were presented at SCOS14. Some authors responded to one theme and some authors to the other theme. Some of the papers represented the author's passion more than a conference theme. Thus, I had an unusually diverse mix from which to cull papers for this volume. The conference concluding session was designed to elicit future themes among the conferees' research plan and thus the volume's 'emerging conundrum' concept was begun. Passion and engagement were more important as selection criteria than merely thematic fit. I wanted to highlight the variety of issues and approaches presented and planned and to create a slightly different (perhaps a postmodern) twist to the development of the book's "structure." The book is divided into untitled sections with interstitial material at the end—not the beginning. Thus readers are encouraged to make their own way through the book. The individual abstracts that precede each of the papers are intended to provide readers with sufficient clues so that they can select the order in which they wish to read the book. In this case, the story can be read differently and interpreted uniquely by each reader.

Before turning to the book proper, I want to clarify and demystify two terms—post industrial and postmodern. These terms to many seem almost interchangeable. To me, the terms are conceptually very different in origin and intent. Post industrial refers to the basic structure of the economy. This structure can be simply thought of as the shifting ratio of industrial jobs to service and other jobs in an economy. Commonly, we think of economies as hunter/gathering, agrarian, industrial and post industrial. Each structure creates different demands on location and yields different social systems. Industrial work requires that workers congregate at the location of the factories. Thus employment demands of industrial work demanded migration from rural areas to cities and the social fabric was rewoven. Service work requires workers to de-congregate and locate near the customers. Thus industrial economies require and permit much centralization while service economies require and permit much decentralization.

In contrast, postmodern refers to organizational structures that no longer model the industrial world of discipline, measurement, supervision and hierarchy. Postmodern thus refers to a way of organizing. In postmodern thought new issues of fragmentation, reflexivity, membership, locus of control and others become issues of concern. Once this looser sense of organization appears many new issues arise for organizational theorists. This is a description of the impact of the postmodern condition as viewed by an organization theorist. The causal factor according to Walter Anderson is when people all over the globe recognize that there are many beliefs and even many kinds of beliefs and in fact many ways of believing. All else follows from this fundamental change in the knowledge bases of the global society.

Neither postindustrial nor postmodern ideas exist in pure form. Fast food franchises, for example, are clearly postindustrial as they represent decentralized service. They are also clearly modern as they represent close measurement, supervision, and clear hierarchy. Thus concepts that evolve from postmodern thought can be identified within modern organizations and vice versa. With this said let me turn to the real work of a preface.

In the process of writing this book I became deeply impressed with the struggles and successes of the authors included within the text. They struggle with the search for knowledge, they struggle with the selection of a point of view, they struggle with communication. They succeed in producing work of robust character and compassion. They are prodigiously creative in their abilities to approach such basic issues from so many unique avenues and I am honored to be able to use their work within this compendium.

Thanks are also highly appropriate. Financial support for the LA SCOS Conference was provided by several sources. UCLA's Center for Business Education and Research (CIBER) through the good offices of Professor José de la Torre has been a long term supporter of this work. The Sidney Stern Foundation was a key supporter and I extend my thanks to Marvin and Betty Hoffenberg. The Graduate Division of UCLA through the good offices of Dean Robin Fisher was very supportive throughout the planning year and I am very grateful. Additionally, the staff at the Anderson Graduate School of Management, UCLA were incredible in their knowledgeable support and ability to provide the infrastructure necessary for all conferees.

The confidence expressed by the Standing Conference on Organizational Symbolism (SCOS) and its membership, one and all, by selecting the UCLA site and by attending the conference with such zeal created a truly exciting relationship and a memorable event. I particularly wish to compliment the chair of SCOS, Heather Höpfl for her support and encouragement. More directly related to this publication, I need to thank Bill Hicks, Publisher of The New Lexington Press, who from early on showed interest in the work but also skillfully brought to bear an expertise of unusual perspicuity. Similarly, my in-house copy editor and companion (read wife) Ann Pollack made *immense* contributions to the task of producing the book. Most specially, the book's quality is based upon the thoughtful and skillful work of some 30 wonderful authors. I have learned greatly from reading all the papers in fine detail and from this effort I have become increasingly impressed by the work of my colleagues!

1

EMERGING CONUNDRUMS IN MODERN ORGANIZATIONS: EXPLORING THE POSTINDUSTRIAL SUBCULTURE OF THE THIRD MILLENNIUM

Richard A. Goodman

The spirit of Barry Turner permeates this volume. His commitment to process and to play is clearly evident. Barry knew he was on a journey but he was unsure of where it was leading and never expected to arrive. There was a "Mosaic" quality to his work and life. Within this spirit, this book is a work-in-progress; a series of steps; some forward, others to the side.

Barry's spirit provides a springboard to the future rather than an anchor to the past. Thus, this *festschrift* features both new and established authors. Some authors knew Barry very well; others know only of his work; others know of his work as undocumented conventional wisdom in the field of organizational culture and symbolism. The force of his work flows through these many paths. As a result the process and substance of Barry's contributions appear both consciously and unconsciously within it.

Symbolically, Barry's book, *Exploring the Industrial Sub-culture* is the major touchstone of this work. Its publication marked the start of serious interest in the culture and symbolism of the Industrial Period. *Modern Organizations and Emerging Conundrums: Exploring the Postindustrial Subculture of the Third Millennium* plays upon this idea and marks a latter-day interest. The postindustrial context, arising amidst many social revolutions and embedded within earlier contexts, emerges slowly. The possible nature of this evolving subculture is the focus for this work.

The linear nature of text limits the structure of this exploration as culture is a gestalt. The use of specific techniques or points of view cannot fully take into account a rich gestalt. The medium of reporting what was 'seen, sensed, felt, etc.,' further limits the full appreciation of the culture. Finally, by bringing their own perspective to the work, readers further alter the meaning articulated by the various authors. Thus, the book is designed to permit readers full play between the authors and themselves.

Before describing the design in detail it is important to think about what we know and what we can communicate. S. I. Hayakawa in his *Language in Thought and Action* clearly employs issues of encoding and decoding limitations as significant barriers between what one *knows* and what one can *communicate*. Toni Morrison, in her Nobel lecture, further elaborates the limitations of language in the conveyance of meaning. To make some progress in overcoming these limitations this book works at many levels and from many angles.

Each section is composed of several papers. The way in which papers are clustered reflects my point of view. This essay and the structure of the sections create a framework for the exploration. But, in the spirit of inquiry, readers can approach this volume on their own terms. They can read the papers in any order. To encourage the reader to be an active participant in this exploration I have presented my perspective as concluding rather than introductory essays. In this manner, readers have the initial opportunity at sense making.

Perhaps the book structure can best be described through a weaving metaphor. This introductory essay delineates the warp and woof of the fabric. Sometimes the threads will cross one way to make up a pattern; at other times the threads are woven into a very different pattern. Although reading within sections will be satisfying, reading across sections may be intriguing as well. Selecting bits and pieces from several papers will allow readers to create unique points of view. Most importantly, within this volume the "meaning" of postindustrial subculture is highly dependent on the individual reader's use of several such frames.

THE PLATFORM

I look at the issues related to postindustrial subculture through the eyes of an organizational scientist searching for central features. I care most about features of the situation that empower or constrain action. Sometimes, I view this from the point of view of management and the manager. Sometimes, I focus on the employee. Other times I consider the issues of the student of organizations. In postindustrial terms it seems to me that organizational work and study must focus on heightened concern for the individual and for basic values.

To my mind the basic platform of the postindustrial subculture is the increased dignity offered to *individual interpretation* of events. Only this view permits different interpretations of the organizational scene from individual actors or from systematic observers to be accepted for their own worth. Acceptance of different inter-pretations is a newly articulated organizational phenomena and has impact for man-agers, employees, and organizational scientists. For the organizational actor the dig-nity afforded individual interpretation is consistent with a view that people select their behaviors with respect to their own interpretation of what they see and believe. For the organizational scientist observed behavior can be interpreted through several lenses and can accommodate the actor's interpretation as well as the observer's.

Support for this position derives from a blending of the many arguments and dis-cussions I have held with colleagues over the course of the past three decades. Time and space constraints allow me to refer to only a few—Eric Trist, Anne Huff, Ian Mitroff and Mary Jo Hatch. A very intriguing thesis that Eric wrote in the mid-six-ties argued that the basis of social power (or truth, in the Kluckhohn and Schrodt-beck sense) had shifted from the empirical to the paradigmatic. Theories rather than data became the touchstone of truth and action. While Eric's observation was at a high level of abstraction, he drew his data from observable shifts in scholarship at universities and in public policy debate. In the academy raw empiricism has since been de-emphasized and paradigm-driven work encouraged. For instance, the par-adigmatic quality of McKelvey's population perspective provides more insight into organizations and their environments than does Hannan's extensive empirical analysis and curve-fitting work on population ecology. Today paradigms help shape organizational activities to a far greater extent than the empirically derived work un-derpinning the paradigms. Similarly, organizational economics has more leverage as a system of thought than any of the empirical studies based upon it. The shift from empiricism to paradigm reinforces the concept of individual interpretation.

Ironically, as a paradigm matures it transforms into a constraint on individual interpretation. For instance, Giovanni Dosi speaks of paradigm-driven technolog-ical trajectories that specify the permitted questions and the permitted methods of answering. The mature paradigm then limits the nature of inquiry.

Anne Huff begins from a very different stimulus. She focuses on sense-making, asking How do individuals and companies make sense of their worlds? Starting with an 'intelligence' model, Anne asks How do uncommon events become inte-grated into cognition (conscious or otherwise)? These questions relate to organi-zational as well as individual cognition. Richard Normann used Fritz Heider's work to formulate a "domain–distant environment" dichotomy that foreshadowed Anne's interest in sense-making. Both Huff and Normann assume that sense-making is an individual interpretation of events or data points.

Ian Mitroff pursued parallel work when he studied moon scientists before and after the first Apollo moon landing. Ian's controversial book on the subjective side of science provided interesting empirical support for Anne's work. Whereas some scientists, when faced with the uncommon event of holding a piece of the moon in their hands, used this as data to revise their models of the moon, others rejected the uncommon event as too limited a sample for readjusting their views. Thus, in-dividual interpretation of the facts represented by a piece of the moon served to drive each scientist's ensuing research efforts. Some radically changed their course of inquiry; others continued on their current path.

From her early studies in Copenhagen, through work in California and back to Europe, Mary Jo Hatch has sharpened her focus on central questions of organizational theory. In her teaching, her research and her recent book she has focused upon individual interpretations of events and argued persuasively that they are a central issue for organizational analysis. She is concerned with what individuals see and how they place what they see into a mental model of the organization.

Of course this is my individual interpretation of these scholars' work. It is very personal and thus I symbolically represent my individual reading of the organizational literature by writing in the first person. Parenthetically, over time, I have begun observing a clear trend toward dignifying the individual's interpretation in the realm of management and action and within some arenas of organizational science.

The postindustrial subculture also seems to focus on values. If the touchstone of the industrial model is efficiency, perhaps the hallmark of the postindustrial model is effectiveness defined in the Barnardian sense. Barnard used the concept of effectiveness to refer to organizations in which people want to participate and with which they want to interact. Later sections of this essay will broaden this view and stretch it beyond its admittedly modernist origins.

In modern organizational design there have been innumerable steps that edge toward valuing the whole person. Some of these include flex-time, cafeteria-style fringe benefits, telecommuting and the creation of virtual organizations. Each recognize that individual needs must be included in the organization of the workplace and the work effort if effectiveness is to be enhanced. (Design for increased diversity in the workforce furthers the acceptance of individual differences on some rather basic levels.)

In many ways the postindustrial subculture appears to be moving toward accommodation of personal space, family space and workspace. The integration of personal values is slowly increasing in the industrial workplace and in the invention of new organizations that incorporate serious value-based propositions into their basic design. These values represent movement within the industrial subculture, a shift in emphasis from efficiency toward effectiveness. This focus can only be explored however by looking at extreme examples of postindustrial organizations or tendencies within an industrial model. As tendencies, this postindustrial movement is difficult to identify and often appears in subtle rather than dramatic fashion.

THE METHODS

The dignity of individual interpretation and the appearance of holistic values require increasingly robust methodical approaches for the study of postindustrial subculture. Traditional methods from ethnography to historiography continue to contribute, but narrative techniques, gendered research methods, and multi-interpretive material all shed different kinds of light upon the work of the field. Deconstruction as an approach clearly represents an individual interpretation. But the inherent difficulties in the search for 'meaning' coupled with the limitations of words and symbols to express 'meaning' almost require a personal interpretive basis to organizational science.

The methodical challenge is further exacerbated by rapid shifts in the media of the postindustrial subculture. The shift is occurring in both communications and organization structure. It facilitates inter-penetration of meaning from cultures around the world and across the city. This shift drives new media-related analytic methods.

An example of this is seen in the final performance of a dance workshop I recently attended, which featured some forty college students from Asia. The student were the authors, the designers and the choreographers of the performance. The imagery and mimicry of Occidental culture in their dances was accurate and natural. While most of the performance was clearly of Asian character, the inter-penetration of foreign culture was presented with ease. It is obvious that the resultant inter-penetration of artifacts and meanings must be part of the warp and woof of this volume.

THE SUBSTANCE

What is really going on in the postindustrial subculture? More and more I see *teams,* I see *cross-organizational* teams, I see *international* teams. I see increasing numbers of *service and leisure organizations*—some based on an industrial model, others based on a postindustrial model. I find substantial impacts of *information technology* and the creation of *virtual organizations.* I see various impacts of *media* qua media and of media qua *carnival;* of bigger-than-life impacts reflecting on organizational behavior and organizational expectations. I see *ideas that exploit* as well as *illuminate.* And, I see organizations investing more in the idea of the *whole individual.* These represent my vision. I encourage readers to look at this vision from other angles in order to weave their own tapestry.

The platform is a logical beginning. A commentary on methods is a logical next observation. The remaining categories are not so logical. They are placed here in Mondrian-like blocks with some limited connections to the other blocks within the overall fabric.

TEAMS, CROSS-ORGANIZATIONAL TEAMS, INTERNATIONAL TEAMS

Viewing organizations as monocultural is becoming increasingly problematic. Viewing organizations as multicultural is becoming more prevalent over time. Traditional cultures such as ethnicity and nationality, and task-oriented cultures such as finance or marketing or human resources, may co-exist. Or the cultures may be the mix of subcultures that each individual brings to the organization every day. This view leads to increasingly complex organization theories.

One response to the complexity of task and traditional cultures—of members, of customers, of markets, of stakeholders—is the increasing use of cross-organizational teams. Some teams are deployed as temporary systems for specific objectives. Others are established as permanent methods for handling the tasks of the work place. In my view, a prominent feature of postindustrial subculture is the increasing employment of cross-organizational teams.

Teams are found within and across function. Teams are found within and across organizations. Teams are found domestically, regionally and globally. We now realize that teams have a higher variance in make-up and operation than previously examined by traditional industrial organizational theorists. Complex organizational and trans-organizational teams are an artifact of the postindustrial subculture.

An interesting artifact of the trans-organizational are some of the acronyms coined to describe this phenomenon, such as Mike Lawless's DIOS (Directed Inter-Organizational Systems) or Rosabeth Kanter's PALS (pooling, allying, linking across companies). Only when the monocultural view of organization begins to weaken can the real complexity of organizational life emerge. The team phenomenon suggests that organizational boundaries begin to blur and organizational members are thus placed in ambiguous situations. The team member doesn't always know whether the functional manager or the team manager is the boss. This ambiguity is often unresolved organizationally and permits the team member to exercise personal judgment by default. Organizational ambiguity empowers the individual and this, I believe, is another central feature of the postindustrial subculture.

SERVICE AND LEISURE ORGANIZATIONS

The most common Sunday supplement view on the postindustrial subculture is the increase in leisure time and the concomitant increase in service organizations. This journalistic speculation is fascinating and, in fact, the data has supported this trend for decades.

Paging through the local Sunday newspaper provides an interesting glimpse into the postindustrial subculture. The preponderance of articles highlight not-for-profit organizations rather than for-profit ones. These organizations range from government to social action to religious. A far greater number of these organizations focus on leisure and service rather than production. Some are loose associations, others tight formal ones. Some are clearly postindustrial and other may be. Since I first did this newspaper scan in the early 1970s, if anything the number of organizations in the not-for-profit arena has proliferated.

The 'for' and 'not-for' dichotomy, of course, is only a way to make a point simply. In reality, many for-profit organizations are in the service and leisure industries and increasingly many of these have social objectives as well as profit motives. Thus, many organizations resist pure categorization.

In parallel is the evolving postindustrial service metaphor that implies an adaptive capability which permits an organization to recreate itself in order to provide customer satisfaction. As a result, one of the clear conflicts plaguing emerging postindustrial organizations is the internal tension between the efficient and the effective. This conflict is felt most keenly by the front line members of the organization—those who actually deal with customers. They are frequently caught between the organizational metaphor of service and the older industrial measures of efficiency. Central to this cultural conflict is member discretion—whether permitted or not; whether exercised or not. Thus, within the postindustrial subculture there is significant pressure on individual members to exercise judgment and opportunities for individual discretion. These are two facets of the postindustrial subculture that require balance between conflicting organizational foci.

IMPACTS OF INFORMATION TECHNOLOGY AND THE CREATION OF VIRTUAL ORGANIZATIONS

Information technology (IT) *creates culture* and drives the *inter-penetration* of that culture globally. It occurs through its pan global reach. Opportunities for IT to transcend boundaries effectively have opened the door to the *creation of a wide range of 'virtual' organizations*. Both features of information technology—the creation and the inter-penetration of culture—have dramatic effects on postindustrial subculture.

Information technology has multiple impacts that unify and mystify. For instance, Microsoft software has provided users with shared experiences that traverse organizations and with results that we reify and vilify. In the early days of IBM (Big Blue), many of the same concerns were articulated. These technologies, by their very structure, permit and demand inter-penetration of culture across international boundaries. In conversations about function keys and work-arounds, bits and bytes, information technology provides a shared experience on the one hand, and a structured language and thought pattern on the other.

Technology itself and the language of technology are socially constructed. When the technology itself is endemic, the way we talk about it becomes a world language, an area of shared concern. Concerns about user friendliness, using MAC or WINTEL machines, using desktops or laptops, are some of the common issues we all discuss and which shape the discussion of information technology.

Over time, questions of concern shift to new words and concepts with equally elusive meanings. Is it client server architecture? What level of interoperability can we anticipate? The cultural artifacts of these "created" issues are widely represented. These are the problems with which we wrestle when we choose to purchase hardware or software. IT provides enhanced communication capabilities and has permeated the globe. Hence it focuses part of our attention on the means of communication and in this fashion becomes a central artifact of our organizational setting.

Even globally shared artifacts do not necessarily have the same socially constructed meanings and require serious investigation before underlying cultural attribution can occur. Thus the elusive character of the concepts permit a wide range of understanding and misunderstanding; and substantial variance in literal and symbolic meaning.

In the Zen sense, when 'distance' shrinks, cultural disparity shrinks and overlaps among cultures increase. Increased knowledge is exciting but the potential extinction of differences is abhorrent. Nonetheless, these dichotomous counter tensions are clearly a central feature of the postindustrial landscape.

Information technology also has direct organizational effects. The relative efficiency of the electronic communication environment permits the creation of a myriad of virtual organizations and quasi-virtual organizations. Let me describe a few.

Several years ago four editors decided to start a publishing company. They then discovered that each wanted to live in a different locale. Since the manuscript acquisition process requires significant travel, they quickly realized that even if they established a central office they would not spend a lot of face to face time together. Since much of their communications could be handled by IT, they decided create a centerless organization, bow to personal preferences about individual locations and use a centrally located airport as a meeting point when needed.

Papers delivered at the 14th Standing Conference on Organizational Symbolism held in Los Angeles were available online to all participants with a web browser. While insufficient to the task of SCOS, it was widely praised as an effective method of organizing. To date it remains on-line, facilitating post-meeting efforts and allowing other scholars to visit the site. The pre- and post-participation in the SCOS community has greatly increased without requiring the full face-to-face interactions available at the conference itself.

These two vignettes are primarily about the ability to work together from a distance while staying in your own locale. The role of the individual is strengthened by such arrangements. IT can have a substantive and enabling impact in the postindustrial subculture.

IMPACTS OF MEDIA AND CARNIVAL

Media depicts organizational life willy-nilly. The characters are ensconced in organizations of all types. These situations broadcast diverse images of organizational life both good and bad. Daily, the images thus created are carried to work by viewers. Frequently it is these images that form the basis of the viewer's organizational expectations. Whether the expectations are good or evil, realistic or romanticized, real or surreal, they have impact. Viewers observe more behaviors in organizations through endemic exposure to media then they would normally experience first-hand. Thus, typical or stereotypical organizational behaviors are created for viewers who use those images as models for determining whether behaviors in their organization are congruent or discrepant to media-formed expectations. Media plays an increasing role in the formulation of organizational expectations, thus providing a platform for the inter-penetration of culture from outside the organization and from outside local cultural bases.

The role of media is, itself, controversial. It is perceived as a means by which culture can be attacked and behavior effected. With rare exception the controversy is couched in negative terms—i.e., it is a threat. Media is not often seen as a social force that protects culture or improves behavior.

Media can create enabling conditions for organizations to become reified in the image of their public leadership. Organizations and organizational individuals play roles that are clearly carnival-esque in the Bakhtinian sense. In a perverse fashion, the mediated organizational leader becomes an example of the acceptance of the whole person and the integration of life with work. Because media permits many more impacts of symbol and imagery in the postindustrial subculture it is simultaneously a cause and an effect.

THE WHOLE INDIVIDUAL

The Quality of Life (QoL) movement in the sixties, the cafeteria fringe benefit movement of the eighties, the leadership seminars of the sixties and the nineties all have in common the sense that organizational members bring their 'whole' life to 'work' each day. The QoL movement was driven by concerns for the working class and developed from the shop floor up. Other concerns were driven from a human-resource perspective but were essentially top down. The sources of all these concepts are clearly modernist. But their evolution reflects an increasing sense of the whole individual—one that permits emotion, passion and spirit to be reflected in the arrangements between people and their associations.

IDEAS EXPLOIT AS WELL AS ILLUMINATE

Exploitation is central to the ever-changing definition of the economic systems under which we operate. The concept of efficiency originated in European scholarship—Weber, Fayol, etc. The social construction of the economic system in European, in Asian, in North American, in Eastern European, in Latin American and in African are very different and the evolution of these systems has led to efficiency and exploitation, to expectations and disillusionment, etc. The basic economic systems ideas were illumination in some instances and exploitation within others. Punk music, for example, while embraced by the blue collar disenfranchised in Europe, is a music of the wealthy alienated in North America. Democracy (whatever that means) is an anathema to some and a boon to others. The forces of change, social movements, etc. are imperfectly worked out by their disciples, uneven in their short-run effects, and often uneven in their long-run effects. But ideas like paradigms specify the questions that can be asked and the methods that can be used to formulate responses. Thus the imperfection of the ideas underlying ideals can lead to exploitation and abuse in the eyes of the actors or the observers.

POSTINDUSTRIAL SUBCULTURE

I find that the postindustrial experience involves a shift from Weber and Taylor's hierarchy to Hedlund's heterarchy. Its organizational response to complexity in parallel with increasing recognition of the dignity of individuals create a break-down of traditional structures and even of definitions of organizations and/or their boundaries. This involves a transcendent vision of organizations that invokes idealism, carnival, and the gestalt of life. Perhaps in some way McLuhan's global village is a good metaphor.

2

IN SEARCH OF WHAT IS LEFT OUT IN THE MEDIUM OF WORDS

Ulla Johansson

I often think about "words."

I find myself focusing, not on words, but on what is left out by words.
What does the discourse of "words" repress?
I fumble after the perspective,
I find myself in a country where I have no idea about the borders,
in a countryside without contours.

I only know there is another side that is not the opposite side,
but the repressed side.
I have encountered a side where emotions,
feelings, and moods are
not only essential,
not only the essence,
but the very IT.

Once I found it difficult to separate emotions from words.
Words and emotions were almost the same.
I found it difficult "only to feel,"
my deeper feelings were almost always accompanied by words,
or by thoughts that were geared by words
I had difficulties
in having emotions without words.

I know this intellectualizing only because I know the surprise I felt
when someone talked about emotions without words.
Do they exist?
I am not sure.
Emotions, even when I do not have a single word in my head,
are shown to be social constructions,
carrying the world and attitudes
constructed by institutional and taken for granted thought structures,
constructed unconsciously from early childhood and onwards.

How can I say whether my emotions exist without words or not?
That is a question impossible to answer,
maybe even a non-interesting one.

What fascinates me, is the very fact that I am able to construct this
division
between emotions and words.
I am also drawn by fascination to the connections between the two of
them,
but even more fascinated I am by the fact that it is
only when the division,
only when the separation first is done
that the connection can be discussed.

So separation becomes the prerequisite for connection.
If I were an engineer or a positivist scholar,
I would perhaps look for a simple relationship,
a formula,
a bridge.
Because they are two different countries, aren't they?
Or are they?
They are two universes and one in the same.

I am not an engineer I am not a positivist,
I am a social constructionist who asks myself
how to construct these complex multidimensional dimensions
between something that is separated and united at the same time,
between something that is one and many at the same time?
This is my question.

If I had a simple answer,
I would be a liar.
There are no simple answers to such questions.

However, I think it is those questions where you find no answers
that are the triggering questions,
the questions to be posed,
the questions to be elaborated,
the questions to construct multiple answers toward
to elaborate and unfold perspectives around.
It is, as Asplund says, not the answers that are the most important,
but the questions that are posed.

Though I agree with Asplund,
I sometimes think that what is most important
is not the questions
but the grounds on which the questions rely,
the ground from which they are posed,
the assumptions that are taken for granted,
the world to which they belong and lush and rest
like something heavily relying, something almost impossible to move away
from that ground to which it is connected like having roots in it.

If I am interested in words and emotions
I have to explore and walk around in the world of them separately.
At least I think so.
But maybe it is not possible,
maybe it should be regarded only a wish to elaborate
the construction of these worlds,
a wish that should not be realized because it is not possible to realize,
or maybe not desirable.
At least I must be open towards that possibility . . .

Luce Irigaray talks about words that have always been around,
Marie Cardinal talks about words that deliberate.
Though I feel very sympathetic with both of them,
words have in my mind a very ambivalent place.
My emotional conception of words is schizophrenic.
Using words is like breathing the air,
and with the help of words I can throw both hate and love
through the air, through paper or through electronic mail.
Words carry or evoke emotions.
Words are an important part of communications;
actually almost the only one accepted for academic seminars and
examinations.

Words can open doors and set free.
But words can also oppress and imprison.

Imprison both the aware and unaware me,
both my conscious and unconscious self.

Sometimes I love words,
but often I am afraid of them.
Words in communication can help me center myself,
but sometimes they also rinse me away from the center of life.

If I shall be honest, I must confess that the most magical time,
the most interesting loving parts of life
are when there are no words whatsoever in my head,
when my head is empty,
when my being and my feeling is in the whole body,
when I can feel the vibrating life in my body and don't bother about
words.

My words and my talking is subjective
talking constitutes myself,
I construct my world view with help of words.
But sometimes, when I have no words,
when my ego almost dissolves,
I become myself even more,
separated or lonely
and an integrated part of the universe
at the same time.

These moments I would like to catch.
I would like to catch them
without words.
I try to say yes to them as soon as they come.
But I also try to formulate these universes
that I have no words to formulate,
that I am not, at least not yet, able to formulate
to give words to.

I have a wish. Only the future can tell whether this wish to capture in words, something that might not be captured in words, can be so.

Because sometimes words are like birds.
With the help of words I can sometimes remember the feelings
I once had but no longer have.
When I dress these feelings in words,
words become messages,

messages that at the very same time are the message itself.
Messenger and message merge like for the angels.
Sometimes similar feelings as I once had,
can evoke in myself,
or in another person.
The feelings and the situations, sometimes can be reconstructed.
But it is not a copy,
it is not the same.
It is a re-construction,
a construction that is made again
but inspired by the situation that did evoke them.
Therefore birds are not bringing what was there,
but as the birds are metaphors,
what the birds bring are also metaphors,
images and pictures of something that is actually neither images nor
pictures,
but feelings.

In Edinburgh library in November 1995 there was an exhibition called
"words." But the interesting thing with it was that it was not words
that were shown.
It was illustrations of words,
it was pictures,
coverings to books, advertisement pictures,
that was picturing and illustrating words.
It was showing something that was neither opposite nor same as words,
but just another dimension,
something complementary to words,
something with even more of essence,
more concentration,
with more abstraction and yet more concrete than words.

When seeing that, I wonder . . .
these discourses of words and pictures,
what do they oppress?
These pictures show something else than words,
but what "else," what other dimensions were not shown
while showing these?

In our conference we can progressively use not only words
but also chose to illustrate our worlds with pictures.
It is coming more and more.

But what is not coming?
What do we still leave out?
What illusions of wholeness do we create
by expanding into pictures and images?

In my mind taste comes first.
The taste of wine,
the taste of salt and sugar,
the smelling.
Yes, you can have a book about wine.
And yes, a book about wine can be much more dense and essential
if it is also illustrated with photos and pictures.
The pictures and photos of wine can give something that is
hard to capture with words.
But those pictures and words can hardly substitute the taste of wine.
The words around wine
and the taste of wine becomes almost meaningless
for a person that never tasted a glass of wine.
The audience constitutes the performance
and the connoisseurness of the audience constitutes
what is connected or associated to the text and the picture . . .
Not only the performer but also the audience is totally crucial
for the construction of the performance.
If the voice isn't heard, or the vibrations not seen
the body,
the emotions,
the voice becomes mute.

Gilligan talks about another voice,
a voice that is to be listened to.
I would like to go further,
to embrace life into what is mute,
constructing perspectives of what has been overlooked,
not seen,
not heard
. . . and embrace it all with words.

The day before I went to the exhibition about words, I bought a book
about
dance.
That book was only words.
It was words about the anthropology of dance,
about style,

about feminism and dance,
about the body.
There are few such books.
Maybe one reason is that dance is neither words nor pictures,
neither a smell (except for maybe sweat) or a taste (except for as a
metaphor).
Dance is something else, another dimension.
A dimension that is not one, but many.
Different dances do not communicate the same,
do not speak the same languages.
There are lots of languages, different richness, different rules.
I think dance is a language that is not a language.
Since dance is not only a communication, but also something else.
It is something else, it is the place of the other country, or the
universe of emotions.
And it is that universe of dance that fascinates me.
Yes, dance is communication.
But not only communication with the audience,
dance is also a communication with yourself.
Not only a communication with your aware self,
dance is also surprising yourself.
Dance is uncapturable in words,
and of course in some paradoxical ways
possible to capture at the same time.
I think that my challenge in this LA conference will be
to capture dance in words
as much as I can,
and try to capture and give to the audience, to my colleagues,
some conceptions of what dance is to me.
To make myself aware of what it is
and try to communicate this in the media of dancing to my colleagues.
But not only that . . . because I am not a marvelous dancer,
and it is not a dance conference.
It is a conference about organizations,
and I am fascinated by the relations of these hidden dimensions
and whether similar hidden dimensions are there to be explored in
organizations.

Then I come back to the universe of emotions.
Emotions without words . . . that is what organizations are filled with.

Emotional structures in organizations
was the title of PO Berg's dissertation

(one of the SCOS founders).
It shows that the emotional structure is something
that is structuring the conversation,
structuring the organization,
structuring even the organizational charts
and the agenda of strategic development.

The world of emotions is not something obscure,
not something remote,
maybe remote from the aware academic seminars.
They do exist there too, of course,
though a lot of time, as we all know, in a very negative form.
They do exist in organizations but in positive and in negative form.
But we sometimes treat them as if they were taboo.

I would like to reflect around why they are taboo.
I would like to explore these taboos and their relations.
The relations to words.
And if I with help of words, could show some new perspectives,
could open up and unfold,
or maybe even connect the world of emotions with what . . . ?

I do not even know what bridges are to be constructed,
since I do not know where to put the separations,
do not know the lines of demarcation that Popper thought so important.
I only know that there is something oppressed,
maybe not so much in organizations necessarily (as Argyris told us),
because out in organizations, in praxis, they live.
They are there.
Oppressed more in the academic discourse
than in the reality that we do not picture
but that we reconstruct in our academic reality.

I would like to reflect around the differences of these two universes
and
what dimensions are left out when we move from the one to the other.
I would like to put more questions,
because it is only through constructing questions that it is possible to
give answers
to at least some of them. But the answers lie within the
questions.

---

and some other thoughts about love and social sciences:

Questions we don't ask
or
Where did the love perspective on science go (discursively repressed)?
Where is the love perspective in social sciences?

We all know by our own experiences
that the world looks different
depending on what mood we are in.

If we are angry, happy or sad,
the mood and emotions influence what we see
and how we construct our reality.

We all know that a text written in anger
looks different from one written with love.
That the emotional platform
influences what we see and how we talk and communicate
about the reality we perceive and construct.

We have learnt to analyze the paradigmatic grounds
for our scientific constructions, for our texts,
but why haven't we learnt to analyze
the emotional platform
from which a text is constructed?

And what would happen if a researcher
would have to take responsibility
for that platform
and defend
the emotional ground on which
his or her text is constructed?

And what would happen if the texts in human sciences
were written from a love perspective?

In social sciences today
a critical perspective is, for good reasons, encouraged.
But what about the love perspective?

SECTION ONE

3

THE COMPLEX CULTURE OF
INTERNATIONAL PROJECT TEAMS

Richard A. Goodman, Margaret E. Phillips and Sonja A. Sackmann

Project teams have become increasingly important in dealing with non-routine, complex, interdisciplinary, and international tasks. In this chapter the project team is used as a case example for exploring the cultural milieu of the multicultural project. Employment of a viewpoint that recognizes the simultaneous existence of geographically based cultures, societal sub-groups, cross-organizational, organizational and sub-organizational cultures permits increased insight into the cultural complexity of the international project team and development of themes for future research.

INTRODUCTION

Project teams are a frequently used approach to address non-routine, complex, interdisciplinary and time-limited tasks that cannot be handled by the firm's regular organization (Goodman, 1981; Steinbuch, 1987). With trends toward internationalization and globalization, project teams become increasingly international in their objectives and their membership.

While the technical aspects of managing projects have been addressed by both researchers and practitioners (Steiner and Ryan, 1968; Goodman, 1981; Madauss, 1991), the functioning of the project team itself and its effects on the team's performance have received significantly less attention (Goodman 1981; McCaskey,

1983). Virtually ignored have been the added complications inherent in international project teams. Selected in part for their diversity, it is that diversity of individual members that must be tapped and tempered if the group is going to coalesce into a well-functioning 'team.'

Part of the diversity of the project team is the multiplicity of cultures that various members bring with them. Part of what encourages their coalescing is that they already share certain cultures in common. As the members proceed with their task, part of what evolves is a unique way of thinking and doing their work together: *a distinctive project team culture.*

Diverse cultures, shared cultures, evolving cultures—all are part of the complex, multifaceted cultural context of international project teams. To address questions about the way multiple cultures impact on the development and functioning of project teams, we present a description of an international project team. We explore it from both the widely held traditional view of culture and from an expanded cultural perspective.

THE EUROFIN TEAM

The EuroFIN project team convened for the first time. They entered the conference room, gathered around the large table, greeted old colleagues and introduced themselves to new ones. Some knew others, having worked together in pairs and in groups on other projects within their own companies over the past several years. Some had communicated with one or a few of the assembled individuals solely through telephone and FAX. One had been recently hired; some were newly promoted. All were pleased to accept assignment to the project team that was to develop the new software package for distribution by SoftPak's European subsidiary, EuroPak. The product, currently dubbed "EuroFIN," was actually an adaptation of a highly successful financial software package—SoftFIN—introduced in the U.S. by SoftPak three months earlier. Several members of the group that had produced that winning product were around the table that day. All had anxiously anticipated this first meeting of the new project team.

THE TRADITIONAL VIEW OF CULTURE

Traditional cross-cultural management literature (Adler, 1991; Hofstede, 1980; Nath, 1988; Trompenaars, 1994) leads us to believe that the complexity experienced by international project teams is represented largely by the different passports carried by the team members: specifically, the U.S.-based SoftPak culture and the several European *national cultures* represented by the EuroPak participants. In this still-dominant view, culture is bound by national borders and observed differences are ascribed strictly to national cultural differences.

More recent research indicates that cultural differentiation based solely on national context is too coarse (Boyacigiller et al., 1996; Sackmann, 1997). Explorations into *organization*-based *cultures* (Frost et al., 1985, 1991; Jones et al., 1988; Schein, 1985, 1992; B. Schneider, 1990; Trice and Beyer, 1991) remind us that culture may exist at the organizational and sub-organizational level. When applied to the scenario presented above, distinct SoftPak and EuroPak cultures may exist. Additionally, the cultural residue of the *prior project team* may also be present, carried by those members of the original SoftFIN team assigned to this new team. Thus, we have an expanded list of those cultural groups whose mindsets may influence the development and functioning of this new EuroFIN project team—national, organizational and sub-organizational groups.

With only this minor reconceptualization, we can see that the cultural milieu of a newly formed project team is substantially more complex. To gain an even broader understanding, we must take a truly *cultural perspective* (Boyacigiller et al., 1996; Phillips and Sackmann, 1992) on project team life. To do so, we start with a general definition of culture and explore its implications for the scenario presented above.

A GENERAL DEFINITION OF CULTURE

Culture is a set of assumptions shared by a group of people. The set is distinctive to the group. The assumptions serve as guides to acceptable perception, thought, feeling, and behavior, and they may become manifest in the group's values, norms, actions, and artifacts. The assumptions are tacit among members, are developed through and evolve from group experience, are learned, and are passed on to each new member of the group (adapted from Phillips, 1994:384).

Here we characterize *"culture"* as a *dynamic, shared mindset*. We probe to its deeper core. We go beyond the physical symbols and artifacts of culture; beyond its behavioral and verbal manifestations, and the formal and informal norms into which it is encoded. We even go beyond its mores, ethics, and values, to those tacit, shared meanings that serve as the basis for "the collective mind" (Sackmann, 1991a)—a unique set of assumptions. For each culture impacting upon the project team, it is this set of assumptions that must be identified as we explore the team's cultural context (Sackmann, 1991b, 1992).

This definition implies that *a unique collection of assumptions distinguishes one cultural group from another*. In identifying cultures relevant to a project team's environment, attention must be paid both to the variety of assumptions that form a particular culture's core *and* to the elements of the assumption sets that differentiate cultures from one another (Sackmann, 1992, 1997). From this delineation, it may be seen that overlapping, superimposed, and/or nested cultures may exist around, across, and/or within project teams. Also, as it evolves, a team may develop a shared set of assumptions unique to their group (McCaskey, 1983)—*a project team culture*.

To determine the way these cultural groups are realized within the project team environment, we must consider another implication of the definition: that *culture is a group phenomenon enacted by individual members*. As they come to the group setting and as they approach the task, individual members of the project team bring with them various cultural mindsets acquired outside the team and even outside the organizational setting. It is by virtue of their possible enaction in the team setting by an individual team member that a culture becomes relevant to the project team's cultural milieu.

We must also recognize that the *team members themselves are carriers of multiple cultures*. Project team members are not citizens of simple, mono-cultural societies, but rather of contemporary complex society (Sackmann, 1989). And contemporary society, "instead of [a single] all embracing 'design for living', involves its members in many such designs" (Van Maanen and Barley, 1983:3). As such, individual team members may not consistently use a single set of cultural assumptions. Rather, they may shift their cultural identity depending on the issue at hand, drawing from the different mindsets they carry. Thus, the project team itself can be characterized as the potential carrier of a multiplicity of separate, overlapping, superimposed, and/or nested cultures, with team members maintaining simultaneous membership in any number of these cultural groups.

To identify these multiple cultural groups that have the potential to impact on project team life, we return to the scenario of the newly formed EuroFIN team and apply this perspective to the collection of individuals around the table at the first EuroFIN team meeting.

THE CULTURAL CONTEXT OF EUROFIN— AN EXPANDED VIEW

RAUL RODRIGUEZ, project team leader, was undertaking his first team management assignment. A pivotal member of the original SoftFIN team, Raul had been hand-picked to lead this new team because of his extensive knowledge of the product, his experience adapting several other SoftPak products for the European market, and his outstanding organizational and human relations skills. His recent promotion to management had been long in coming and had been achieved subsequent to a move from SoftPak's Houston office. This was despite the fact that Raul was an exceptional software engineer (a profession with which he identified wholly) and that his potential management skills were well recognized among his peers. Constantly aware of being the only person of Mexican descent in the Texas office, Raul had a lingering feeling that he might have been promoted faster had he been situated at one of SoftPak's other locations.

Thus, Raul brings to the table, at minimum, his *national culture* (United States), his *ethnic culture* (Mexican-American), the culture of the software engineer which is *professionally* based, the SoftPak *organizational culture,* and the SoftFIN *project team culture.* Concurrently, he may also be learning the SoftPak *managerial culture.*

HANS KELLER, a long-time EuroPak employee, was one of the firm's most senior software designers and was the senior engineer in the company's small Frankfurt office. He had worked closely with Raul on several previous project teams, modifying U.S. products for the European market. Hans enjoyed working on these multi-national teams and especially working with Raul, whom he regarded as the consummate software engineer. However, both EuroPak and SoftPak had been unable to lure Hans away from his homeland to a permanent assignment in the former's Paris headquarters or London regional center or the latter's Silicon Valley headquarters.

Hans carries to the EuroFIN team his *German national culture,* the EuroPak *organizational culture,* the *software engineering culture,* and, possibly, *previous project team cultures.* Hans' project teams' cultural mindsets may include those that he shares with Raul.

CAROLYN CONROY, a newly minted computer scientist, had begun her career only a few months earlier with SoftPak. An MIT graduate, she was fully accepted in her technical role by the engineering staff. She found, however, that she was not fully accepted by the secretarial staff, who were noticeably reticent about doing work for her. In completing her previous assignments, Carolyn was constantly shifting between being a "member of the technical staff" and one of the "girls"—never knowing exactly when each behavior was appropriate or whether it really made any difference. She trusted that she would be perceived by her fellow EuroFIN team members as she was by her SoftPak engineering colleagues, although the team was an otherwise all-male, international group. She was wary, however, as she was aware that EuroPak's professional ranks were exclusively male.

Carolyn clearly brings a *gender-based cultural mindset* to the team, which may become salient both in relation to the male team members and in relation to the female clerical support staff. She may also carry the *software engineering culture* and, in contrast to the German Hans, an American *cultural mindset.* By virtue of her years at MIT in Boston, she may also bring a variation on the American mindset— the *regional culture of the Northeast United States.* A new hire, Carolyn is probably still learning the SoftPak *organizational culture.*

JOHN DOUGLAS had been hired by SoftPak several years earlier specifically to work on the development of the original SoftFIN product. Most of his work life had been spent designing software in the aerospace industry in Southern California. John was approached by SoftPak because they had learned of his extensive experience designing and maintaining financial software for project monitoring, a skill not possessed by other SoftFIN team members. Yet, despite John's ability to make a unique contribution to SoftFIN, opposition to hiring him exists. "We never hire anyone from aerospace; their 'performance first' way of thinking ends up costing us too much money in development and brings us too little benefit in the commercial marketplace" was the argument mounted by his opponents.

John might still be viewed by some as the carrier of the *aerospace industry culture.* In fact, he may still actually use that mindset under certain circumstances.

Like Raul, Hans, and Carolyn, John also brings to the table the *software engineering culture,* and like Raul, he may carry to this new project the culture of the previous SoftFIN *project team.* John is also the carrier of the *American national culture* and the *California regional culture.* And, although working strictly with the SoftFIN team during his time at SoftPak, he almost surely has become acculturated into the larger SoftPak organizational *culture.*

> *The new team's marketing experts, DENNIS MALLORY and MARCO BENEDETTO, had worked together on the international marketing campaign for the firm's successful word processing program. Also, both were graduates of UCLA's MBA program, although they had attended the program in different years. An Italian, Marco had been a product marketing manager working out of the EuroPak's Paris headquarters for the past five years. Dennis, an African American and a native Californian, had been a SoftPak product marketing manager for eight years. Most recently, Dennis had served on the SoftFIN project team and had been largely responsible for the marketing campaign that launched that product.*

It is certain that Dennis and Marco each bring their *national cultural mindsets*— American and Italian, respectively—to the table. They most likely share the *UCLA management school organizational culture* and a *marketing management culture,* as well as that of the *word processing program project team.* Marco most likely carries the *EuroPak organizational culture,* while Dennis carries that of the American-based *SoftPak organization,* although both ostensibly could have in common the culture of the larger *SoftPak/EuroPak global enterprise.* Dennis may also bring both his *ethnic* (African American) and his *regional* (Californian) cultural mindsets to the table and, like Raul and John, probably also carries the residue of the *SoftFIN project team culture.*

> *Peter McMorris, project controller, had spent the last eight years of his career working as a budget officer in SoftPak's Route 128 office just outside of Boston. Peter's recent promotion to the controller's office at the company's Silicon Valley headquarters, and his assignment to this new project team, were the result of his outstanding work on several intermediate-sized international projects (Raul and Hans had been on the team of one of these projects). Born and raised in Boston, Peter felt somewhat out of place in his new California environs. But he was pleased that he had negotiated into his new contract release time to pursue a graduate degree, and he had recently enrolled in a well-regarded MBA program for working professionals at nearby San Jose State University.*

Our seventh project team member, Peter, may bring to the table the *finance cultural mindset* often characteristic of controllers, financial analysts, and budget officers. Like Carolyn, he may bring a *Northeastern U.S. cultural perspective* to the group. Peter probably carries the *SoftPak organizational culture* and cultural remnants of the *previous international project teams* with which he worked, some of which may be held in common with Raul and Hans. Concurrently, he also is learning an *MBA culture* that may already be shared by Dennis and Marco.

Raul, Hans, Carolyn, John, Dennis, Marco, and Peter—an obviously diverse group. Each brings to the new project team a variety of cultural mindsets, some of which are shared with other group members, some of which are not. All are present in the current situation and may come to bear in the developing and evolving culture—that of the *EuroFIN project team.*

Table 3.1 illustrates what we have learned about the cultural milieu of the EuroFIN project team by delineating some of the many cultures represented by the seven individuals in this scenario. It provides an overview of the complexity of the cultural milieu of the EuroFIN project team. Five levels or layers of culture may impact the EuroFIN environment. These are *geographically based* (e.g., national, regional), *societal sub-groups* (e.g., ethnic, gender), *cross-organizational* (e.g., industry, professional, discipline), *organizational,* and *sub-organizational* cultures (e.g., functional, hierarchical, project-based). These set of assumptions all potentially impact the development and functioning of project teams. Thus they may influence the team's and team members' perceptions, thoughts, feelings, and behavior in the future.

Having introduced this expanded and more complex cultural context, the key question arises:

In what way does this cultural perspective contribute to our understanding and managing of project teams, as compared to the currently held traditional perspective?

TRADITIONAL VS. EXPANDED VIEW OF PROJECT TEAM CULTURAL CONTEXT

Current dominant views in international cross-cultural and organization management literatures differentiate two levels of culture: nationally based and organizationally based cultures (Boyacigiller et al., 1996; Frost et al., 1991; Martin, 1992; S. Schneider, 1988). While these two cultural levels are important, their distinction offers only a crude tool for understanding the complexity and dynamics of life in today's project teams. Table 3.2 shows the EuroFIN project team from currently held perspectives.

When compared to Table 3.1, Table 3.2 indicates the limitations of currently held perspectives in understanding the culturally complex environment of project teams. In their daily work, project team members may draw upon sets of assumptions that are neither nationally nor organizationally based. If these other potentially important cultural assumptions are not evident to their co-workers or manager, misunderstandings are likely to occur. The expanded view of the cultural context may serve as a basis for a much finer-grained analysis and, thus, a better understanding of the dynamics of the project team in action.

Table 3.1. The EuroFIN Project Team Cultural Milieu

General Type of Culture	Specific Culture	Members of the Culture
Geographically based cultures		
national	American	Raul, Carolyn, John, Dennis, Peter
	German	Hans
	Italian	Marco
regional	Californian	Dennis, John
	Northeastern U.S.	Carolyn, Peter
Cultures of societal sub-groups		
ethnic	Mexican-American	Raul
	African-American	Dennis
	Caucasian-American	Carolyn, John, Peter
	Caucasian-European	Hans, Marco
gender-based	female	Carolyn
	male	Raul, Hans, John, Dennis, Marco, Peter
Cross-organizational cultures		
industry-based	computer-software	Raul, Hans, Carolyn, Dennis, Marco, Peter
	aerospace	John
professional/ discipline-based	engineer-software	Raul, Hans, Carolyn, John
	MBA	Dennis, Marco, Peter
Organizational cultures		
SoftPak		Raul, John, Dennis, Peter
EuroPak		Hans, Marco
SoftPak/EuroPak	global enterprise	Raul, Hans, John, Dennis, Marco, Peter
UCLA		Dennis, Marco
Sub-organizational cultures		
functional/hierarchical	management	Raul
	engineering	Raul, Hans, Carolyn, John
	marketing	Dennis, Marco
	finance	Peter
project-based	SoftFIN	Raul, John, Dennis
	word processing	Dennis, Marco
	other teams	Raul, Hans / Raul, Hans, Peter
	EuroFIN (evolving)	Raul, Hans, Carolyn, John, Dennis, Marco, Peter

Table 3.2. The EuroFIN Project Team Cultural Milieu Viewed From Currently Held Perspectives

General Type of Culture	Specific Culture	Members of the Culture
National cultures		
national	American	Raul, Carolyn, John, Dennis, Peter
	German	Hans
	Italian	Marco
Organizational cultures		
	SoftPak	Raul, John, Dennis, Peter
	EuroPak	Hans, Marco
possibly:	SoftPak/EuroPak	
	global enterprise	Raul, Hans, John, Dennis, Marco, Peter

For example,

- regionally based cultural assumptions may have a strong effect in EuroFIN with regard to the relative informality in interactions of the Californians, as compared to those team members from the Northeastern U.S. and Europe (Weiss and Delbecq, 1987);
- potential commonalties in perspective shared by Marco and Dennis may be overlooked and possible synergies untapped if their shared UCLA cultural heritage and their marketing culture is ignored and focus placed solely on their national (Italian and American, respectively) or organizational (EuroPak and SoftPak, respectively) cultures;
- marketeers and engineers are likely to clash when they draw unconsciously upon their functional mindsets without considering the different priorities that come with their different cultures (Dubinskas, 1988; Sackmann, 1992).

Though these examples demonstrate its value, little empirical work has been conducted to support this expanded cultural perspective (Boyacigiller et al., 1996; Phillips and Sackmann, 1992). If it is to be considered the "normal" environment of project teams, several new questions and issues arise that need to be addressed in future research. For example,

- Many different cultural mindsets are brought to the table simultaneously. Which ones will become salient, when do they become salient, and under which conditions may salience change?

- What types of diversity, and how much, are relevant in the development of a project team?
- What needs to happen to ensure that the existing diversity results in constructive dialogue and synergy from which project teams may benefit?
- What is the impact of an evolving team culture on the cultural milieu? Does it necessarily reduce the cultural complexity of the team environment?
- When and why are different cultural mindsets "attributed" to others during project work, and how can attribution errors be overcome?
- To what degree must the complexity of the cultural milieu be understood for project teams to be effectively managed?

Exploring these questions may also shed new light on the entire area of work groups and group dynamics from a truly cultural, and not merely international, perspective.

REFERENCES

Adler, N.J. (1991) *International Dimensions of Organizational Behavior,* 2nd Ed., Boston: PWS-Kent Publishing Company.

Boyacigiller, N.A., M.J. Kleinberg, M.E. Phillips, and S.A. Sackmann (1996) "Conceptualizing Culture" in B.J. Punnett and O. Shenkar, eds. *Handbook for International Management Research,* Cambridge, MA: Blackwell.

Dubinskas, F.A. (1988) "Janus Organizations: Scientists And Managers In Genetic Engineering Firms" in F. A. Dubinskas, ed., *Making Time: Ethnographies of High-technology Organizations.* Philadelphia: Temple University Press, 170–232.

Frost, P.J., L.F. Moore, M.R. Louis, C.C. Lundberg, and J. Martin (1985) *Organizational Culture,* Beverly Hills, California: Sage Publications.

Frost, P.J., L.F. Moore, M.R. Louis, C.C. Lundberg, and J. Martin (1991) *Reframing Organizational Culture,* Newbury Park, CA: Sage Publications.

Goodman, R.A. (1981) *Temporary Systems.* New York: Praeger.

Hofstede, G. (1980) *Culture's Consequences: International Differences in Work-Related Values,* Beverly Hills, CA: Sage Publications.

Jones, M.O., M.D. Moore, and R.C. Snyder (1988) *Inside Organizations: Understanding the Human Dimension,* Newbury Park, CA: Sage Publications.

McCaskey, M.B. (1983) "A Framework For Analyzing Work Groups" in L.A. Schlesinger, R.G. Eccles, and J.J. Gabarro, eds. *Managing Behavior in Organizations: Text, Cases, Readings,* New York: McGraw-Hill, 4–24.

Madauss, B.J. (1991) *Handbuch Projektmanagement* [Handbook of Project Management], 4th Ed., Stuttgart: C.E. Poeschel Verlag.

Martin, J. (1992) *Cultures in Organizations: Three Perspectives.* New York: Oxford University Press.

Nath, R., ed. (1988) *Comparative Management: A Regional View.* Cambridge, Massachusetts: Ballinger Publishing Company.

Phillips, M.E. (1994) "Industry Mindsets: Exploring The Cultures Of Two Macro-Organizational Settings" *Organization Science,* 5 (3), 384–402.

Phillips, M.E. and S.A. Sackmann (1992) *Mapping the Terrain Of Culture Research: Current Boundaries And Future Directions,* Working Paper #92–05, CIBER, Anderson School, UCLA.

Sackmann, S.A. (1989) *The Framers of Culture: The Conceptual Views from Anthropology, Organizational Theory, and Management,* Paper presented at the Academy of Management Annual Meeting, Washington D.C.

Sackmann, S.A. (1991a) *Cultural Knowledge in Organizations: Exploring the Collective Mind,* Newbury Park, CA: Sage Publications.

Sackmann, S.A. (1991b) "Uncovering Culture In Organizational Settings," *Journal of Applied Behavioral Sciences,* 27 (3) 295–317.

Sackmann, S.A. (1992) "Culture and Subcultures: An Analysis of Organizational Knowledge" *Administrative Science Quarterly,* March, 1992 140–161.

Sackmann, S.A. ed. (1997) *Cultural Complexity in Organizations: Inherent Contrasts and Contradictions.* Thousand Oaks, CA: Sage Publications.

Schein, E.H. (1985) *Organizational Culture And Leadership,* San Francisco: Jossey-Bass.

Schein, E. (1992) *Organizational Culture And Leadership,* 2nd Ed., San Francisco: Jossey-Bass.

Schneider, B., ed. (1990) *Organizational Climate And Culture.* San Francisco: Jossey-Bass.

Schneider, S. (1988) "National Vs. Corporate Culture: Implications For Human Resource Management" *Human Resource Management,* 27 (2), 231–246.

Steinbuch, P.A. (1987). *Organisation,* 6th Ed., Ludwigshafen (Rhein): Kiel Verlag.

Steiner, G.A. and W.G. Ryan (1968) *Industrial Project Management,* New York: Macmillan.

Trice, H. and J. Beyer (1991) *The Cultures of Work Organizations.* Englewood Cliffs, NJ: Prentice-Hall.

Trompenaars, F. (1994) *Riding the Waves of Culture: Understanding Diversity in Global Business,* Burr Ridge, IL: Irwin.

Van Maanen, J. and S.R. Barley (1983) *Cultural Organization: Fragments of a Theory.* Paper presented at the Academy of Management Annual Meeting, Dallas, Texas.

Weiss, J. and A. Delbecq (1987). "High-Technology Cultures And Management: Silicon Valley And Route 128" *Group and Organization Studies,* 12 (1), 39–54.

4

THE SUBCULTURE OF INTERNATIONAL WORK TEAMS: TOWARD INTERNATIONAL PROFESSIONAL CULTURES?

Sylvie Chevrier

With increasing frequency, executives, engineers or employees work with counterparts from different nations and cultures. As they work on projects together the way they deal with cultural differences eventually emerges into a unique international work team subculture. A qualitative study of three European engineering teams demonstrates that each cross-cultural team forms its own subculture depending on its activities, nationalities, organizational context, etc. These specific subcultures have two common denominators: high tolerance for diversity, preventing disintegration, and shared professional cultures, playing a major cohesive role.

INTRODUCTION

The postindustrial society is becoming more and more cross-cultural and business management plays a significant role in this process. Going global, internationalizing activities, relocating facilities abroad are among the repertoire of contemporary managers. An increasing number of executives, engineers and employees are required to work with counterparts from different cultures.

This chapter presents the conclusions of a qualitative study of three European teams of engineers working respectively in the telecommunications, computer science and electrical engineering industries. Field work (interviews and attendance

34

at meetings as a participant-observer) was conducted between March and November 1993. The quotations throughout the paper are taken from interviews of the members of the three international teams.

The careful comparison of these teams demonstrates that each cross-cultural team creates its own subculture depending on its activity, the nationalities involved, the organizational context, etc. However, these specific subcultures proved to have two common denominators: first, a kind of 'international mindset' that prevents the teams from disintegrating, and second, a shared professional culture that plays an overwhelming role in the cohesion of the teams. This article focuses on both dimensions of the subculture of cross-cultural work teams.

THE SPECIFIC MINDSET PERVADING
INTERNATIONAL TEAMS

Members of international teams are able to engage in common work despite cultural barriers because they share an open turn of mind and implicitly apply a special 'rule of common interests and friendship.' This refers to the strong will to overcome differences either by marginalizing them or by valuing and respecting them. Common interests and friendship drive these teams.

Members of successful international work teams are torn between two opposite attitudes. On the one hand, they tend to minimize the influence of cultural differences on collective work.

We no longer think in cultural terms. At first, I thought: I speak to my Portuguese or Yugoslavian colleague. Now, it does not matter any more.

They claim that they are able to go beyond cultural differences to focus on professional issues. Cultural perceptions, if ever mentioned, are depicted with caution and sometimes even guilt. Drawing upon a universalist view, participants strive for the utopia of cross-cultural harmony and assert that national identities are irrelevant in professional relationships. In this view, cultural systems are reduced to sets of marginal particular behaviors. Some participants with extensive international experience say that cultural differences are no big deal and become rather blasé (Gruère and Morel, 1991).

On the other hand, some participants suggest that cultural differences play a significant role in the dynamics of international teams and that diversity should be respected. Understanding different cultures is a source of personal growth. The members of international teams fight against ethnocentrism, explicitly reject prejudices and stereotypes. Rather, they advocate adoption of an 'exotic attitude,' meaning that the other's value is systematically enhanced. Exchanges through cultural barriers sustain cross-fertilization and are supposed to benefit to both partners.

We get a general culture, an open mindset out of cross-cultural experiences. We can have a broader view of problems. We learn a lot.

The selection of cross-cultural team members may account for this attitude. Joining a cross-cultural work team is often a matter of choice. Most of the team members interviewed sought the exotic and thus were interested in international careers. Furthermore, more than 50 percent of team members had previous international experiences. This process of self selection of participants who are *a priori* curious and open to other cultures drove the creation of a turn of mind based upon recognition and respect for cultural differences. Such participants take diversity of thinking and action among their colleagues for granted and are ready to make more adjustments than in 'mono-cultural' teams.

In international teams, it is not always possible to enforce one way to do the job. Participants are bound to accept the coexistence of different ways of communicating and working. For example, engineers noted that German participants prepare extensively for meetings and stick strictly to the agenda, while Latin participants are ready to improvise and feel free to start on unexpected topics. Latins also speak their minds easily even to say that they agree with a proposal while the Scandinavians feel they need to express themselves only if they have objections to make or if they disagree with a decision.

In our country (Portugal), you get consensus when everybody agrees. Here consensus is reached when nobody speaks. It took time to adjust.

Observations show that some participants try to find solutions to problems through a pragmatic trial-and-error approach, while others have a linear conceptual approach that starts with elaboration of a model, the formal deduction of a theoretical solution that leads to the implementation of the solution, etc.

Participants are sometimes irritated by behaviors that would not be acceptable in their own culture, but make continuous efforts to put up with them and to avoid clashes.

In a European project, we tolerate more from the others. We have to be more patient with sixteen partners. Meetings cannot be very efficient.

Working in an international team is a state of mind.

THE RULE OF SHARED INTERESTS AND FRIENDSHIP

Goodwill, pragmatism and resignation are necessary but not sufficient conditions for finding common ground in an international work team. Collective work can be achieved if participants expect valuable results for themselves. Cross-cultural teamwork relies on the balance of the stakeholders' interests. Adjustment endeavors should be rewarding.

We work together to benefit from advanced techniques. I like to have people working on the same problem. It really helps to make progress.

Participants deal with real individuals, not with abstract cultural systems. Progressively, they begin to understand the particular behaviors and interpretations of their counterparts and make a series of pragmatic interpersonal accommodations to find a *modus vivendi*.

If the diversity of cultural frameworks leads to misinterpretations, most of them are overcome through deeper mutual knowledge. Trust cannot be established spontaneously when people do not share common references and do not understand their counterparts' behaviors. Trust arises after a long process of exchanges, during which participants become familiar with one another. Eventually, each team sets up a local frame of references to counterbalance the lack of shared cultural frameworks.

Last year, there was not so much trust. People did not come from the same previous projects and there is mistrust between projects because they are competing. Now, the partners know each other better. It works well. Relationships are informal and there are not too many hair-splitting people.

In one of the teams studied, the development of informal interpersonal relationships was systematically fostered by the work organization. During the weeks devoted to meetings of all team members, dinners were opportunities to create friendship. Senior participants declare that over the years, they have made friends within the team.

From the previous project I got to know the people. Now relationships are quite relaxed. We know each other well, we have some friends. Work is much easier, meetings go on better, the common work is good. We have no inhibitions to pick up the phone to call each other.

But this analysis of the process of cross-cultural adjustment also suggests the frailty of arrangements in cross-cultural teams. The balance of interests can be questioned at any time and any imbalance threatens common work. Cross-cultural teams are always about to collapse abruptly. If for any reason any of the stakeholders feel that their interests are damaged, the whole common construction might fall. The role of the interpersonal dimension may not be sufficient to prevent the team from disintegration. On the contrary, in case of conflict, friendship is questioned and there is a permanent risk to accusing others on the basis of supposed intentions.

People, especially those willing to work in an international environment, are not entirely dependent upon culturally predetermined behaviors. Within one culture, participants making the most of their freedom of action are able to respond differently to a given situation. This phenomenon, called 'oscillation' (Demorgon, 1993), means that team participants can choose to make efforts to adjust to cultural differences which do not directly clash with their system of basic values. The context—*i.e.,* the balance of interests and the friendly relationships—prompts the participants to be open-minded or to demonstrate cultural flexibility.

THE ROLE OF PROFESSIONAL CULTURES

Professional cultures also proved to be a powerful cement in international work teams. One's occupation may be a deep source of identity, providing status and social recognition. The job may also generate specific ways of thinking and acting and induce a special conception of the technical environment. Intimate acquaintance with a physical and human milieu makes professionals highly sensitive to its dimensions. Over time they learn to distinguish subtle nuances hidden from neophytes. An occupation also requires an accurate language to describe technical tasks and the specific work experiences. Finally, the occupation gives rise to new norms of behaviors and new values appropriate to the special work environment.

Each trade can be associated with an occupational culture made up of a complex set of know-how, knowledge, professional lexicons, values and social representations. This knowledge and know-how, peculiar to an occupation, are the constituents of the professional's identity. Such technical cultures help overcome cultural barriers.

The Culture of Engineering

In the three teams studied, the engineering culture played a leading role in federating all members around a common core of knowledge, know-how and representations.

Engineering basically relies on mastery of a technique, *i.e.,* the implementation of advanced knowledge and know-how adapted to particular circumstances. Technique, mastered and implemented, allows the creation of industrial installations and gives engineers the pleasure of achievement. Even though engineering is primarily conceptual in nature and requires copious writing, papers are only the starting point for the concrete realizations that are a source of pride for the engineers.

Technical matters are the only points of interests for some engineers who dislike the commercial, administrative and managerial elements of their job. Engineers who focus on technical issues tend to become experts, able to solve intricate problems in a narrow field. But technique remains interesting only if it is not taken for granted, if there remains something new to learn and if experts can still increase their expertise. The project that runs smoothly after initial problems have been fixed no longer arouses enthusiasm. Technique is associated with learning, innovating and constantly searching for new solutions and procedures.

Engineering is creative and future-oriented. The best place to be is at the state-of-the-art using advanced techniques. Engineers routinely speak about first-, second-, and third-generation products as the notion of progress is deeply rooted in the engineering culture.

In one of the teams studied, the rapid evolution and high technical complexity of the product sustained the interest and the enthusiasm of engineers throughout the project period. For them, a project is an opportunity to test new concepts, new functions and to take part in the development of new technologies. Indeed, not all new functions generate the same excitement: the more complex and sophisticated they are, the more enthusiastic engineers are about conceiving and testing them. Similarly, in another team, advanced research played a leading role in motivating engineers. Participants there were interested in models and prototypes as well as in new concepts and future perspectives.

Interest in technical matters and taste for scientific problems go hand-in-hand with logical reasoning. To reach a theoretical solution and get actual results, engineers respect method and follow logical paths. Innovation requires intuition which relies on extensive knowledge but also on rigor and the capacity to discriminate between truth and error. Scientific determinism applies to technical matters, which can be analyzed through patterns and figures and can be tested.

Technical skills and scientific knowledge can easily be evaluated and make up the ultimate authority. In their concern to remain rigorous, engineers generally do not speak up about issues they have not mastered entirely. The overwhelming influence of the technical logic reveals itself in the discourse of several engineers interviewed. In one team, for example, the authority stemming from technical abilities seems to overshadow the hierarchical authority: decisions are not implemented because they have been made by the executive board but because they fit in with the technical logic.

Technical work is most often carried out through teamwork marked with intense moments (contract closures, launches, tests, etc.) that meld the engineers in a tightly knit professional community. Collective projects are made easier by the shared occupational culture, but concurrently, they contribute to its development. The shared trade fosters cultural integration while simultaneously, collective work consolidates the common bases of the professional culture.

Professional Cultures as Catalysts of Cross-Cultural Work

Professional cultures act as catalysts facilitating cross-cultural communication. They help to cope with cultural barriers because they provide several conditions favorable to international communication, *i.e.,* a content for exchanges, a common language to formulate this content and an environment fostering the development of good interpersonal relationships.

Professionals from within the same industry share some preoccupations, experiences and questions. Exchanges with other professionals are a source of enrichment and the intellectual proximity of the members of a professional community enable them to have deep technical discussions.

> *It often surprised me that we have the same ideas. Technically we are close, maybe because of common readings.*

The special vocabulary that conveys the different dimensions of a given professional world is shared as well. Technical issues are discussed with a jargon well known by professionals. The diversity of languages is not a real obstacle as far as technical lexicons are concerned because all engineers are familiar with them. Furthermore, English words do not always have accurate translations in other languages, which often incorporate them as they are. The professional culture provides the medium for cross-cultural communication.

Eventually, occupational culture fosters mutual respect based upon the acknowledgment of colleagues' competencies. As mentioned earlier, in the technical world, skills and abilities can be easily appraised. Technique is something with which you cannot cheat. One can not be fooled with a prototype: it works or not. Thus, relationships within a profession are based upon mutual respect directly connected to knowledge. Such respect is more favorable to open communication on touchy issues than within traditional hierarchical authority.

The Limits of International Professional Cultures

The federating power of the professional culture should not be overestimated. Within a profession, there are multiple sub-specialities. This means that talking about the culture of a branch may be sometimes more accurate than talking about a uniform professional culture.

Issues, vocabulary and methods differ significantly among specialities. From such divergence arise heated technical discussions. The technical dimension of the professional culture brings together engineers from different origins but the social dimension of their jobs tends to separate them. Professions are grounded in specific technical activities but also provide an identity in the society. The social identity of engineers is not the same in all countries.

In Germany, for instance, many engineers are trained in technical schools (Technische Hochschulen). Even engineers trained at the University have a practical training and are oriented towards shop problems. Thus, they perceive a continuation between their knowledge and know-how, and that of workmen and technicians. The salary gap between workmen and engineers is not large and working for the powerful German industry is considered prestigious by blue-collar and white-collar workers. Engineers think of themselves as workers and are more often affiliated with the large national trade unions (DGB) than with the corporate union representing exclusively engineers' interests (ULA).

In the United States, the emergence of engineers as a social group is part of the global trend of 'professionalization,' which refers to the establishment of bodies of highly skilled professionals called 'corporations.' These corporations recruit and select their members on the basis of their professional degree. While ensuring the competencies of their members they also enforce professional ethics summed up in a charter and are preoccupied as well with the role the profession should play in the society. In the United States, engineers, like nurses or attorneys, identify themselves more with their peers than their company. They also tend to question the traditional model of hierarchical authority and refer instead to the judgment of their peers. American engineers are experts with specialized academic training, whose social identity relies on allegiance to a professional community acknowledged for its skills; a social identity that results from a kind of horizontal division of labor between professions.

In France, the title 'engineer' ensures the technical skills of the holder but also provides a status. This title is closely associated with the notion of 'cadre.' Engineers, whatever their real activities and their hierarchical span of control might be, benefit from the prestige of the French education system. Initially the schools created to train French engineers were designed by governments to build a modern technical administration for the state (Grelon, 1993). The competitive entrance exams at the '*Grandes Ecoles*' and later at the '*Grands Corps*' are designed to select candidates able to attend advanced scientific courses. They aim at severely selecting an elite destined to accept the highest State responsibilities and rise to the top management of large companies. Thus, a French engineer has a passion for sciences and technique but is also a generalist who identifies with the ruling class.

These three examples clearly show that the perfect cross-cultural engineer does not really exist, since engineers of all countries resort to specific national references to build their social identities. The technical dimension alone appears universal. Yet in a cross-cultural work team, professional culture can be a useful starting point for defining the common core of the group and sustaining a feeling of community within the team.

CONCLUSION

From a practical perspective, this empirical study of cross-cultural teams sheds light on the role of the international project manager. Besides being cosmopolitan, a good communicator, a successful negotiator, etc. (Harris and Moran, 1991; Thiederman, 1991), the manager of a cross-cultural team has to be aware of the dynamics underlying such a team, making the most of the factors of integration to balance the main features impeding the cohesion of the work team (cultural differences, diversity of languages, mistrust). More specifically, he should attend to what is at stake for each partner so their interests converge as much as possible, foster the development of interpersonal relationships to increase mutual knowledge and avoid misinterpretations and create trust among team members. The team manager should also use the professional culture to support cross-cultural communication. Finally, at the same time the manager must enlarge the common ground of team members and show respect for cultural peculiarities.

From a theoretical point of view this research points out that the actual dynamics of cross-cultural teams cannot be thoroughly explained using solely a universalist or a cultural-relativist view. The universalist view tends to underestimate the real cross-cultural difficulties of the participants. Cross-cultural adjustments cost dearly for the persons involved. On the contrary, the cultural-relativist view underlines the incompatibility of the cultural systems of interpretations and assumes that cross-cultural encounters are bound to fail. The analysis of cross-cultural work teams shows that reality falls somewhere between these two theoretical views. For lack of some conditions the universalist's dream of the melting-pot can be turned into the nightmare of the Tower of Babel.

BIBLIOGRAPHY

Demorgon, J. (1993) "Vivre Et Penser Les Cultures Dans La Mondialisation En Cours", *Intercultures,* n°20, janvier 93.

Grelon, A. (1993) "European Models of Engineers: Origins and Prospects", in *The Culture of Engineering in a Rapidly Changing World,* International Symposium, proceedings, November 93, Berkeley, California, 30–32.

Gruère, J.-P. and P. Morel (1991) *Cadres Français Et Communications Interculturelles,* Paris: Editions Eyrolles.

Harris, P. and R. Moran, (1990) *Managing Cultural Differences,* 3rd Ed., Houston: Gulf Publishing Company.

Hofstede, G. (1980) *Culture's Consequences: International Differences in Work-Related Values,* Beverly Hills: Sage.

Thiedermann, S. (1991) *Bridging Cultural Barriers for Corporate Success,* San Francisco: Lexington Books.

5

UNDERSTANDING MULTICULTURAL ACQUISITIONS THROUGH AMBIGUITY AND COMMUNICATION[1]

Anette Risberg

This paper offers an alternative perspective on mergers and acquisitions by acknowledging the cultural differences and ambiguities that occur in the cultural encounter. A conceptual framework has been developed using 'communication throughout the acquisition process' to produce and negotiate meaning from ambiguities and cultural differences. This perspective gives us an additional explanation of why acquiring management's expectations often fail to be fulfilled.

AMBIGUITY AND COMMUNICATION

Merger and acquisitions are complex phenomena with high failure rates (Larsson, 1990; Napier, 1989). Within the behaviorally oriented literature, cultural clashes between the two merging companies is a common explanation for failure (Buono and Bowditch, 1989). Martin and Meyerson (1991) argue that corporate culture researchers using a consensus model oversimplify the complex phenomenon of culture. To them cultural ambiguity, rather than full understanding and consensus, is an important element for the study of organizational cultures.

[1]This study has been funded in part by Tore Browald's Research Foundation for Social Sciences, The Foundation for Support of Economic Research at Lund University, The Foundation for Export Development, and The Lars Hierta Memorial Foundation.

43

In this chapter I argue that studying acquisitions through a cultural ambiguity frame not only helps us to understand the complexity of these phenomena, but may also prevent some of their undesirable outcomes. In the turmoil caused by the acquisition, the ambiguity of communication is often overlooked. When this occurs, rumor mills begin and 'worst scenarios' often emerge, frequently increasing anxiety (Sinetar, 1981; Mirvis and Marks, 1986).

Insufficient information causes uncertainty and ambiguity (Kahn et al., 1964) and many post-merger problems develop from lack of sufficient information (Marks, 1982). In examining the role of ambiguity and communication difficulties in the context of cross-national acquisitions, I argue that the amount and consistency of information provided by management is important in creating meaning from the uncertainty and ambiguity in these acquisitions.

ORGANIZATIONAL CULTURE AND ACQUISITIONS

Previous acquisition research focused upon the fit between the combining companies (Salter and Weinhold, 1981; Lubatkin, 1983; Jemison and Sitkin, 1986). Some have looked for similarities in management styles (Marks, 1982) and culture (Nahavandi and Malekzadeh, 1988). Their underlying assumption is that a matching partner will result in a successful acquisition (Jemison and Sitkin, 1986; Mirvis, 1985). The same theme is found in the implementation research, where related companies with similar cultures are expected to reach the highest degree of acculturation (Nahavandi and Malekzadeh, 1988). The underlying assumption is that best outcomes arise when the two companies are culturally integrated (Shrivastava, 1986). Traditionally, the acquired company is forced to adapt the acquiring company's culture and routines (Napier, Simmons and Stratton, 1989).

The view that an acquired company should be assimilated into acquiring company's culture is grounded in existing organizational theories but it does not account for cultural differences *within* the organization (Fine, 1991). Rather, in these theories organizational culture is viewed as something that homogenizes the members (Martin and Meyerson, 1991) through the assimilation of the cultures (Nahavandi and Malekzadeh, 1988; Berry, 1980).

An organizational culture rarely has values and assumptions that are shared by all members. Instead it consists of different subcultures that may have quite conflicting assumptions about reality (Schein, 1993; Martin and Meyerson, 1991). Martin and Meyerson (1991) suggest three different paradigms that might be used to study corporate culture: integration, differentiation, and ambiguity, and understand acquisition literature.

Integration emphasizes consistency among cultural manifestations and organization-wide consensus among cultural members. This view means that the members of the combining companies *deny* their differences.

Differentiation stresses the inconsistency and lack of consensus in the culture.

Failure is explained by cultural clashes (e.g., in acquisitions see Buono and Bowditch, 1989). These clashes occur when the members of the two companies *deny* their similarities.

The ambiguity paradigm argues that cultural manifestations are neither wholly consistent nor wholly inconsistent with each other. Within the ambiguity model, corporate culture is viewed as fragmented. When the two cultures meet, the ambiguity is acknowledged and sometimes made the focus of attention. A culture when viewed from an ambiguity perspective cannot be characterized as harmonious or inharmonious. Instead, individuals share some viewpoints, disagree about some, and are ignorant of or indifferent to others (Martin and Meyerson, 1991).

AMBIGUITY . . .

According to Feldman (1991:146) ambiguity occurs when there is "no clear interpretation of a phenomenon or set of events." Many different interpretations of a phenomenon or a set of events may exist, and different individuals experience ambiguity at different times, and of different types.

March and Olsen (1976), Cohen and March (1974), and Kahn et al. (1964) describe several types of ambiguity, which are explored in this summary.

Ambiguity of purpose (Cohen and March, 1974) occurs when the organization does not have a clear goal for its business activity. If what the organization intends to do is ambiguous, the organization is characterized by inconsistent and ill-defined preferences and decisions become much more difficult and ambiguous (March and Olsen, 1976).

Power ambiguity (Cohen and March, 1974) occurs when the official leader and the informal leader are different. In matrix organizations, power ambiguity is purposeful but sometimes allows different managers to issue contradictory orders.

Role conflict (Kahn et al., 1964) can be compared to ambiguity of power. Role conflict occurs when a:

> *lack of agreement or co-ordination among role senders produces a pattern of sent expectations which contain logical incompatibilities or which takes inadequate account of the needs and abilities of the focal person.* (Kahn et al. 1964:21).

For example, a middle manager asked by his manager to increase productivity and by his subordinates to increase breaks is facing role conflict.

Ambiguity of understanding (March and Olsen, 1976) occurs when there are competing ideas about appropriate organizational action (Feldman, 1991). This makes it difficult to understand the connection between organizational actions and consequences, making the entire situation difficult to interpret.

Ambiguity of experience (Cohen and March, 1974) arises when it is difficult to determine how the organization should make inferences about its experience.

Organizations should learn from past experiences, but it is often difficult to know what those lessons really are.

Ambiguity of success comes from not knowing whether a certain outcome represents success. Individual successes and rewards are usually judgmental and success criteria change with changes in supervision—creating ambiguity.

Ambiguity of organizations (March and Olsen, 1976) arises from ever-changing decision makers. Participation of different individuals in different choice situations is fluid and it is not always the same individual who pays attention to decisions.

Role ambiguity (Kahn et al., 1964:25–26) is summarized as follows:

> *Role ambiguity is conceived as the degree to which required information is available to a given organizational position. To the extent that such information is communicated clearly and consistently to a focal person, it will tend to induce in him an experience of certainty with respect to his role requirements and his place in the organization. To the extent that such information is lacking he will experience ambiguity.*

Ambiguity of cross-cultural communication occurs when different cultures use different languages (Schein, 1991). This is fundamental: a) to translation problems as meaning can seldom be perfectly translated and b) to the issue that language itself reflects fundamental cultural orientation.

. . . AND COMMUNICATION

An implicit, and sometimes explicit, theme running through the ambiguity literature is insufficient information and communication. Kahn et al. (1964:23) define ambiguity as "the lack of clear, consistent information." Frost, et al. (1991) state that ambiguity is presumably resolvable by the provision of more information. These definitions indicate a relationship between organizational ambiguity, information and communication. Shared information is an effective device for decreasing ambiguity.

The fact that organizations are in Martin and Meyerson's (1991) terms ambiguous must be acknowledged (Fine, 1991) before different cultures can understand each other. Communication across cultural boundaries facilitates these understandings (Schein, 1993). Communication can acknowledge multicultures within an organization and facilitate the co-operation between the cultures. Most importantly, communication can be used as a device to produce and negotiate meaning for the individuals involved (Davis and Jasinksi, 1993).

Communication is also a device for managing change within an organization. Young and Post (1993) found communication was important in reducing employee resistance to change. During the first phases of an acquisition consistency in communication is a vital process because opinion formation about the acquiring company occurs early. Events and actions taking place before the actual acquisition affect people's attitudes towards the acquisition and the acquiring company.

To fully understand cultural encounters, both ambiguity and communication must be considered. Two cultures can work well together if they acknowledge ambiguity in values and assumptions. Communication should be used to produce and negotiate meaning from the encounter. In this model differences are acknowledged and the acquired company is not forced to fully adapt to the parent company. Instead it is allowed to retain its differences within the frame of an overall corporate culture. Moreover, communication is continuously used to reduce uncertainties and ambiguities. This framework will be used to reinterpret previous acquisition research.

AMBIGUITY AND UNCERTAINTY IN ACQUISITION LITERATURE

Individual Effects

Clearly, current research on acquisitions demonstrates its potentially severe effects on managers and employees (Marks and Mirvis, 1985, Mirvis and Marks, 1986, Walsh, 1989). Marks and Mirvis (1985:50) call this reaction the merger syndrome. According to them, the syndrome is caused by:

> *a combination of uncertainty and the likelihood of change, both favorable and unfavorable, that produces stress and, ultimately, affects perceptions and judgments, interpersonal relationships and the dynamics of the combination itself.*

Acquisitions tend to cause stress, ambiguity, anxiety disorientation, and confusion (Buono and Bowditch, 1989). These feelings occur as the acquisition unsettles the ordinary life conditions and create feelings of uncertainty for all concerned (Sinetar, 1981).

Walsh (1989) found acquisitions cause increased turnover among top management who often deal with resultant ambiguities by leaving the company. Mirvis and Marks (1986) found target management turns to crisis management behavior in reaction to the acquisition. They centralize decision making and begin making decisions in an authoritative mode. Moreover, they tend to reduce their accessibility to employees and colleagues and reduce the flow of communication. When managers withdraw from daily operations after the acquisition, employees feel alienated and isolated. Subordinates no longer recognize their 'old' company nor feel they belong. This often leads to a morale decline and decreasing employee commitment (Sinetar, 1981) that, in turn, leads to dwindling efficiency and productivity, and finally to sales shortfalls (Marks and Mirvis, 1985).

What is important here is that subordinates' reactions are affected by their supervisors' actions. Employees watch their supervisors carefully, and interpret their reactions as guidelines for their own behavior. These reactions to the acquisition affect not only internal matters, i.e., relations between hierarchical levels, but also efficiency, sales, and quality.

The acquisition affects the employees on both a professional and a personal level. On the personal level employees often experience lowered personal confidence and self-esteem (Sinetar, 1981). Stresses caused by acquisition can also lead to sense of loss, psychosomatic difficulties, and marital discord (Buono and Bowditch, 1989). On a professional level the reaction could be shown as lowered commitment and productivity, increased dissatisfaction and disloyalty, high turnover and power struggle among managers (Buono and Bowditch, 1989; Schweiger et al., 1987; Haspeslagh and Jemison, 1991b).

Organizational Effects—Implementation

Common among top management in acquiring firms is to immediately state that nothing will change. A well-known phrase is "We contemplate no changes in personnel" (Austin, 1970). These statements are designed to avoid worries and anxiety. Although the intention might be good, the effect is often the opposite. People usually expect some changes to take place in an organization that has just been acquired. If top management declares that nothing will happen, employees will believe they are hiding something (Haspeslagh and Jemison, 1991a). Such behavior from the top management undermines their credibility (Buono and Bowditch, 1989).

One way to minimize ambiguity is through open communication between the companies, and within the acquired company from managerial level to lower levels. According to Schweiger and DeNisi (1991), the only way for managers to deal with anxiety is to communicate with employees as soon as possible. Further, they say that it is not changes after an acquisition but the uncertainty about the future that is most stressful to the employees. The absence of any communication leaves employees with a great uncertainty about the future and the lack of full and frank communication usually leads to rumors and other informal communication (e.g., Sinetar, 1981; Mirvis and Marks, 1986).

To reduce anxiety, communication should begin early in the merger process (Marks, 1982; Shrivastava, 1986). Schweiger, Ivancevich and Power (1987) found most people were concerned with the shortage of timely and accurate information regarding the future for both employees and the company. Marks (1982) says most post-merger problems develop from the lack of sufficient information, and this could be avoided by communication with acquired personnel throughout the whole acquisition process. Sinetar (1981) also argues for communication throughout the process, starting as early as the pre-merger phase (Shrivastava, 1986). Haspeslagh and Jemison (1991a, b) believe integration should be preceded by a stage-setting period to ground the coming integration. While there are many activities going on during this period, all of them are linked by a common theme: managers "need to communicate and then communicate again" (Haspeslagh and Jemison, 1991a: 173), even when they themselves do not have sufficient information (Mirvis and Marks, 1986).

APPLICATION OF THE CONCEPTUAL
FRAMEWORK ON ACQUISITIONS

The conceptual framework and the ambiguity categories discussed earlier will now be applied to acquisition situations to provide an alternative interpretation. What differentiates ambiguity in acquisitions from ambiguity in general is that the focus goes beyond the individual level and includes the collective level.

An alternative interpretation of traditional acquisition research is summarized in Table 5.1.

Role overload (Kahn et al., 1964) can occur in an acquisition situation. Management of the acquiring company is very likely to exert role pressures that require all members to change their behavior in one way or another to adapt to the acquiring company's procedures.

Pre-acquisition ambiguity and *ambiguity of communication* (Kahn et al., 1964) also focus on the way attitudes change under conditions of conflict and ambiguity. It commonly occurs when the acquiring management contends (unrealistically) that no changes will take place (e.g., Haspeslagh and Jemison, 1991a; Buono and Bowditch, 1989; Levinson, 1970). This contradictory behavior from the new management tends to undermine their credibility (Buono and Bowditch, 1989).

The pre-acquisition phase and the beginning of integration is important for setting employees' attitudes towards the acquiring company. Negotiating and implementing managers must be careful about how they communicate, as people often form lasting impressions from initial encounters.

Ambiguity of cross-national communication occurs in international acquisitions, as the interpretation of what is communicated can vary widely depending on the cultural context. Haspeslagh and Jemison (1991a) found that sent information, after it had been decoded, was often not interpreted the way the sender intended.

Ambiguity of purpose arises when acquiring management is unclear about goals for the newly acquired company. Working in a company without clearly articulated goals can make it difficult for members to make decisions (Sinetar, 1981; Marks and Mirvis, 1985). If intentions are not clearly communicated, the working situation remains ambiguous and making plans for the future and even for day-to-day work becomes very difficult.

Ambiguity of power may occur if the old top management leaves the company in conjunction with the acquisition (Walsh, 1989). It is then not clear who is the leader and who gives orders.

Ambiguity of understanding commonly occurs during an acquisition as boundaries between responsibilities and authorities often remain unclear. Management of the acquired company does not know if they are supposed, or are allowed, to continue making decisions. It is also more difficult to predict the outcomes of the decisions as the new owner might interfere and give counter orders or have differing opinions.

Ambiguity of experience. When everything is new, it is hard to know which

Table 5.1. Traditional and Alternative Frameworks

Traditional M&A Literature Explanations of Outcome	Alternative Interpretation; The Conceptual Framework
"We contemplate no changes" syndrome → resistance to change	Pre-acquisition ambiguity → affects ambiguity of communication
Misunderstandings	Ambiguity of communication; ambiguity of cross-cultural communication
Inactivity—"nothing happens"; crisis management	Ambiguity of purpose; ambiguity of power
Unwillingness in making decisions	Ambiguity of understanding
Unwillingness to abandon old practices	Ambiguity of experience
Changes in reward system	Ambiguity of success
Managers leaving the company	Ambiguity of organization

experiences count. Are the acquired company's old experiences valuable and useful, or should they change and adapt to 'their' way? This ambiguity can be moderated if the strategic motive behind the acquisition is clearly communicated.

Ambiguity of success. Rewards may change to fit the new owner's policy, but different kinds of behavior may be rewarded in the new situation. Individuals need to know about new demands on them, what new owners expect of them, what action will be rewarded, etc., as the old organizational norms and expectations are replaced with new ones (Buono and Bowditch, 1989).

Ambiguity of organizations. Participation may change after the acquisition, as people might leave or join the company. Typically, the owners, or at least top management, do the negotiation and planning, but often leave the company after the selling is done. Thus, middle managers who are left running the business have little information as they are rarely involved in the acquisition negotiation and the integration planning process (Pritchett, 1985; Shrivastava, 1986; Jemison and Sitkin, 1986; Haspeslagh and Jemison, 1987).

DISCUSSION

A common theme within these examples of acquisition situations is the issue of communication. Communication seems to be least present during the early phases of the acquisition, when attitudes towards the acquisition and the acquiring company are formed. Thus, if communication had been the focus throughout the whole acquisition process, many of the resulting ambiguities might have been avoided or lessened. Moreover, if the different cultural backgrounds had been acknowledged, some of the ambiguities might have been avoided.

The conceptual framework presented here provides a new perspective for analyzing mergers and acquisitions that can explain, to some extent, why so many acquisitions do not meet management's expectations. The framework and its application are not yet fully developed, but when they are they may lead us one step closer to explaining why mergers between companies that seemed to be a good fit still do not work out.

BIBLIOGRAPHY

Austin, D.V. (1970) "Merger Myths: We Contemplate no Changes in Personnel" *Mergers and Acquisitions,* 5, 5, 20–21.

Berry, J.W. (1980) "Acculturation as Varieties of Adaptation" In A.M. Padilla ed. *Acculturation—Theory, Models and Some New Findings.* Boulder Colorado: Westview Press.

Buono, A.F., J.L. Bowditch (1989) *The Human Side of Mergers and Acquisitions* San Francisco: Jossey-Bass.

Cohen, M., J.G. March (1974) *Leadership and Ambiguity—The American College President,* Second edition, Cambridge, MA: Harvard Business School Press.

Davis, D.K., J. Jasinksi (1993) "Beyond the Culture Wars: An Agenda for Research on Communication and Culture" *Journal of Communication* Summer, 141–149.

Feldman, M.S. (1991) "The Meanings of Ambiguity: Learning from Stories and Metaphors" in Frost, P.J., L.F. Moore, M.R. Louis, C.C Lundberg, J. Martin, eds., *Reframing Organizational Culture.* Beverly Hills, CA: Sage.

Fine, M. (1991) "New Voices in the Workplace: Research Directions in Multicultural Communication" *The Journal of Business Communication,* 28, 3, 259–275.

Frost, P.J., L.F. Moore, M.R. Louis, C.C Lundberg, J. Martin, eds. (1991) *Reframing Organizational Culture.* Beverly Hills, CA: Sage.

Haspeslagh, C., B. Jemison (1991a) *Managing Acquisitions—Creating Value Through Corporate Renewal,* New York: The Free Press.

Haspeslagh, C., B. Jemison (1991b) "Postmerger Integration: The Crucial Early Steps" *M&A Europe,* 3, 5, 47–57.

Haspeslagh, C., B. Jemison (1987) "Acquisitions: Myths and Reality" *Sloan Management Review.* Winter: 53–58.

Jemison, D.B., Sitkin, S.B., 1986, "Acquisitions: The Process can be a Problem" *Harvard Business Review,* March–April, pp. 107–116.

Kahn, R.L., D.M. Wolfe, R. Quinn, J.D. Snoek (1964) *Organizational Stress: Studies in Role Conflict and Ambiguity,* New York: Wiley.

Larsson, R. (1990) *Coordination of Action in Mergers and Acquisitions: Interpretive and Systems Approach Towards Synergy,* Lund University Press, Lund.

Levinson, H. (1970) "A Psychologist Diagnoses Merger Failures" *Harvard Business Review,* March–April, 139–147.

Lubatkin, M., (1983) "Mergers and the Performance of the Acquiring Firm" *Academy of Management Review,* 8 (2), 218–225.

March, J.G., J.P. Olsen (1976), "Organizational Choice under Ambiguity" in March, J. G., J.P. Olsen (1976) *Ambiguity and Choice in Organizations,* Bergen: Universitetsforlaget.

Marks, M.L. (1982) "Merging Human Resources: A Review of Current Research" *Mergers and Acquisitions,* 17, 2, 50–55.

Marks, M.L., P. Mirvis (1985) "Merger Syndrome: Stress and Uncertainty" *Mergers and Acquisitions,* 20, 2, 50–55.

Martin, H.J., D. Meyerson (1991) "Organizational Cultures and the Denial, Channeling and Acknowledgment of Ambiguity" in Pondy, L.R., R.J. Boland, H. Thomas, eds., *Managing Ambiguity and Change,* New York: Wiley.

Mirvis, P. (1985) "Negotiations After the Sale: The Roots and Ramifications of Conflict in an Acquisition" *Journal of Occupational Behaviour,* 6, 65–84.

Mirvis, P., M.L. Marks (1986) "Merger Syndrome: Management by Crisis" *Mergers and Acquisitions,* 21, 1, 70–76.

Nahavandi, A., A.R. Malekzadeh (1988) "Acculturation in Mergers and Acquisitions" *Academy of Management Review,* 13,1, 79–80.

Napier, N.K. (1989) "Mergers and Acquisitions, Human Resource Issues and Outcomes: A Review and Suggested Typology" *Journal of Management Studies,* 26, 3, 271–289.

Napier, N.K., G. Simmons, K. Stratton (1989) "Communication During a Merger: The Experience of Two Banks" *Human Resource Planning,* 12, 2, 105–122.

Pritchett, P. (1985) *After the Merger—Managing the Shockwaves,* Homewood, IL: Dow Jones Irwin.

Salter, M.S., W.A. Weinhold (1981) "Choosing Compatible Acquisitions" *Harvard Business Review,* January–February, 117–127.

Schein, E.(1993) "On Dialog, Culture, and Organizational Learning" *Organizational Dynamics* 22, 2, 40–51.

Schweiger, D.M., A.S. DeNisi (1991) "Communication with Employees Following a Merger: a Longitudinal Field Experiment" *Academy of Management Journal,* 34, 1, 110–135.

Schweiger, D.M., J.M. Ivancevich, F.R. Power (1987) "Executive Actions For Managing Human Resources Before and After Acquisition" *Academy of Management Executive,* 1, 2, 127–138.

Shrivastava, P. (1986) "Post-merger Integration" *Journal of Business Strategy,* 7, 1, 65–76.

Sinetar, M. (1981) "Mergers, Morale and Productivity" *Personnel Journal,* November, 863–867.

Walsh, J.P. (1989) "Doing a Deal: Merger and Acquisition Negotiations and Their Impact upon Target Company Top Management Turnover" *Strategic Management Journal,* 10, 2, 307–322.

Young, M., J.E. Post (1993) "Managing to Communicate, Communicating to Manage: How Leading Companies Communicate with Employees" *Organizational Dynamics* 22, 1, 40–51.

6

ASIAN MODERNITY OR 'CREOLIZATION': WITH WEBER TO SINGAPORE AND BACK AGAIN

Gro Kvåle and Elisabeth Pettersen

Some claim that Weber must have erred when claiming Eastern culture is incompatible with modern economic development and the rapid economic growth in Southeast Asia is proof of this error. Singapore, a multi-ethnic trade and financial center (a virtual form of commerce) with distinctly 'modern Asia' features can be described as a cultural crossroads, a cultural blend that goes well beyond multiculturalism to a kind of 'creolization.' This chapter discusses the conditions of a 'creolized,' spaceless subculture, and how it applies in the Singapore case to the diffusion of standards, ideas and ideals of organization and management.

INTRODUCTION: 'CONFUCIAN COMEBACK'?

On October 26, 1994 an *Asiaweek* article claimed that Max Weber must have been wrong when he said that Eastern culture is incompatible with modern economic development. The article, entitled 'Confucian Comeback,' claimed Eastern culture and philosophy paved the way for this development, and the proof of the premise is the rapid and extensive economic growth over the past couple of decades in Southeast Asia.

A 'Confucian Comeback' is only one of several possible explanations of the Eastern economic 'miracle.' It could be that Southeast Asia only recently met Weber's conditions for success and thus economic rationalism and administrative efficiency is only now spreading from West to the East. Or, that Asian culture and Confucian philosophy are not as different from Western rationalistic values as Weber and *Asiaweek* hold them to be. Or, possibly Asian values have been modified, reinterpreted and redefined over the years to fit into a model of modern economic development.

But perhaps the opposite is true. Western modern ideas have been modified and translated into 'Asian.' This would mean that elements not considered modern in traditional Asian ways have been de-emphasized, and those compatible with modern, rational economic development have been stressed. Perhaps 'Asian modernism' is best understood in terms of a mix that is genuinely Asian and genuinely modern at the same time. Best termed 'creolized' (Hannerz, 1992a; Eriksen, 1994), this mix is characterized by the diffusion of ideas moving West to East as well as East to West.

The city-state of Singapore has become an object of interest and admiration worldwide (Pettersen and Kvåle, 1995; *Fortune,* November 13, 1995; *Asiaweek,* July 13, 1994). It is one of the most successful of the newly industrialized countries, claiming to put its own specific social and cultural values to effective use to accelerate economic growth.

It is interesting to note that both Weber and *Asiaweek* think that cultural, moral or religious background influence economic development and modernization. But the perception of cultural conditions determining development seems to be taken for granted, and other interpretations seem to be overlooked in the discourse, both popular and academic, about the 'economic miracles' of East Asia.

METHOD

This chapter is based primarily on printed or electronic information. There has been little traditional fieldwork, although a visit to Singapore and Malaysia in the summer of 1994 permitted the authors to experience, in the conventional way, the smells, tastes, atmosphere—the little things that make a difference when deciding what is interesting, exciting and meaningful. Singapore appeared familiar and foreign at the same time. This mix of a modern city with its international, spaceless features and local subcultures proved very intriguing.

Academic and popular literature, official reports and statistics, and international media were used to explore the discourse on development in Southeast Asia. By systematically reading the electronic editions of Singapore newspapers such as *Business Times* and *The Straits Times* during March, 1996, the authors had access to the official version of the 'Singapore model.'

Our intent was not to evaluate this image in terms of instrumental or moral standards. However, we do not claim to be objective and neutral. We are fully aware that we see things through the eyes of female social scientists, with a neo-institutional and macro-anthropological theoretical frame of reference, from the periphery of Europe and the (social) democratic West.

MODERNITY: WESTERN, ASIAN OR CREOLIZED?

The concept of individuals and organizations, societies and cultures, as autonomous and singular, pure and unique, coherent and consistent, is becoming increasingly problematic as a meaningful way of understanding the way social entities work (Meyer et al., 1994). A cosmopolitan view of culture is arising in more and more areas. The image of culture as a 'coral reef,' with traditions, stability and continuity, is challenged by a view that culture has no clear boundaries, spreads in all directions, is constantly in motion and changing. Under these new conditions, time and space are no longer preconditions for inter-relatedness (Eriksen, 1994; Meyer et al., 1994; Strang and Meyer, 1994).

From this perspective, ideas travel fast and far—more or less without friction (Czarniawska and Joerges, 1994; Røvik, 1995). Ideas consistent with the hegemony of the Western, rationalistic, institutional order probably stand the best chance of being spread in this way (Strang and Meyer, 1994; Meyer, 1996; Røvik, 1995). At the same time, local translations (Czarniawska and Joerges, 1994) or reconstructions of these ideas are likely to take place. In Kjell Arne Røvik's (1995) words: we are dealing with 'global components and local compositions.'

Western Hegemonic Power

An alternative explanation to a 'Confucian Comeback' is that Western modernity has spread to the rest of the world. One obvious reason for this assumption is the legacy of the European colonial powers. The presence and power of European imperialists created historic-institutional linkages to the West, and to certain understandings, norms and solutions. Over the years numerous Asian leaders have been educated at Western universities, school systems have been modeled after Western standards, and former colonies have adopted or taken over Western political institutions.

Kishore Mahbubani, Permanent Secretary of Singapore's Ministry of Foreign Affairs and Dean of the Civil Service College, observes:

> It is difficult for Europeans and North Americans to understand the momentousness of the psychological revolution in East Asia because they can not step in to Asian minds. Their minds have never been wrapped in colonialism. They have never struggled with the subconscious assumption that perhaps they were second-rate human beings, never good enough to be number one. (1995:103)

For a long time everything that was 'new,' 'trendy' and for many 'worthwhile' was associated with the West. But now reconstruction and reinforcement of an Asian identity is taking place. Only recently has this changed as new pride and consciousness of genuinely Asian ways and ideas have followed in the wake of the economic success.

A New Asian Identity?

It seems paradoxical that some of the former colonies in Asia have been more successful in applying capitalist methods to their economies than the Europeans and Americans (Aftenposten, August 16, 1995). Peter L. Berger (1988:4) argues that the development of these countries is a 'second case' of capitalistic modernity, and that 'Their economic successes have powerfully impressed themselves on the consciousness of people everywhere.' In Kishore Mahbubani's words: 'The growing realization of East Asians that they can do anything as well as, if not better than, other cultures have led to an explosion of confidence' (1995:103).

Quick and successful economic growth is an important element in changing Asian identity. However if these changes represent solely the adoption/imitation of Western goals, means, standards and values, it wouldn't make much sense to describe a specific 'Asian' identity. It is important, therefore, to seek explanations in the genuine cultural traditions and heritage of the region, as well as within the narratives about the ways that Asian cultural uniqueness leads to development and prosperity.

Traditional Confucianism

Like many Western countries that share Judeo-Christian values, many East-Asian countries share a Confucian heritage. Within Confucian ethics, family is regarded as first and most important (Berger and Huang, 1988; Bell et al., 1995; Somjee and Somjee, 1995). Obligation among family members is seen as the key to a good life and a key value for social and political participation later in life. *Asiaweek*'s stories (March 2, 1994) on 'The Asian Way' and 'Asia's new thinkers' claims that 'To many of them, Asian success begins at home.' More duties and obligations are fulfilled because of fealty to family members and for the sake of personal well-being in the process than is common in the West (*Economist,* May 28, 1994).

'The Asian way' emphasizes respect for authority, consensus in decision-making and the supremacy of community over the individual. This Confucian ethos is the essence of the genuinely Asian contribution to the new identity. Aside from the 'authentic' Asian values, the problems and failures the West are facing—perceptions of moral decay, increasing divorce and crime rates, etc.—and economic stagnation (Pettersen and Kvåle, 1995) are additional and important justifications for the new identity.

Western Skepticism

This new Asian identity, promoted by Asian politicians, officials and intellectuals, is to a certain degree a provocation to some Western commentators. For example, *The Economist* (May 28, 1994:13) states, somewhat sarcastically, that 'There is nothing distinctively Confucian about the extended paternalistic families of East

Asia, unless Sicilians (for example) are closet Confucians.' In *The Economist*'s special issue 'The World 1996,' Brian Beedham wrote: 'Both Islam and the West may be heading for an argument with materialist authoritarianism (and the racialism) that seem to lie behind 'Asian values', the concept so popular among modern politicians in the old Confucian culture zone' (p. 13).

Another article, entitled 'The Myth of the Orient' (Davis and Richardson, 1996:16), in the same magazine asked:

> *Why are Asian values so much in vogue? It is paradoxical, because economic growth is undermining those values and ultimately threatening the authority of those at the top. Asian values may in fact tell us more about the fears of their powerful proponents than about the societies that are supposed to thrive on them. They are in effect, a reaction to the successes of capitalism.*

And they continue their comments about alternative non-Western models for economic development with the conclusion that 'As the East grows more prosperous and more capitalist, it will begin to look—for better and for worse—more like the West.'

'Modified' Confucianism and 'Translated' Modernism

Thus, a new Asian identity, characterized by a higher degree of self-consciousness, seems to be emerging. It is an up-to-date and modified version of traditional Asian identity that includes the selective adoption of Western values (*Asiaweek,* March 2, 1994). This means that the cultural basis for economic development in Southeast Asia is portrayed as genuinely Asian, but the characteristics emphasized in the article (education, loyalty, etc.) are not significantly different than those of other modern projects. David Li Kwok Po, a Hong Kong banker, questioned the uniqueness of Asian values, by pointing out that 'No one has yet demonstrated that the values labeled as 'Asian' are so different from those long espoused by the West' (Asian Business, 1996:1). The values he refers to are family ties, education and hard work within the Protestant work ethic: 'A comparable ethos can be found in other cultures. No matter what these values are called, they are good for business.' In other words, what is not modern in Confucianism is de-emphasized or rejected. The key is combining the 'London School of Economics' with 'Asian values'.

Lucien Pye (1988:88) reminds us that Confucian philosophy was never really interested in business and trade and that, to the extent this cultural heritage has anything to do with economic growth, it is a paradox. He concludes that the 'new mandarins had to be schooled in the wisdom of Western economic theories and practices.' *Asiaweek* also recognizes that 'Confucius held business to be a lowly occupation' (October 26, 1994:22). They say that part of Confucian philosophy has led to disastrous economic conditions in the past, and therefore has to be rejected in the modern application of 'the Master's' thoughts. This is an example of Asian values being modified to a certain degree and transformed to fit into the modern and capitalistic world order.

The 'Wonders' of Multiculturalism

Former Asian colonies and European colonialists share a common history and destiny, and there are still significant institutional and normative ties between them. At the same time more or less violent and dramatic breaks with the imperialists make the relationship ambivalent for both parties. For example, many Asian countries have directed their attention toward the U.S. away from Europe in the period since the second World War (Mahbubani, 1995). At the same time a new regional identity, 'The Asia Pacific,' has formed and also directed towards the U.S., increasing the penetration of elements of the American way:

> *The Pacific community will be a completely new creation. It will not be Asian nor will it be an American community. If the Pacific region emerged as one of the most dynamic regions of the world it is because it has drawn on the best practices and values from many rich civilizations, Asian and Western. If the fusion continues to work there will be an explosive creativity on scale never before seen.* (Mahbubani, 1995:107)

David Li Kwok Po argues similarly:

> *I am not suggesting that Asian managers change their core business ideals or personal values. I am suggesting a yin and yang of management, a harmony between our internal values—the beliefs that make us who we are—and the external values of the culture in which we operate. If we can achieve this, we will be multinational, international and transnational. We will no longer be 'Asian' managers, but successful multi-cultural managers.* (*Asian Business*, 1996:1)

These statements, emphasizing the mix of values and cultural forms and practices, move us toward the concept of 'creolization' to which we now turn.

Creolization

Asian modernity is an overly simplified explanation of Asian cultural evolution. Cultural complexity, rather than purity, seems a more fruitful description. Common conceptualizations of cultural complexity and blends borrows metaphors such as 'fusion' from physics and the botanical 'hybridization,' but the linguistic metaphor of 'creolization' is preferable to either of these as it is derived from processes that involve social activities, relations and interaction. Creolization as a metaphor for cultural complexity is an ambiguous and contradictory concept, because it involves change and stability (Eriksen, 1994). Creolized cultures have the potential to be bridges connecting more or less stable 'cultural islands' in a temporary equilibrium. Thus, creolization is a 'grey area' vis-à-vis identity, roots, and/or cultural and spatial boundaries.

The cultural forms of modernity, like markets, bureaucracies and mass consumption, exist in globalized, spaceless rooms (Eriksen, 1994). They are non-places or 'a third culture' that serve as mediators among different cultures. The ultimate creolized cultures are international business hotels, airports and shopping malls where throughout the world the same set of easily accessible rules can be applied by anyone who has learned them, regardless of their national origin. Eriksen (1994) depicts the globalization process as a 'big planer that planes off all differences and unevenness' resulting in homogeneity. This homogeneity or 'post-plurality' (Strathern, 1992) facilitates smooth communication and interaction. It does, however, allow for new creativity and combinations (Hannerz, 1992a, 1992b; Strathern, 1992; Eriksen, 1994) and is an open-ended process, where participants and outcomes are unpredictable (Hannerz, 1992a, b; Strathern, 1992). There is a contradiction between the predictability of homogenization, and this more anarchic and unpredictable situation. The fact that creolization allows for multiple interpretations is exactly what makes the metaphor fruitful and useful. Thus, the condition of creolization represents a modern or even postmodern subculture.

THE SINGAPORE CASE

Singapore is often mentioned in the literature as a particularly successful example of economic development (Pettersen and Kvåle, 1995). A recent survey of executives in *Fortune* (November 13, 1995) shows Singapore ranked as the best city in the world for business. Reporters, statesmen, scholars and businessmen visit to understand and to learn. They ask what the city-state did to achieve its goals, what price it paid to make this happen and how such a high rate of development is maintained (Somjee and Somjee, 1995). The city state's super efficiency and highly pragmatic approach has become a wished-for standard for many countries both developed and undeveloped.

Confucianism and the State as Driving Forces

Singapore has changed remarkably in recent decades. Its ecomony, once based on trading and shipping, is now a global financial, high-tech, shipping and computer center. It changed from a British colony of traders and laborers to a city-state with one of the highest standards of living in Asia (Somjee and Somjee, 1995). Most narratives about Singapore development describe former Finance Minister Goh Keng Swee, former Foreign Minister S. Rajratnam and former Prime Minister Lee Kuan Yew as the founding fathers of the country (Bell et al., 1995; Somjee and Somjee, 1995) and the main architects of Singapore's success (*Asiaweek,* July 13, 1994). Together these top leaders initiated government goals and created solutions that were implemented by an efficient bureaucracy. With pragmatism and meritocracy they aspired to turn the micro-state into a global city. Singapore authorities are quick to point out that these approaches were original solutions and not imitations of foreign models and solutions (Somjee and Somjee, 1995).

Singapore is a multi-ethnic society. Its population of 3 million inhabitants consists of 75 percent Chinese, 14 percent Malay, 8 percent Indian and 3 percent of other origin. Because of the Chinese majority, Confucianism has had a strong impact on society, politics and business (Bergerand Huang, 1988). In 1989 the government identified four official core values: communitarianism, familism, decision-making by consensus and social and religious harmony (Bell et al., 1995). Factors that are important to ensure national unity. The authorities in Singapore also use traditional Confucian values like respect for authority and family, social cohesiveness, reciprocity, social discipline and hard work to achieve their goals. They are in fact giving Confucianism a modern interpretation (Somjee and Somjee, 1995).

'The Singapore Model': Technocratic Management

The other core issue is a strong central, technocratic government built upon a 'recipe' known as the 'Ten Easy Steps to Success' (*Asiaweek,* July 13, 1994). Number one is 'Strong Government' with decisive leadership that provides a societal stability regarded as essential. Number two, long-term planning, has kept the economy on track. The Singapore government, a major provider of communications, media, infrastructure, education and industrial estates, is the country's largest employer. They control wages, unions and own 75 percent of the land in the country (Tremewan, 1994; Somjee and Somjee, 1995).

Number three is the welcoming of foreign investment and overseas multinational corporations. Creating incentives to attract foreign companies has been one of Singapore's central strategies (Somjee and Somjee, 1995).

Number four is 'Clean Administration.' It is important to maintain the reputation of honesty and correctness. In fact, civil servants can be punished more severely than others. Recruitment to public administration is handled carefully to get 'the best and the brightest' by offering very high salaries and demanding honors degrees in most fields (Singapore Government Net Site; Booth, 1994). As Somjee and Somjee puts it:

> *Decision makers were brought in from the corporate world, industry, commerce, academia, the professions and so on, and persuaded to work in the highest offices in the land and later moved on to create a place for the new generation of men and women who had achieved distinction in their respective fields.* (1995:18)

A corollary effect is an efficient, continually improving civil service. 'Budgeting for Results' (BFR) (*The Straits Times,* March, 12, 1996) is one innovation. Another is posting Administrative Service officers to private companies, statutory boards, and government-linked companies in order to 'help sensitize these officers on how Government could be facilitator and nurturer, not just regulator and controller' (Deputy Prime Minister Tony Tan, in *The Straits Times,* March 29, 1996). For the most part, the big national Singapore enterprises are now or have been publicly owned or government-linked. They are extremely successful and efficient. Even so, there is a strong trend towards privatization, perhaps modeled on the European experience. Privatization creates a better international image (Toh Tian Ser, 1994) and encourages entrepreneurship and creativity (*Asiaweek*, March 2, 1994).

Number five, 'Education for all,' supports an efficient civil service. The educational system emphasizes technical and instrumental expertise in management. In Singapore, major political and economic decisions are not made in an open and free debate but rather by highly esteemed bureaucrats chosen on the basis of educational qualifications and professional competence.

In 1975, the Singapore government launched an educational program to upgrade the economy and keep up with the technological development (Tremewan, 1994). Today these professionals are working within the government bureaucracy and in government-linked industries and organizations. Some argue that this has been at the expense of developing 'an intellectual tradition' or 'spirit' (da Cuhna, 1994), while others warn that instrumentalism stands in the way of creativity and entrepreneurship (Devan and Heng, 1994; Chan Kum Wah, 1994).

Number six is 'No Welfarism.' Singapore has rejected Western-style welfare policies. Instead the government 'gives budget surpluses back to the people' (*The Straits Times*, March 11 1996), much the way other businesses distribute dividends to their shareholders. The beneficiaries of this program are not only students and old people, but also shopkeepers, stall holders, and charitable self-help groups.

Number seven, 'Family Values,' and 'No Welfarism' together are a direct connection to Confucianism. Family values also stress respect for authority, and aids the government in implementing policies with little open dissent.

Number eight, 'Law and Order' is the next 'logical' step. Severe punishments even for minor offenses are credited with keeping the crime rate low.

Number nine, 'Communal Harmony,' stresses sensitivity to other cultures in a multiracial society. Learning two of the four local languages is compulsory.

Number ten is 'Nationhood,' and national identity is emphasized above ethnic allegiances.

In sum, the Singapore model might be called 'The Administrative State' (Chan Heng Chee in Somjee and Somjee, 1995), whose main objective is to determine the common good and secure growth and prosperity. Foreign investments and multinational corporations are attracted to the most modern infrastructure in the world (Naisbitt, 1996). The public does not have to 'worry about politics' or 'get involved in public affairs' (Bell, 1995), because a rationalistic technocratic management runs the state as a paternalistic, meritocratic, hierarchic and elitist 'corporate enterprise' (*Asiaweek*, July 13, 1994:25).

Singapore the 'Pacesetter'

In spite of great success, there is a certain degree of ambivalence towards the new situation and the new self. Government officially claims that Singapore is not yet ready to apply for membership in the OECD. Allegedly because they are afraid that establishment as a developed country will slow the drive to be best and to maintain and strengthen the economic results. This ambivalence is also closely connected to OECD's market economy and pluralist democracy requirements. The second of these demands has not been fulfilled in Singapore and the government is reluctant to meet this requirement 'before they are ready.' In addition, there is a peculiar argument from the prime minister that the Singaporeans are not yet civilized—they have to 'learn manners' and 'Some Singaporeans still behave as if they were in the Stone Age' (*Asiaweek,* February 2, 1996). This is more than a little inconsistent with the image of Singapore as 'a brand name for success' (*The Straits Times,* March 8, 1996) and the new Asian identity.

The government's main concern is maintenance of Singapore's economic growth and its reputation as a success. Says Home Affairs Minister Wong Kan Seng: 'It was this reputation that drew investors from other countries as well as people who wanted to study the Singapore 'model'. 'Our people are diligent, our Government is honest, our civil service is efficient, our society is stable and cohesive, and the Government and people work as a team' (*The Straits Times,* March 8, 1996).

Singapore and the international press flaunt Singapore to foreigners with regularity. In *Asiaweek* July 13, 1994, managing director of STIC (Singapore Technologies Industrial Corporation), Wong Kok Siew wrote: 'Singapore has good relations with multinationals. They believe in the Singapore style of management and the support we provide.' S. Ramakrishnan, Vice President in Indian Tata Group continues, 'Singapore is an ideal bridge between the West and Asian countries.' In *Business Times* (March 9, 1996) the president of the Norwegian company Nycomed Asia Pacific stated that 'We were considering Hong Kong and briefly Kuala Lumpur. I was concerned about the cost of being here, but this is the logical place—communications are good and it's possible to attract qualified people.' The year before, a managing director of Siemens was quoted in *Fortune* saying that 'We are comfortable wherever they sell the Singapore way of doing business' (November 13, 1995).

These statements all convey the impression that Singapore fits the needs of modern enterprises, and that its features make doing business smooth and easy.

The Singapore Experience: A Case of Creolization?

Singapore, the small city-state and former British colony, can be described as a cultural crossroads where different cultures meet and mix. With its multi-ethnicity, trade, and financial activity, its 'modern Asia' features become distinct. The normal state of affairs is a blend that goes beyond multiculturalism into a kind of 'creolization.' Because of its lack of natural resources and its increasing reliance on computerized trade and financial activity Singapore is in a way 'spaceless.' It exists in 'virtual space' (Lim, 1994). The narratives of the Singapore experience as a global city, 'communications facilitator' and mediator between different cultures, is a kind of 'third culture' which becomes the Singapore identity. In short, a 'post industrial' condition of creolization and 'virtuality' can be what gives meaning to Singapore as a provider of 'good' solutions for (economic) development.

DIFFUSION: MEANING AND MEDIA

Social scientists usually focus on diffusion as a relational phenomenon. Meyer and Strang (1994), however, argue that this is not an adequate basis for understanding institutional conditions and mechanisms for diffusion. In today's world many things are diffusing without overall policy, specific places, or arenas, within which the ideas spread. They argue, that to explain diffusion we need 'to formulate the wider conditions under which expanded social relationships lead to rapid diffusion' (Meyer and Strang, 1994:103). This understanding is based on culture and the extent of social actors' knowledge of diffusion theory.

According to Meyer (1994), modern organizations are embedded in a wider context of rationalized environments at 'the world level,' a context characterized by the lack of supernational hierarchy and superorganizational authority: 'It lacks a collective actor at the center and is instead made up of fragmented organizational and professional systems that function as rationalizing agents or others rather than actors' (Meyer, 1994:31). In relation to this case, it seems as if modernity, with its lack of international hierarchy, globalization and advanced technology, paves the way for the diffusion of a creolized alternative like the Singapore experience.

One aspect of this rationalized environment is the stratification systems that make up the organizational world (Meyer, 1994, 1996) that consists of a successful elite of organizations, followed by an imitating mass. Diffusion is one outcome of the logic of following fashion (Røvik, 1996). Another aspect is the nation-state with its regulatory power over licensing and sanctioning organizations according to the public good. A knowledge system of sciences and professions is a third part of the rationalized environment affecting organizing and management (Meyer, 1994). Meyer (1996) labels these as 'Others' in contrast to 'Actors,' occupied with talk rather than action. They are 'rationalized' because they 'validate universalistic rationality as a collective good' (p.352). According to Meyer they 'discuss, interpret, advise, suggest, codify and sometimes pronounce and legislate. They develop, promulgate and certify some ideas as proper forms, and ignore or stigmatize other ideas' (p. 348).

There are some indications that Singapore is a promoter of its own successes and features, the modern, rational, efficient and Asian methods. As *Asiaweek* put it: 'It is management' and 'proven formulas for success' (July 13, 1994), and the slogan 'Nothing succeeds like success' (*The Straits Times,* March 16, 1996) indicates that Singapore realizes how these processes work. Meyer (1996:349) finds it a little strange that modern organized entities 'put themselves forward as general models, and promote the copying process' considering the conditions of competition. The answer seems to lie in the need to legitimize and strengthen oneself as living up to universalistic, rational and modern standards, and to be recognized as an innovator.

Conventional wisdom suggests that the power of the nation state is losing its importance. Yet, as a modernist city-state, Singapore has made the most of the role of the government's regulatory power. It is also a postmodern perception that city-states are taking over the role of the modern nation-states. Besides, Meyer (1996:354) indicates that ' . . . ideas of a cultural kind are located in meaning, rather than concrete power.' This statement suggests that the role of conventional decision-makers and actors has to be de-emphasized.

What Types of Ideas about Organization and Management Diffuse?

A 'perceived similarity' seems to underlie the process of diffusion. But according to Strang and Meyer (1994), interaction and exchange is no precondition for a notion of similarity between social entities, or for diffusion. This argument is compatible with the creolization metaphor's emphasis on spacelessness.

Cultural theorizing, or:

> *the development of abstract categories, and the formulation of patterned relationships such as chains of cause and effect* (Strang and Meyer, 1994:104)

is the process that creates perceptions of similarity and thus diffusion. Often the constructs of sciences and professions simplifies theorizing and provides causal accounts of social units like organizations and of concepts of organization and management, and thus promotes diffusion. The most important of these concepts is 'modernity,' and practices consistent with modernity are most likely to become widely spread because modernity in itself is seen as an important cultural aspect. Because of this, the more modern an organizational feature or practice is perceived, the more likely it will be that this practice will diffuse. As Røvik (1995) put it, it is the idea of modernity itself that fosters the spread of modern ideas, or 'institutionalized standards.'

'Asian values' or 'Neo-Confucianism' are labels employed as an alternative to Western thought, but are general, abstract and theoretical enough to be acceptable anywhere. Most importantly they are backed by the grand narratives of the economic miracles, development and general prosperity of East Asian actors, and are thus powerful rationalizations. As for the generalization of the Weberian bureaucracy, the 'dragons' of East Asia are also known for their efforts to avoid corruption. All this could of course be typical features of Asian culture that are important for success, but accountability, responsibility, a sharp distinction between private and public affairs in administration, etc. are just as 'Weberian' as Asian. The attention directed towards Singapore makes it a possibility that 'clean administration' and 'technocratic management' will become a 'new' standard of business and administrative affairs that diffuses beyond The Lion City. Perhaps it can be said metaphorically that: "Weber is on his way back from his 'journey' to East Asia?" In that case it strengthens the hypothesis that bureaucracy is alive and well, as some kind of a super standard (Røvik, 1992) for the effective, rational management of modern organizations.

CONCLUSION

Our point of departure was to discuss the conditions of a creolized, spaceless subculture, and how it applies to the Singapore case and to the diffusion of ideas, standards and ideals of organizing and management.

In the context of modernization and globalization, we discussed the 'culture as essence' perspective of the 'Confucian Comeback,' in contrast to the creolization metaphor of modern cultural forms. We also discussed the challenge of the Western hegemonic power by a new Asian confidence that has emerged as a result of the economic development in East Asia, and as a cause for these 'miracles.' It is in this context, that the essence of Singapore can be defined as creolized. Besides the traditional features of a creolized society—multi-ethnicity and multiculturalism— this city-state is characterized by its attempt to achieve modernity and to build and maintain a reputation of success. It is more of a corporation than a community, and has to be run accordingly. The authorities' mission is to create conditions for economic prosperity both for its citizens and for foreigners, to realize even more success. One outcome of these efforts is an easily accessible, smooth and 'spaceless' mix that serves as a 'user-friendly interface.' According to neo-institutional theory on diffusion, ideas or theories spread most easily by 'rationalized others' in a spaceless, modernist context. The Singapore experience can be interpreted as one such generalization, a relatively simple narrative about success in modernization and economic prosperity and thus spread easily. A creolized society that is an 'open' and modern society, lacking boundaries, seems a perfect metaphor for culturally globalized world with no hierarchy to slow down, or guide the flow of information— leading to a more rapid spread of ideas and concepts.

In a state of 'creolization,' as in the Singapore case, a generalized, simple set of rules applies—which means they are easily mediated and easily accessible for everyone who wants to adopt, or imitate. One example of this is the 'Ten Easy Steps to Success', which has found its way from *Asiaweek* (July 13, 1994) to John Naisbitt's bestseller *Megatrends Asia* (1996), to our desks and into this paper.

In titling this chapter 'Asian Modernity or Creolization: With Weber to Singapore and Back Again,' we indicate that Singapore is Asian, modern and creolized. When it comes to Max Weber we had no intentions of proving him right or wrong, although he is probably both when he argued that capitalist modernism is most likely to occur in the Protestant West, and least likely in the Orient. Right because modern capitalism occurred first in the West and wrong because he could not foresee the second capitalism emerging in Asia, nor the mixed modern cultural forms transmitted by global technological development.

BIBLIOGRAPHY

Beedham, B. (1996) "A Dangerous Century Ahead" in *The Economist: The World in 1996,* London: The Economist Group.

Bell, D.A., D. Brown, K. Jayasuriya and D.M. Jones (1995) *Towards Illiberal Democracy in Pacific Asia,* Oxford: St. Martin's Press.

Berger, P.L. and M. Hsiao Hsin Huang, eds. (1988) *In Search of an East Asian Development Model* New Brunswick, New Jersey: Transactions, Inc.

Booth, A. (1992) "Privatization May Not Be The Best Answer" *Sunday Times* 23 February 1992.

Chan, Kum Wah, D. (1994) "Kiasuism And The Withering Away Of Singapore Creativity." In D. da Cunha, ed. *Debating Singapore,* Singapore: Institute of South East Asian Studies.

Czarniawska, B. and B. Joerges (1994) in Bacharach, S. and G. Pasquale, eds. *Research in Organization Sociology,* Greenwich, CT: JAI Press.

da Cunha, D., (1994) "The Intellectual's Role In Society" in D. da Cunha, ed. *Debating Singapore,* Singapore: Institute of South East Asian Studies.

Davis, K. and G. Richardson (1996) "The Myth Of The Orient" in *The Economist: The World in 1996,* London: The Economist Group.

Devan, J. and G. Heng (1994) "A Minimum Working Hypothesis Of Democracy For Singapore" in D. da Cunha, ed. *Debating Singapore.* Singapore: Institute of South East Asian Studies.

Eriksen, Hylland, T. (1994) *Kulturelle veikryss: Essays om kreolisering.* Oslo: Universitetsforlaget.

Hannerz, U. (1992a) *Cultural Complexity: Studies in the Social Organization of Meaning.* New York: Columbia University Press.

Hannerz, U (1992b) "The Global Ecumene As A Network Of Networks" in A. Kuper, ed. *Conceptualizing Society,* London: Routledge.

Lim, L.M. (1994) "The Invisible Singapore" in *Trends Business Times,* Weekend Edition, June 25–26 1994.

Mahbubani, K. (1995) "The Pacific Way" in *Foreign Affairs,* Volume 74 No.1 January/February 1995.

Meyer, J.W, J. Boli, and G. M. Thomas (1994) "Ontology And Rationalization In The Western Cultural Account" in W.R. Scott and J.W Meyer and Associates *Institutional Environments and Organizations. Structural Complexity and Individualism,* Thousand Oaks, CA: SAGE.

Meyer, J.W. (1994) "Rationalized Environments" in W.R. Scott and J.W. Meyer and Associates *Institutional Environments and Organizations. Structural Complexity and Individualism.* Thousand Oaks, CA: SAGE.

Meyer, J. W. (1996) "Otherhood: The Promulgation And Transmission Of Ideas In The

Modern Organizational Environment" in B. Czarniawaska, and G. Sevon, eds. *Translating Organizational Change,* New York: De Gruyter.

Naisbitt, J. (1996) *Megatrends Asia: The Eight Asian Megatrends That Are Changing The World,* London: Nicholas Brealey.

Pettersen, E. and G. Kvåle (1995) "Den Singaporske erfaring some forbilde" *Internasjonal politikk* Nr. 21995 53. Oslo: Årgang.

Pye, L. (1988) "The New Asian Capitalism: A Political Portrait", in P.L. Berger and M.H Hsin Huang, eds. *In Search of an East Asian Development Model,* New Brunswick, NJ: Transaction, Inc.

Røvik, K.A. (1992) "Institusjonaliserte standarder og multistandardorganisasjoner," In *Norsk statsvitenskaplig tidsskrift 8, 4,* 261–284.

Røvik, K. A. (1995) "Globale komponenter og lokale komposisjoner: Om organisasjonsutforming i en flyktig verden." Unpublished manuscript, University of Tromsø, Tromsø, Norway.

Røvik, K. A. (1996) "Deinstitutionalization And The Logic Of Fashion" in B. Czarniawska and G. Sevon, eds. *Translating Organizational Change,* New York: De Gruyter.

Somjee, A.H and G. Somjee (1995) *Development Success In Asia Pacific,* London: Macmillan.

Strang, D. and J.W. Meyer (1994) "Institutional Conditions For Diffusion" in J.W. Meyer, et al *Institutional Environments And Organizations: Structural Complexity and Individualism.* Newbury Park, CA: SAGE.

Strathern, M. (1992) "Parts And Wholes: Refiguring Relationships In Post Plural World" In A. Kuper, ed. *Conceptualizing Society,* London: Routledge.

Toh Tian Ser (1994) "Creating New Urban Elites For Singapore." in D. da Cuhna, ed. *Debating Singapore,* Singapore: ISEAS.

Tremewan, C. (1994) *The Political Economy of Social Control in Singapore,* London: Macmillan.

Newspapers, Weekly Magazines and Websites

Aftenposten, August 16, 1995

Asian Business: 1996:1. http: //www.asia1.com.sg/

Asiaweek: March 2, 1994. July 13, 1994. October 26, 1994. September 29, 1995. November 24, 1995. February 2 1996.

Business Times: March 9 1996.

Economist: May 28, 1994.

Fortune: November 13, 1995 No.22.

The Straits Times: March 8 1996. March 11, 1996. March 12, 1996. March 16, March 29, 1996.

Singapore Government Net Site 1996: http: //www.gov.sg

7

SECTION SUMMARY:
WHEN SUBCULTURES MEET

Richard A. Goodman

The fabric of this section is woven from the warp of personal experience and the woof of research problematique. My career has led me into "foreign" engagements far more often then I imagined as a callow researcher. By personality, I engage more with my senses than my persona; that is, I observe more and participate less. This distances my learning and highlights my sense of not really understanding what I am seeing, but it is also a far less judgmental position. What is clear is that I journey more and more frequently into settings that are inherently puzzling and thus I am more and more challenged to make sense of what I see.

The increased frequency of this phenomena in modern life can be illustrated through a personal vignette. I had always thought that my father was born in Brooklyn. Only after reaching adulthood did I learn that he had actually emigrated from Latvia to the U.S. After arriving at Ellis Island in 1910 he remained on the U.S. mainland until 1974—not traveling abroad until he was 72 years old. By this time my brother and I had begun our own foreign travel. But my real insight only came in 1987, a year when my eldest daughter traveled to Managua, my son visited Monterrey and my 16-year-old daughter was in Moscow. Concurrently, all three were abroad visiting places usually characterized as exotic and unlikely destinations. In only three generations our family's pattern of international experience had changed dramatically. In fact, this pattern changed within a single generation but affected three generations.

What is unique about this story is that it is American in nature since the U.S. is a nation bounded by thousands of miles of oceans. Because the European geography is so very different, the European experience is also quite different; foreign travel is more widespread and less phenomenal. In Asia or Latin American or Africa different phenomena might be remarked upon. But, the story's implications are also *misleading*.

First-hand experience with foreign cultures is limited primarily to certain jobs and categories of citizens. In any culture a significant portion of the population never has opportunities to travel. Second-hand experience with foreign cultures through immigration, tourism and media is more commonplace. Through second-hand experience, a fairly wide portion of the population is exposed to various foreign experiences. Unfortunately, second-hand exposure without the benefit of first-hand experience is a serious source of distortion and evokes stereotypical responses. Even first-hand experience does not guarantee foreign understanding for reasons of cultural receptivity, language barriers, and the tacit nature of culture. Thus the potential for culture clash and for culture distortion in the postindustrial world is an important issue.

One of the predominant features of the postindustrial subculture is the increased inter-penetration of cultures. Globally, people are becoming increasingly sensitive to the existence of other cultures. World travel and marketing products to other nations are much easier. Thus, more and more organizations—whether they are government, business or educational—have global perspectives. It follows that more and more people from different cultures are working together in various forms of transaction.

Is this phenomenon actually new? No. Throughout the current millennium hordes of conquerors and traders have swept over Europe, Asia, Africa and the Americas. The phenomena has served to intermix language and cultural elements and helped to create new but differentiated cultures, developed by accretion and rejection over a long period of time. Because the process is slow, we often accept these different cultures as if they are stable and natural. Nevertheless, movement among peoples has continued and cultural inter-penetration has deepened.

What is new is the more frequent contact between cultures occasioned by improved communications. Telephone, print media, film, television, and the Internet create increased frequencies and potency for cultural images. While the media has not concerned itself with the accuracy of these images, small children in Accra, Rangoon or Tblisi know that other cultures really do exist even though their knowledge of different cultures is often based on image and rather than reality.

At the same time, opportunities to engage on a global scale are also rising. Globalization increases the need to work with representatives of many cultures. These opportunities are usually limited to a small portion of the firm's population. While the majority of employees continue to labor in blissful ignorance of the needs and determinants of the firm's global position.

The basic conundrum at the organizational level is achieving effectiveness in cross-cultural engagements when real cultural differences create both natural barriers and artifactual barriers. Perhaps the most easily identifiable of these barriers are personnel who have distorted or little understanding of other cultures. I am reminded of an untravelled American engineer who couldn't understand that a readable but smeared part number, while consistent with U.S. standards to avoid over-design, might be interpreted as evidence of shoddy quality in other cultures. I know an Italian engineering firm that didn't understand why their American customer needed 'firm' delivery dates for critical components. And I know an English manufacturer's representative who didn't understand the urgency to supply repair parts needed for full restoration of a customer's manufacturing capabilities. These simple examples highlight the fact that cultural differences and cultural distortions have more than an academic impact.

When Maggi Phillips, Sonja Sackmann and I wrote the introduction to this section, "The Complex Culture of International Project Teams," we felt we were staking out a researchable domain. We approached the paper as a module for discussion to highlight three issues. The fundamental issue was the concept that individuals are usually members of multiple cultures. This seemed to us to be a sounder starting point for future work than a monocultural assumption. It led us to ask: "If an individual is a member of multiple cultures, which culture dominates behavior at a specific point in time?" Phrased another way, we asked, "What triggers the salience of one or another culture?" This naturally led to the third question, "What actually happens when two or more people with different cultural sets and different salience thresholds work together?"

Having begun this exploration, we were very excited to learn of the work of Sylvie Chevrier, as she was testing some of the same ideas in "The Subculture of International Work Teams: Toward International Professional Cultures?" She found that cultural differences did in fact impact the "process" of working together but not necessarily the "results." This finding supports some of the implications of our own work. But Sylvie's work sheds light on other issues as well. She found that the high technology groups shared "a common problem solving culture." That is, their formalized, engineering design paradigms had more salience than national cultural differences. The design paradigms served as a meta-level cultural touchstone that permitted problem resolution to occur and allowed the teams to achieve their basic objectives. An additional finding was that successful international work team members self-select for other international projects. She concluded that a segment of the organizational world is becoming 'professionalized' as internationalists. This self-selection process reduces the global inter-penetration of cultures because it limits the impact of such a phenomena to a small set of organizational members. This finding, of course, is consistent with the conundrum of difference and distortion.

A strong form of culture inter-penetration and potential clash is the merger and acquisition process. Unlike evolutionary multicultural organizations such as the European Union, the merger process is intensive and demanding. Descriptions of the process of blending two firms raises elements of the postmodern within the postindustrial. Anette Risberg focuses on these issues in her chapter, "Understanding Multicultural Acquisitions Through Ambiguity and Communication."

While conventional wisdom recommends rapid establishment of a dominant culture, Risberg argues that there is a fatal flaw in this thinking. She contends that each culture provides substantial benefit to the organization and further, that understanding other cultures is a better process for amalgamation than forcing one's culture on others. In this way ambiguity between cultures provides an opportunity for mutual exploration. Living with and experiencing the ambiguity of cultural differences becomes a diagnostic tool that allows differences to surface and to be explored. This position suggests that the appropriate objective is not dominance but rather synergy, or the 'effective' inter-penetration of culture. Risberg's work represents a basic and counter-intuitive organizational challenge to the prevailing notion of the ways partners 'should' approach the explicit merger of two organizational cultures.

The first two chapters focused on the team level of analysis while the third paper was at the interorganizational level. Gro Kvåle and Elisabeth Pettersen address these ideas at the societal level in their contribution "Asian Modernity or 'Creolization': With Weber to Singapore and Back Again." As a starting point, they note that the Singapore government is an unusually dominant factor and the Singapore population is marked by a high level of Confucian-based homogeneity. Within their work, Kvåle and Pettersen struggle with questions about whether Confucian ethics and Weberian modernity are antithetical. While they effectively raise several very different explanations that range from win/lose to post-hoc reinterpretation, they conclude that the mix of cultures in the form of several ethnicities, the English institutional heritage and the shift into global commerce fostered by transportation and communication revolutions, has resulted in a creolized society. Thus Singapore represents a rather high level of inter-penetration which has evolved through a sensitivity and respect for differences and the use of ambiguity as a diagnostic tool. Even though Singapore has a very strong central government committed to a significant role in Asia and the world, the creolization process has gone on without serious impediment.

Language is only one source of limitation, but it is a powerful one. In a public presentation to a large group of US business executives, Jean Claude Usunier pointed out that the business language of Europe is "broken" English. Once while attending a meeting of the Economic Commission of Europe, I realized that most of the complex negotiations of the meeting were being carried out in each delegate's second language. The Swedes and the Finns were speaking English, Romanians and the Hungarians were speaking Russian, the Tunisians were speaking French. I listened to the professional translation from Spanish to English of papers I had written and was surprised by the inaccuracies of the translations.

These vignettes are intended as reminders that the inter-penetration of culture is inhibited by language unfamiliarity. Typically, an educated member of any society has a 30,000-word vocabulary. But the second language vocabulary of most fluent international travelers is only 5,000 words. Thus, in multi-language settings the common language must be restricted to a much smaller vocabulary than participants have in their native tongues. As a result, robust communication is severely handicapped in crossing cultures. This enhances ambiguity and provides many surprises.

The postindustrial subculture can be characterized as a world of inter-penetrated culture but this appears to be more of an in-process viewpoint than an end-state viewpoint. Cultural identity is protected and preserved by many explicit and tacit forces, by various isolating mechanisms, and altered by multiple forces requiring interaction between cultures and supporting cultural inter-penetration. Clash and distortion, uneven cultural development, resistance and self-selection pose complex problems for the next millennium.

SECTION TWO

8

MASTERS OF SYMBOL: MY TRAVELS IN THOUGHT AND WORK LIFE IN THE CZECH REPUBLIC

Kathryn S. Rogers

A nation in the midst of turbulent change and actively involved in reconciliation with its own past seems especially ripe for observing the messages embedded in symbols. Information about "who we are" and "who we are not" takes on great significance as normative boundaries are redrawn to stabilize fragile new institutions and to encourage new patterns of behavior.

COMPREHENDING THE PRESENT

Physical artifacts permit access to the sensory and aesthetic dimensions of corporate life (Gagliardi, 1990). Because they are representational they simultaneously reinforce meaning on cognitive (logos), moral (ethos) and sensing (pathos) levels. They provide the structural muscle and connective tissue that link complex and abstract ideas with patterns of behavior and action. But as, Jung would say, inevitably some part of the meaning of any symbol is inarticulate, vague, and inaccessible except to the subconscious mind.

People look to the past to comprehend the present. They choose to understand history in terms of their current experiences. They select among historical possibilities things that appear to be valuable analogies. While discussing images of dragons within different cultural contexts and time periods, Sievers (1990) suggested that tradition is not a force emerging from and "preserving" history, but rather an influence on the social construction of historical events in the "present."

It is likely, if not inevitable, that association of historical images with certain symbols gives rise to new definitions of cultural order and new expectations about organizational roles and memberships. In this way history is a compilation of artifacts whose interpretations change. Through a self-constructed narrative, the particular selection of the artifacts that are invoked and their current interpretation tell us who we are, what we value, and subconsciously influence what we feel, see, and find touching.

In this chapter I use the metaphor "remnants of suppression" as a way of understanding current events in the Czech Republic. While living and working in and around Prague during the spring of 1996, I observed a variety of deliberately chosen artifacts used in a paradoxical fashion to overlay the past with a "new" identity while concurrently affirming Czech history. Selective evocation of historical and mythological figures in artifacts such as money, schools and theater combine with the new admiration of capitalist ethos to reinterpret Czech history as a continuous, proud but stifled, heritage that is congruent with an economically prosperous and independent future.

Forging this amalgam effectively involves building on the society's "traditional" values and preferences for accommodation, subtlety, conflict avoidance, and wit. These habitual behavior patterns provide coping mechanisms that encourage the simultaneous honoring and critiquing of symbolic elements that are being invoked to reinforce the new culture. They also deliberately heighten the ironic recognition of what might be yet another form of passive acceptance of foreign occupation (U.S. capitalism).

These observations are necessarily superficial; as a neophyte in the study of central Europe and a non-Czech speaker, I can hope only to identify some curious paradoxes and prompt questions about what the ongoing economic transition means to the survival of the Czech nation and/or to individual Czech interpretations of their history. Perhaps these speculations will also provide data to further investigate the way in which artifacts, especially deliberately chosen artifacts, contribute to the endurance and resiliency of organizations.

MONEY

When a regime changes, money is frequently reissued, for both practical and political reasons. Old debts may be canceled or currency revalued to insulate the new political system from the sins or obligations of the past. Less frequently noted are the new images chosen to adorn the coins and bills. These images convey important and sometimes subtle messages that mark the division of one time period from another. Money is crucial in the conduct of modern life, and it is rare that an emergent political system neglects this opportunity to honor the icons of the new order. On the other hand, everyone uses money and routine handling of these images usually makes them quickly invisible as explicit conveyors of cultural messages.

I became interested in the images chosen for currency by the new Czech Republic in 1992. Most people thought this was quite irrelevant to changes taking place. New currency had been issued just prior to the Velvet Revolution in 1989. Most of the images on the bills remained the same. An exception was the 100-crown Gottwald note. One side featured a portrait of the former communist head of state and on the other a famous nineteenth-century etching of the Charles Bridge in Prague. According to one tale about the old note, many people would partially deface it by tearing it through Gottwald's face before spending it.

Its replacement, issued in late 1989, shows the face of Charles IV with the jeweled crown of King Wenceslas (Vaclev I) on the obverse. The image of a resented modern communist puppet bureaucrat was replaced by that of a kind, intelligent, charismatic, powerful, and innovative but relatively remote national leader. Charles IV, who ruled in the mid-1300s as both king and Holy Roman Emperor, represents the cultural zenith and only example of Czech power. He was the last to unify Czech lands under one rule and presided over a time when arts, education, and public works flowered. The choice of so beloved a leader seems innocuous until seen as a deliberate substitution and put-down of the modern communist regime.

More currency changes were necessary after the split of the Czech Republic from Slovakia. New territorial boundaries, a new national name, and new Parliament made a reissuance of currency imperative. Interestingly, the selected images came from a previous national competition. They were rejected in 1988 by the communists and were resurrected from a vault. Both the expense and the design of these notes were major considerations in the fragile economy. Because of this some interesting remnants of old identities coexist with the new. The 100-crown Charles IV note was retained with minor modifications. Other images show a mixture of men and women known for their wisdom, kindliness, and foresight. The group includes the ancient king Premsyl Otakar I, St. Agnes (a spiritual martyr and aunt of Wenceslas), Jan Amos Komensky (a famous international educator), and from the nineteenth century a woman novelist, linguist and historian.

Other images include a newly developed four-part coat of arms, selected to replace the unified Czech-Slovak one, and a variety of folk, spiritual, and mythic images. To an American the absence of politicians is remarkable. In fact, it is a marked contrast to coinage from the first Czechoslovakian republic in which modern national leaders were celebrated. Massaryk, President of the first republic and a noted scholar, is included in the 1992 issue, but only at the 5,000-crown level.

One somewhat remarkable remnant of suppression remains on all bills currently in circulation. It is the tiny emblem, a stylized C/S, printed on both sides of all bills as a security check. This is a reference to the now defunct state of Czechoslovakia. It is a remnant of a checkered past that included the bartering of Czech lands to appease Hitler and more significantly the creation of the Czechoslovak nation after the collapse of the Hapsburg empire, Austria-Hungary, following World War I. The image no longer has a specific referent but has yet to be removed from the bills.

These symbols seem to suggest desire for continuity with an ancient past as a source of energy and inspiration for the difficult task ahead. At a time of uncertainty, they also emphasize the life of the mind and of individual and artistic pursuits above service to the state. The connection to the current symbolic head of state, playwright Vaclev Havel, is unavoidable here.

These images may serve to shore up the tentative government and help create confidence that culture, if not the nation, will continue to survive. They also evoke a nostalgic past and do little to articulate ways of sustaining the current political regime. Compared to American moralisms such as "E pluribus unum," the Latin saying printed on one-dollar bills and coinage, or simplistic presentations of socialist realism and Marxist-Leninist ideology, little here defines obligations or provides explicit civic instruction. The message is a puzzle that must be more subtly decoded. Doing so is voluntary, irrelevant, fun, and freer than in earlier times because playing with multiple meanings is an exercise of freedom and subversion.

CELEBRATING ABSENCES

Some symbols were noticeable by their absence. Most people remembered with horror the red stars that were seen on most houses and buildings during communist days. The weariness and conformity implied by these emblems has been replaced by a cacophony of banners, leaflets, and advertising that creates both confusion and litter. Tourist guidebooks are apt to celebrate Czech political humor by recalling the "liberated" World War II Soviet tank that was proudly exhibited and then later painted pink in honor of the revolt of 1968. Or they recall the Trabant, an East German automobile, that was placed on four legs to ridicule the cowardice of those who sought refuge at the German embassy in 1989 or who left the country in these common and inexpensive cars. Both of these icons of subversion have now been removed.

Still present is the "monument where nobody came." It is an attractively designed but empty niche in a Prague park. In it the statue of the new Hapsburg emperor was to have been installed in 1918 after the death of Franz-Joseph of Austria. Instead, World War I ended, the empire fell, and no new emperor arrived. The niche remains empty as an ironic reminder of a brief period of absence from foreign control.

ENVY AND FEAR AMONG CONSUMERS AND EMPLOYEES

Posters in subway stations where blank walls or ideological directives were posted are now a colorful array of advertisements to buy, learn, spend, save, or vote. Typically, the posters are beautifully designed and visually appealing. In Prague, higher priced luxury goods are imaginatively displayed in shop windows. By way of contrast, window displays in smaller towns tend to emphasize availability. There is a double message here. First, the influx of tourist business favoring expensive consumer goods occurs largely within the capital. Second, luxury ads as well as piles of soup cans in the windows of provincial shops reinforces the envy and penury that Czechs are so used to. The infrastructure of the small towns is still horribly neglected. Although there are no shortages and consumer goods are not rationed, Czech citizens are used to small and outwardly dull apartments, poor maintenance, everyday shopping, and expect that the high-design or electronic items they favor will be very expensive. The messages to Czechs consumers are to save money in hard currency or in savings banks and to continue to envy the West.

FEAR OF EXPLOITATION BOTH IN THE FUTURE AND THE PAST MAY PARTIALLY EXPLAIN SOME DEFENSES

I was teaching at the Czech Management Center (CMC), an institution jointly supported by US, Czech and Canadian government funds. Its mission is to prepare managers through American-style management practice to participate successfully in the transitional economy. This "partnership" of governments to prepare Czech managers is simultaneously revered and resented. No one makes entirely clear what managers are being prepared to do. Is it to become assistants to foreign capitalists? Or to run their own firms? Or to move away from home and into the "global" economy? Such ambiguity contributes to ambivalence about the program goals and apprehension about the relevance of the program to the local scene.

It does not help that the CMC is housed in a former Communist party training center. It does not help that the brass plaques listing contributors emphasize the stakes that foreign firms and investors have in producing receptive management practitioners. The format is very familiar. Partnership boards at CMC merely mimic the prominent displays of brass plaques on Prague buildings where foreign wealth is represented in the form of corporate tenants and investors who hold the most desirable office space.

Other links to the fear of exploitation are found in advertising. Czechs advertise aggressively, on painted buses, subway signage, on T-shirts, promoting banks and investment funds and vacations. Most of these campaigns are aimed at both tourists and Prague residents. This reinforces the feeling of invasiveness.

Resentment and anger are usually masked, but may come out in poor service, minor graft, and in subverting or ridiculing authority. This shadow side of Czech behavior is hard to detect since feigning affability coexists with the curious and naive openness that can make Americans believe Czechs are much like them. Resistance persists, however, in almost undetectable non-cooperation and the avoidance of uncomfortable emotional involvement.

Outbursts of anger in public are rare. Czechs are taught from early on to be compliant, polite, and quiet, unless drunk. If dissent or subversion is expressed it is most likely to take an indirect or teasing form. Visual puns, bizarre and surreal images, perhaps graffiti, and other forms of non cooperation are the habitual behaviors that this patently secretive society relies on to assert itself and express its identity.

HOW AND WHAT SHALL WE LEARN?

A common image of learning and teaching is that of Jan Amos Komensky (also known as Commenius). His image is on many school buildings and on the 200-crown bill. An early advocate of internationalism and student-centered learning, he has had an enduring influence on education. Some texts he wrote in the seventeenth century were still in use after World War II. A political dissident as well as educator, he went underground to avoid persecution by the king.

Students are expected to take pride in Commenius' depth of curiosity and breadth of knowledge. They are expected to practice the arts and be well-rounded. Sports, gymnastics, dancing, and theater are supposed to coexist with studying for the final exams after high school. Nevertheless, the actual form of schooling does not follow the liberal Komensky model. School programs are likely held in lecture formats with arbitrary oral examinations. These contrast sharply with imaginative after-school music and art programs that provide extra income for working artists and are still often partially supported by the state.

Music, theater, poetry and art are important to the Czech people. Thus, playwrights, linguists, historians, novelists, and composers are far more likely than political figures to be honored on public monuments or in museums and celebrations. For example, Smetana's patriotic opera, *Libuse,* was performed in the National Theater on the building's opening day in the 1870s and is often repeated on other symbolic occasions, such as the recent May 8th celebrations of liberation day, marking the end of World War II. *Libuse* honors the wise mythical seer who founded Prague and became queen. She is revered for her ability to resolve and avoid conflicts both with her advisors and among her people and to see the glorious future of the country.

I admired a statue of Jan Tyl, a dramatist and poet, who incidentally and embarrassingly to Czechs composed the Czech national anthem. The anthem "Where is my Homeland?" represents repressive political authority and is seldom sung. In fact, Olympic athletes have conspicuously protested singing it. Nevertheless, Tyl is honored for his artistic imagination.

PASSIVE DISSENT

Desire to criticize silently, to use subterfuge, or to convey a double message is a widely practiced and functional response to the blatant imposition of outward power and the need to accommodate to the quirks of culturally different and powerful authorities. Czechs see this behavior, which reinforces passivity and avoids conflict, as normal, appropriate, and not problematic. They take pride in being more subtle, more graceful in their criticisms, and more in control of their emotional responses than others, especially Americans. The triumph of Czech humor and passive resistance is gaining full credit and recognition for engaging in subterfuge, merely pretending to do something; sometimes to the point of being honored by authorities while simultaneously undercutting them.

CELEBRATED DATES

The final example of public symbols that embed and employ remnants of suppression in helping to define "who we are now" can be seen in the choice of dates designated for the country's various spring celebrations. May 1, the traditional communist Labor Day, is now hardly marked. Outside of Prague, a few small parades sponsored by conservative idealists of the labor movement are held. Most Czechs go on picnics or to horse races and relish the freedom from enforced attendance at the parades that used to characterize the day.

May 5 was celebrated rousingly in Plzen to commemorate General Patton's liberation of the city in 1945. In Prague and throughout the rest of the Czech Republic, May 8 is the day selected to celebrate the end of World War II in Europe. This date has been designated the official holiday since 1990.

Prague was not liberated until the Russians arrived on May 9, 1945. Thus, during the years of communist rule, May 9 was the date of commemoration. But Russian tanks as well as Russian "liberation" soon took on a different meaning and in order to "get the red stain off the day" the new regime has changed the date to May 8. History and even the calendar needed to be cleaned for the Czech nation to move forward into its future.

Removing or reinterpreting the remnants of suppression is evidently a long-term process. It is likely to continue for a long time as the country and individual citizens try to find integrative ways to understand and to gain pride and self-esteem from their complex and confusing recent narrative histories. Restoring a remote past that they can honor may provide solace but it may actually serve to delay the job of reinterpreting these images so they may become avant-garde and seen in a new light. Returning to the words of Sievers (1990:221):

[T]he function of avant-garde in mythology or symbolism could be to look at the apparently assured interpretations of our ancestors from a different perspective, i.e. to recognize again as unknown and surprising what has been regarded as evident and familiar. To create such a new tradition often means recognizing the social as well as the unconscious dimensions these images refer to and are built upon as parts of a common culture. This, for example, means that ancient images often carry latently, so to speak, more crystallized meaning than we are able to reactivate contemporarily or that we, in a non-conscious manner, are referring to earlier images; we may even quote from them without being aware of the fact or of its sources.

The creation and construction of tradition seems to be happening on a daily basis in the Czech republic. Defining behaviors and setting examples for consumers, employees, students, and citizens does not mean that these examples are always understood or willingly followed. The next task is to decode those symbols more thoroughly and to understand better the way in which they might affect the future.

BIBLIOGRAPHY

Gagliardi, P. ed. (1990) *Symbols and Artifacts,* Berlin: De Gruyter.
Sievers, B. (1990) "Curing the Monster: Some Images of and Considerations About the Dragon" in P. Gagliardi, ed. *Symbols and Artifacts,* Berlin: De Gruyter.

9

THE SEXY BIOTECHNOLOGY: A POSTMODERN PHENOMENOLOGICAL OBSERVATION OF CONTRADICTION AND MEANING

Martin Fuglsang

This chapter looks at an array of conflicting organizational practices characterized by great uncertainty. In situations like this, there is an infinity of choices—each conditioned by contingency and ambiguity. There are several lexicons at work and hence multiple possible perceptions. The context is phenomenologically post-modern because it renounces the role of insight, a fixed Archimedean point for developing aging reason and contemporary rationality.

INTRODUCTION

He has been standing on a corner with something on his mind for many years. He has almost been forgotten and his message has drowned in the infinite flood of universal meaning and order. Though his voice is now lowered to an almost inaudible whisper he repeats himself endlessly. His eyes reflect serenity as if he knows his time has come. He thinks that somewhere someone has heard him and continues his tale through the infinite flood of meaning, but he is not quite sure. So he resumes saying: "I, the Cretan Epimenides claim, as I have always done, that all Cretans are liars." In a reflexive moment he thinks that the world must be able to understand that the basis of all our thinking is paradoxical. That is exactly why I have remained in my corner. Not to tell the world what has happened, like Kant, but by my mere presence to tell what has been forgotten or ignored.

Finally I have been heard. Well yes, mutters the hawk and scavenger Derrida, you have been heard old friend, but there is something you have misunderstood. While the paradoxical nature of thinking is basic, the problem is not the logic but the nature of modernity. Modernity's universal rationality and unambiguous meaning is its last agony. There is no essence to which the text refers other than itself. Because meaning is always radically unstable, the present is always kaleidoscopic and fragmented. Metaphysical elements such as truth, singular meaning and reality do not exist. All that exist are patterns of games, differences in the expression itself, differences between differences, and traces of traces.

The philosophical text and the instructions for our kitchen appliances are equal, differing only in genre. Our task is deconstructing any text that purports to be something other than text. As Nietzsche always said, when he senses a feeling of creeping malaise slowly penetrating the muscles of his spine, he gets up and leaves the room and goes out into his garden. It is beautiful, he thinks, and the creeping malaise gradually leaves him. But before it is all gone, the cynical nihilism resumes its usual place. Farthest back in his consciousness the thought strikes him that perhaps postmodernism is more than deconstruction. Perhaps it also cherishes hopes that are not rooted in the universal, but in the linguistic being itself, in the very construction. He shakes his head. Once more the garden sets his mind at rest, this garden with all its order.

Epimenides smiles a little as he slowly moves away from his corner to take a well-deserved rest. Even you, dear Derrida, Epimenides thinks, with your cynical deconstruction you will never let go of the paradoxical nature of thinking. For if meaning is radically unstable, what is then the status of this absolutist proposition? Even you, dear friend, are captured by this self-reflexive paradox, and now his smile fades and he laughs shrilly.

CONTRADICTION AND MEANING

This chapter attempts to make sense of conflicting organizational practice characterized by great uncertainty and an infinity of choices. All choices are conditioned by contingency and ambiguity and thus there are several lexicons at work permitting multiple possible perceptions. The organizational context is postmodern, because it renounces the place of insight, a fixed Archimedean point for the developing reason and contemporary rationality. The context is simply phenomenological in a postmodern sense.[1]

---

[1]Use of postmodern phenomenology in this context should be viewed as an attempt to merge three perspectives: the language philosophy of Wittgenstein, the phenomenology of Heidegger and Merleau-Ponty, and the Frankfurter School's focus on the importance of the social-historical context to our thinking. The Frankfurter School recognizes that 'radical' constructivism can be viewed as a contemporary expression of the historicity of epistemology. And it is the postmodern phenomenology's merging of

Before discussing these contradictions, it is important to clarify 'context' in a postmodern phenomenological sense. The basis of organizational context in the scientific sphere is language. The position of observation cannot be detached from language and life. Thus postmodern phenomenology is an intrinsic part of the linguistic philosophical terminology of the twentieth century.

Postmodern phenomenology directly opposes the dualism dominating West European philosophy and science. It opposes Descartes' surgical cut, dividing body and mind. It challenges the 'philosophy of consciousness' concept of full self-reflexivity by inactive entities. It also challenges the constructed contrast between consciousness and the world—or between experience and reality—in which empiricism portrays consciousness or experience as a passive element. It opposes the rationalist picture that applies universal maxims to transform experience into undisturbed and undistorted knowledge.

A postmodern phenomenological position confronts the perception of a reality independent of experience. Thus it is a confrontation of the claim that scientific data can exist outside ourselves as 'raw data,' that we can observe, explain, and predict in a neutral and unaffected way. Scientific data are within ourselves as interpretations and perhaps, at best, as a community of interpretation, as a (con)-text.

We can never place ourselves outside of our context. Therefore, recognizing and committing oneself to the reflections of language is identical to endorsing Wittgenstein's paragraphs in "Philosophical Investigations." What Kirkeby (1995) expresses as the 'I can' in thought is that language games are the way we play with words and concepts to shape events [*Ereignis*] and worlds, while life form reflects our cultural heritage, and create our routine movement and practice.

Language games and life forms express themselves in an almost dialectic interplay, or more precisely, as an interwovenness, from which we understand the common, the real, and the possible. The mutual shifts in language games and life forms create change and variability. This is Heidegger's 'linguistic being' [*Sprachwesen*] which shares the possibility and limits of everything. Language is both the infinite scope of our freedom and our prison. We cannot talk about meaning in which language functions as a transparent medium or as a logic of reason having the same form as the outside world. Only through language can we talk about meaning. Meaning presupposes the phenomenon meaning as a linguistic category delimiting non-meaning. Thus, language brings us reality, and reality is language as formulated by Kirkeby (1994) in his discussion of postmodern phenomenological epistemology.

We are always situated within a context of meaning and potential meaning. The

---

these ideas, elaborated by the Danish philosopher Ole Fogh Kirkeby in his doctoral thesis "Begivenhed og Krops-tanke" [Event and Body-Mind], that is one of the most important Danish contributions to philosophy in the twentieth century.
This is expressed in a more secular version in his prolegomena "Verden, ord og tanke" [World, Word and Thought] and expressed almost lyrically and poetically in his recent book "Selvnødighedens filosofi" [The Philosophy of Selfcessity].

situation itself is often a struggle for meaning in which questions of fact are a complex interaction between me and others. I do not control the parameters creating the situation or that which makes the situation an event. Nor do I control the point at which essence becomes existence and signification is ascribed.

We are socialized into history, into existing language games and life forms from which we have no existential hope of fleeing. Like Sarte's humanistic existentialism claims, the choices we make are already limited by our own historicity. Through the situation we are always incorporated into the world. What we are is always saturated with meaning before we can adopt a reflexive attitude, therefore, in our existence we have already been read, spoken and thought.

This represents the premise for my search; a search for meaning in a conflicting practice. We create such a practice subtly through observing practice and our attempts to empathize with what we assume to be outside ourselves. There are forms of practice in which the meaning appears to be less singular, more tentative and in perpetual motion: a practice which is characterized by high innovative action and in which closure is a desirable condition, but in where consistent motion of meaning seems to increase the potential for conflict.

BIOTECHNOLOGY: AN INNOVATIVE PRACTICE

Let's take a close look at private biotechnological research in two companies, 'Institute for Drug Analysis' and 'Neuro-Search.' The former develops medical products based on plants and the latter develops drugs for the central nervous system.

Biotechnology now is what alchemy was in the Middle Ages—mysterious, surprising and incomprehensible to us standing on the outside. We are in the forefront of science; on the borderland of the unpredictable, and thereby the spoken. With biotechnology, we have actualized and realized Dante's idea of a world in which man is half divine and half secular. Biotechnology not only discovers the natural, it creates the natural.

Biotechnology is an organizational context whose attractive force seems to be the sensual and sometime intense dance of knowledge [*Erkenntnis*] and technology. While dancing they create harmonious contrasts. When one is red the other doesn't want to be blue, but they are both a precondition of black. The Institute of Drug Analysis and Neuro-Search can be viewed as manifestations of this phenomena and simultaneously the precondition each other. When one unwraps the other, the other wraps up the one, and the partial nature of determinism is thus dissolved. It is in this perpetual change at an increasing rate, that biotechnology becomes sexy. Speed is the sexological fix point of the nineties. In the context of such high-speed movement the basic organization appears to be conditioned by uncertainty, turbulence and ambiguity.

Managers and employees must be capable of anticipating these phenomena to develop tools for managing the unmanageable, controlling the uncontrollable, and predicting the unpredictable. There is a large body of literature on organization and management. Explanations are provided, organizational change described and possible actions suggested, but we are seldom furnished with explicit explanations. Large parts of the literature view certainty, stability, and unambiguity as givens; their negation is viewed as unnatural, threatening, and undesirable.

For the Institute for Drug Analysis and Neuro-Search it is not a question of going from uncertainty to certainty, from turbulence to stability, and from ambiguity to clarity. Rather it is a matter of exploiting the contingencies and surprises created by these conditions while simultaneously attempting to reduce their complexity.

It is as if the Institute for Drug Analysis and Neuro-Search can't resist these conditions but would rather appropriate them. It is as if the two organizations simply cannot contain the activities they unfold. They resemble a chameleon that not only changes color at incredible speed, but also changes form, depending on which biotechnological activity is underway.

To observe these biotechnological projects, we must move beyond the way in which we usually think about the Institute for Drug Analysis and Neuro-Search. When we study their productive activity, the genesis and maturing of the biological projects, we can do it in multiple ways. We can observe formal cooperation with other firms and hence other actors, where formal boundaries are broken down by informal exchange of information, or we can study informal exchange of information between actors from competing organizations that follows an implicit language codex.

This could mean that the linguistic demarcation between the organization and its environment is far more blurred and changeable than anything we have seen before. Describing and understanding what is inside and what is outside is becoming increasingly difficult where organizational environments are continuously changing. Both the organization and its environment are perpetually being redefined and reinterpreted. Thus, the organization's permanent state may simply be an arbitrary linguistic convention.

We tend to view systems as if they cyclically close in on themselves to reduce complexity and later reopen themselves to the environment to find new situations or dissolve. But in biotechnology our reality approximates a kaleidoscope, producing colorful figures and configurations which disappear when shaken and are replaced with new different colorful configurations.

Using postmodern phenomenology, biotechnology is a situation where researchers are in a state of 'meaning' and 'potential meaning': ideas that are consistent with a concept of social system inspired by the works of the German sociologist Niklas Luhmann (1984) and the French constructivist Michel Callon (1986). Biotech researchers operate in a space where meaning is often at conflict between individual actors and the artifacts around which they are centered. It is a world in which we find practice expressing itself in conflicting ways but simultaneously creating a subtle emergent consistency. We can observe action that is conflicting and meaningful at the same time.

Biotechnology researchers in the private sector often participate in networks in which they have to collaborate and compete in the same time and space. That is, they must engage in what I term 'paradoxical conduct': to get information they must give information, yet to survive they must simultaneously keep information secret. A biotechnology researcher from the Institute for Drug Analysis reflects on this type of conduct: "Since my organization is a network organization I lose control, and how am I to handle this uncertainty?"

He answers: "I suppose one learns to live with it, because I live from it. This type of collaboration is a delicate balance; there are things which I must keep to myself, my basic knowledge I must keep to myself—that is my means of survival," and he continues: "It is a dilemma; on the one hand, I need information from people in my network, and in order to get that I must depart with some knowledge, and in order to survive I have to strike the right balance."

The individual actor is forced to choose between two extremes: to pass on information or conceal information. This is consistent with traditional organizational sociology where the individual is governed by conflicting perspectives and these various interests require reflexive adoption of a position followed by making the 'right' decision. There is no empirical data to support this idea clearly but there are two cognitive frames of reference, or more precisely two different discourses at work simultaneously: a scientific and an economic one.

In simple form, science as discourse can be centered around the medium true/false (Luhmann, 1990). In the scientific discourse, communication is ultimately tied to the demand for openness, for publishing results in order to create 'closure,' to turn the object/phenomenon into an objective form. In similar simple form the economic discourse is centered around the medium profitable/unprofitable. In this basic utilitarian moral philosophy, communication ultimately attempts to protect and conceal the organization's domain of knowledge and production.

The network, or the social system, demands that communication be tied simultaneously to both alternatives. In this perspective, network communication appears to be a dichotomy, the two poles constitute mutually exclusive demands on the actors' action. But, quite to the contrary, I found that biotechnology researchers participating in various networks seem to display an extreme degree of mobility. They appear capable of managing mutually exclusive demands in the same time and space and with an admirable naturalness.

First we must understand that action is not the problem. As Wittgenstein stresses, action exists as a pre-linguistic condition. The problem is the interpretation and meaning of subsequent action. Biotechnology researchers display paradoxical conduct. This is what Cameron and Quinn (1988) call an organizational paradox. Paradoxical conduct is action within the context of contradictions. An organizational paradox is an analytical category, a linguistic construction, based on paradoxical conduct. An organizational paradox is, therefore, a reflexive concept of the second order; it is a concept of meaning, not action.

In my view, organizational paradox is a reflexive perspective that functions as an analytical knife to make sense of actions that appear to be mutually exclusive. We can make sense of the context, characterized by uncertainty, turbulence, and ambiguity. This is different than the 'meaning' usually ascribed to action using traditional organizational sociological perspectives.

The two discourses, or more concretely the two alternatives, constitute a duality in which each alternative creates a contradictory pole. Actors must choose between passing on or withholding information. From this perspective, the two poles are continuously interchanged. From a perspective supported by a dualist view action appears formally logical (Ford and Backoff 1988). The individual actor places himself at the intersection of location of insight and decides reflexively, which of the two alternatives is the most suitable. This is an expression of a purposive rationality, difficult to meet in the complex interplay visualized by network participation. The general criticism leveled against the organizational sociological perspectives, that divides the poles into either/or dichotomy, is that they reduce, or rather remove totally, the sphere of tension created by this duality. This perspective simplifies both the biotechnological networks' action flow and the action's dual bond to two contradictory demands.

Several studies have stressed the necessity of maintaining contradictions both in the scientific analysis (Westenholz 1994; Fuglsang and Schmidt 1994) and in organizations where contradictions exist (Cameron and Quinn 1988; Hampden-Turner 1990). The organizational sociological paradox is this kind of perspective, characterized by a lack of dualism, breaks with formal, logical linearity by introducing a lateral form of cognition. The observations thus created are systemic. In it the internal relationship between the two poles of the duality constitute a complementary contrast that generates equilibrium in relation to the surrounding systems. Thus the organizational sociological paradox perspective is supported by what Oscar Ichazo (1982) calls trialectic logic.

Trialectric logic breaks with the assumption that contradictions are inherent, claiming that as users/carriers of language we create these contradictions as immanent variations in the language itself. We make sense through the use of concepts and their negation. Language functions as a maker of distinctions. To understand cold we construct its negation warm. To understand open we create its negation closed, etc. Meaning emerges through the active construction of opposites. Based on this assumption, perspectives which perpetually remove one of the two poles of duality appear to be meaningless.

On the other hand, the organizational paradox perspective insists on opposites. It supports the paradox that the network is a medium for both passing on and concealing information in the same time. It is this very contrast that makes the network viable as a social ecological system. We can understand the necessity for passing on information to ensure that the network can create 'closure' and appreciate the need to conceal information to ensure the survival of the individual biotechnological actor. This does not imply that the individual actor doesn't experience it as a conflict and a tremendous dilemma, but he operates in the sphere of tension suspended between complementary opposites.

The paradox perspective encompasses numerous interpretations of the social context, creating an opening for contradictory constellations and alternatives in the contextual setting. It should be seen as an attempt to capture what logically seems illogical, contrasts that are apparently mutually exclusive in the same time and space and which function as a reflexive concept of the second order.

BIBLIOGRAPHY

Callon, M., J. Law and A. Rib, eds. (1986) *Mapping the Dynamics of Science and Technology,* London: Macmillan.

Cameron, K.S. and R.E. Quinn, eds. (1988) *Paradox and Transformation,* Boston: Ballinger.

Ford, J.D. and R.W. Backoff (1988) "Organizational Change In and Out of Dualities and Paradox" in Cameron and Quinn (1988) *Paradox and Transformation,* Boston: Ballinger.

Fuglsang, M. and M. Schmidt (1994) *En Akademisk Fortælling* [An Academic Story], Copenhagen: Handelshøjskolen i København.

Hampden-Turner, C. (1990) *Charting the Corporate Mind,* Oxford: Blackwell.

Heidegger, M. (1926) *Being and Time.* New York: Harper and Row.

Heidegger, M. (1959) *On the Way to Language,* New York: Harper and Row.

Ichazo, Oscar (1982) *Between Metaphysics and Protoanalysis.* New York: Arica.

Kirkeby, O.F. (1994) *Begivenhed og Krops-Tanke* [Event and Body-Mind], Copenhagen: Forlaget Modtryk.

Kirkeby, O.F. (1995) *Verden, Ord og Tanke* [World, Word and Thought], Copenhagen: Handelshøjskolens Forlag.

Kirkeby, O.F. (1996) *Selvnødighedens Filosofi* [The Philosophy of Selfcessity], Copenhagen: Forlaget Modtryk.

Luhmann, N. (1984) *Social Systems.* Stanford, CA: Stanford University Press.

Luhmann, N. (1990) *Die Wissenschaft der Gesellschaft,* Frankfurt am Main: Suhrkamp Verlag.

Westenholtz, A. (1994) Modeller af arbejdsmarkedsdemokrati efter 2. Verdenskrig. [Models of Workplace Democracy since the Second World War] Copenhagen: Handelshøjskolen i København.

Wittgenstein, L. (1958) *Folosofiske Undersøgelser.* Copenhagen: Munksgaard.

10

RESEARCHING THE EXPERIENCE OF WOMEN IN "MAN"AGEMENT ACROSS CULTURES: A FEMINIST STANDPOINT APPROACH

Iiris Aaltio-Marjosola and Sarah Williams Jacobson

Cross-cultural studies of scientific modernist design sometimes reinforce or create stereotypes about national character and organizational life rather than heighten cultural awareness. Specifically, these stereotypes mask the life-world of women. We suggest an alternative approach—one grounded in a "feminist standpoint." The research project we will describe here, conducted in Finland and the United States, countries with very different cultural features, illustrates the "feminist standpoint" approach and demonstrates the importance of considering both gender and context in attempting to describe the work lives, private lives and career development of women managers.

INTRODUCTION

As the economies of most countries become more global, recognition of "other"—other norms, habits and cultural ways of doing business—is becoming increasingly important. Recently, focus on the other has turned to consideration of the role women managers will play in an expanding world economy (Adler and Izraeli, 1994). Most of this work, much of it conducted as large-scale survey research, focuses either on cataloging and explaining the limited economic participation of women managers or advocating for their inclusion based upon "traits and orientations traditionally associated with women, the female and the feminine" (Calás and Smircich, 1993). Some have argued that cultural analysis and comparisons such as these, rather than reflecting universal truths, are inextricably bound to both temporal and geographical contexts. Within this perspective, universalization of the terms management and woman manager is both inappropriate and misleading. The contingent nature of analysis must be bridged in some way (Calás, 1994; Boyacigiller and Adler, 1991; Steers, Bischoff and Higgins, 1992).

One suggested way to bridge understanding of the experience of the "other" is through the use of ethnographic techniques—observation, interviewing, and "thick" descriptions (Geertz, 1973; Boyacigiller and Adler, 1991). However, while these techniques may be helpful in mitigating the inappropriate application of culture-bound theory, it is also important to recognize that such analysis is itself inevitably rooted in the cultural context and life experiences of the researcher(s) who produce it.

Therefore, we advance the argument that being more reflective about the complex and deep effects of culture must constitute a part of the "validity" of any cross-cultural project regardless of the topic or specific methodology employed. This argument is theoretically positioned from a "feminist standpoint" (Harding, 1987; Fletcher, 1994; Calvert and Ramsey, 1992).

FEMINIST STANDPOINT THEORIZING: IMPLICATIONS FOR CROSS-CULTURAL RESEARCH

While scholarly work using the feminist standpoint has varied in focus (Fletcher, 1995; Jacques, 1993; Grant, 1988; Rosener, 1990), it all shares at least three assumptions: (1) an acceptance of gender differences and the understanding that these differences neither imply nor legitimate inequality; (2) a challenge to the traditional foundations of organizational and *man*agement knowledge that emerged from an historically "masculine" view of the world; and (3) a belief in the importance of moving beyond critique to incorporate knowledge created from the unique experience of women.

Gender Difference

Foundational organizational scholarship, much of it created in the United States, was designed by men, for men, to explore the experience of men. After the passage of equal opportunity legislation and increasing presence of women in organizations and management positions, research turned to examination of ways in which women might be similar or different from males—along a series of previously established variables. Few differences were identified (Powell, 1988, 1993). When differences did surface, they were explained as the product of an archaic gender socialization process undergoing transformation as a new age of equality dawned.

While liberal feminists focused on the documentation of "no difference," more radical scholars (Firestone, 1970; Dinnerstein, 1977) emphasized inherent differences between men and women, claiming that true social change would come only when the masculine was devalued and dethroned and the feminine extolled and elevated.

A gender difference/similarity debate continues among feminist scholars in all academic disciplines and has increased since the development of a comprehensive theory of gender difference by psychologists Nancy Chodorow (1978) and Carol Gilligan (1982). These authors describe female "self-hood" as "a complex web of interacting psychological and social forces that place women's early development in a context of communion (expressiveness, connection, relatedness) whereas men's early development occurs in a context of agency (independence, autonomy, instrumentality)" (Fletcher, 1994).

Aptheker (1989) summarizes the implications of this difference: "Women have a distinct way of seeing and interpreting the world. This is not to say that all women have the same consciousness or share the same beliefs. It is to say that women of each particular culture or group have a consciousness, a way of seeing, which is common to themselves as women in that it is distinct from the way the men of their culture or group sees things" (p. 12).

Miller (1986) reframed these personality characteristics as representing a unique "female advantage." Like-minded scholars have suggested that incorporation and greater valuation of characteristics associated with "women's voice" or a "female advantage" would bring much-needed softening and connection to organizational life (Grant, 1988; Rosener, 1990; Calvert and Ramsey, 1992) and offer competitive advantage in an age of global competition (Adler and Izraeli, 1994).

Critique of the female-advantage perspective was not long in coming. Liberal feminists (Powell, 1993) contend that a focus on gender difference represents retreat and restatement of past gender stereotypes. Kolb (1992) argues that because characteristics associated with the female and the feminine are and have been devalued in organizations, reinforcement under the banner of the female advantage will serve to keep women in devalued positions. Others (Calás et al., 1991), speaking from a feminist post-structuralist position, argue that

> promoting the female advantage co-opts women, encouraging them to use their skills to advance bureaucratic management goals while diverting energy from the larger struggle to challenge and question the very nature of these goals and the knowledge production procedures that created and maintain them as natural, right and unassailable. (Fletcher, 1994)

Still others (Collins, 1991; Bell, Denton and Nkomo, 1993) find fault with the female advantage perspective because it universalizes the experience of white, middle-class academics in the United States—obfuscating the influences that membership in specific categories such as race, class, national origin, sexual orientation, etc. have on lived experience. More recently, Joyce Fletcher (1994:75) has initiated a critique of the female advantage position grounded in "feminist standpoint" theory. This critique

> *maintains that there is a female advantage or alternative perspective that has the power to transform our way of thinking about organizing. However, it asserts that the transformational power of this alternative perspective has been degendered. The problem with the female advantage raised in this critique is not that gender differences are mere illusions nor that feminine strengths are being co-opted by organizations but that the essence, the truly transformative power of women's voice, is missing from popular representations of these strengths.*

In support of the logic of the female advantage, there is little doubt that the life experiences of most women are different from those of most men. While those differences are modified through membership in other social categories, and vary based on context and historical period, the powerful interweaving of biology, status and power differentials, cultural images and influences, and related child-rearing practices ensure that this is so. The result is that women see and experience the world in special ways. If encouraged, this perspective could bring unique positive strengths and advantages to organizational life and research.

This line of thinking must be pursued with caution, however. Organizational practices are deeply entrenched and universalizing within gender categories is a dangerous trap. Reified representations of "gender," "women" and the "feminine" should be looked upon with suspicion as legitimating and extending present relationships of power. We believe, therefore, that any scholarship that seeks to examine the experiences of women managers must be designed to live within this tension—on the one hand accepting differences in experience based on membership in a gender category and, on the other, recognizing that those differences are unstable, conditional, and ultimately capable of change. Linda Nicholson (1994:99–100) summarizes the implications of this tension in the following way:

> *As we search for that which is socially shared, we need to be simultaneously searching for the places where such patterns break down. My argument thus points to the replacement of claims about women as such or even women in patriarchal societies with claims about women in particular contexts. I want to suggest that we think of the meaning of woman as a word whose meaning is not found through the elucidation of some specific characteristic but is found through the elaboration of a complex network of characteristics.*

The "Masculine" Nature of Knowledge Making

A feminist standpoint critique of knowledge making rests upon this uneasy assumption of gender difference. Early feminist scholars in the United States and Europe challenged existing institutions and social practice as patriarchal. This critique was later extended to include knowledge production, specifically the scientific method itself as both a product and legitimator of patriarchy (Haraway, 1988;

Millman and Kanter, 1987; Harding, 1986, 1987; Keller, 1984). In this argument, science is characterized by values traditionally associated with masculinity and males in Western society. The notion that science is itself masculine is difficult for some to accept and the rejection of the scientific method is far from universal among feminist scholars. For example, psychologist Toby Jayaratne (1983:160–161,159–158) argues that

> *there must be appropriate quantitative evidence to counter the pervasive and influential quantitative sexist research which has and continues to be generated in the social sciences. Feminist researchers can best accomplish this. If some of the traditional procedures used to produce that needed evidence are contrary to our feminist values, then we must change those procedures accordingly. In the process of change we not only must remember to view our research in a political context . . . but we must support one another against the academic and professional pressures to compromise our standards.*

These positions are not necessarily antithetical. If the values of science are assumed to correspond to a single subset of human experience then supposedly real criteria of objectivity, reliability, validity and statistical significance can be seen as value-based. Reliance on these criteria limits both the nature and range of topics that can be studied to phenomena that are finite, observable and measurable. It also limits the kind of knowledge that is produced. We are not, however, suggesting that the scientific method and the use of quantitative data in social research are always useless, inappropriate and/or sexist. Far more important is the notion that research conducted from within the perspective of science constitutes but one way of knowing. We argue that there are additional and equally valid standards.

A "Feminist Standpoint" Perspective

A feminist standpoint approach to conducting research offers one alternative perspective on knowledge making. We share with Shulamit Reinharz (1992:4) the opinion that "Instead of orthodoxy, feminist research practices must be recognized as a plurality. Rather than there being a 'woman's way of knowing,' or a 'feminist way of doing research,' there are women's ways of knowing." Each appropriately designed to address the specific problem and context in which the creation of knowledge is occurring. It is at a deeper level that the feminist standpoint perspective shares common themes, setting it apart from non-feminist research.

Reinharz (1992:240) identifies these themes as characteristics of feminist research,

it is a perspective not a method . . . uses a multiplicity of research methods . . . involves an ongoing criticism of nonfeminist research . . . is guided by feminist theory may . . . be transdisciplinary . . . aims to create social change . . . strives to represent human diversity . . . includes the researcher as a person . . . attempts to develop special relations with the people studied, and defines a special relationship with the reader.

In addition, research conducted from a feminist standpoint approach is specifically grounded in qualities of vulnerability, reflexivity, receptivity, empathy, collaboration and appreciation of context. These qualities point to the following design implications (adapted from Fletcher, 1994).

(1) *Vulnerability/Reflexivity.* A scientific approach to knowledge making requires objectivity and distancing. In feminist standpoint research, a deliberate effort is made to reduce the distance between researcher and research subject. This effort requires that researchers suspend their expert role in order to "hear" the other's story with naive ears—creating the possibility that in learning about the "other," the researcher may actually learn more about him or herself. In this sense research may offer transformative power for the researcher as well as for the reader and the researched.

(2) *Receptivity/Openness/Empathy.* The ability to immerse oneself and to connect on some level beyond the merely intellectual is an important element in feminist standpoint research. Fletcher (1994:77), in describing this quality, says, "empathy is an affectively and cognitively complex response that is characterized by creativity and mutuality. Most important, it depends on a capacity to freely and wholeheartedly engage with another's subjectivity while maintaining and being in touch with one's own."

Such openness ultimately relies on the recognition that all knowledge-making is at some level rooted in one's own life experience. Reinharz (1992:259) notes that "feminist researchers use the strategy of 'starting from one's own experience' for many purposes. It defines our research questions, leads us to sources of useful data, gains the trust of others in doing the research, and enables us to partially test our findings."

(3) *Collaboration.* While historically, organization and management science has valued independent work, the feminist standpoint approach recognizes that collaboration, while generally more difficult and less "heroic" than independent production, is both essential and inevitable in the research process even when such collaboration is unacknowledged or unrecognized.

(4) *Contextualizing.* The norm in social science research is simplification, measurement of a few discrete, easily quantified variables across as large a "sample" of individuals as possible. A feminist standpoint approach recognizes the dangers inherent in generalization and focuses on the particular at the expense of the general. A more holistic approach is adopted. Complexity rather than simplicity is emphasized. Thus, for example, in establishing context, the complex linkages between private and public life augment isolated experiences within organizations.

Employing these qualities, feminist standpoint research agendas are liberatory in the sense that their goal is to open up possibilities for understanding many equally valuable and valued ways of existing. In feminist standpoint work, however, it is important to first challenge that which has gone before within the scientific value perspective outlined above. Therefore, before describing our research project, we begin with consideration of past work that has examined the experience of women managers across cultures.

Crossing Cultures—The Hofstede Story

Perhaps the best-known, most widely read, most often cited, cross-cultural organizational research in the literature is that of Geert Hofstede and his associates. While not specifically focused on the experience of women managers, Hofstede's work has had a profound influence on all international research and theorizing dealing with topics relating to them. Hofstede has noted that he only "accidentally became interested in cultural differences" (1991, p. ix) when he revisited a study drawn from an internally funded attitude assessment of IBM employees. This study was conducted twice (once in 1968 and again in 1970) across the countries in which the company was then doing business. As IBM's "chief psychologist," Hofstede's assessment design evolved into a data bank that eventually included 117,000 subjects.

Based on the size of his sample and the large number of countries included in the research, his findings constitute a highly credible foundation for subsequent research in this domain. His findings are increasingly employed as a convenient tool for the attempts of practicing managers to understand the "other." Hofstede believed that patterns of values within a national culture are widely held by its members. Using factor analysis, he identified four such dimensions of variation, described as follows:

(1) *Power distance*—the ways in which societies deal with inequality, prestige, wealth and power.

(2) *Uncertainty avoidance*—the ways in which societies differentially use rules, norms and rituals to reduce or live with uncertainty.

(3) *Individualism*—the ways in which societies differentially balance the needs of the individual and the collectivity.

(4) *Masculinity/Femininity*—the ways in which individuals in societies differentially endorse stereotypically masculine values (e.g., paid work as a central factor in life, a preference for more salary to shorter work hours, a strong achievement motivation) or stereotypically feminine values (e.g., good interpersonal relationships and service to others).

Finland and the United States were among the countries included in the study. Finns were characterized as having a small power distance and as being individualistic. Americans also favored a small power distance but were characterized as being individualistic in the extreme, being the highest such culture in the world. In terms of relative level of uncertainty avoidance, Finns were characterized as being above average while Americans were well below the median. Additionally, Hofstede identified Finland as among the least "masculine"/ most "feminine" cultures of those considered. On this dimension, Finland ranked 47/53 while the United States was ranked above the median in 15th position.

Delving more deeply, we considered the assumptions underlying the masculine/feminine dimension. A number of these items reflect historic stereotypes about male and female work orientations [*i.e.*, men are achievement-oriented and want challenge and advancement in their work while women are supportive and cooperative, put their families first and seek security]. These concepts, first advanced by Frederick Herzberg in the 1950s, assert advancement and challenge are necessary for "genuine" work motivation, whereas fulfillment of security needs and the presence of a cooperative working community only create an absence of what might be called "unmotivation." The statements support an understanding of the premise that those adhering to a "feminine" work orientation are not really motivated by their work. A statement that, when loaded on female bodies, offers an absurdly inaccurate generalization that all women share this pattern.

Theorists have suggested alterations to the Hofstede findings in subsequent theorizing and research (Adler, 1986; Adler and Jelinek, 1986). However, this has been done "without ever acknowledging that both the meta-theoretical discourse—i.e., Hofstede's dimensions—and the corrected theoretical discourse emerge from the same cultural assumptions—i.e., from the same understandings—of the original" (Calás, 1994). One way to challenge these understandings is by carefully re-reading Hofstede's work from a feminist standpoint perspective.

There are few who would argue with the premise that life in the workplace and at home has changed remarkably in the years since 1970 when Hofstede last surveyed IBM employees. These changes have occurred in Finland as well as in the United States. Tuija Parvikko (1990:99) notes that, as late as the 1970s, "the discussion on women's position in [Finnish] society was often linked to discussion on social and family policy." Thus, it is quite possible that opinions registered with regard to gender issues in the Hofstede questionnaire made in 1970 in Finland might be entirely different today. And yet, the myth of permanence, once institutionalized, is tacitly perpetuated.

The Hofstede study has some additional and more basic limitations. It has been persuasively argued (Haraway, 1988; Millman and Kanter, 1987; Harding, 1986, 1987; Keller, 1984) that research questions, research methods (often quantitative) and research situations, deriving from an academic tradition of historical male presence and control, can systematically illuminate certain kinds of information while preventing the emergence of other equally important knowledge. Mills (1988) more specifically argues that techniques used in organizational studies often produce information that is seriously biased by gender considerations. In an Appendix to his 1984 book, Hofstede (1984:287) notes that "research into values cannot be value-free—this book reflects not only the values of the HERMES employees and IMEDE course participants, but between the lines the values of its author." Although Hofstede compares his values to those identified through the factor analysis and describes the impact of his upbringing on his scholarship in a fairly self-revelatory manner, he does not examine the degree to which this standpoint position may have influenced the intent of the research, the design of the survey instrument or the manner in which interpretation was accomplished. When he writes, "the distribution of sex roles in our family is rather classical; my wife has a university education and a broad intellectual interest, but so far has never built up any continuous career of her own" (1984:288), we can't help wondering about the effect this experience may have had on Hofstede's concepts of gender roles and value systems. This lack of deeper reflexivity has the effect of legitimating survey items, the project and the interpretation of results as themselves value-neutral when they actually never can be.

Despite the attention and prestige attached to large-sample research and the kind of sophisticated quantitative analysis that Hofstede employs, generalizations that effectively hide the life-world of organization members (female as well as male) are unavoidable. While Hofstede's conclusions suggest that male organizational members in Finland may be "softer" (i.e., more feminine) than their colleagues in the United States, actual life experiences remain unknown.

Identification of the gender-related aspects of cultural and organizational value systems is a potentially powerful idea. However, Hofstede's masculine/feminine dichotomy sustains and creates stereotypes as it closes down useful dialogue around alternative possibilities for the lived experience of men and women. Thus, within intercultural social relations at a practical level oversimplified stereotypic images may narrow rather than broaden understanding. While globalization and the accompanying need to understand "the other" have led to the proliferation and an increased volume of cross-cultural research, generalized over-simplification actually leads to even less understanding!

Situational theories about cross-cultural differences are needed. To produce these theories, we need to study people both in terms of their cultural background, as well as in their historical and organizational locations. It is also important to determine if there may be a way to conduct cross-cultural research so that mutual understanding can be increased without finding, creating or sustaining stereotypes and/or static descriptions of national character.

Crossing Cultures—A Feminist Standpoint Story

In telling the story of this research project, we will use "normal" type to represent the voice of the American author while using italicized text to capture the dialogue between the American author and the Finn who served as the silent collaborator in the original work. In adopting this conversational manner of writing, we hope to illustrate the way in which cross-cultural knowledge production and learning itself is strengthened through open-ended conversation and the blending of "insider/outsider" (Louis and Bartunek, 1992) perspectives.

METHODOLOGY

Curious about the differences between women managers in Finland and the United States, I studied the work and private life experience of groups of women bank managers from each country. Based on interviews, I developed with the participants two separate naturalistic Q-sorts (Brown, 1986). The women then ranked the items from "most true in my career and in my life" to "least true." Results were combined and factor analyzed.

Q-methodology renders "subjective communication amenable to objective analysis and understanding" while "ensuring that self-reference is preserved rather than compromised or confused with an external frame of reference brought by an investigator" (McKeown and Thomas, 1988:5). It is a good tool for cross-cultural organizational and management research because:

1. It offers the possibility to cross cultures in an open and receptive manner without imposing *a priori* notions about things that researchers are likely to find.
2. It permits the development and testing of research concepts by the participants allowing insiders to reflect upon their own experience.
3. It provides a method for breaking with the established tradition of comparing against a previous standard established from researching male managers in the United States.
4. It honors the fact that although research participants construct the Q-sort items from a subject position, their stories emerge from and are based on specific cultural, institutional and organizational arrangements that are themselves objective in nature.

The final step in the analysis involved a subjective process of abstracting from the factors. In this analysis the factors were thought about as "scripts," borrowing the notion from Barley (1989:53) who explains the idea in this manner:

> *Scripts may be thought of as plans for recurrent patterns of action that define, in observable terms, the essence of actors' roles. To the degree that institutional forms influence ongoing action via the enactment of scripts that encode the institution's logic, the institution can be said to be reproduced, for institutions can have no existence independent of instantiation in daily life.*

Use of the notion of careers as scripts provides a means to connect the "micro" and "macro" levels of analysis in a holistic and logical way and express experience of concrete individuals as a reflection of the broader context.

FINDINGS

As a result of conducting the project in this way, I found that although many surface similarities could be found, career scripts were parochial in nature and reflected the values and institutions of each country. In Finland, a country said to value "harmony" and high social identity (Jakobson, 1987), women described their lives as being "balanced" and justified ways in which their lives as managers were "different" from other Finnish women who, they said, held "just jobs." The women studied were highly educated and in positions of considerable authority. They thought of themselves as "pioneers" departing from traditional role definitions.

> *IIRIS: No, this is not quite right. I do not think that when Finnish female managers talk about "balance" they want to emphasize differences with their sisters who "just hold jobs." Perhaps they wanted to say that they are ALSO women, part of the female culture within their managerial positions, and that they can combine their roles in a satisfactory way. This combining of public and private life has been a central ideal in the family policy in Finland. Balance and harmony are not synonyms to me!*
>
> *SARAH: You may have a point. In the United States, where a "balanced" life seems almost an impossible dream, the notions of harmony and balance are tightly related, i.e., "If I could achieve balance in my life it would be more harmonious." I obviously heard the Finnish stories with American ears. I am not sure we can ever completely agree on my interpretation of this point.*
>
> *What is clear to me, however and something I think we can agree on, is that this group of women represents something new within Finnish banking specifically and Finnish business generally. Although women have been employed in large numbers in the Finnish economy for some time, only recently have they become managers. With this comes a need for new ways of speaking about experience.*

Many of the women spoke of a desire for "autonomy," "freedom," "promotion to senior levels of the hierarchy," and for some "stress in their work"—all of which seem to fall within Hofstede's description of masculinity. However, these desires must be understood in a context in which such aspirations are reserved for the few and the "special" where one must ask "Can I grow in this job, bearing in mind that the bank must benefit too?" This sense of individual possibility within a framework of corporate and group responsibility (perhaps what Hofstede described as feminine) mirrors notions of Finnish culture described earlier by Berry (1995:19):

> A cultural analysis of the Finnish myth of frontier demonstrates that "we" are individuals bounded by a sense of collective identity based on shared language, ethnic roots, religion, history and identity with the same local (sic). Our log cabin is a sauna. It symbolizes roots—the results of a successful effort to carve out a zone of comfort in the forests of the North—and a meeting place for members of the community. In the sauna the superficial symbols of social status are put aside for the moment. We own and defend our own space and the collective space known as Finland. We aren't going anywhere except to visit, and we don't want anyone coming here, except to visit. We are bounded by group but not by social hierarchy. This makes us different than others.

In the United States, storytelling rationalized choices within and about career with those made in the balance of life, often using the metaphor of "juggling" (Bateson, 1989). This rationalization emerged, I believe, from tensions between internalized middle class notions about the importance of achievement and the possibility of in-dividual choice (perhaps what Hofstede described as "masculine") with ideas about being a "good" woman and/or a "good" mother drawn from childhood experiences when most middle-class mothers stayed at home. The Finnish women, working in a country where lengthy parental leaves and subsidized day care are mandated, and where most were the daughters of working women, spoke of "balance" in ways that were very different and perhaps impossible within the American experience.

The rhetorical strategy employed by the American women represented an at-tempt to set themselves apart as "individuals," "unique," and "self-determining," both affirming and acclaiming personal responsibility for the complexities of "jug-gling" demanded in their lives. Not one woman suggested that the bank or the gov-ernment might play a role in helping her to bring her life into balance. To pose such a notion in the US would be to challenge the very foundation of individual-ism that forms a critical part of the historical construction of its society. Berry (1995:19) describes American notions of success in this way:

> *A cultural analysis of the American myth of frontier . . . demonstrates that "we" are "unique" individuals bounded by "communication" of shared feelings and values of "rights" and "opportunity." We have no shared roots, regions, history nor identity with the same local (sic). Our log cabin symbolizes individual opportunity that evolves from rugged life and movement across space to opportunity. . . . We are somewhere on the trail or the highway to a better life. . . . This makes us different than others.*

With the exception of the youngest women studied, nearly all the women in Finland were married and most had children. This was not true of the women in the United States sample. In the US most of those who had children said they were not sure that devotion to career and proper child care were both possible and/or desirable, though many indicated that financial considerations would keep them in the workplace. While organizations in the United States might be characterized as "masculine" using Hofstede's schema, many women as well as men legitimize those values, standards and lack of support as appropriate and inevitable.

While liberal social benefits and private life support available for the women in Finland might seem like paradise to their harried American counterparts, their ex-istence may be related to factors other than the "feminization" of Nordic culture. Entrance of women into the Finnish workforce during the second world war was mostly due to a shortage of men. As Finland shifted from a largely agrarian nation to an industrialized state in the years following WWII, women remained in the workforce. Their labor contribution was necessary. Today more than 80 percent of women are employed in Finland; a majority of them work full-time. In the United States about 50 percent work. High standards of living and tax rates in Finland seem to reinforce this pattern of employment, but, women in the study, apparently in an effort to legitimate the seriousness of their career interests, were quick to point out that "they were not working just for the money."

IIRIS: Careful. Remember that Sweden didn't enter World War II, yet 80 percent of women there also work. So, what is the explanation for this? In my mind, it is important to remember that values and economic systems are closely related (as, in fact, Hofstede has argued). The feminization of the work force in Sweden and Finland is a complex phenomena. Both history and economic systems have a profound effect on the value systems, and they work in interrelated ways. This is the reason that war is not primary, I think; it had some effect, but not as straightforward an influence as you describe.

SARAH: You are probably right. I forgot the major point of this chapter, which is that all social phenomena have multiple and complex causes. I was oversimplifying.

Over the years, in response to severely declining birthrates and the continued shortage of labor, decision-makers in the Finnish government have continued to mandate increasingly generous welfare services for families. Several of the Finnish participants suggested that these supports may be related more to a desire to maintain homogeneity of the population and to discourage immigration, an alternative source of labor, than to enhance opportunities for women. This opinion is supported by the fact that legislation banning discrimination in employment, requiring equal opportunity for women, and mandating equal pay were not in place within Finland until 1987.

IIRIS: I wonder if these comments were made by women who spoke Swedish? In fact, I think the number of Swedish women managers you interviewed may have affected many of your findings. I think that it is more accurate to say that welfare services for Finnish families have not only been provided to enhance opportunity for women, but also for other reasons, like avoiding high rates of immigration.

SARAH: I realize that living in Finland as a Swede-speaking Finnish must influence life experience in ways I did not examine. As you know, this particular bank has always had close ties with the Swedish-speaking community and several of the women in the study were Swedish-speaking—they had been recruited to the bank by a senior manager who was also Swedish-speaking. Although the government goes to great lengths to ensure equal treatment for the small minority of citizens who are Swedish-speaking, they remain apart from their Finnish-speaking counterparts—living in separate neighborhoods/communities, maintaining separate educational systems, and separate churches etc. Several spoke no Finnish. This layer of complexity in what appears to the world to be a homogeneous country should be acknowledged.

Osterberg and Hedman indicate that women in Finland spend approximately 13 hours more per week on household work than men. This disproportionate load is further complicated by the fact that household work appears more time-consuming in Finland than in the United States. Food shopping is done frequently in a series of small neighborhood stores, clothes dryers and frost-free refrigerators are still uncommon, and ironing remains the norm.

IIRIS: If you are arguing that women in the United States spend less time in household work than those in Finland, you should find some statistical data to support the statement.

SARAH: Actually, that wasn't my point. I only meant that the world may perceive Finland (as described by Hofstede) as a place where men and women are quite equal—fulfilling similar roles both in the workplace and at home while the Osterberg and Hedman statistic and other data indicate that this is not the case. Hochschild (1989) and others say that working women in the U.S. spend about 11 hours more per week on household tasks than their male partners. Thus, employed women in both countries do more housework than men.

IIRIS: I cannot agree that household work is more time-consuming in Finland than in the United States. I find that dependence on superstores and automobiles is very time-consuming while defrosting the refrigerator takes only a couple of hours every year. To understand why clothes dryers are uncommon is also complex: electricity is relatively expensive, environmental values are also important and people want to save electricity, many people think machines are prone to breaking down, drying clothes indoors is seen as healthy etc. So attitudes are different—home work takes time in both the United States and Finland!

SARAH: I suppose it is mostly a matter of what you are accustomed to—and, you are correct, maintenance of private life is time-consuming world wide. Perhaps we can agree that those tasks are generally assumed by women in greater proportion than by men, even in the countries Hofstede has characterized as "Feminine."

Hofstede also described as masculine cultures with a divided value atmosphere, where males and females exhibit very different behaviors and assume separate roles; men are seen as "tough," rational and keen on a materialistic orientation towards life, while females are more irresponsible, caring and "soft," emphasizing life's quality aspects. Findings from the research described here indicate that within the United States the belief system and experience of women, at least of those in one time and in one place, can scarcely be generalized in this way. Further, by feminine, Hofstede meant a society characterized by more equal values for men and women, where both are responsible, caring and "soft" and emphasize quality of life. The findings of this study indicate that this description is quite over simplified.

EXTENDING THE LOGIC

We are not arguing that Hostede's findings are totally inaccurate nor that they might be supplanted with other more accurate conclusions. We are suggesting he was "somewhat" right although somewhat limited in his conclusions and, more importantly, that his is "just one possible knowledge claim among others" (Calás, 1994).

Scholarship located within an objectivist epistemology requiring, as it does, simplification and dichotomization of purportedly measurable variables, always illuminates some concepts while obscuring others. If the underlying purpose of the research lies within the domain of prediction and control this may seem less problematic than if understanding and potential for change is the purpose.

This study, focused on an interpretation of the subjective, contextual experience of a few women, will never win attention for size of sample or breadth of international coverage, nor does it attempt to create a useful schema for global management. What it does do, however, is to point out the dangers of universalizing, dichotomizing and simplifying research as it illustrates the manner in which complex lived experiences may depart from supposed stereotypic norms. In the Finnish case, the study illuminates the experience of being a female manager in one of Hofstede's "feminine" countries, breaking the stereotype that their work culture is, indeed, quite ideal and provides equality for women. At the same time, by comparing this group of women managers with counterparts in the "masculine" United States, we find that social policy and organizational practice often makes more difference in terms of women's ability to participate than laws that mandate equality.

A deeper consideration of context challenges the notion that neither organizations nor values and experiences of participants are mere reflections of the values of the wider culture. Rather, organizations are just as responsible for this emerging creation as the political, educational or family sources to which they are traditionally attributed. The bank in Finland is consciously reinventing the role of its women managers despite historical practice in the wider society. Additionally, managers not only reflect the values of a given society, but they also create new values by making organizational decisions. Documentation of specific exemplary organizational practice creates potential for shifts in social arrangements and offers the possibility for change in gender roles, identification and values.

We also learned, and should acknowledge, that female managers, even if their experiential world differs as it does in the U.S. and Finland, have much in common. The history of the countries and their social policies may be different but not as different as might be expected from Hofstede's work. It is important to realize that in documenting "differences"—those factors which unite experience across cultures are necessarily left out or not described—and may often be just as meaningful.

Fundamental to the approach adopted in this project is the notion that the measure of the success of any cross-cultural research lies in the ability to assess what has been learned and how findings may differ because the research has been conducted this way. Obviously researchers can never truly depart from the fundamental socialization in their own culture successfully enough to allow the experience of the "other" to be interpreted in other than idiosyncratic ways. Thus, an additional claim of this chapter is that no cross-cultural research can or should be an individual effort—despite the mythology surrounding the production of scholarship in general.

While notions of vulnerability, receptivity, empowerment, collaboration and attention to context may reflect a feminist standpoint epistemology, they are also critical elements in any cross-cultural project that seeks to better understand not only the "selves" that a culture produces and displays to the world, but a deeper sense of the context in which those life experiences are carried out.

BIBLIOGRAPHY

Adler, N.J. (1986) *International Dimensions of Organizational Behavior,* Boston: P.W.S. Kent.

Adler, N.J., and M. Jelinek (1986) "Is 'Organization Culture' Culture Bound?" *Human Resource Management* 25: 73–90.

Adler, N.J., and D. Izraeli (1994) *Competitive Frontiers: Women Managers in a Global Economy,* Cambridge, MA.: Blackwell.

Aptheker, B. (1989) *Tapestries of Life: Women's Work, Women's Consciousness, and the Meaning of Daily Experience.* Amherst, MA: University of Massachusetts Press.

Barley, S. (1989) "Careers, Identities and Institutions: The Legacy of the Chicago School of Sociology" in M.B. Arthur, D.T. Hall and B.S. Lawrence, eds. *Handbook of Career Theory,* Cambridge: Cambridge University Press, 41–66.

Bateson, M.C. (1989) *Composing a Life,* New York: Atlantic Monthly Press.

Bell, E., T. Denton, and S. Nkomo (1993) "Women of Color in Management: Toward an Inclusive Analysis" in E. Fagenson, ed. *Women in Management: Trends, Issues, Challenges in Managerial Diversity,* Thousand Oaks, CA: Sage, 105–130.

Berry, M. (1995) "American and Finnish Myths of Frontier: Implications for Concepts of Individualism" *Unpublished manuscript.* Helsinki, Finland.

Berthoin Antal A., and D. Izraeli (1993) "A Global Comparison of Women in Management: Women Managers in Their Homelands and Expatriates" in E. Fagenson, ed. *Women in Management: Trends, Issues and Challenges in Managerial Diversity,* Newbury Park, CA: Sage.

Boyacigiller, N.A., and N.J. Adler (1991) "The Parochial Dinosaur: Organizational Science In A Global Context" *Academy of Management Review* 16: 262–290.

Brown, S.R. (1986) "Q technique and method" in W. D. Berry and M. S. Lewis-Beck, eds. *New Tools for Social Scientists,* Beverly Hills, CA: Sage.

Calás, M.B. (1994) "Love and War in the 'Feminine Language': Communicative Strategies for Organizational Analysis" part of the Academy of Management Showcase Symposium, *Language: A Barrier to Organizational Understanding?* Annual Meeting of the Academy of Management, Dallas, Texas.

Calás, M.B., and L. Smircich (1993) "Dangerous Liaisons: The 'Feminine-in-Management' Meets 'Globalization'" *Business Horizons* March–April: 71–81.

Calás, M.B., S. Jacobson, R. Jacques, and L. Smircich (1991) "Is A Woman Centered Theory Of Management Dangerous?" Paper presented at the Academy of Management Annual Meeting, Miami, FL., August.

Calvert, L.M., and V.J. Ramsey (1992) "Bringing Women's Voice to Research on Women in Management: A Feminist Perspective" *Journal of Management Inquiry* 1(1) March: 79–88.

Chodorow, N. (1978) *The Reproduction Cf Mothering,* Berkeley: The University of California Press.

Collins, P.H. (1991) "Learning From the Outsider Within" in M.M. Fonow and J. A. Cook, eds. *Beyond Methodology: Feminist Scholarship as Lived Research,* Bloomington, IN: Indiana University Press, 35–60.

Dinnerstein, D. (1977) *The Mermaid and the Minotaur: Sexual Arrangements and Human Malaise,* New York: Harper and Row.

Firestone, S. (1970) *The Dialectic of Sex,* New York: William Morrow.

Fletcher, J. (1994) "Feminist Standpoint Research and Management Science" *Journal of Management Inquiry 3(1)* March: 74–82.

Fletcher, J. (1995) "Radically Transforming Work for the 21st Century: A Feminist Reconstruction of 'Real' Work" Paper Presented at the Academy of Management Annual Meeting, Vancouver, August.

Geertz, C. (1973) *The Interpretation of Culture,* New York: Basic Books.

Gilligan, C. (1982) *In a different voice,* Cambridge, MA: Harvard University Press.

Grant, J. (1988) "Women As Managers: What They Can Offer To Organizations" *Organizational Dynamics* 16(1): 56–63.

Haraway, D. (1988) "Situated Knowledges: The Science Question In Feminism And The Privilege Of Partial Perspective" *Feminist Studies* 14(3) Fall: 575–599.

Harding, S. (1987) "Is There a Feminist Method?" in S. Harding, ed. *Feminism and Methodology,* Bloomington: The University of Indiana Press, 1–15.

Harding, S.(1986) *The Science Question in Feminism,* Ithaca, NY: Cornell University Press.

Hofstede, G. (1991) *Cultures in Organizations: Software of the Mind,* London: McGraw Hill.

Hofstede, G. (1984) *Culture's Consequences,* Beverly Hills: Sage.

Hochschild, A. (1989) *The Second Shift,* New York: Viking.

Izraeli, D., and Y. Zeira (1993) "Women As Managers In International Business: A Research Review And Appraisal" *Business and The Contemporary World,* 3, 35–36.

Jacobson, S. W. (1991) *Careers in Cross-Cultural Context: Women Bank Managers in Finland and in the United States,* Ph.D. Dissertation: The University of Massachusetts, Amherst.

Jacques, R. (1993) "Nursing As A Basic Service To Society—The Caring Phenomenon" *Nursing Adminstration Quarterly* 17(2): 1–10.

Jakobson, M. (1987) *Finland: Myth and Reality,* Keuru, Finland: Ottava Printing Works.

Jayaratne, T. (1983) "The Value Of Quantitative Methodology For Feminist Research" in G. Bowles and R.D. Klein, eds. *Theories of Women's Studies,* Boston: Routledge and Kegan Paul, 140–161.

Keller, E.F. (1984) *Reflections On Gender And Science,* New Haven, CT: Yale University Press.

Kolb, D. (1992) "Women's Work: Peacemaking In Organizations" in D. Kolb and J. Bartunek, eds. *Hidden Conflict In Organizations: Uncovering Behind The Scenes Disputes,* Newbury Park, CA: Sage, 63–91.

Louis, M.R., and J.M. Bartunek (1992) "Insider/Outsider Research Teams: Collaboration Across Diverse Perspectives" *Journal of Management Inquiry* 1, 2, June, 101–110.

McKeown, B. and D. Thomas (1988) *Q Methodology,* in the series *Quantitative Applications in the Social Sciences.* Newbury Park: Sage.

Miller, J.B. (1986) *Toward A New Psychology Of Women,* 2nd ed., Boston: Beacon.

Millman, M., and R.M. Kanter (1987) "Introduction To Another Voice: Feminist Perspectives On Social Life And Social Science" in S. Harding, ed. *Feminism and Methodology,* Bloomington: The University of Indiana Press, 29–36.

Mills, A. (1988) "Organization, Gender and Culture" *Organization Studies* 9, 3, 351–369.

Nicholson, L. (1994) "Interpreting Gender" *Signs* 20, 11, Autumn, 79–104.

Osterberg, C., and B. Hedman (1988) *Women And Men In The Nordic Countries: Facts On Equal Opportunities Yesterday, Today And Tomorrow,* Copenhagen, Denmark: The Nordic Council of Ministers.

Parvikko, T. (1990) "Conceptions Of Gender Equality: Similarity And Difference" in M. Keranen, ed. *Finnish UnDemocracy: Essays On Gender And Politics,* Helsinki: Finnish Political Science Association.

Powell, G.N. (1993) *Women And Men In Management,* 2nd ed., Newbury Park, CA: Sage.

Powell, G.N. (1990) "One More Time: Do Female And Male Managers Differ?" *Academy of Management Executive* 4, 3, 68–75.

Reinharz, S. (1992) *Feminist Methods In Social Research,* New York: Oxford University Press.

Rosener, J. (1990) "Ways Women Lead" *Harvard Business Review* 68, 6, 119–125.

Steers, R.M., S.J. Bischoff, and L.H. Higgins (1992) "Cross-Cultural Management Research: The Fish and the Fisherman" *Journal of Management Inquiry* 1, 4, December, 321–330.

11

TEXT, GENDER AND FUTURE REALITIES

Monica Lee

Science fiction presents forms of future reality, either heroic or symbiotic. These appear gender-linked, present two very different forms of societal aspiration, and hold different implications for an individual's 'identity.' Research is the creation of meaning and is clearly heroic. This chapter focuses on the question of whether it is possible to envision the 'creation' of a symbiotic society through heroic means.

INTRODUCTION

This chapter questions the extent to which 'identity' is confirmed, molded, or denied through one's chosen text. It evolved from and contains a paper originally presented in 1995. The original was interesting, thought-provoking, rigorous, analytical, well-received and widely used but unpublishable. That paper questioned what kind of society we promulgate by adherence to the 'textual norms'? It was written in a different text—one searching for authenticity, rather than authority. I was experimenting but it was more to me than a casual game.

TEXT AND IDENTITY

There are three main types of management literature. The majority build upon a tradition of knowledge. Some of these are deep theoretical tomes, while others provide recipes and models of organizational worlds. Each provides the surety of an ordered causal reality in which planning and control lead to anticipated outcomes.

'Identity' is a known and measurable phenomena and unitary identities are ascribed to organizations and individuals. Arguments are validated through rigorous reference to other sources (textual and empirical) interpreted from within the context of an existing body of knowledge.

A sizable minority discuss management in a different way. They question and deconstruct traditional knowledge. They present alternative accounts of 'reality' that cannot be uniquely defined since it is a function of perceptions. Causality is questioned, and planning and control are presented as illusory—chimera created to satisfy needs for security. Some talk of the role that myths and metaphors play in stabilizing and promulgating organizational life. Some talk of emotions and values. Individual and organizational 'identity' is seen as socially constructed and relative. Artificial conceptual boundaries between the individual and the organizational are eroded. The arguments are validated through rigorous reference to other sources (textual and empirical) interpreted from within the existing body of knowledge.

These two types of literature offer very different world views but contain strong similarities. The adoption of either one requires a leap of faith. In both cases, authors call upon a higher power to validate their thoughts. Support is derived from the peer group—'as Smith and Jones (1999) suggest', or 'following Derrida (1999).' This is more than a textual artifice; it is a source of authority. As one academic acknowledged she often refers to 'Bull and Jackson' when unsure of her ground. Although these frequently quoted (by her) authorities are the neighborhood cleaners, whom she has overheard chatting, much of what they say makes sense and it has become an 'authoritative' reference. At issue, however, is the question of what makes this charade necessary?

It is instructive to distinguish between the personal spark or drive that creates the text, and the 'voice' in which it is written. The text presented in this section has been written in a distant voice. It does not use 'I' in the personal sense, yet clearly, the writer has a unique world view and mix of needs, motivations and beliefs. This distantly voiced 'I' has, in working through the communicative effort required, thought of the 'other' and the impact or influence the emergent text might have upon the 'other.' In thinking about the 'other,' the 'I' has understood better the thoughts that are evolving through the process of writing. Though distant from the text, the 'I' is central to its creation. In addition, the self-perception of the 'I' changes and develops through the creative process. The malleable 'I' resides behind all interactions, but is normally hidden. It is a safer, less-exposed position from which to operate.

The creation of text is essentially an attempt to communicate. For some, this may be communication with self. For many, the recipients of the communication may be known or imagined others. The nature of the anticipated recipient influences the form and intended function of the text. The act of writing involves 'self' and 'intent' to influence a selected target group. Both types are normally designed to further the body of knowledge to which they relate. The target group is an anonymous body of knowledge whose adherents patrol its boundaries. There are rules and regulations for influence that must be enforced and those on the inside are jealous of their maintenance responsibilities.

The understanding of life to which the body adheres through subsumation of its members within a collective mind-set would be threatened or challenged by a strong statement of 'self' on the part of another body. A supplicant to the body can minimize this apparent threat by referring to the 'truth' that the body upholds—using textual cues that evidence right of membership as if they were elements of a drug designed to suppress the immune system and minimize chances of organ rejection.

Of the two types of literature presented above, the first is, at least, consistent in its assumptions and enactment of a unitary body of knowledge. The second is inconsistent in its cry for inconsistency. The boundaries of the second type of literature are patrolled in a highly consistent manner, one which regulates and reifies the 'body' of knowledge. It is intriguing to consider the way the espoused principles would look if they were to be enacted.

There is a third type of literature on the shelves—a type rarely associated with academe (let alone, management). It is the realm of stories—ideal vehicles for the exploration of identity and emotion, myths and metaphors—dust-covered and rarely visited. Escape for a short while into the story.

THE STORY

I wish to tell you a tale of love and hate, escapism and addiction, and how an idealistic young girl grew into a woman compelled to justify idealism. I shall tell it of myself, but, as you are listening, multiply the one to many—as many have taken the journey. This tale might, at first, appear divorced from the 'reality' of organizations, but it has a bearing on it and we will come to it before the end.

I have, since early childhood, been fascinated by visions of other ways of being. I started on a diet of mythology. From the age of seven or eight I would scour the local library to feed my habit. Initially my parents were pleased that I appeared precocious in my tastes. I devoured mythology, moving through the Nordic complexity of heroes and villains, in which the individual's life is led in a blaze of glory, the supporting cast benefits from reflected light, and the hero (and his genetic line) is remembered to eternity, fighting to the cry of death (and eternal reward) before dishonor. I then widened my repertoire to include myths that focused more upon environmental symbiosis—Indian and Eskimo myths in which all things have their place and name, a rabbit is as 'valuable' as a man or woman and death is an inevitable part of life. These were less acceptable to my parents, as they accorded less with the way in which they viewed life, but were seen as a minor aberration on my part.

As I grew older I understood there are many ways of representing the past. Despite the normality of my existence relative to my acquired mythological heritage, my life within the family was recountable within mythological terms. Family histories were micro-myths conceived and retold as control mechanisms to influence the future. Mythology is timeless. Though rooted in the past, it played an active part in my present and in molding my future.

By the age of twelve I was hooked on science fiction. My allegiance to myths located in the past shifted to myths of the future—to ways of envisaging future 'realities' and the practical, ethical and philosophical implications these might have for my present and future existence. I became less discreet, and started to withdraw from family life (particularly the chores) in order to read in privacy. My pocket money disappeared at second-hand book stalls. I was truly addicted. My father saw it as infantile escapism and pressured me to break the pattern. There was a tall Yew tree that only I was able to climb, and I spent many hours up there, on a level with a wild dove's nest, cool in the summer's heat whilst my siblings searched for me, or tossed around in the autumn storms whilst my parents shouted for me. None thought to look upwards. I invariably had a tatty paperback hidden up there and I would read and think, and read and think, and escape. As reality became more unpleasant I became increasingly involved in alternatives. My life became one of 'what if?'

By fourteen I saw my life in terms of control and rebellion, hate and rejection. I was a rebellious female in an intensely patriarchal household; a doubter of organized belief in a strictly religious community; an idealist in a world of practicality—in short, I questioned. I was not alone in the questioning process—my siblings also questioned, but each of us was alone in the form of release we sought, and it took nearly twenty years before we began talking about it. Exploring alternative forms of future was now central to my way of thinking and my identity. I was continually denigrated for this approach and was a focal point for much of the conflict. Then things became really dirty and I was disinherited. My mental instability as evidenced by my passion for science fiction was cited *as one* of the bases for this decision. This monologue represents, in part, an attempt to justify such mental instability.

Futuristic Fiction

To those who are not addicts it is hard to describe the fascination or even the wide range of forms that science fiction (SF) can take. I have created a new category that I call futuristic fiction. This genre is about creating and exploring the implications of alternative forms of reality.

Reading these works enhanced my personal understanding, just as living in a different culture often increases understanding of one's own culture. There is something about relaxing the constraints of reality that fires the imagination while minimizing personal threat. The inherent symbolism and mythology is often not truly appreciated until later reflection: 'Science Fiction writers are limited only by human potential, not human actualities. SF can serve to show women, and men, how large that potential can be' (Sargent, 1977).

Increasingly, reviewers comment more upon the author's ability to create believable multi-level microcosms and less upon the quality of scientific ideas. Take, for example, these reviews about *Beauty* by Sheri Tepper: '*Beauty* lives up to its name in all ways. It is a story of mankind and magic, fairies and fairy tales, future and fantasy all intertwined into a complex collage about the downfall of Earth. It is a story you can float away in" (*Time Out*). Or from the *New York Review of Science Fiction:* '*Beauty* slips its message like a knife through skin and brain and bone. It is brilliant and subtle and fabulous.'

Or these of *Raising the Stones,* also by Sheri Tepper: 'Sheri S. Tepper has given us a genuine SF novel of ideas about religion and fanaticism, legends and heroism, and men and women (among other things), reminiscent at times of Le Guin, Vance, Cordwainer Smith and Frank Herbert. It's too good, too strongly felt and imagined to ignore' (*Locus*). And from *Kirkus Reviews:* 'Tepper effectively combines satire, inventive social engineering, strong main characters, and a plot that works on both internal and external levels in what may be her best novel to date.'

The description of a particular form of future might popularize it and make it more realizable. For example, Nicholls (1993a) suggests that 'the US government could never have got away with budgeting such large amounts of the national income on the space programme had the desire for space flight, largely catalysed by SF, not been so great.' Similarly, some authors, such as Cordwainer Smith, an army intelligence officer and US Governmental advisor, have held positions of power from which they could influence the future of society. Some authors, such as H.G. Wells, George Orwell or Isaac Asimov, have used the genre to support political fantasies, deliberately written to influence society.

Future Realities

For the purpose of this account I wish to explore the view of humanity carried by SF. In doing so I am following McHale's (1987) footsteps when he argues that SF is 'perhaps the ontological genre par excellence. We can think of science fiction as Postmodernism's non-canonised or "low art" double, its sister-genre in the same sense that the popular detective thriller is Modernism's sister-genre.' And in those of Broderick (1993), who suggests that 'SF is, of all the genres, the one that constructs "realities" as a matter of course.' Within the many variants there are two main, but not mutually exclusive, archetypes (using the word 'archetype' as discussed by Doty and Glick, 1994)—the heroic and the symbiotic.

Heroes, Villains, Gods and Predetermination

For we wrestle not against flesh and blood, but against principalities, against powers, against the rulers of the darkness of this world, against spiritual wickedness in high places
(Ephesians, 6:12)

SF toys with notions central to metaphysics, and the values underlying heroic vision are 'religious' in nature. Nicholls (1993b) notes that 'god' is the word most commonly used across all SF titles.

I see this type of SF as a vision focused around power and impotence—in which super-entities with abilities to create and manipulate whole worlds abound. The narrative form is usually the quest for an emblematic object. Characters most commonly work within a dualistic system where good confronts evil or where they are trapped in a pattern that fulfills a predetermined destiny. Writers portray the God-like theme in different ways, questioning the interrelationship between god and man (*Downward to the Earth,* Robert Silverberg); questioning the nature of 'god-liness' (*Dune* series, Frank Herbert); exploring the evolution of man into god and the generation of quasi-gods (*Childhood's End,* Arthur Clark); or developing the role of the young accidental hero in a world whose 'rules' are driven by gods or god-like powers.

Extreme examples of this can be found in Survivalist fiction—described by Clute (1993) as

> male-action story, set in post-holocaust venues where law and order has disappeared, and where there is effectively no restraint upon the behaviour of the hero, who therefore kills before he is killed, demonstrating his fitness to survive through acts of unbridled violence (which very frequently descend into prolonged sessions of rape and sadism).

This type often demonstrates apocalypse pathology where life is conducted in anticipation of surviving the holocaust. It represents a political agenda in which civilian values are defeated when the real world bares its teeth. It also contains elements of predetermination where the man who is able to realize his true (predetermined) nature survives.

The emblematic nature of the genre clearly extends to the role of women and of villains.

> Not allowed the variety or complexity of real people, women in SF have been represented most frequently by a very few sexual stereotypes; the Timorous Virgin (good for being rescued, and for having things explained to her), the Amazon Queen (sexually desirable and terrifying at the same time, usually set up to be 'tamed' by the super-masculine hero), the Frustrated Spinster Scientist (an object lesson to girl readers that career success equals feminine failure), the Good Wife (keeps quietly in the background, loving her man and never making trouble) and the Tomboy Kid Sister (who has a semblance of autonomy only until male appreciation of her burgeoning sexuality transforms her into Virgin or Wife). (Tuttle, 1993)

It is almost as if women are portrayed as an alien race linked to man but threatening and thus deserving of metaphorical subjugation. Women lead men astray from the true path:

Wisdom hath builded her house, she hath hewn out her seven pillars (Proverbs, 9:1) . . . Give instruction to a wise man, and he will be yet wiser: teach a just man and he will increase in learning. (Proverbs, 9:9) . . . A foolish woman is clamorous: she is simple and knoweth nothing. For she sitteth at the door of her house, on a seat in the high places of the city, To call passengers who go right on their ways: Whoso is simple, let him turn in hither: and as for him that wanteth understanding, she saith to him, Stolen waters are sweet, and bread eaten in secret is pleasant. But he knoweth not that the dead are there: and that her guests are in the depths of hell. (Proverbs, 9:13–18)

And Adam said, This is now bone of my bones, and flesh of my flesh: she shall be called Woman, because she was taken out of Man. (Genesis 2:25). And the Lord God said unto the Woman, What is this that thou hast done? I will greatly multiply thy sorrow and thy conception: in sorrow thou shalt bring forth children: and thy desire shall be to thy husband, and he shall rule over thee. (Genesis 3:13 and 16)

Female heroes are cast in a male world, their main interactions are with men, they are placed within high power-distance scenarios and given a 'masculine' approach to a fight for or against power. In Robert Heinlein's "Friday" (1983), the hero is a genetically engineered woman who is assured that she 'can take pride in the fact that *all* of you were most carefully selected to maximize the best traits of H. sapiens.' She has augmented powers and weaves her way through political plots, fights 'anarchists,' kills, suffers torture and rape with casual aplomb, uses sexual manipulation, and, of course, looks fantastic. Upon completion of her tasks, she is given to say, 'I no longer think about my odd and sometimes shameful origin. "It takes a human mother to bear a human baby," Georges told me that long ago. It's true and I have Wendy to prove it. I'm human and I belong.' Visions that portray women as 'equals in the fight' tend to be incomplete, and fail to address the wider implications of societal maintenance. Even in Cyberpunk (a sub-genre epitomised by William Gibson's *Neuromancer* series), where women regularly play central and relatively equal roles, all but the main characters fail to exist at any depth.

Cyberpunk is also important because of its reliance on virtual reality. It became popular in the 1980s, and creates a future in which 'industrial and political blocks may be global rather than national and controlled through information networks; a future in which machine augmentations of the human body are commonplace, as are mind and body changes brought about by drugs and biological engineering' (Nicholls, 1993c). In Cyberpunk, the world's data networks form a machine environment into which a human can enter by jacking into a cyberspace deck and projecting 'his disembodied consciousness into the consensual hallucination that was the matrix' (*Neuromancer*). It is a world in which the role of the anti-hero becomes heroic. Cyberpunk consciously places itself within virtual realities that themselves exist within alternate realities. Its denial of neat aesthetic or moral wrap-up means that it lends itself to being seen as the SF sub-genre closest to postmodernism. Jameson (1991) suggests that Cyberpunk is 'the supreme literary expression if not of postmodernism, then of late capitalism itself.'

Postmodernism can be portrayed as a shift in approach that reflects 'being' as opposed to 'knowing' and is linked to a qualitative rather than quantitative search for meaning and a recognition that the world of human experience is multiple and open-ended. Placement of Cyberpunk within this archetype is therefore a provocative act on my part because I believe that the underlying values within Cyberpunk (and postmodernism) remain heroic endeavors.

On the surface Cyberpunk is anti-religious, however, at a basal level the machine becomes God and cyberspace his playground. The ethos is clearly one of survival. Augmented individuals might learn the rules that allow them to commune with God and acquire favored status. The presenting villain is normally the faceless manipulator, but the real villain is naiveté: and that is punished immediately—often by a gory death.

Heroes require villains. In this genre, the nature of villainy has changed as a reflection of the fears and bigotry of the societies from which it emerged. For example: the mad scientist and loss of humanity (Stevenson's Jekyll and Hyde) indicating fear and suppression of the darker side of human nature; the idea of alien species and hive mind (*The Midwich Cuckoos,* Wyndham) in which individuality is subjugated to demands of the mass; the uncontrollable robot, indicating an anti-technology theme; and the faceless, behind-the-scenes manipulator, exploring a fear of computerized society.

An underlying theme central to this archetype is that of paranoia: the fear of the unknown and uncontrollable, fear of loss of the integrated self, in which lack of control equals chaos. Something, someone, some pre-destined future is out there or within us and we are but tools of a force that is bigger, cleverer and more powerful we are. We need to understand and control it to sustain our physical, emotional or spiritual well being, without which we will split asunder.

To ensure our longevity, we need to become big, clever and powerful. This is as true for Cyberpunk (and reified postmodernism) as for other examples of the genre. The big bad thing is the collective focus upon knowing; the proposition of multiple ways of being then becomes as draconian a way of knowing as that which was being reacted against. Heroes exist to demonstrate that overcoming temptation from the path of wisdom avoids ultimate doom.

Existence, Symbiosis and Relationships

I usually associate the symbiotic archetype with female authors. I was not searching for a gender split when I began but it crept up on me. Authors I see as symbiotic clearly question rather than play with our cultural norms, gender biases and existence and the heroic, power-related base from which they are derived. In creating an alternative reality they attempt completeness—exploring the implications for maintenance of that society, its procreation and its interrelationships.

While some visions are heroic in form (as of *Jack the Bodiless* by Julian May, or *Heroes and Villains* by Angela Carter) the majority are pastorally based. They are divorced from the pastoral-idyll sub-genre because they contextualize the dark-side as a natural facet of existence—to be embraced rather than feared. Perhaps the epitome of this is Ursula Le Guin's *Always Coming Home*. She creates a liberal utopian vision, rendered far more complex than the term utopian usually allows. She creates a sense of human suffering by weaving together stories, poetry, and other aspects of a fictional culture in order to 'force a dialogue with the here and now' (*New York Times Book Review*). Take, for example, the following quote:

> *It is hard to remember how little I knew. Now that I am learned in such matters, it is my old ignorance, in itself valueless, that is valuable, useful, and powerful. We have to learn what we can, but be mindful that our knowledge not close the circle, closing out the void, so that we may forget that what we do not know remains boundless, without limit or bottom, and that what we know may have to share the quality of being known with what denies it. What is seen with one eye has no depth.* (Le Guin, 1993)

The archetype works towards completeness—there is striving but not of the heroic kind. All is pattern and interrelationships. An example can be seen in Storm Constantine's three books of the "Wraeththu." The saga depicting the struggle for recognition of a mutant class that eventually spreads throughout the world is definitely not peaceful. It is one of patterns of relationships between authentic beings, who love and hate, to adjust to their circumstance and develop within an interacting and mutually dependent existence.

> *We have the future now, no need to cling to the past . . . Once it (power) lived in man, but men and women couldn't experience the light and dark of their natures without fear. Perhaps Kamagrian and Wraeththu are the answer. We shall certainly try. Our races as we know ourselves are just the beginning; there is so much more to come, and if we are wise, we shall greet it gladly.* "The Fulfillments of Fate and Desire," Storm Constantine.

Another (and perhaps less mainstream) example might be Flynn Connolly's *The Rising of the Moon*. This tale of rebellion in twenty-first century Ireland focuses on the interrelationships between women, women and men, and the patriarchy. It depicts a strife-torn but interrelated and complete society in which individuals choose, and accept responsibility for, their actions without resorting to the heroic or the villainous. This theme can also be seen in *A Plague of Angels* by Sheri Tepper, where the heroic myth is directly challenged and reversed. The main characters are authentic and developed as such. They act as archetypes based upon their own heroic myths within the wider belief of a heroic, star-traveling past. The angels are hunger, war and sickness:

> *The last thing they asked me was this: 'Since man was so intransigent, why was he allowed to go to the stars?' Man never went to the stars . . . His star journey was only a myth. Another in an endless series of man's heroic myths of his own past. Glorious stories to make man the hero, for man always has to be the hero . . . There is an archetype we never had*

in any of our villages . . . The Mysterious Stranger. The one who comes and goes, who sees everything, learns everything. He is needed in this new world . . . Something within him shuddered and sat up straight, substituting one vision for another. Instead of glory and power, instead of a gleaming shuttle pushed by its tail of fire, this slow creaking wagon behind this flatulent horse. How far to Rigel, or to Betelgeuse? Or did one aspire to a different destination? . . . room perhaps for a Mysterious Stranger. A storyteller.

Similar real and interconnected archetypal characters can be seen clearly in Cordwainer Smith's work. He is one of few male writers I would place in this symbiotic category. His writing epitomizes many of the symbiotic issues, and he appears to explore female sexuality from a 'feminine' point of view (as defined by my own preferences) in which sex is less about explicit domination and challenge, and more about implicit knowing and being: 'With ordinary telepathy, it would have been frightening. But this was not communication. It was being. She was following the Hunter's mind as his awareness rushed through her body, drank it up, enjoyed it, loved it all over again, this time from inside out.' ('The Dead Lady of Clown Town,' Smith, 1965).

A female approach to sex in Megan Lindholm's *Cloven Hooves* hardly mentions the act. It is instead a journey of self-development and understanding fostered by relations with others in which sex is an integral part. The whole book is about sexuality yet it is hard to find one quote that directly refers to it. Sexuality is about self—a state of being. Sex, both enjoyable and painful, is one of the constants in life alongside death and birth.

Both Lindholm and Cordwainer Smith address the dark side of existence in a similarly factual and necessary manner. 'The Dead Lady of Clown Town' for example uses the myth of Joan of Arc to address deviance, heresy and death. D'joan is a genetically engineered dog fighting for the rights of the underpeople. She adopts passive resistance as an inevitable part of her dog-like nature, and eventually is burnt at the stake—by which time all lives are irrevocably altered. This brief description does very little for the complexity and depth of the existential dilemmas—the relationship between pre-determination and free choice, identity and collectivity, humanity and prejudice, longevity and death, task and enjoyment—and the inevitable role of the accidental hero and the power of the weak that are addressed within the short story. He writes of heroism, but from a symbiotic perspective in which the heroic endeavor is the recognition and reestablishment of the dark side—thereby revalidating the light:

The bear-man Orson had been kept to the very end. He died oddly. He died laughing. His laughter is warm, generous, relaxed—like the friendly laughter of a happy foster-father who has found a guilty and embarrassed child, knowing full well that the child expects punishment but will not get it. "Shoot, man. You can't kill me, man. I'm in your mind. I love you. Joan taught us. You are the unlucky one. You are going to live. And remember. And remember. And remember. I'm saving you, man. I'm turning you into a real human being. With the power of Joan. The power of love. (Smith, 1965).

I am making a clear connection between maleness and the heroic myth, and femaleness and symbiosis, but I do not see this split as necessarily causal. Women adopt the heroic pattern and men the symbiotic. In general, however, women tend to tell a different story than that told by men.

If women's work is organised differently from men's, if the day is structured differently, if space is inhabited differently, if styles of verbal communication are different, then it follows that women will have a different sense of beauty and pleasure. Whether this shows up in literature depends on the extent to which women's literary forms are derived from a female culture, rather than determined by literary tradition and critical response. (Register, 1980).

Furman (1985) argues that the recurrence of topics, themes, images and metaphors in the literary works of women is linked to the search for an emancipated self by individuals who react in a collective manner to a common social reality. If the central focus in heroic literature is the preservation of the unified self, then in contrast, the focus is upon acceptance of the many sides of the non-unified self. Given that history and myths are recounted by the winners and that women are traditionally the non-winners, we live with a cultural heritage that supports the archetype of the patriarchal hero and preservation of the unified self.

Future Realities and Organizations

Futuristic fiction addresses alternative forms of organization. Many, such as *The Land Beyond* by Gill Alderman or *Raising the Stones* by Sheri Tepper or *The Wanderground* by Sally Gearhart, use stories of dissatisfied people who attempt to establish a vehicle for exploring alternative forms of existence. All futuristic fiction addresses the human condition and displays the authors' beliefs about its source, management, and extrapolated future. However, the more complete representations also explore conditions for and modifiers of that future.

We are raised on a diet of heroic endeavor. Organizational vision, a future myth based upon the past myths, is a control mechanism reinforcing status quo. The system is pre-determined: our organizational pattern recreates the aspirations of the founding father (Salama, 1991). We will climb the corporate ladder if we augment our powers and learn to understand the system. There is little place for questioning. The deviant might be accepted if sufficiently close to the higher powers, but the heretic is burnt (Harshbarger, 1973). To question the myth is heresy.

We talk of paradigm shifts, and of questioning rationalist, modernist approaches. We talk of the multiplicity of forms of knowing and being, but, as with cyberpunk, we exist within our basal myths. We replace surety of knowledge with rapid communication, flatter structures, and power shifts. The search for meaning and expertise becomes a heroic endeavor. The street-wise knowledge worker becomes the hero.

This has two important elements, the way in which the heroic myth encapsulates or at least correlates with predetermination and disempowerment, and the potential impossibility of being able to step outside our mythological heritage. Instead of symbiosis we find ourselves in ritualized harmony:

- Who do we accept in our colony, our society, our organisation?—*those who believe as we do.*
- Who leads the organisation?—*those who epitomise our beliefs and thus our existence.*
- How do we know our beliefs?—*by sharing, telling each other of their existence and meaning.*
- How do we reinforce our beliefs?—*by reward and punishment, promotion or exclusion.*
- How do we know what to do?—*by seeking clues, anticipating our leaders' responses.*
- What of the learner, the children?—*they will be helped to understand, and to emulate our leaders.*
- What if we make a mistake?—*we avoid this, by narrowing our potential response we remain safe.*
- What if we still make a mistake?—*we are less worthy, we cannot yet aspire to grace.*
- What if others make a mistake?—*they are either weak learners, deviants or heretics.*
- What proof do you need for these things?—*the perceptions of trusted others (or rumours of these) is sufficient.*
- What of the deviant?—*individual interpretations of our beliefs are misguided and need help.*
- What of the heretic?—*who? they don't exist here.*
- How do we accommodate difference?—*we look to our leaders and our beliefs for judgement.*
- How do we accommodate change?—*we have our past and thus our future mapped out.*
- What of unexpected change?—*we have our ways of working, it will not happen.*
- What if our leaders are wrong?—*they cannot be, as we aspire to be like them.*
- What if our beliefs are wrong?—*we all agree that they are not. You challenge. You are no longer we.*

This is not Orwell's *1984*. Rather it is my experience of a work group that espouses collective decision making and a supportive environment that is situated within a wider bureaucratic environment that espouses freedom of speech and inquiry, and the development of potential, and which is, in turn, situated within a national culture that espouses supportive social structures and the facilitation of creativity and innovation. Each is trapped by the heroic myth, by the systems of stabilization that developed alongside the myth, and by the heroic rhetoric associated with betterment.

The question of available alternatives is central to futuristic fiction and one that the symbiotic archetype attempts to address. This archetype poses a clear and irrevocable distinction between empowerment and power. Power is the search for betterment over others, the creation of in-groups and out-groups, structures of control and reward, and the inevitability of existence. Empowerment is about equality for all things, a realization and acceptance of the dark side, an appreciation of interconnectedness, freedom of choice, responsibility for that choice, and a belief in the openness of the future. Instead of heroes and villains, good and evil, all is patterns—interconnected patterns of love and hate, life and death. The problem is that far-reaching empowerment would have profound effect and would lead to a society that eschews much of which we hold dear.

For me it is more than just fiction. I direct a research-based Masters in Human Resource Development, designed in part to focus reflexively upon the group's workings as a 'live-case.' We create and examine the forms of personal power and influence that each member brings to the group. Each carries externally derived power. The tutors carry formal power. The fee-paying students have their own agendas and want their goals met. We are not, therefore, divorced from the wider world.

Issues such as the relationship between the individual and the collective; influence and equality; power, empowerment and responsibility; self-development and the meeting of predetermined goals; sub-groups, prejudice and alienation; and methods of control and reward are central to the discussion and are emphasized by the manner in which the group *lives* them. One person's frustration about time-keeping when linked to another's procrastination leads to a wide-ranging exploration of the decisionmaking processes. A call for the 'leaders' (in this case the tutors) to take responsibility is matched by the tutors' refusal to do so and with others' disagreeing with the call for a variety of reasons. It elicits an explosion of emotion; an exploration of the different understandings of roles and responsibilities within the group and the wider world; discussion about whether we are hierarchically or consensually managed, whether either is really possible. In other words, it is a messy and interactive business, confusing for both tutors and students. There is no clear agenda and no clear rules. As tutors we foster reflexivity in the belief that research and learning are synonymous: that a questioning approach to the interaction minimizes the blame and acknowledges the pain. At each workshop, 'issues' arrive from nowhere and impact us all.

The reflexive period in each workshop is balanced by 'expert' input: specialists talking of their own research around the topic of the workshop, by explicitly focusing upon individual concerns in action learning sets and by work-based activities (*i.e.,* projects, dissertation, etc.). The emphasis changes over the period of the course. Initially, the participants report that specialist sessions and action learning have value, but they are skeptical about the value of reflection. Toward the end, they emphasize the particular long-term value of the reflexive periods.

This 'live case' is NOT a pastoral idyll—it is one in which individual influence, interactions, pain and authenticity are acknowledged in a relatively open manner. It is not divorced from the outside world, nor is it totally task-free. The tasks and the external influences are brought in by the participants based on their relevance to them as individuals rather than imposed by a higher power. Perhaps, sometimes, we approach a level of symbiotic working.

My experience here is not unique. This symbiotic sense exists in my interactions with other groups, and I am sure it exists in many other places. It does, however, seem hard to capture and deliberately foster, particularly in larger organizational units. This seems to be a function of the systems of management and control that larger units feel the need to create. It is, perhaps, not just chance that this example is derived from a group of people focusing upon HR *development* as opposed to *management.*

Chasing the Tail

I seem to be plodding along, despite my mentally unstable preference for futuristic fiction. I still hide to read and lose myself in reverie. I welcome the recent influx of mainly female authors who force me to question my assumptions while presenting me with a view of existence with which I can empathize.

I have set out to justify my idealism—arguing that my individual idealism is mirrored by all who question the mythology of our existence and that a growing number interpret it as I do. I have suggested that with changing patterns of work, this questioning will increase and that the individually idealistic but collectively disillusioned might together challenge the systems of control and reward. I have presented this as an inevitably growing force, a challenge to the heroic myth that will confront us all. I agree that a minimum of this needs to be understood, but, preferably, should be explored and embraced. I have right on my side!

In other words, I have established myself as the down-trodden heroine, who, developing some ability with words, attempts the heroic endeavor (late into the night, at cost to body and soul, risking peaceful family fulfillment) to place herself within the parameters of the system by getting another paper published, a step toward achieving wider recognition and securing immortality. Take the description of the work group I am involved in, I continue to collude with the expectations and established parameters. I treat others in the way in which I am treated. In the 'live case' described above—we are all consenting adults, yet the power is not equal. Examination of group process was justified as a necessary part of the course—the implicit message was 'if you want the qualification you do what I say.' I am trapped by my own mythology.

This is, perhaps, more noticeable because I have chosen to speak in the first person—to impose my views on others. In reality, is not the establishment of one's own view part of the heroic archetype? I could have pretended objectivity '60 percent of the respondents,' or tried the third person, 'once upon a time there was a little girl who.' Do we become Sheri Tepper's Mysterious Strangers—storytellers who replace one basal form of myth with another? Are all myths heroic in essence? I am, at least, trying to be obvious and honest in my attempt to influence others. However, taken to the logical conclusion, the idea of symbiosis also entails responsibility to ensure that others develop their own views of life. Can I really keep quiet and not impose my views on others? If we question the basal myths of research will our jobs remain? Is research therefore irrevocably welded to the heroic archetype? Is the realization of anything patterning onto the symbiotic archetype a logical impossibility?

There is no end to this story, only questions. Given my heritage, however, I cannot leave it at that. As a symbiotic sort of male friend once said: 'I'm glad I don't have good taste. I can, at least, enjoy life.'

Text and Identity

To recap, the third type of literature is the story; an account that is deliberately designed to engage the 'self' of the recipient through the 'authenticity' of the author. It provides the recipient freedom to make their own sense of the 'meaning' contained. From this perspective, the 'story' just recounted is a poor example as it has no clear purpose. It is told, in part, to emphasize the different textual forms associated with the same intended message. However, it is also noticeable that the 'story' form allows greater flexibility or layering of intent than formal research texts. Certainly, feedback from those who have read or worked with the 'story' indicates that a multiplicity of threads of meaning can be derived from it—the majority of which were unknown to, or go beyond, the author's intention when writing it.

The notion of 'authenticity' is problematic. A truly 'authentic' account might be one of emotional expression of the transient 'self' but it is likely to have little to offer recipients other than an idea of how the 'author' was feeling at that moment. While this may constitute valid communication, it is unlikely to have lasting impact upon others' sense-making. The urgent debates that pervade the corridors of academe about what is meant by rigor and validity, and about 'choice' of methodology and method, illustrate the complex relationship between personal preference and authenticity, sense-making and research, and influential dissemination and authority. Can any academic account ever be fully authentic? How do we cope with the 'need' for authority if we move beyond the second type of literature?

The 'story' does employ 'authority' through the use of references, although not those normally associated with management literature. And, while the first section attempts to play with other 'authoritative cues,' as an author, I find it hard to gauge what the effect of such 'playing' has upon the reader. So I shall leave you with some thoughts and questions.

I am clear about the genesis of my initial disquiet about needing to change my textual form. The way I write is an expression of, development of, and reaffirmation of, my 'self.' When I write in a form that is intended to be acceptable to the 'body of knowledge' I am effectively adopting a different persona, and in doing so my development and reaffirmation are skewed toward making me 'acceptable' to those who patrol the boundaries of the authoritative mind-set. I am, perhaps, becoming too old and too crotchety to do this willingly.

I am also sufficiently self-indulgent to attempt to put this on the agenda for others. I have justified this by questioning whether we need to move beyond post-modernism, by suggesting that if this is the case, then we need to do so in textual form as well as in content—in our 'acceptance criteria' as well as in our methodological approach. I play with the idea of stories as a possible vehicle for this, but what would it do to the 'body of knowledge' if stories were to become an acceptable means by which to seek membership? Would the rules change, or would the 'body' become so dis-embodied that membership criteria no longer existed?

BIBLIOGRAPHY

Alderman, G. (1992) *The Land Beyond: A Fable,* London: HarperCollins.

Broderick, D. (1993) "Postmodernism And Science Fiction" in J. Clute and P. Nicholls, eds. *The Encyclopaedia of Science Fiction,* London: Orbit.

Carter, A. (1969) *Heroes and Villains,* London: Penguin.

Clark, A.C. (1953) *Childhood's End,* London: Pan Science Fiction.

Clute, J. (1993) "Survivalist Fiction" in J. Clute and P. Nicholls, eds., *The Encyclopaedia of Science Fiction,* London: Orbit.

Connolly, F. (1993) *The Rising of the Moon,* New York: Ballantine.

Constantine, S. The Wraeththu Trilogy: 1) (1988) *The Enchantments of Flesh and Spirit;* 2) (1988) *The Bewitchments of Love and Hate;* 3) (1989) *The Fulfilment of Fate and Desire.* London: Futura.

Doty, D.H. and W.H. Glick (1994) "Typologies As A Unique Form Of Theory Building: Toward Improved Understanding And Modelling" *Academy of Management Review,* 19, 2, 230–251.

Ephesians (1958) *The Holy Bible,* King James Version, London: Collins.

Furman, N. (1985) The Politics of Language: Beyond the Gender Principle? in G. Greene and C. Kahn, eds., *Making a Difference: Feminist Literary Criticism,* London: Routledge.

Gearhart, S. (1985) *The Wanderground.* London: The Womans Press Ltd.

Genesis (1958) *The Holy Bible,* King James Version, London: Collins.

Gibson, W. The 'Neuromancer' series: 1) (1984) *Neuromancer;* 2) (1986) *Count Zero;* 3) (1986) *Burning Chrome;* 4) (1988) *Mona Lisa Overdrive.* London: HarperCollins.

Le Guin, U. (1993) *Always Coming Home.* London: HarperCollins.

Harshbarger, D. (1973) "The Individual And The Social Order: Notes On The Management Of Heresy And Deviance In Complex Organisations" *Human Relations,* 26, 2, 251–269.

Heinlein, R. (1983) *Friday,* Hodder and Stoughton: New English Library.

Herbert, F. The 'Dune' series: 1) (1965) *Dune;* 2) (1969) *Dune Messiah;* 3) (1976) *Children of Dune;* 4) (1981) *God Emperor of Dune;* 5) (1984) *Heretics of Dune;* 6) (1985) *Chapter House Dune,* London: New English Library.

Jameson, F. (1991) *Postmodernism Or The Cultural Logic Of Late Capitalism,* Durham, NC: Duke University Press.

Lindholm, M. (1993) *Cloven Hooves,* London: HarperCollins.

May, J. (1991) *Jack the Bodiless,* London: Pan.

McHale, B. (1987) *Postmodernist Fiction,* New York: Methuen.

Nicholls, P. (1993a) 'Prediction'; (1993b) 'Gods and Demons'; (1993c) 'Cyberpunk', in J. Clute and P. Nicholls, eds. *The Encyclopaedia of Science Fiction,* London: Orbit.

Orwell, G. (1949) *Nineteen Eighty-Four, A Novel,* London: Secker and Warburg, 1949.

Proverbs. (1958) *The Holy Bible,* King James Version, London: Collins.

Register, C. (1980) "Review Essay: Literary Criticism" *Signs: Journal of Women in Culture and Society,* 6, 2, 268–82.

Salama, A, (1991) "Privatisation And Cultural Change", *International Conference on Privatisation: Strategies and Practices.*

Sargent, P. (1977) "Letter to *Frontiers: A Journal of Woman's Studies*" cited in Tuttle, (1993) 'Women as Portrayed in Science Fiction' in J. Clute and P. Nicholls, eds. *The Encyclopaedia of Science Fiction,* London: Orbit.

Silverberg, R. (1971) *Downward to the Earth,* London: Gollancz.

Smith, C. (1965) 'The Dead Lady of Clown Town' in *Space Lords.* London: Sphere Books.

Stevenson, R. L. (1886) *The Strange Case of Dr. Jekyll and Mr. Hyde,* London: Longmans, Green.

Tepper, S. (1992) *Beauty,* London: HarperCollins.

Tepper, S, (1991) *Raising the Stones,* Bantam Spectra.

Tepper, S. (1994) *A Plague of Angels,* London: HarperCollins.

Tuttle, L. (1993) "Women as Portrayed in Science Fiction" in J. Clute and P. Nicholls, eds. *The Encyclopaedia of Science Fiction,* London: Orbit.

Wyndham, J. (1957) *The Midwich Cuckoos,* London: Penguin.

12

ACCOUNTING FOR THE CAPRICES OF MADNESS: NARRATIVE FICTION AS A MEANS OF ORGANIZATIONAL TRANSCENDENCE

Burkard Sievers

This account of madness is based on the author's experience as director of a Group Relations/Leicester-style working conference. It is an account of an organization dominated by a high degree of paranoia. Within this particular conference attempts by the staff to explore the group's psychotic psycho-social dynamics were unsuccessful until we began using narrative fiction to contain the fear that had been blocking learning. This analysis is a rare opportunity to examine the use of narrative fiction to transcend and replace anxieties and to make reparation and reconciliation possible. It clearly demonstrates that narrative fiction can provide a unique tool for action research.

INTRODUCTION

There is no account for the caprices of madmen. (Poe, 1938:318)

With increasing frequency I have used ancient mythology, narrative fiction and theater in my research and writing, drawing on these non scientific sources to conceptualize, reflect upon and understand situations I encountered (Sievers, 1989, 1993, 1994, 1995, 1996a,b).

This chapter describes the way a working conference staff dealt with a psycho-social organizational dynamic of madness (i.e., the fear of going mad and the desire to drive others crazy) that predominated the event. A systemic perspective of psychoanalysis known as the 'Leicester Model', a group relations conference approach originating from earlier work of the Tavistock Institute (Lawrence, 1979a, b; Miller, 1989, 1990a, b; Rice, 1965), was employed. The staff were well trained to work with the unconscious, but the collective preoccupation with madness in this particular working conference was so intense that the staff was unable to disentangle or explore the situation until they began to work associatively with narrative fiction. By looking for shared meaning in the ongoing quarrel about a socially shared perception of reality, the narratives became 'objects' and thus 'potential forms of transformation' (Bollas, 1993; Ogden, 1986).

The more I reflect on my experiences as a manager and a consultant, the more evident it becomes that 'caprices of madness' are a common phenomenon, by no means limited to these working conferences. Just as discrimination in psychiatric hospitals between inmates and wardens is not always congruent with the distinction between madness and sanity (Luske, 1990; Rosenham, 1973), it is not always easy to discriminate between madhouses and other types of organizations. This exploration provides further insights towards a better understanding of peoples' fate and the psycho-social dynamics they experience in other 'houses of madness'.

The emphasis of the group relations conference is on the systemic and organizational dimensions—the way people, consciously and unconsciously, articulate their inner and outer worlds in attempts to manage themselves (Lawrence, 1979c), how they assume or avoid leadership and authority, and how, on the basis of individual and collective fantasies and assumptions, they socially construct a common reality. In contrast to the encounter movement—primarily a therapeutic intervention—the group relations approach provides learning opportunities about how people as members of social systems create and sustain their individual and systemic relatedness. Personality and character features are seen as private matters whose exploration is left to the initiative of individuals.

Despite the explicit social and political orientation of the Leicester working conferences, fear that temporary learning organizations might produce casualties has increasingly preoccupied potential participants and staff. The fact that people have, during or after working conferences, been admitted to psychiatric hospitals or have had to undergo therapeutic treatment may appear strange and even disturbing, especially since a reasonable number of staff are trained psychoanalysts and/or are engaged professionally as therapists. The phenomena can only be understood in light of deliberate decisions by conference organizers not to provide therapy within the context of the learning opportunity. 'Our working hypothesis is that any increase in the individual's disturbance is a product of projections from the group—which is adept at spotting and exploiting the vulnerable member' (Miller, 1989:28).

Time and time again, this fundamental premise has proven important in face of the common tendency of individuals to avoid or to spoil the required investigation of socially constructed realities by expressing the wish for personal treatment or by quickly personalizing or pathologizing political and organizational dynamics and conflict. This preoccupation precludes participation in the unconscious rhythms of everyday experience (Bollas, 1995), and, in particular, of a working conference. While casualties cannot be prevented with certainty, the underlying didactics do not aim at producing casualties, nor do the conference staff run the irresponsible risk of causing casualties.

From the very few occasions I have been involved in processes that resulted in casualties, I have come to the conclusion that they occur when two factors coincide. The first element is a strong individual predisposition caused by an extreme biographical, social or political constellation of traumatic conflict that, in the subjective experience of the conference participant, is repeated at the conference. The second element is a failure of management to provide necessary security and containment to allow enough work on the psycho-social dynamics of the conference and its unconscious dimensions (i.e., failure in the staff's attempt to manage the tasks, roles and boundaries the working conference requires).

A HOUSE OF MADNESS

Immediately after my introductory presentation as conference director, one participant almost shouted a question at me. She asked if it was true that during previous conferences people had gone mad and had been admitted to a madhouse. She wanted to know how we, the staff, would be able to prevent such an incident this time. She seemed to be unconsciously raising the question on behalf of a larger number of participants and seemed to be saying that she considered the staff, particularly the director, to be taking a careless and irresponsible risk. Covering her own fear behind a facade of vociferous contempt towards us, she denied us any claim to competence.

Later that evening, when we began exploring our first-day experiences, I began to realize the extent to which the staff and I had already gotten caught in what proved to be the predominant dynamic of the conference. Though we were not clear about what the powerfully expressed fear of going mad actually meant and what it stood for, we were becoming increasingly aware of the extent those basic anxieties had already begun to interfere with everyone's fantasies. This gave early rise to the unconscious fantasy of contagion and contamination, as if a toxin had cast its shadow over the conference.

The more we understood the participants' hidden desire to blame us for driving them crazy, the more we had to let the participants take back the responsibility they had projected onto us and to share our impression with them that they were actually trying to stage madness. The pathological notion of normality to which they were unconsciously attuned had predisposed them to trick madness by making it appear normal (Gruen, 1987), or as 'surface sanity' (LaBier, 1986:62), a kind of 'rational madness' that covers the anxiety of the chaos which is inescapably connected with the traumatic impact of change when organizations are being reconstructed (Lawrence, 1995; Jacobsen, 1959).

The predominant fear of madness was not the exclusive concern of the participants. The staff became progressively aware of the way this fundamental fear had
affected us. This awareness and the anxiety it expressed increased the symbolization of our staff role as management. The greater our awareness of participants'
preoccupation with madness as a defense against learning, the more we assumed
our managerial responsibilities to ensure that intended learning could take place.

During the course of the conference we moved closer and closer to grasping at
what might be described as mature management (Sievers, 1994). Still, the fear of
going mad and the desire to drive others crazy had become a constituent part of
the staff's unconscious dynamic. This was not an easy concept to grasp, and we
were only gradually, and to a limited extent, capable of doing so.

Despite our individual and collective limitations, we were fully aware that the
predominant conference dynamic had to be perceived inescapably as psycho-social. Individual preoccupation with the fear and desire for madness had, from the
very beginning of the conference, been turned into a social marshaling yard, in the
sense that everybody became affected by it. In so far as actions were 'driven by energy derived from the split off parts of personal experience and personal identity,'
an 'effective network' was installed, 'an exchange system of human emotions and
identity, of reified bits of human beings' (Hinshelwood, 1989:79, 82). It was also
obvious this preoccupation with madness had to be seen and conceptualized as a
collusion in which both sides—participants and staff—were inescapably engaged.
In retrospect, the fact that this fear was covered up for some time indicated that it
enabled both 'parties' 'to be of mutual service to each other'(Steiner, 1985:169).

Although the notion of collusion was never explicitly conceptualized among the
staff or in our interpretations of the different conference events, it had become the
guiding metaphor for ongoing attempts to understand better the predominant collective preoccupation. The more we were able to follow this collusion line, the more
we became aware of the implicated falseness knowingly used as a basis for action
which, as Goffman (1969:359) states, is a constituent dimension of every collusion.
We began to realize that to a certain extent we all were caught in the game of not
playing a game (Laing, 1971). Similar to the dynamics of participation of management and workers in business enterprises (Sievers, 1994), the potential of learning
in this particular case had turned into a process of mutual collusion among participants and staff. As such, it had both 'resonances of playing and deception' and increasingly had become 'a game of counterfeiting a relation' (Laing, 1969:108).

Though the staff was able to develop a certain 'capacity for tolerating frustration'
that 'enables the psyche to develop thought as a means by which the frustration that
is tolerated is itself made more tolerable' (Bion, 1962:307), it took some time to
overcome the fragmentation of our experience and thoughts as the outcome of 'the
mating of our preconceptions with our frustration' (*ibid.*). Although we unknow-
ingly began working with 'collusion' as an 'unthought known' (Bollas, 1995, 1987;
Armstrong, 1995), it was difficult to overcome the preconceptualization and to link
it with other thoughts and the common attempts of thinking.

THE INSTITUTIONAL EVENT

We finally succeeded in grasping meaning beyond the mutual collusion of madness by the coincidence of a special event and our ability to use narrative fiction to engage with the primary conference task and this special event.

The basic design of the conference usually includes two events involving the system as a whole (Rice, 1965; Miller, 1989, 1990a). The explicit focus of the conference's final 'institutional event' was the relatedness among participants and staff in their double role as management and consultants (Guereca, 1979). The event design incorporated various subsystems formed by participants and staff. This time it provided us with an extended frame to further experience and to explore the predominant psycho-social dynamic of madness.

Since the institutional event is an experiential event, the development and search for new meanings and their potential discovery is not a matter of one party arriving at the truth and teaching this perspective to the other parties. Rather it is action research at its best. Members develop working hypotheses from the exploration of their own feelings, assumptions and fantasies. In the course of the event, they are tested, improved or refuted. The conference is based on the assumption that the learning of each participant will be unique. Everyone decides with their own authority what they will take as important or what they will refuse. Within these conferences there is no need to arrive at any objective or collectively shared 'truth'. If truth can be found, it can only be derived from serious questioning of individuals' subjective experiences and of their attempt to relate it to meaning in mutual exploration. The learning in the institutional event is based on serious attempts at experiencing one's own and others' experience.

To experience is not a rational, one-way process of arriving at a solution, but rather a series of iterative attempts at increasingly integrating what had been previously unconsciously denied, displaced, rejected or, through projection, invested into others. This reduces the potential pathogenic character of this suffering by converting it into a creative experience (Dejours, 1990; Sievers, 1995) that ultimately arrives at new discoveries about oneself and about the relatedness with others.

DECONSTRUCTING ORGANIZATIONAL EXPERIENCE WITH THE HELP OF NARRATIVE FICTION

As the institutional event began, it seemed as if the predominant dynamic had almost vanished. It soon became clear that by still playing the game of not playing a game, many of the participants were repressing the irrational madness upon which they had openly acted earlier in the conference.

This was especially obvious within the participant subsystem that included the woman who had first spoken. Instead of interacting with other subsystems, this subsystem remained within its boundaries for quite some time. The extent to which they were content with each other was symbolized by their chosen name: group-sex. The predominant style in which this subsystem presented itself was sustained in an almost carnevalesque manner. The subsystem thus seemed to be a paranoid system (Cameron, 1943; Lemert, 1974), expressing the state of paranoid delusions felt by many of its members. As they were stuck in defense of 'eroticized anxiety' (Devereux, 1986:343), they were only able to hold on to an 'image of the organization (and the institutional event, in particular) as an absurd farce' (Gabriel, 1995:486). They appeared to act out madness in an attempt to avoid engaging with the reality of the event and thus to avoid experiencing their experiences (Green, 1978).

The tendency among participants and staff to refer to fictional literature and films as an additional source of interpretation was an invaluable part of our explorations. Since image can be regarded as 'the first step necessary for the production of ideas which can be incorporated in a relational system of thought' (Puget, 1988:126) and metaphor, in particular, as 'a process by which new perspectives on the world come into existence' (Schön, 1979:254), this tendency supported the hope that the organizational reality of the conference might be perceived beyond the narrow frame of a madhouse.

In our repeated attempts to explore the predominant psycho-social dynamic and the collusion created, the staff began to refer to Herman Melville's (1855/1969) story *Benito Cereno* as a metaphoric frame which could possibly contain our experiences of hopelessness and despair until we were more capable of facing and understanding the predominant dynamic. The story, in contrast to the more common metaphorical use of an image, provided an extended plot with its respective history and dynamic.

Melville describes a meeting of two ships, the *Bachelor's Delight,* commanded by Captain Amasa Delano from New England, and the *San Dominick,* with its Spanish Captain Benito Cereno, along the Chilean coast in 1799. When Delano visits the *San Dominick,* once a fine merchant ship but now a slave ship, he finds dilapidation and disrepair. The passengers are wailing aloud about a long and painful sea voyage. The young Spanish captain, apparently exhausted and sick, lets his Negro servant Babo do most of the talking for him. Benito Cereno's 'conduct is so strange that it suggests madness' (Fogle, 1952:157). Babo 'directs a masquerade of order that deceives both Captain Delano and the reader about who is actually in charge' (Rogin, 1985:209). Delano recognizes signs of a mysterious inconsistency, the whole vessel appears to him as an uncanny, enchanted palace. 'The vessel was completely a death ship, in appearance and history' (Howard, 1951:220).

The true nature of the situation is only revealed after Delano leaves. Suddenly, as his men begin rowing away, the Spaniard,

with a wild leap . . . throws himself in Delano's boat, followed by his faithful black, dagger in hand; and the black aims his dagger, not at the Americans, but at his Spanish master. When the American crew finally pulls to safety a harrowing story comes out (Mumford, 1929:245).

Some time before, the *San Dominick* slaves had mutinied, overpowered the crew, killed most of the Spaniards and kept the remaining crew on board. Since the slaves did not know how to navigate, they forced the whites to help, demanding that they return them to Africa. The *San Dominick's* slaves had staged a masquerade during Delano's short stay to create the illusion of normality and order, an event devilishly directed by Babo. Ironically, it was the New England captain's own naiveté that saved him from a certain death had he discovered the truth while still on the vessel.

This brief sketch provides limited insight into the almost inexhaustible symbolic significance of Melville's tale. It is hardly surprising that we were only able to remember parts of the story and its potential symbolic implications. The story gave us an idea of how the participants—in some parts of our imagination—might take over the conference. Lacking, metaphorically speaking, any further knowledge of navigation, they might have forced us to return to the continent from which they originated (and with which they were more familiar), the university department and the rational ways of learning to which they were accustomed. This image allowed us to explore further our own counter-transferences within the staff and, at least tentatively, to express the unthinkable notion that the participants may have mistaken the conference invitation for a violent attempt to enslave them into a kind of learning in which they actively refused to participate.

Although drawing upon associations and playing with Melville's *Benito Cereno* provided us with a vehicle for understanding the predominant dynamic, we felt that we were not yet exactly on target. The slave masquerade that successfully deceived Delano and the subversive obedience into which Cereno and his mates had been forced did not correspond closely enough to what we unconsciously knew to be the conference dynamic. The metaphoric frame left us with a sense of hesitation and uneasiness.

Further acknowledgment of revolution and mutiny on board of the *San Dominick* would inevitably have raised feelings of vigorous violence and the powerful anxieties of vengeance, hate and guilt with which we could not yet cope. It might equally well have been that we were censoring our own counter-transferences about the participants, and therefore were unable to acknowledge that they, at least to a certain extent, had turned us into slave holders through projective identification.

In the subsequent session of the institutional event, we, the staff, publicly worked with the metaphoric frame sketched above. As usual we worked with what came to mind and related this to what actually was presented to us. We were still very uncomfortable with the frame provided by *Benito Cereno.* Then a staff member referred to another narrative writer, Edgar Allan Poe, in whom she had been keenly interested since childhood. As if opening her eyes for the first time, she began to tell the story of Poe's (1938) *The System of Doctor Tarr and Professor Fether,* the tale of an early nineteenth century visit to a private lunatic asylum in the south of France. The narrator is the first visitor in many years to be allowed access by the superintendent, Monsieur Maillard. The 'system of soothing', upon which the institution had become famous, was built on the presupposition that 'all punishments were avoided' and

> *that the patients, while secretly watched, were left much apparent liberty, and that most of them were permitted to roam about the house and grounds, in the ordinary apparel of persons in right mind* (p. 308).

Only a few weeks earlier, the system was replaced due to its inherent dangers. The former system is described by the superintendent

> *as one in which the patients were ménagés, humored. We contradicted no fancies which entered the brains of the mad. On the contrary, we not only indulged but encouraged them; and many of our most permanent cures have been thus effected. There is no argument which so touches the feeble reason of the madman as the reductio ad absurdum. . . . We affected to treat each individual as if for some ordinary physical disorder; and the word 'lunacy' was never employed* (p. 309).

Monsieur Maillard offered to take the visitor on an after-dinner tour. At dinner, the visitor shares the company with some twenty five to thirty people, apparently of rank and high breeding and rather extravagantly dressed and bejeweled. But, much to the visitor's surprise, 'the topic of lunacy was a favorite one with all present' (p. 312).

Suddenly, a series of loud screams from elsewhere on the premises drowned out the dinner party and 'they all grew as pale as so many corpses, and shrinking within their seats, sat quivering and gibbering with terror, and listening for a repetition of the sound' (p. 315). Never in his life had the visitor seen 'any set of reasonable people so thoroughly frightened' (ibid.). The sounds recurred several times before the visitor 'ventured to inquire the cause of this disturbance' (ibid.). But Monsieur Maillard played down the incident as a bagatelle. Some ten lunatics in their charge occasionally got up a howl in concert.

The fact that the whole scene was 'growing gradually worse and worse' and 'became at length a sort of Pandemonium in petto' (p. 317) did not prevent Monsieur Maillard from explaining further that he had developed the new system based on some critical elements from Dr. Tarr and the celebrated Professor Fether. Referring to the danger inherent in the old system, Monsieur Maillard explained:

> *There is no accounting for the caprices of madmen; and, in my opinion, as well as in that of Doctor Tarr and Professor Fether, it is never safe to permit them to run at large unattended. A lunatic may be 'soothed', as it is called, for a time, but, in the end, he is very apt to become obstreperous. His cunning, too, is proverbial, and great. If he has a project in view, he conceals his design with a marvelous wisdom; and the dexterity with which he counterfeits sanity, presents, to the metaphysician, one of the most singular problems in the study of mind. When a madman appears thoroughly sane, indeed, it is high time to put him in a straight jacket* (p. 318).

The old system was renounced when one of the lunatics had gotten out of hand and, with the help of his fellow patients, had initiated a revolt which ended when

> *one fine morning the keepers found themselves pinioned hand and foot, and thrown into cells, where they were attended, as if they were the lunatics, by the lunatics themselves, who had usurped the offices of the keepers. The keepers and kept were soon made to exchange places. Not that exactly either—for the madmen had been free, but the keepers were shut up in cells forthwith, and treated, I am sorry to say, in a very cavalier manner* (p. 318).

Only toward the end of the story, when the drama reaches a catastrophic climax, does it become evident what really had happened. The people at the dinner party were overpowered by a gang of ten: 'stamping, scratching, and howling, there rushed a perfect army of what I took to be Chimpanzees, Ourang-Outangs, or big black baboons of the Cape of Good Hope' (p. 320).

When the tragedy was over and the soothing system restored, the visitor was able to conclude:

> *Monsieur Maillard, it appeared, in giving me the account of the lunatic who had excited his fellows to rebellion, had been merely relating his own exploits. This gentleman had, indeed, some two or three years before, been the superintendent of the establishment; but grew crazy himself, and so became a patient. The keepers, ten in number, having been suddenly overpowered, were first well tarred, then carefully feathered, and then shut up in underground cells. They had been so imprisoned for more than a month. At length, one escaping through a sewer, gave freedom to all the rest* (p. 320f.).

Our colleague provided a brief version of Poe's story but one that conveyed its main elements. The tale appeared to offer a much better metaphoric frame than we had found in *Benito Cereno* and provided us with enormous relief.

Poe's story allowed us to come to grips with the collusion of madness in which we had all been caught for so long. The meaning we finally derived from the tale no longer referred to either 'them' or 'us' as patients or keepers. Rather we identified more with the visitor who was ultimately able to realize how he had been severely mistaken. Unlike the Negro slaves in *Benito Cereno* who had successfully concealed from the visiting Captain Delano the fact that they actually took over the vessel, the inherent notion of madness in Dr. Tarr's and Professor Fether's system provided us reference to a meaning that went beyond any accusation of who was to be found guilty and who to be handed over to the courts for further sanctioning.

Considering Poe's phrase, that 'there is no argument which so touches the feeble reason of the madman as the *reductio ad absurdum*' (p. 309), allowed us—in a most paradoxical manner—to deconstruct the former 'collusion of madness' and reestablish the possible reality of 'sanity'. By seriously addressing and working through the displaced irrationality of rational madness, we were ultimately able to go beyond the shadow of insanity that previously threatened us, and thus to increase our perception of the shadow as a constituent dimension of any 'normal' reality.

From this perspective, we were able to reinterpret the main elements of the conference's history. When viewed through this metaphoric frame, the episode in the opening plenary appeared in a new light. The student who rationally voiced her concerns about other participants being driven crazy occupies a role that can be compared with Monsieur Maillard's. Like the former superintendent of the madhouse in Poe's story who went mad himself and then initiated a revolt that he later legitimated as 'the new system', she appeared to have later lost control of her initial 'rational madness'.

In her mind she was able, together with her fellow participants, to turn the staff from its role as conference management into prisoners who were shut up in underground cells. Like the superintendent in Poe's story, she and her fellow participants had kept the management imprisoned for the following week of the conference. Like the real keepers in Poe's story, both the fact of the imprisonment itself and the conversion of managers into persecutors had to be sealed unconsciously. Just as the keepers in Poe's story did not escape for more than a month, conference staff rather than containing this projective identification, became entangled in the persecutory role into which they were projected.

I am convinced that our use of narrative fiction and of Poe's *System of Dr. Tarr and Professor Fether* ultimately allowed staff and participants to reconstruct the fiction of the madhouse and the previously prevailing psycho-social dynamic of madness. Nevertheless, I still have some doubts as to whether all the participants were, in fact, in a position to liberate themselves from the traumatic experience of having been temporarily confined in a house of madness. I am sure some will remember the conference as a nightmare which seemed to prevent all learning.

At the same time, I would like to think that the ongoing, often painful effort undertaken by the conference management to symbolize 'mature management' kept alive the possibility of creatively transcending the unavoidable suffering that is inescapably related to any serious attempt at learning from experience. For me, this indicates that the search for new meanings can become a consequential and necessary venture.

THE CAPRICES OF MADNESS

The conference dynamic is most likely a dynamic of all organizations—only differing in its intensity. The notion of madness in work is often expressed in the Xerox lore of most enterprises (Gabriel, 1995). The joke culture mirrors a broader unconscious fear that working in an organization may be bad for one's health. It also expresses the general conviction that it is not oneself, but others, and those at the top in particular, who really are crazy.

Just as family in capitalist society has become a psychotic institution (Kovel, 1984; Hoggett, 1992), so too

much, if not most of our group behavior and institutional arrangements, are quite specif-
ically and exquisitely designed to avoid consciously experiencing psychotic anxiety. More-
over, the psychotic processes are in danger of breaking through from moment to moment
(Young, 1994:156).

As 'bureaucracy and organization are the rationalization of the cultural containment of anxiety' (Alford, 1990:26), individual and collective abilities to manage
these unconscious anxieties and their defenses are always at risk. Madness can, in
this context, be understood as a psychotic anxiety about one's inability to operate
as the manager of one's unconscious (Bollas, 1995). It is the experience of imprisonment and regression that goes along with imprisonment that usually contributes
to the experienced lack of managerial capacity (Jacobsen, 1949). Goffman writes,
'There is a multitude of reasons why someone who is not mentally ill at all, but
who finds he can neither leave an organization nor basically alter it, might introduce exactly the same trouble as is caused by patients' (1969:386).

Without 'the rationalization of the cultural containment of anxiety' (Alford,
1990:26) and the defense function of organizational structures and mechanisms
(Menzies, 1988) we would not be able to survive the resulting chaos and accomplish the functional tasks of organizations. There is little doubt that the cultural
containment of anxiety via rationalization is usually built on fundamental internal
splitting processes of the members that must be described as being mad.

To the extent that the rationality of organizations is based on the necessity to
separate thinking and feeling, both the organization (Ramos, 1981) and these fundamental human capacities become instrumentalized. According to the underlying instrumental logic, it appears almost natural that people distance themselves
from their own experience to perform required tasks. Within most organizations
people are not only supposed to hide their own feelings, but to give the impression that they are not feeling at all.

This fundamental splitting and the inherent madness, however, are permanently
concealed through the impression and emphasis on normality and sanity. As 'the
chaos that could come from each individual releasing his own secret world' of feelings (Brook, 1993:99) becomes neutralized or negated, the negation itself has to
be turned into a reflexive one. To ensure that even the feelings that are related to
such a betrayal of both oneself and others can be successfully concealed, the double denial of feelings and madness has to be declared normal.

The potentially mature individual is forced to identify himself and to be identified with what Bion (1962:309) calls 'a willfully misunderstanding object'. To appear normal and reasonable, the individual is supposed to willfully misinterpret his
own experience of himself. The organizational member tends to infantilize himself and to be infantilized. This has to be concealed through the perpetuation of
immaturity via leadership (Sievers, 1994). To the extent that the individual is supposed either to deny his mature capacity for toleration of negative experience and
is forced to reduce his own psychic qualities, his capacity for being capable of

thinking is not only reduced but is substituted by 'reasonable' thoughts that seldom are deeper than conventional wisdom.

The organization in general, and those commonly regarded as management in particular, encourage individuals to substitute their own psychic anxiety of going mad with reasonable conviction, that if one has to cope with these anxieties, it is exclusively because there are people (and those at the top, in particular) who have the capacity or even the explicit intent of driving their subjects crazy.

Ultimately, madness has to be regarded as a metaphor. Still the experience of this particular conference taught me that the anxiety of going mad and the desire to drive others crazy should not only be treated as if they are real, but as the predominant—or even exclusive—reality to which people appear capable of relating. Despite the fact that the organizational reality, built upon such a social (de)construction of reality, does not appear ultimately as a fiction, any serious attempt to reconstruct the fictitious reality in order to transcend it has to take that fictitiousness as if it were real. Like fantasies, fictions are especially real when they are socially constructed and maintained for the purpose of hiding the reality of those archaic anxieties from which they are ultimately derived. It seems to me that these psychotic anxieties, not only in the case of schizophrenics in 'madhouses', but equally in contemporary organizational 'houses of madness' are expressions of a quality of anxiety that Searles (1959) aptly and frankly describes:

> *The effort to drive the other person crazy can consist, predominantly, in the psychological equivalent of murder; that is, it can represent primarily an endeavour to destroy the other person, to get rid of him as completely as if he were physically destroyed* (p. 5) . . . *The effort to drive the other person crazy can be motivated predominantly by a desire to externalize, and thus get rid of, the threatening craziness in oneself* (p. 7).

Clearly, if we want to take madness seriously, we have to perceive madness as a social category. Elias (1985:54) describes the concept of meaning and how the concept of madness must be understood 'as a social category referring to a plurality of inter-related people as its subject and which, as a category, cannot be understood if it is only related to an isolated individual' (Sievers, 1994:27). Because of its inherent fear of the end or the destruction of meaning, madness can be considered a futile attempt to survive in spite of the apparent turmoil and loss of what has previously been regarded as meaningful. Just as the necessity for meaning can be derived from the fact that we, as human beings, are inescapably mortal and must ultimately die, madness can be understood as the expression of the archaic anxiety that, one day, we will either be killed or will find ourselves in a situation where suicide is the only option. To protect our own invulnerability and immortality, these mortal anxieties have to be denied and the fear of being killed has to be turned against others in an attempt to kill them by driving them crazy.

It is important to understand that madness is related to mental pain. It is, as Waddell (1989:13) puts it, a defense against 'feelings which are very hard to bear—the conscious phenomena of unconscious psychic pain' that people would inescapably experience if they allowed themselves to actually face the experience of pain. It is the fear that acknowledging the pain that people feel for themselves and others within normal situations will inevitably lead to going mad. Madness is thus conceived as 'a state equivalent to mental death, which for the mature ego seems to be more intolerable than physical death' (Puget, 1988:121). An equivalent to psychic death, madness is the representation 'unprovoked by forces linked to destruction which come from another' (p. 126). This essence is precisely expressed by Foucault (1971:16): 'Madness is the déjà-là of death.'

ACCOUNTING FOR THE ACCOUNT OF MADNESS

Any attempt to end this account of madness with a traditional conclusion seems premature and rash. The potential implications of the foregoing account leave me with a considerable amount of thinking and meaning yet to be explored. My 'books', and probably those of my former colleagues and the conference participants, cannot be 'balanced' yet.

Using narrative fiction, we discovered an important dimension of psychoanalytical science. Whereas traditionally the discipline has been primarily limited to analysis of the narrative as a piece of art, and to examining its creative process, reception and interpretation (Schönau, 1991), our use of narrative as metaphor can be considered as an expression of applied psychoanalytical science. As such, it is evidence that narrative fiction may be a meaningful tool in psychoanalytically oriented approaches to action research.

The elaboration of the predominant psycho-social dynamic of madness illustrated for the staff the efficacy of narrative fiction in disentangling the cobweb of emotions, fantasies and behavior presented at the conference. As a result, first Herman Melville's story *Benito Cereno* and later Edgar Allan Poe's tale *The System of Dr. Tarr and Professor Fether*, provided us with a kind of container. This container temporarily allowed us not only to contain our fears—derived from the paranoid schizoid position and the pity, as the emotion of the depressive position—but also to relate them to a much broader 'fictional' reality. The fictional reality allowed a metaphoric frame for realizing both the inter-relatedness of these emotions and their effect on the psycho-social dynamics in the systemic contexts of the respective tales.

These tales helped us generate insights and conceptualizations more in accord with our unconscious impressions and the fantasies. Mobilized by our own depressive anxiety of not being good enough to provide learning in face of the persecutory anxieties in the conference, we initially projected our own fears into Melville's representation of the external world. Then we were able to deposit our anxieties, feel partly liberated from them, and thus permit an unconscious search for a more appropriate container and a better understanding of the nature of the anxieties in which most conference members appeared caught.

The account of madness offered here seems limited, not only in terms of my analysis, but in respect of the description and further exploration of actual phenomena treated. I was reminded of this every time I mentioned the subject in conversation. The number of episodes recounted by my companions is almost endless, and they almost always refer to other people's madness or to the madness of organizations in general. This confirms the impressive extent to which feelings of madness cannot be owned by the self, but rather the pathology is projected onto others or perceived as basically persecutive. It seems as if the notion of madness is close to unbearable:

> *In discovering and allowing our own individuality, marginality and madness, we not only become more prepared to admit these to others; we even become more convinced that facing madness and chaos as a substantial part of our internal and our common reality probably is the necessary precondition to individually and collectively continue to struggle for meaning.* (Sievers, 1994:180)

It well may be that our preoccupation with madness during the conference was not as much futile as it was mainly an expression that madness itself was inaccessible. This would give space to the idea that the actual experience of madness as a form of knowledge and a different kind of empirical research of the inner and the outer worlds (Cooper, 1978) was substituted or displaced by the major preoccupation with the fear of such an experience. Instead of actually facing madness and its individual and social caprices, we may have been misled by the caprioles of madness. Insofar as the experience of madness unconsciously represents annihilation, we may have been caught in survival strategies mirroring the times in which we live in and the predominant fear of being destroyed. To annihilate one's own fear of annihilation is but another expression of rational normality.

BIBLIOGRAPHY

Alford, C. Fred (1990) "Reparation And Civilization. A Kleinian Account Of The Large Group" *Free Association,* 19, 7–30.

Armstrong, David (1995) "The Analytic Object In Organizational Work" Paper Presented at the 1995 Annual Meeting of the International Society for the Psychoanalytic Study of Organizations, London, July, 7–9.

Bion, Wilfred R. (1962) "The Psycho Analytic Study Of Thinking" *International Journal of Psycho-Analysis* 43, 306–310.

Bollas, Christopher (1987) *The Shadow of the Object: Psychoanalysis of the Unthought Known,* London: Free Association Books.

Bollas, Christopher (1993) *Being a Character: Psychoanalysis and Self Experience,* London: Routledge.

Bollas, Christopher (1995) *Cracking Up: The Work of Unconscious Experience,* London: Routledge.

Brook, Peter (1993) *The Open Door: Thoughts on Acting and Theater,* New York: Pantheon Books.

Cameron, Norman (1943) "The Paranoid Pseudo Community" *The American Journal of Sociology* 49, 32–38.

Cooper, David (1978) *The Language of Madness,* London: Penguin.

Dejours, Christophe (1990) "Nouveau-regard sur la souffrance humaine dans les organisations" in Jeancois Chanlat (ed.) *L'individu dans l'organisation: Les dimensions oubliées,* Laval: Les Presses de l'Universite Laval, 687–708.

Devereux, G. (1986) *Freud and Mythos,* München: Wilhelm Fink.

Elias, Norbert (1985) *The Loneliness of the Dying,* Oxford: Basil Blackwell.

Fogle, Richard Harter (1952) "The Monk and the Bachelor: Melville's *Benito Cereno*" *Tulane Studies in English,* 3, 155–178.

Foucault, Michel (1971) *Madness and Civilization,* London: Tavistock.

Gabriel, Yiannis (1995) "The Unmanaged Organization: Stories, Fantasies and Subjectivity" *Organization Studies,* 16, 477–501.

Goffman, Erving (1969) "The Insanity of Place" *Psychiatry,* 32, 357–388.

Green, Hanna (1978) "Ich hab dir nie einen Rosengarten versprochen" *Bericht einer Heilung,* Reinbek: Rowohlt.

Gruen, Arno (1987) Der Wahnsinn der Normalität, *Realismus als Krankheit: eine grundlegende Theorie zur menschlichen Destruktivität,* Kempten: Kösel-Verlag.

Guereca, Dennis (1979) "A Manager's View of the Institutional Event" in W. Gordon Lawrence, ed. *Exploring Individual and Organizational Boundaries: A Tavistock Open Systems Approach,* Chichester: Wiley, 103–109.

Hinshelwood, Robert D. (1989) "Social Possession of Identity" in B. Richards, ed. *Crises of the Self,* London: Free Association Books.

Hoggett, Paul (1992) *Partisans in an Uncertain World: The Psychoanalysis of Engagement,* London: Free Association Books.

Howard, Leon (1951) *Herman Melville: A Biography,* Berkeley: University of California Press.

Jacobsen, Edith (1949) "Observations On The Psychological Effects Of Imprisonment On Female Political Prisoners" in K. R. Eissler, ed. *Searchlights on Delinquency. New Psychoanalytic Studies,* New York: International Universities Press, 341–368.

Jacobsen, Edith (1959) "Depersonalization" *Journal of the American Psychoanalytic Association,* 7, 581–560.

Kovel, Joel (1984) "Rationalisation And The Family" in B. Richards, ed. *Capitalism and Infancy: Essays on Psychoanalysis and Politics,* London: Free Association Books, 102–121.

LaBier, Douglas (1986) *Modern Madness: The Emotional Fallout of Success,* Reading, MA: Addison-Wesley.

Laing, Ronald D. (1969) *Self and Others,* Harmondsworth, Middlesex: Penguin.

Laing, Ronald D.(1971) *Knots,* Harmondsworth, Middlesex: Penguin.

Lawrence, W. Gordon (1979a) "Die Methode der offenen Systeme für das Gruppenbeziehungstraining des Tavistock Institutes" in *Die Psychologie des 20 Jahrhunderts,* Vol. VIII, Zürich: Kindler, 659–666.

Lawrence, W. Gordon (ed.) (1979b) *Exploring Individual and Organizational Boundaries: A Tavistock Open System Approach,* Chichester: Wiley.

Lawrence, W. Gordon (1979c) "A Concept For Today: The Management Of Oneself In Role" in W. G. Lawrence, ed. *Exploring Individual and Organizational Boundaries: A Tavistock Open System Approach,* Chichester: Wiley, 235–249.

Lawrence, W. Gordon (1995) "Social Dreaming As A Tool Of Action Research" Paper Presented at the 1995 Annual Meeting of the International Society for the Psychoanalytic Study of Organizations, London, July 7–9.

Lemert, Edwin M. (1974) "Paranoia and the Dynamics of Exclusion" *Sociometry*, 25, 2–20.

Luske, Bruce (1990) *Mirrors of Madness: Patrolling the Psychic Border*, New York: de Gruyter.

Melville, Herman (1855/1969) "Benito Cereno" in W. Berthoff, ed. *Great Short Works of Herman Melville*. New York: Harper and Row, 238–315.

Menzies, Isabel E. P. (1988) "The Functioning of Social Systems as a Defense Against Anxiety" in I. M. Lyth, *Containing Anxiety in Institutions: Selected Essay, Vol I*, London: Free Association Books, 43–85.

Miller, Eric J. (1989) "The 'Leicester' Model: Experiential Study of Group and Organizational Processes" Occasional Paper No. 10. London: The Tavistock Institute of Human Relations.

Miller, Eric J. (1990a) "Experiential Learning in Groups I: The Development of the Leicester Mode" in E. Trist and H. Murray, eds. *The Social Engagement of Social Science: A Tavistock Anthology, Vol. I: The Socio-Psychological Perspective*, London: Free Association Books, 165–185.

Miller, Eric J. (1990b) "Experiential Learning in Groups II: Recent Developments in Dissemination and Application" in E. Trist and H. Murray, eds. *The Social Engagement of Social Science: A Tavistock Anthology, Vol. I: The Socio-Psychological Perspective*, London (Free Association Books) 186–198.

Mumford, Lewis (1929) *Herman Melville*, New York: The Library Guild of America.

Ogden, Thomas H. (1986) *The Matrix of the Mind: Object Relations and the Psychoanalytic Dialogue*, Northwale, NJ: Jason Aronson.

Poe, Edgar Allan (1845/1938) "The System of Doctor Tarr and Professor Fether" in *The Complete Tales and Poems of Edgar Allan Poe*, New York: Modern Library, 307–321.

Puget, Janine (1988) "Social Violence and Psychoanalysis in Argentina: The Unthinkable and the Unthought" *Free Associations* 13, 84–140.

Ramos, Alberto Guerreiro (1981) *The New Science of Organizations. A Reconceptualization of the Wealth of Nations*, Toronto: University of Toronto Press.

Rice, Kenneth A. (1965) *Learning for Leadership: Interpersonal and Intergroup Relations*, London: Tavistock.

Rogin, Michael Paul (1985) *Subversive Genealogy: The Politics and Art of Herman Melville*, Berkeley: University of California Press.

Rosenham, D.L. (1973) "On Being Sane in Insane Places" *Science* 179, 250–258.

Schön, Donald (1979) "Generative Metaphor: A Perspective on Problem Setting in Social Policy" in A. Ortony, ed. *Metaphor*, Cambridge: Cambridge University Press, 254–283.

Schönau, Walter (1991) *Einführung in die psychoanalytische Literaturwissenschaft*, Stuttgart: J. B. Metzler.

Searles, Harold F. (1959) "The Effort To Drive The Other Person Crazy: An Element In The Aetiology And Psychotherapy Of Schizophrenia," *British Journal of Medical Psychology*, 32, 118.

Sievers, Burkard (1989) " 'I will not let thee go, except thou bless me!' Some Considerations about the Constitution of Authority, Inheritance and Succession" in Faith Gabelnick and A. Wesley Carr, eds. *Contributions to Social and Political Science*, Proceedings of the First International Symposium on Group Relations. Washington, D. C. (A. K. Rice Institute), 155–173.

Sievers, Burkard (1993) "Love in the Times of AIDS" Arbeitspapiere des Fachbereichs Wirtschaftswissenschaft der Bergischen Universität Wuppertal, Wuppertal No. 163.

Sievers, Burkard (1994) *Work, Death, and Life Itself: Essays on Management and Organization,* Berlin: de Gruyter.

Sievers, Burkard (1995) "Characters in Search of a Theatre: Organization as Theatre for the Drama of Childhood and the Drama at Work" *Free Associations* 5, 2, 34, 196–220.

Sievers, Burkard (1996a) "Greek Mythology as a Means of Organizational Analysis: The Battle at Larkfield" *Leadership and Organization Development Journal* 17, 6, 32–40.

Sievers, Burkard (1996b) "Accounting for the Caprices of Madness. Narrative Fiction as a Means of Organizational Transcendence" *Arbeitspapiere des Fachbereichs Wirtschaftswissenschaft.* Bergische Universität Wuppertal, Wuppertal, No. 176.

Steiner, John (1985) "Turning A Blind Eye: The Cover Up For Oedipus" *International Review of Psycho Analysis* 12, 161–172.

Waddell, Margot (1989) "Living In Two Worlds: Psycho-Dynamic Theory and Social Work Practice" *Free Associations* 15, 11–35.

Young, Robert (1994) *Mental Space,* London (Process Press).

13

SECTION SUMMARY: METHODS OF ENGAGING SUBCULTURES

Richard A. Goodman

I have selected a number of papers that reflect an array of robust methods of engaging with postindustrial 'organizational' subcultures. These papers could easily have been placed in other sections of the volume as each carries a message that goes substantively beyond the details of technique and method. But these papers are gathered here to represent one of the most interesting aspects of the postindustrial period—the increasing opportunities to engage with many different organizational forms. No longer is there simply an organization and a client. The world has become much more complex. Organizations now come in a wide variety of guises and structures. Organizations are local, national, global and transnational. Organizations are logical wholes, networked, or virtual. Organizations are permanent, quasi-permanent or temporary. Alliances exacerbate goal fuzziness. Individual membership is local or cosmopolitan, direct or by secondment. They are permanent or transitory. And thus their exploration requires a variety of appreciative approaches.

Earlier this complexity was highlighted when the question of cultural salience was raised. The idea that organizational participants can simultaneously be members of several cultures had only limited academic interest until the complexity of organizational forms also became salient—as it recently has.

As a professor I confront this question in the classroom everyday. Are my students customers, products or co-evolutionists? On what basis should I or the university listen to their concerns? They tend to embrace the experience in a limited fashion that is consonant with their self-interests. As temporary members of a community they most often challenge tradition rather than become a part of it. This handicaps both the student and the faculty and creates enduring conundrums for the administration. Students enter into a strange culture, the university, with no formal tools for cultural assessment and thus with serious limitations on their abilities to cope and navigate. (In general, faculty also have diagnostic limitations but presumably they are more or less conversant with the dominant culture.)

Are we, as professionals, any better? Of course we are! As illustrated in this section, we have a wide range of tools for assessing culture and cultural impact. And even though discerning the "truth" about tacit knowledge is always problematic and tricky we do have robust skills available with which we can engage these issues at many levels.

This summer I traveled to Riga, Warsaw and Prague for the first time. I was confronted with "foreign" situations and struggled afresh with personal sensemaking. I returned home with only tentative insights and substantial uncertainty about most of my experiences. One tentative insight from this trip is that national identity is not as important as local identity and thus I use city names rather than country names. City, of course, is not exactly correct either but it is symbolic of a another conundrum of the postindustrial period—the question of defining the "correct" boundaries of analysis.

Personal sensemaking is our usual starting point. It is unencumbered with techniques and systems on the one hand and filled with tacit worldviews and search paradigms on the other. I have often used such a simple "go and see" technique as a starting point to help me figure out what questions I would like to pursue on subsequent trips. This starting point then creates a stimulus for studying tentative conceptualizations and for deeper analysis. This evolving and deepening model of engagement was reflected in this section and it is the reason that I began the section with Kathryn Rogers' work "Masters of Symbol: My Travels in Thought and Work Life in the Czech Republic."

Kate provides us with an introduction to the conundrum of initial scanning. She demonstrates how a skilled, new traveler might reflect upon her journey. Her main mission to the Czech Republic was not one of research into the nature of national culture. But as a skilled professional she did pick up and salt away cues and then find ways of presenting the issues based on both the presence and absence of cues. In this case she used symbolism as her theme precisely because this was a transitional period in the history of the Czech Republic. The formation of a new nation requires conscious attention to the selection of new symbols. These symbols appear explicitly in the form of flags and in the design of currency and are reflected by their use in publications, displays and such. The new symbols have to compete for attention with older symbols embodied in design, statuary and buildings. A fascinating thought in this paper is the idea that the Czech Republic itself has been the subject of so many transitory alliances that the current government chose to reach far back into history in its quest for appropriate symbolism.

While the Czech Republic can be described as an "organization" (read: nation) of many transitory alliances, other postmodern forms can be seen in the inherent structure of biotechnology. The biotechnology industry has very different operational requirements and unusual cross-boundary interdependencies as compared to the long-linked technologies attributed to the modernist period. Martin Fuglsang captures this well in "The Sexy Biotechnology: A Postmodern Phenomenological Observation of Contradiction and Meaning." In biotechnology, conflicting membership issues take a very different form as firms must collaborate with their competitors for various technologically based strategic reasons. Thus individual members of a firm are never certain if they are really working for their own firm or that of a competitor.

Postmodern phenomenology reminds us that categories produce their opposite "not-categories" and that point-of-view is constrained by the ability to "express" point-of-view, which itself changes the point-of-view in a Heisenberg-like phenomena. So too in biotechnology uncertainty, turbulence and ambiguity lead to rapidly changing relationships among scientists and firms. This description is consistent with postmodern phenomonology as describing and understanding what is "inside" and what is "outside" a firm becomes increasingly difficult. Both the organization and its environment are perpetually being redefined and reinterpreted. In a later section Christina Garsten further explores these membership conundrums at the individual level.

This section began with personal sensemaking and then focused on deeper methods of phenomenology at the organizational/industrial level of analysis. It then moved up one half step of generalization to workforce diversity. Organizational diversity reflects the broad multi-level penetration of subcultures into the work force. At the moment the more robust methods of studying diversity effects within the gender category have evolved through the advent of a feminist standpoint.

The increasing numbers of women in significant organizational roles requires the development of new ways of researching organizational cultures. Iiris Aaltio-Marjosola and Sarah Williams Jacobson in "Researching the Experience of Women in 'Man'agement Across Cultures: A Feminist Standpoint Approach" remind us that "modern" and "male" used to be more or less equivalent and that a feminist standpoint reveals different organizational issues than modernist male analysis does. The modernist approach masks the life-world of women. In fact, the modernist approach based frequently on a monocultural stance and reporting on central tendencies masks the life-world of any subculture. Iiris and Sarah demonstrated the importance of considering both gender and context in describing the work lives, private lives and the career development patterns of women managers. Much of the work in this volume, in fact, eschews monocultural assumptions and demonstrates the importance of considering other sources of cultural relevance. An additional contribution to their work is the study of two national cultures with two voices (the authors) in dialogue. This technique further explores cultural ambiguity by testing insights against a "native" source. This dialogic approach provides deeper insights into each culture as the native informants are both professionals.

The fourth chapter, Monica Lee's "Text, Gender and Future Realities," explores society as a whole through the textual analysis of a lifetime passion for science fiction. Note, that in many of these chapters the key analytic instrument is often the author. This is certainly true in my construction of the book, in Kate's exploration of Czech Republic, and in Iiris and Sarah's study of banking in Finland and the U.S. Here Monica explored the construction of "future realities" or new societies. Her textual analysis of the new societies revealed heroic and romantic themes where evil is conquered in the literature of male authors. By contrast, the literature of female authors contained the themes of evil as immutable. This distinction between the romantic and the pragmatic is reflected in other experiences as well.

I am reminded of an international diplomacy vignette that I encountered at the SCOS Saarbrucken annual meeting. The English language contains words for problem-solving. It is clearly a heroic language. Middle Eastern languages apparently do not have problem-solving words; instead, they have words for reshaping problems. When Western diplomats meet with Middle Eastern diplomats the two sides have very different "innate" understanding of what they are trying to accomplish in the regional negotiations. These differences are similar to the ones derived from Monica's paper although it is not a gender difference.

Monica's use of textual analysis is focused on the future, albeit the future in a "fantasy" world. She detects a bit of influence from the current social context of the authors. A further look at textual analysis, this time from "past to present" is seen in chapters written by Michèle Bowring and by Louise and Bernard James and contained in a later section. They have focused their work on the relationship of the social context to authors' choices of themes and discourse style.

The final chapter, Burkard Sievers' "Accounting for the Caprices of Madness: Narrative Fiction as a Means of Organizational Transcendence," provides another method of understanding culture. This time the view is from within the culture. In the early 1960s Sam Culbert wrote "It Takes Two to See One," a monograph that reflected on the need to step outside of oneself in order to see oneself. This is the essence of Burkard's approach. His chapter is about a set of professionals working within a "temporary" culture that they created and of a type in which they have worked before. In this instance, though, the experience was so strongly gripped by various events that normal distancing was not possible. Burkard describes a conceptual approach that uses narrative to escape the blinders insiders normally wear. The narratives in his story released emotional blocks to understanding and allowed an examination of the situation "as if" insiders were really organizational outsiders working on the inside.

I include this work in the methods section for reasons of personal insight. I have often asked my students to describe their firm or regional culture. They are often puzzled about how to respond. As insiders they are aware of tremendous variety and have trouble feeling comfortable with definitive statements of central tendencies. My personal thought is that narratives have a tremendous power for richly conveying knowledge about a situation and providing a starting point for sharing perceptions with people who are not of the culture. The narrative approach can thus be very effective in helping us see ourselves.

Each of these chapters described a standpoint for analysis and deployment of personal tools for that analysis. The insights drawn by professionals were perceived as imperfect in all cases, but approaches were identified that served as levers for the confluence of professional insights as well as to conclude in a non-heroic fashion that imperfection can be ameliorated with some help but cannot be solved.

SECTION THREE

14

DANCES WITH SHADOWS, DANCE CLUBS, MIRRORED BALLS AND REFLECTED PLEASURES

Ian Atkin and Mike Lowe

Just as mirrored balls refract light over the dance floor, dancers bend the shadows of moral and legal conduct that shape the meaning of pleasure through the phenomena of "re-eroticization." As "places of tolerance" night clubs provide a bounded arena where management's delicate balancing of legal and illegal demands provide clubbers with the potential for pleasure. It is through shared meaning that both administered pleasure and re-eroticization are "decentered."

INTRODUCTION

Life's but a walking shadow, a poor player,
That struts and frets his hour upon the stage,
And then is heard no more; it is a tale
Told by an idiot, full of sound and fury,
Signifying nothing.
(William Shakespeare, *Macbeth*)

The study of work organizations has focused primarily on manufacturing and industrial society. As a result, consumer services that operate outside the daytime economy have been overlooked. We believe that the interwoven flow between the organization, leisure, and night-life pleasures creates an organizational form distinct from its day-light counterpart.

We offer three interpretations of the information provided by research collaborators in the style of Gramsci's (1971) unfinished notes. One interpretation positions the dance clubs as "manufacturers" of cultural happenings for consumption. By producing products in cultural form (Adorno and Horkheimer, 1979), organizations attempt to balance controlled and mimetic, decontrolled events and experiences (Elias and Dunning, 1986). It is through this balance that individuals and groups who visit dance clubs acquiesce to the available pleasures.

A second interpretation views dance clubs in terms of spectacles, events and immemorials. This interpretive frame suggests that individuals become witnesses who create their own active meanings of authentic pleasure through personal and group processes of re-eroticization (Burrell, 1992).

Finally, we can explain dance clubs as flows of play that open a movement between these two fixed positions. Flows from dance clubs' attempt to provide music, sound, lighting, and legal and illegal activities to maximize pleasure while these same conditions are the basis from which active meanings of re-eroticized pleasure are sought, witnessed and appropriated.

"WHEN THE NIGHT COMES FALLING FROM THE SKY" (BOB DYLAN)

Statements that "represent the 'organization of organization'" (Cooper, 1990: 196–197) do not often comment on differences between the light of day and the fall of night. Statements about the organization (Cooper and Burrell, 1988:91) tend to ignore the differences in the tenor of life between day and night. The unique conditions of the night are emphasized here to invite debate about organizational forms that become increasingly visible in the dark. By concentrating on nocturnal entertainment and amusement, the hidden aspects of night time organization is illuminated.

Often night-life entertainment is not limited to a single organization. Rather, joy, passions and play are sought and given meaning through visits to a number of organizations. Malinda, a research collaborator, provides illustrations of the journey to and around organizations, "say you are going out to pubs, you may only take an hour to get ready, or something, and maybe go to a selection of pubs, and then we'll go home" (Malinda: semi-structured interview).

By "artificially distinguish[ing] some inseparable elements" (Debord, 1970:11) from other organizational settings, the conditions of night and night-life pleasures can be studied. Eco (1987:79) provides an illustration of night living:

> *In the Middle Ages a wanderer in the woods at night saw people with malevolent presences; one did not lightly venture beyond the town; men went armed. This condition is close to that of the white middle-class inhabitant of New York, who doesn't set foot in Central Park after five in the afternoon or who makes sure not to get off the subway in*

Harlem by mistake, nor does he take the subway alone after midnight (or even before, in the case of women).

Pleasure and "some kindred notions such as desire, love, jouissance and play" (Burrell, 1992:66) can be experienced in heightened form when people are actively engaged in night life. Some of these pleasures, such as violence, can be coarse, expressed and experienced directly: "all the Wigan punks would gather there (the Empress) and really go for it with a vengeance. Beer fights that would see the dance floor covered in blood, snot and broken glasses" (McKenna, 1996:56–57). Concern for personal security is part of night time experiences.

Tim observed that dance clubs offer the opportunity "to get drunk (and) if you are single to tap up" while Sophie noted "that one function of a club was if you aren't single to tap up" (focus group). The search for romance, love or sex is also associated with night life. Clarke and Critcher (1985:162) note that

It is a commonplace (if often unarticulated) observation that much of leisure is 'about sex.' The promise of meeting someone of the opposite sex, or of confirming an existing relationship, is inherent in the structure of parties, discotheques, night-clubs, not to mention pubs, restaurants and cinemas.

While some people must work to provide the organized pleasures of the night, most participants in night life are not pursuing leisure in terms of idle relaxation but simply putting their non-work time to active use (Thompson, 1967). Rojek (1995) notes that this understanding of leisure-demands involve the arousal of passions and tensions and the balance between aggression and restraint. Within this context, Elias and Dunning (1986:89) suggest that a principle function of leisure is the "arousal of pleasurable forms of excitement."

Urban night life can be described as an heightened encounter with life in the raw. Yet it also involves a degree of suspension from the direct, material urban landscape of the night. Vaneigem (1983:11) notes that "the history of our time calls to mind those Walt Disney characters who rush madly over the edge of a cliff without seeing it: the power of their imagination keeps them suspended in mid-air, but as soon as they look down and see where they are, they fall." The power of the imagination is also critical in seeking out urban night-time pleasures. At night, the urban landscape appears to be imaginistic rather than tactile and spatial.

Plant (1992) notes that the engagement between the material world and subjective experience is important. Emotions, desires, and experiences of all sorts differ according to the architecture of space and arrangements of colors, sounds, textures, and lighting with which it is created. "The situationists pointed to the forms of conditioning imposed by shopping malls, night clubs, adverts . . . as evidence of the existence of a plethora of techniques by which experiences, desires, attitudes and behaviour are presently manipulated" (57). The corporate mainstream administers and regulates respectable urban dance clubs for the masses (Thornton,

1995), repackaging the sensibility (Dyer 1990) of certain dance cultures as segments of a mass market. The "spectacle" of the mainstream dance club offers slots for distinct sensibilities.

This is illustrated by Malinda, when distinguishing between the mainstream and specialist clubs: "I was there for the three hours, and the need was there for three hours, not just for that general half hour, that you'd get in a club, maybe not a specialist night club" (semi-structured interview). Toni also makes this distinction "raves are more purely for the dance thing. Ravers are more likely to be dancing on their own. It is more of an individual thing, not a group thing; whereas something like the 'Irish Rover' is a group thing, where you're jumping up and down together" (focus-group discussion).

It is important to use the concept of "dance subcultures"—that is, specialist clubs and their organizational forms. According to Thornton (1995), dance subcultures can be understood as the almost constant seeking out of an "authentic" dance club experience incommensurable with the mainstream. Mark comments that "this club I went to, most people were just dancing, which was hip-hop, funk, rare grove night, and you just know that sort of music is going to attract the sort of people who are just going to dance and have a good time" (focus group). Yet while appearing to be outside the mainstream, dance clubs are often incorporated into the repackaging of the club experience through its commodification. Cream, a "clubbing empire" in Liverpool, now organizes national tours, produces CDs and merchandises them (Prince, 1995).

What was once the other is now the mainstream. The "superclub" is, for example, an extension of the attempt to find the authentic: "Goa trance nights, jungle nights and the newer, harder acid jazz nights are all packing in London's clubbing hardcore at converted pubs, tunnels under a railway viaduct or small obscure bars" (Armstrong, 1996:10–11). Given changes in the organization of dance clubs, Thornton's (1995:3) observation seems especially relevant: "that clubs, and indeed raves, house ad hoc communities with fluid boundaries which may come together and dissolve in a single summer or endure for a few years."

THE CASTING OF SHADOWS

This exploration *centers* on those cultural, economic, political and social conditions that produce urban night life pleasures. In this regard, the "appearance" of dance clubs and their contested organizational forms are the main focus of attention. Lighting, colors and sounds are used to differentiate these domes of pleasure in architecture and arrangements of space. Emotions, experiences and feelings are directed in an attempt to enhance pleasure. However, these attempts to manage pleasure can be confounded by clubbers striving to satisfy "moral" and/or "immoral" desires.

The spontaneity and danger associated with enjoyment places clubbers in a position to subvert and even overthrow the managed administration of pleasure. The notion of flow is a useful metaphor for interpreting the contest between the spectacles that situate pleasure, its administration and the meaning of those attending dance clubs. Just as the mirrored ball over the dance floor refracts light, clubbers have the potential to bend the hegemonic administration that hangs over their meanings of pleasure through re-eroticization. In this context, the nocturnal world of the dance club plays host to shadows whose duration depends on the intensity of the light.

Pirsig (1991:26) identifies something of the event of dance clubs: "Then the music started again and the disco lights rotated and Lila looked at him in a curious way. It was just a glance, and the disco light moved on but in just that moment he noticed what a beautiful pale blue her eyes were." When immediate moments slip away they are either lost forever or form an "immemorial." For Lyotard (1984), the immemorial is that which cannot be remembered in consciousness. At the same time, an immemorial disrupts forever any pre-existing understanding of the organization of night life pleasures. Nothing will be the same again.

Not all events or immemorials happen in the fleeting illumination of light inside dance clubs. Light can also peer into and project shadows. The shadow is a non-presence; a fear arising from a perceived menace, something that is not present yet appears in the mind's eye as a presence.

Denhardt (1981) and Bowles (1991) are useful here. Drawing on Jung, Denhardt applies the shadow concept to organizations. Managerial dependence on a rational discourse gives rise to organizational shadows that directs the values it associates with work, efficiency and the design of the organization. This discourse fails to account for the non-rational meanings people give to actions. It represses the "feeling function" that moves the organization toward success. The more this "feeling function" is repressed, the less likely it is that an individual, or indeed the organization will be able to call on that function in the future.

According to Denhardt (1981) the "feeling function" represents unconscious material that can show itself in a harmful and caustic form when the shadow is released. The organization shadow is normally directed towards particular groups who challenge management and even its supremacy. For individuals this can be manifested as explosions of temper, violence and even the arousal of pleasure.

Shadows and the Control-Decontrol of Dance Club Organization

For Adorno (1991), the culture industry manufactures products for mass consumption. In adopting the word "industry" he argues that characteristics associated with the rational manufacture of standardized products for exchange are being appropriated for the organization and administration of cultural products. Dance clubs, both those in the corporate mainstream and dance subcultures, represent a branch of this industry.

Adorno and Horkheimer (1979) criticize the culture industry for its tendency to bring culture down to the level of mass amusement. Within this critical perspective pleasure means not thinking about anything, forgetting suffering, etc. It is flight, not from a wretched reality, but from the last remaining thought of resistance (Adorno and Horkheimer, 1979).

Adorno and Horkheimer (1979) emphasize pleasure as a retreat from resistance; whereas for Elias and Dunning (1986) it is the arousal of excitement and passions. Following Rojek (1995), who interprets the arousal of pleasures in terms of aggression and restraint, it is possible to understand the organization of night-life pleasures as a contest between the advancement and restraint of pleasure seeking.

Attempts to control and regulate "manufactured" night-life pleasures through a network of flows inside and between organizations and institutions are the focus here. We begin by exploring the flows between those institutions of the State that regulate urban night life in general and dance clubs in particular.

It is often assumed that the entire clubbing experience has the sole goal of complete moral corruption (Ferguson, 1993). Thus, the regulation of dance clubs is considered essential. The shadows of law and order and government regulation are obliged to enforce some restrictions on the administration of pleasure in an attempt to appease claims about and confine 'moral corruption.' As a result, "ever since discos and beat clubs began to force dance halls into closure in the 1960s and 1970s owners have found themselves caught between the rock of licensing laws and the hard place of health and safety regulations" (p. 10).

Control through the organization of dance clubs can take several forms. The administration of dance clubs requires that flows between "controlled pleasure" are maintained at a level that attempts to conform to the rules and the legal statutes. Individuals and groups seeking enjoyment are often kept waiting outside the entrance to the club before encountering its pleasures and spectacles, a ritual event consciously built into the club experience. Malinda gives an illustration of this night-time ritual:

> *I waited about twenty-five minutes and it was raining, and it wasn't the fact that it was uncomfortable and I was getting wet. It was nothing to do with that, the fact was that you're standing outside a building and all you want to do is get in there. You can hear everything going on, it's more frustrating, it just builds up the excitement. I suppose cos it's like a restriction from something you want, but you know at the end of it, you know you are going to get it. So you don't get annoyed or stuff like that.* (semi-structured interview)

If part of the administration of dance clubs is deferred gratification, another is the threat of the withdrawal of pleasure. Door staff try to maintain order and clubs' "reputations." Eric observes "I don't know if it's because they (the door staff) have got a reputation for violence, but if the club has a heavy handed presence especially when you're (with) a group of lads (it) can intimidate you, almost put you on edge" (focus group).

This perception of the potential threat from door staff is reiterated by Martin "that atmosphere can antagonize you though, moving around as if they've got this power status" (focus group).

The DJ is also central to the control of pleasure. The DJ directs the way music is played and therefore controls the happenings, experiences and passions of those seeking enjoyment. Mark notes that "the DJ manipulates everyone, he's their (the Club's) control really to some extent, cos he knows what you like, he knows how to deliver, he like mixes it up" (semi-structured interview).

Further, there is the imposed control on the administration of pleasure through the regulation of licensing hours. Mark notes that at the end of the night, "it's like 2.00 (am) (the) lights go up and everyone's still dancing, and the music might still be playing. People start clapping going 'more,' 'more,' and that's quite good, cos everyone's like on the same wavelength, and you get outside, and your so hot you just want fresh air, cos you've been dancing for the last three hours" (semi-structured interview).

The control of the administration of pleasure by the culture industry is not its sole function. Experiencing pleasure, whether it be morally corrupt or not, often requires seeking risk and this involves a complete or partial break from control toward the decontrol of enjoyment. Elias and Dunning (1986) refer to this controlling and decontrolling of emotions in leisure activities; whereby excitement generated in "real" life situations is imitated. In this way the tension between "real" pleasure and the imitation provided through the administration of pleasure is a matter of balancing out tensions. According to Elias and Dunning (1986) it is the tension, or flows, between routinized control and deroutinized mimetic decontrol within leisure activities that are at the root of their dynamics.

A primary source of the tensions between control and decontrol is drug use inside dance clubs. In some cases this decontrol and risk-taking can intensify the transitory experience of pleasure. To the extent that this is a bounded arena within which mimetic decontrol can be exercised dance clubs appear to be "places of tolerance" (Foucault, 1990:4). The internal design of night clubs creates interior boundaries between the lighted areas, such as the dance floor, bar and lounges, and darkened recesses. These recesses are acknowledged and accepted by management as places where "immoral" or illegal shadows are decontrolled and to some degree permitted.

Dale observed that "within the geographical layout of the club these dark recesses play host to drug dealing, there are different dealers in each alcove; the bouncers turned a blind eye. It gives a heightened feeling of anxiety" (semi-structured interview). Mark adds, "there were actually dark corners, you could see people 'skinning up' and stuff" (semi-structured interview).

The administration of night clubs, therefore, involves the delicate art of meeting legal regulation while attempting to rationalize the demands of illegality so as to attain a balance between the flow of control and decontrol. Malinda comments on the difficulty of administering control:

The club is that dark anyway, that they (door staff) are just wasting their time walking around. Cos there is always a way that somebody can find to get around it. You'd have

*to get to the point where you get undercover management to pose as customers and stuff,
and I'd just cannot see the point of it. That maybe, if their attitude is "it's going to go
on anyway," they'd rather have the custom in here than anywhere else.* (semi-structured
interview)

Thus, it can be proposed that the flows between control and decontrol across
and inside dance clubs are linked to legal and illegal regulation. If the legal regulation of restricted time limits for night-time enjoyments act on the administration of pleasure so do illegal regulation. An article in *The Face* magazine suggests
that in Manchester gangs turned to the club owners, offering their services as "security consultants" and doormen on the strength of their ability to deny entrance
to other gangs. If their services were refused, club owners knew their staff and customers might be subjected to violence and intimidation (Anon 1996:129).

Amazing Adventures Inside the Pleasure Dome

The organized spectacles inside dance clubs, the use of music, illumination and the
provision of light and dark spaces direct, through ambiance, the control and decontrol of pleasures. As noted before by Debord (1970) and Vaneigem (1983),
these conditions illustrate ways in which happenings and pleasures can be guided
by the spectacle. Martin illustrates the workings of the conditioned situation, "If
you go into 'Roxy's' you feel confident because you know where all the spots are,
You know the different lighting effects" (focus group).

When the spectacle is new, the organized and conditioned situations of dance
clubs can be disrupted by a non-passive experience of life lived instantaneously.
Martin, when commenting on a visit to a dance club not previously attended, gives
active meaning to this sense of an event's immediate occurrence: "you go in(to)
somewhere else, you don't known what's what. You don't know what groups are in
what corners and how lighting is affected. You become sort of disorientated sometimes" (focus group).

Creation of light and dark spaces inside dance clubs facilitate control and decontrol as they relate to comfort, safety, and the pleasures of "amoral" illegal or violent acts. The organizational "Shadow" (Denhardt, 1981) entices interpretations
from those attempting to gain for themselves a meaning of an event or an immemorial not constrained by administered spectacles. These active meanings can,
in part, be interpreted in terms of re-eroticization (Burrell, 1992). Burrell suggests
a more joyous, playful attitude to life and to fellow humans, where sensuality and
feelings are enhanced and where eroticism plays a more central role in our day-to-
day lives but where "erotic" is seen to be very widely conceived.

Dance clubs are both conventional and "alternative organizational forms" (Burrell, 1992:82) for night-life pleasures and the joyfulness of re-eroticization is basic
to their nocturnal appearance. It can be argued that the spontancity and potential
danger associated with enjoyment offers a chance to create active meanings out-

side those achievable through the controlled and decontrolled administration of pleasure. As a result there is a potential for both individuals and groups to create their own sense of style and express *joie de vivre* in a guise that distances itself from the cultural forms being offered (Hebdige, 1988).

Burrell's understanding of re-eroticization is appropriate to night-life pleasures because people tend to seek out and return to locations of re-eroticization. Used in this sense, the "re" of re-eroticization does not indicate its historical re-introduction; instead it suggests a return to sought-after pleasures.

Burrell (1992) suggests that re-eroticization is "spontaneous, messy, complicated—in other words dangerous" (Burrell 1992:82) and thus not related to control. It is worth noting here that there is an overlap between "re-eroticization" and Vaneigem's "radical subject."

According to Vaneigem (1983), the radical subject opposes the spectacle's seductions by demanding active participation. Through active participation, the radical subject contests the spectacle's claim to encircle reality. Active participation allows for more capacious forms of self-realization. Re-eroticization, lasting as a promise of the break from control, suggests that enjoyment can be connected with pleasure as a disruptive, "it happens," event and the commemorated immemorial. By giving active meaning to the transitory joys of re-eroticized pleasure, individuals and groups are capable of thinking and reacting differently to organized spectacles.

Mark noticed that drug use was not restricted to the dark, hidden-yet-tolerated interiors of the dance club. Rather, this particular organizational Shadow was drawn out into the light, "I saw a couple of people actually 'skinning up' on the dance floor, in front of everyone, but at the time it must have been so widespread. They just got away with it, but later on it becomes more out in the open" (semi-structured interview). While Malinda's experiences was not in strict accord with those of Mark, she observed that, "later on, you see someone walk(ing) with a joint to the toilets but it would just go straight over your head, you wouldn't actually think about it" (semi-structured interview).

The radical subject's spontaneous sense of engagement with an event and/or immemorial is another form of re-eroticization. The radical subject intends to break down the concealments of commodified experience to gain a lived immediate happening. Vaneigem (1983) suggests this because the radical subjects are not spectators in their own life. Rather, by adopting this practice they gain the right to construct their lived situations (Plant, 1992).

Malinda and Mark illustrate this appropriation of the spectacle of night life pleasures inside dance clubs to construct their own joyous and sensual situations:

If you plan something like this (a visit to a dance club) you'll know for at least six hours beforehand that at a certain point, at a certain time, that's how you're going to feel, you know what the end result is, what's going to happen. (Malinda, semi-structured interview)

You don't necessarily know what's going to happen, you know something is going to happen. (Mark, semi-structured interview)

While Malinda and Mark's interpretation might be interpreted as the re-eroti-cization of the immemorial, there is a passion to bear witness and "return to" experiences thought to have been encountered before. Through this practice they re-make situations according to their own judgments and images. A further illus-tration of re-eroticization and the making of an event as situation is provided by Malinda when hearing a cherished song as an immemorial:

> *You get so excited, you get the first couple of notes and you can identify a particular song, that you actually adore something like a tape you've had for years, and all of a sudden, you'll get that massive message back, that you had years ago, and that will be one of those moments. Another thing is, the guy I went with, if you think just a boy and a girl, and I could see. When I wasn't having those moments and he was though we were together en-joying the music, but he's getting the bigger "buzz" or "high" for that particular song funny you just know.* (Malinda, semi-structure interview)

This note identifies two practices through which active meanings of re-eroti-cization are made and re-made. One is the physical, observable, gestures of plea-sure-seekers that flaunt and question the administration of the balance between control and decontrol. The other links the radical subject to spontaneous involve-ment in an event. By using its creative imagination, the spectacle is not accepted by the subject in a passive manner; rather those individuals and groups seeking pleasures inside dance clubs make reflexive, if at times transitory, meanings. This flow tends to throw off-center the approach presented above which views such en-joyment as a "manufactured," cultural product, that is administered and organized as a spectacle. The next intervention will consider "decentering" (Rojek 1995) and flows of play, that link and fail to link these two opposite positions.

Joyful Pessimism

Dance clubs can also be defined as bounded spaces of tolerance that appear and are maintained through flows leading from one another. By using the flow concept we can include the regular organization of new or refreshed dance club subcultures.

These subcultures make a statement about the "traditions" of the mainstream. These statements often arise because traditions weigh heavy and the only way for-ward is to split from the commodification of the recent past and start anew in search of the "authentic" club experience. The term flow avoids privileging of "presence" over "absence."

Rojek (1995:131) notes that Derrida's understanding of "decentering" is as a flow-of-play. We now have to provide an interpretation of an event to reveal the self-disruption through which decentered flows-of-play are opened.

Malinda recounted an immemorial related to the term "buzz," a psycho-social occurrence that provides pleasure to the inner self. Malinda's interpretation of the immemorial can be re-interpreted as a "pleasure given active meaning." A "look-ing back" and the "immediate buzz of direct living" intermingle so that things cannot be the same again. This event is not tied to a manufactured, commodified spectacle offered through the organization of a dance club. Rather, it is Malinda's relation to a particular piece of music that gives active meaning to the commodity. For a few minutes Malinda is not a spectator of the spectacle appearing inside the dance club, instead she is the creator of immediate lived experience.

In the flow of play between the dance music as cultural commodity and immediate lived experience there is always interdependence. As we have already noted, those who direct the playing of music are also in a position to control and decontrol the desires, experiences and passions of those seeking pleasure. The DJ, and live musicians, are in such a position: "Disc jockeys have had a decisive role in conducting the energies and rearranging the authenticities of the dance floor" (Thornton 1995:58).

While Malinda derives an immediate experience that disrupts the spectacle, the very moment of its disturbance is mediated by the DJ, either creating for individuals and popular cultural spirits an "authentic" happening, or a contrived spectacle. That is, the flow of play decenters active meanings of immediate experience, authentic events and the spectacle. The pursuit of a decontrolled musical buzz, for instance, is a pleasure attained when the DJ connects with the audience, while simultaneously the inverse is also occurring.

The pleasures sought inside a dance club are mediated by its organization. One expression of organization is the use of force, and/or consent, to control and decontrol these pleasures. Cooper (1990) suggests that domination, if it is not too strong a word in this context, arises in several guises, not least of which is the control and mastery of the meta-language necessary to rationalize and justify the point of view of organized authority.

The meta-language on the inside of dance clubs organizes space, music, sounds and lighting to influence or help along the enjoyment of pleasures. The perspective developed in this note is pessimistic about the prospects for active meaning. Indeed, it might be that individuals and popular collective spirits seek out spectacles as a part of their night-time non-work entertainment. It is the practice of making active meanings of pleasure that excites. This flow of decentering play exposes individual and popular collective spirits' experiences and active meanings as perceptible traces. Those attending dance clubs keep alive personal and group meanings of pleasure.

In sum, no matter where in time and space organization appears, there is always already a flow of decentered play that allows events and/or immemorials to be experienced and interpreted. The pessimism of this particular section is therefore joyful. Those attending dance clubs are not absolute spectators in their own experiences, there are opportunities for the pleasure of responsible irresponsibility; whereby, the self-disruption of organization can be revealed through the discernible trace of active meanings. It is through this seeking of pleasure that active meanings of decontrol can occur. However, before this alternative is conceived, flows of decentering play, reveals organizational control in its own vagueness.

CONCLUSION

Flows of decentering play reveal the inseparability of active meaning and the organization and administration of both mainstream and subculture dance clubs; yet it is these flows that maintain the appearance of these clubs on the urban nightscape. Individuals and popular creative spirits are not spectators in events and immemorials made by the spectacles of dance club organization, neither are they free agents. Moreover, the relationship between active meanings of pleasure and its administered control and mimetic decontrol is one of joyful pessimism.

BIBLIOGRAPHY

Adorno, T.W. (1991) "Culture Industry Reconsidered" in J.M. Bernstein, ed., *The Culture Industry,* London: Routledge.

Adorno, T.W., and M. Horkheimer (1979) *Dialectic of Enlightenment,* London: Verso.

Anon. (1996) "Fear and Loathing" *The Face,* February, 129.

Armstrong, S. (1996) "The New Underclass" *The Guardian,* Section 2, March 12th, 10–11.

Bowles, M.L. (1991) "The Organization Shadow" *Organization Studies,* 12, 3, 387–404.

Burrell, G. (1992), "The Organization of Pleasure" in M. Alvesson and H. Willmott, eds., *Critical Management Studies,* London: Sage.

Clarke, J., and C. Critcher (1985) *The Devil Makes Work: Leisure in Capitalist Britain,* Houndsmills, Basingstoke: Macmillan.

Cooper, R., and G. Burrell (1988) "Modernism, Postmodernism and Organizational Analysis: An Introduction" *Organization Studies,* 9, 1, 91–112.

Cooper, R. (1990) "Organization/Disorganization" in J. Hassard and D. Pym, eds., *The Theory and Philosophy of Organizations: Critical Issues and New Perspectives,* London: Routledge.

Debord, G. (1970) *Society of the Spectacle,* Detroit: Black and Red.

Denhardt, R.B. (1981) *In the Shadow of Organization,* Lawrence, KS: The Regents Press of Kansas.

Dyer, R. (1990) "In Defense of Disco" in S. Frith and A. Goodwin, eds., *On Record: Rock, Pop and the Written Word,* New York: Pantheon Books.

Eco, U. (1987) *Travels in Hyperreality: Essays,* London: Picador.

Elias, N. and E. Dunning (1986) "The Quest for Excitement in Leisure" in N. Elias and E. Dunning, *Quest for Excitement: Sport and Leisure in the Civilizing Process,* Oxford: Blackwell.

Ferguson, S. (1993) "Filling Glasgow's Midnight Streets with Disco" Cinderellas, *Sunday Times,* June 13th, 10.

Foucault, M. (1990) *The History of Sexuality. An Introduction, Volume One,* Harmondsworth: Penguin.

Gramsci, A. (1971) *Selection from The Prison Notebooks,* London: Lawrence and Wishart.

Hebdige, D. (1988) *Hiding in the Light: On Images and Things,* London: Routledge.

Lyotard, J-F (1984) *Driftworks / Jean-Francois Lyotard* ed. by Roger McKeon, New York: Semiotext(e).

McKenna, P. (1996) *Nightshift,* Dunoon: S.T. Publishing.

Plant, S. (1992) *The Most Radical Gesture: The Situationist International in a Postmodern Age,* London, Routledge.

Pirsig, R.M. (1991) *Lila: An Inquiry into Morals,* London: Black Swan Books.

Prince, D. (1995) "Five Star Clubs" *Mixmag* 2, 58, 58.

Rojek, C. (1995) *Decentring Leisure. Rethinking Leisure Theory,* London, Sage.

Saunders, N. (1995) *Ecstasy and the Dance Culture,* London: Nicholas Saunders.

Thompson, E.P. (1967) "Time, Work-Discipline and Industrial Capitalism" *Past and Present,* 38, December, 56–97.

Thornton, S. (1995) *Club Cultures: Music, Media and Subcultural Capital,* Cambridge: Polity Press.

Vaneigem, R. (1983) *The Revolution of Everyday Life,* London: Left Bank Books and Rebel Press.

15

USING CATEGORIES TO PROVIDE CUSTOMIZED SERVICE: MEANINGS CREATED IN SKI RESORT SUBCULTURES

Wendy Guild

A ski resort is a semiotician's playground. Resort employees are well aware of the equipment, clothing, and demeanor configurations composing a symbolic display and use their interpretations of these cues to facilitate 'customized' service encounters. By observing, showing photographs, and interviewing, I sought Lift Operators' and Activity Center employees' responses to different customers. I then studied their responses to understand the meaning of the categories driving variations in response and assessed the consequences arising from the use of these categories. Thus, the pragmatic aspects of meaning making are explored through the contrast of differential service provided in two occupational subcultures.

INTRODUCTION

A number of scholars have recently considered issues of control and standardization of service work (Benson, 1986; Biggart, 1989; Hochschild, 1983; Leidner, 1993, 1996; Paules, 1991), but few have considered the processes or consequences of *customized* service work. Where workers are granted discretion to provide service 'appropriate' to the customer, they must develop categories for types of customers to manage the response options. This chapter addresses the process of making the categories meaningful and the consequences of their use in two service-interaction sites at a ski resort.

The two occupational subcultures compared shed light on organizational service delivery. Even when employees are charged to customize service, an employer might hope that one customer will receive similar treatment in different service encounters within the organization. Through comparing these two departments, I explore the challenges occupational subcultures present to organization-wide standardization of customization by customer.

In an attempt to make the many different customers feel at home, management encourages Lift Operators to tailor their greetings—to go beyond the simple 'hi.' "What's up?," "Howzit?," "Hey, Champ," "Morning," "Hello" and "Good Morning to you, sir," are among the greetings often heard. To deliver an appropriate response option, employees conduct lightning-fast readings of symbols customers display with types of customers in mind. These service encounters are brief and highly repetitive; clear patterns form through clustered cues creating a limited number of responses.

Employees at the Activity Center have a more complex task; their job is to solve customers' problems. In addition to honoring promotions and discounts, they handle complaints; they are the only employees with authority to grant refunds or complimentary products or services. Although they are spatially and culturally removed from on-mountain operations, their readings rely on cues similar to those used by Lifties. Their readings affect the allocation of discretionary resources and have consequences beyond the actual encounter.

Looking at categories for customers through how they drive responses used (i.e., service delivery) combines the semantic and pragmatic aspects of the employees' semiotics (Eco, 1990). Eco argues that the widespread adoption and perpetuation of Morris' (1957) distinction between syntax, semantics and pragmatics created too narrow a specialization in each area. Too often semanticists attempt to locate the most logically precise dictionary definition for the word at the expense of the contextual or situational shaping of meaning, the purpose of the word use, and the consequences (or responses evoked). Pragmatists, on the other hand, are so successful at decentering meaning in favor of understanding processes that they are often left without a rich sense of the worlds created (Goodman, 1978) through the words used. Without some reference to the semantic 'invoked in the use' and the 'consequences generated', pragmatics make little sense.

This chapter uses the lens of philosophical pragmatism, a tradition articulated by Austin (1962), Dewey (1931), James (1909), Pierce (1878) and Searle (1969), among others. In this view, meaning is created through the use of words and the consequences of that usage; the pragmatic determines the semantic. Yet it is recognized that a semantic is invoked in any word use, a semantic that is simply the historical trace of the word's use. Here Pragmatism shares with the contextual semanticists the idea of meaning as historically contingent and situationally determined (Firth, 1957). Although this study was designed within a pragmatic frame, my understanding of the context strongly informs both my conversations with employees and my analyses.

In what follows, background information on the Lift Operators, the Activity Center employees, and the customers is provided. After a brief comment on methods, the next section details analyses of the two employee groups' categories used, and responses, and consequences of use. Finally I compare these two groups' service delivery consequences for the employees, the organization, and the customers.

CONTEXT

Lift Operators are responsible for greeting customers and assuring that they are safely loaded on the chairs. The operators stand at the end of the lane maze, greeting customers in the two to four seconds after they have been through the maze and before they are whisked up the mountain on the chair. There are usually two employees at the bottom of the chair lift, one loading while another shovels, fixes the maze, or sits in the lift shack. To ensure safe unloading, one employee is stationed at the top, usually out of sight, behind the tinted glass of the shack. Employees rotate positions throughout the day and an additional veteran Lift Operator rides from lift to lift to provide relief.

With eight lifts there can be up to 28 Lift Operators on the mountain at any one time. On a fair weather weekend or holiday, an employee working a 'feeder quad'—servicing beginner terrain and conveying some to a second lift servicing more difficult terrain—will see about 8,000 people and maintain a 15-minute queue for most of the day. However, traffic depends on a number of factors: the difficulty of the terrain serviced, the weather conditions, the day (weekend, midweek or holiday) and any special events. During a midweek storm, an employee at the same chair might see only 800 people, mostly in the morning as these customers tend to stay on the advanced terrain. On weekends and holidays, the resort averages approximately 4,700 skier-visits; on weekdays, the average is 1,800 skier-visits.

Activity Center employees are also affected by these traffic flows. Their small office is the first thing customers encounter as they enter the base area of the resort. As such, the employees are inundated with customers who do not need their specialized services. On weekends and holidays, their office receives a constant stream of customers; between 8:30 a.m., when the mountain opens, until well after 11:00 a.m. In the afternoon, particularly on stormy days, the employees almost exclusively handle complaints.

Although Lift Operators and Activity Center employees are all Caucasian and mostly Californian, they are drawn from two very different social worlds. Thirteen of the fifteen women in the Activity Center are married and in their 40s; the other two are in their 20s. The older women have lived year-round in the mountains for some time and ski infrequently. They have families and full private lives. Aside from the small community of Activity Center staff, they generally do not socialize within the resort community.

The Lift Operators, who are in their early 20s, ride and ski as much as possible and socialize almost exclusively within the resort community. The majority are male and the vast majority ride snowboards. The intense socializing, four or five parties a week as well as days off riding together, creates a strong subculture that identifies with the snowboarder aesthetic and talk. Most Lift Operators work for a season and never return. Many come from middle-class to upper-middle-class families in the San Francisco Bay or Sacramento areas and go back home at the end of the winter. Since the job is entry-level and at the bottom of the pay scale, many receive financial help or have a safety net from their families. Slightly understaffed this year, the Lift Operators sometimes worked six-day weeks to cover all the shifts—even so, they found ways to take a few runs each day.

The customers represent yet another social world. The resort draws from Northern Californian, upper-middle-class, suburban and urban families primarily of Caucasian or, more recently, Asian descent. The resort's family image is facilitated by the intermediate terrain, large base of housing available within a short shuttle ride, operation of a strong ski school program for children, and onsite day care. This resort has a reputation for being the most customer-oriented destination resort in California. Regulars know they can count on the resort employees' Disney-like friendliness. They also know that the resort's standing policy is to 'give away the farm' to most anyone who complains.

METHODS

My impressions on service delivery were first formed during my two winter seasons of participant observation fieldwork at a California ski resort. To examine my hunches more closely, I selected eighteen customer photos to show to the Lift Operators. These photos were chosen for clarity and representation of cues and demography in the customer base. I asked the Lifties how they would greet each customer and I recorded their responses, their comments on salient cues, and the strategies they used in their work. Activity Center employees' service encounters were studied through a combination of observation and interviews. My observations formed the basis for insights corroborated by in-depth, freeform interviews with five employees and the manager.

LIFT OPERATORS' READINGS

In service encounters, Lift Operators used several customer categories and responded from these categories to create certain complex consequences for employees, customers and the organization.

Categories

The categories they delineated were snowboarders, smilers, grumps, 'flailers,' de-mographic groups and comment-begging equipment or clothing.

Snowboarders were identified most frequently. Sixteen of the 20 employees iden-tified snowboarders as a category and 13 used distinct greetings: "I have to go with 'what's up' with snowboarders." A different set of 13 followed on with 'openers.' Openers are conversation starters, in this case, they asked "how's the snow?," "where are the jumps?," "where have you been and how is it?," or "how are you likin' those boots?" With snowboarder openers, employees are often trying to get information about equipment, start a conversation, and/or assess the conditions so they can find good snow and jumps on their breaks. The comments "this guy would be cool," usually implied identification with that group; "if they look cool, I'll be cool back."

People who smile comprised the second most common category. "I would talk to her cause she's smiling, she's having a good day." While a smile is important, the converse, someone who is angry or who doesn't acknowledge the employee will probably not receive a greeting. Angry customers are most often avoided: 'If they are aggravated, I will not say anything. If they are mad, I try not to keep the ball rolling.' Customers who don't acknowledge employees are not avoided, but are considered 'not greetable.' 'I'd get out of this guy's way, he's on the rampage, ready to go. Or You could tell with this dude, if he dropped his wallet, he would just keep going, wouldn't even look back.' These customers are considered serious, in-tent, or in a hurry. Most often no greeting is given.

The third category identified are 'flailers' or 'gapers'; those struggling with their equipment or having problems with muscular coordination. 'I'm more alert with people having trouble getting through the line. You know, losers, people who aren't coordinated or aren't paying attention.' Employees usually call attention to flailing as a form of reprimand. 'This guy looks out of control,' 'you're trouble, get your-self together.' They use subtle signals (humor, assistance) to discourage 'trouble' in the hope that they can head off real trouble that might lead to stopping the lift.

Demography—age, ethnicity and gender—was also a basis for categorization and response. Almost half noted such groups as kids, seniors, Asians and 'ladies'. Kids were called 'champ,' 'buddy,' and 'dude.' Special comments were made to some kids: 'Did your parents take you out of school and drag you up here for the week? Or 'BEHAVE!' Kids get a kick out of that.'

Seniors were often asked, 'what's up young fella?,' or received comments to the effect—'I hope to be still kickin' like that at his age.' Kids and seniors received cheerful greetings and positive comments but Asians were treated as 'other.' 'Where are you from?' was asked by three respondents, while four others said noth-ing, assuming they 'probably don't speak English anyway.' Caucasian ladies re-ceived 'polite and friendly' greetings: 'good morning ladies!' and 'have a great day!'

Finally, employees often commented on unusual equipment or clothing. 'Nice hat.' 'How are those fat boys (powder skis)?' Initially, I thought this kind of greeting only helped employees break the monotony. However, Leidner (1993) has shown that customers are interested in more than a generic greeting. They are interested in a human connection. She notes 'customers or clients often feel resentful when it is clear that a worker is reciting lines from a script and that everyone is being treated exactly alike, because they experience the regimentation as dehumanizing and alienating' (p. 29). One employee went even further with this idea of establishing a human connection when she considered the task of greeting customers: 'I'd compliment her coat. Older ladies, they've bought suits to look nice, they just love it when you say something. Her husband probably bought it for her.'

When I formulated this research idea, I expected the employees to be more verbal about the fashions they read. Around the resort I often heard comments on clothing; the 'sweet' new jacket, the 'fag bag' powder suit, the 'useless' suede Bogner jacket (very expensive and not waterproof). One employee did make such a comment: 'That guy is wearing a Descente suit, he could be a snob. The majority of people wearing Descente suits are grumpy and grouchy.' Another employee used style categories in reading one set of customers: 'These guys don't ski much, but they have all the equipment, they're weekend warriors, gapers.' For the most part, style types were not made explicit, but were used in creating the customer types reported.

Responses

The responses were clustered into eleven major categories. Of those, only six were used frequently; nothing (no greeting), plain and simple casual greetings, snowboarder greetings, polite and friendly greetings, helping the flailers responses, generic openers and targeted openers.

For snowboarders, a special greeting was used almost exclusively and was often followed by a targeted opener. Smilers received a plain and simple greeting with an enthusiastic tone or a polite and friendly greeting followed by a generic opener. Flailers were either ignored or had their own special greeting—the "helpin' the gapers" greeting. The demographic groups received openers that marked their group membership (kid "buddy," senior "young man," Asian "where are you from?," and ladies "have a great day, ladies!"). The customers donning comment-begging equipment and clothing by definition received targeted openers.

Although I had assumed that each employee behaved in very much the same way, the response patterns fell into four distinct strategy types. They were the avoiders, the plain-and-simple repeaters, the category-sensitive greeters, and the creative responders. The one avoider in my sample occupied himself with other tasks (shoveling snow) or simply did not greet customers. The three plain-and-simple greeters recognized different categories of customers, but greeted everyone with "how's it goin?" or "how are ya doin?" The vast majority of the sample were category-sensitive greeters employing many different response types. Their responses form the basis for this report. The three creative responders gave me two or three sentences per photo, occasionally using unusual responses and categories.

Consequences

The patterned use of the categories 'snowboarders,' 'kids,' 'seniors,' 'Asians' and 'ladies' to evoke responses reinforces the strong association of cues to these categories. Identity group marking is perpetuated, in part, by these seemingly inane everyday interactions. Additionally, the repetition of these patterned responses helps define the meaning and generalized treatment of these groups.

The marking of and participation in the snowboarders' identity group seems to be of central concern to the Lift Operators. Many describe themselves as boarders and rely on membership in this group to define their own identity through an aesthetic (e.g. demeanor, clothing tastes, music tastes, objects of sexual attraction, etc.) and through common practices (e.g. riding as often as possible, party participation, smoking pot, listening to music, conversations topics and language used, etc.). The stereotypical aspects of this identity group, its aesthetics and practices, are defined largely outside the context of the employee greeting. The frequency of these everyday instances, however, help maintain the group boundary and bind employees and certain customers.

However, demographic groups do derive some of their meaning from these 'superficial' instances. While kids and seniors are enthusiastically embraced by these employees, Asians are distanced through treatment as 'other' and women are distanced, although to a lesser extent, through respectful formality. This consequence of formal distance and discrimination reproduces the sport of skiing as the domain of the middle/upper class white male, and possibly, his family. Perhaps it is unintended, but only the 'right' people are made to feel at home.

Responding favorably to smilers has consequences at two levels. The customer often enjoys the interaction, except when it is received as scripted and empty. A number of customers commented at day end that the employees were very friendly, 'they really treat you like a person, not like cattle.'

Employees, on the other hand, find that all this friendliness can be emotional work; it is often an act, and can be burdensome. This finding echoes Hochschild's (1983) flight attendants' and bill collectors' experiences: 'I smile at everyone, but it doesn't mean I mean it. I can be polite and pleasant when I have to be; you know a Molly Sunshine, or Susie Chapstick.'

On the other hand, I have heard employees tell stories of the fun they had or the nice customer who came through the line and made their day. Positive experiences of emotion work are consistent with Amy Wharton's (1996) assertion that autonomy (or discretion) paired with this type of work can result in job satisfaction.

Attention to flailers is rife with contradictions as well. Although Lift Operators take pride in the importance of keeping customers safe, many are loathe to actually intervene. Seeing a flailer coming though the maze evokes sighs—sarcastic comments are often exchanged with fellow employees. Not only is it not cool to be a beginner, it is a hassle for the employee. Yet these same employees are heard saying again and again, 'it is so great that you are out here trying to learn a new thing, good for you!'

Aware of the sacrifices in 'coolness' one makes and the mental challenges one confronts when beginning a new sport, the employees show admiration for beginners—especially adults. The beginners also receive the 'helping the gapers' greetings through a host of contractions. The offer of help, in itself, implies that the customer is obviously behind the curve, not a cool or sexy implication in sports. These customers would like help, but don't want to call attention to themselves. Some don't want to acknowledge that they need help and are embarrassed by offers.

Demonstrating stylistic approval of older ladies' jackets because 'they bought suits to look nice and they just love it when you say something' implies that the employees are not, in fact, approving of the style. They are simply trying to be nice. Customers, on the other hand, accept comments as sincere and feel validated in their fashion choices. In the words of a female customer to her husband: 'see, dear, it *was* a good purchase.' It is also possible that the comment is sincere, but only under the consideration that the style is 'nice' for the customer, a rich urban lady in her forties, not for the Lifty. The employee will not adopt these aesthetics, but will instead use those styles as counterpoints to their own self-styling.

ACTIVITY CENTER EMPLOYEES' READINGS

The Activity Center employees' categories and responses were presented in tandem in interviews so I have chosen to present them in this same manner. The consequences of the above are considered in turn.

Categories and Responses

The Activity Center employees are adept at reading a customer's emotional state. They are looking for "eyes darting around the room," a set jaw and an intensity that accompanies rage. 'Many of the people that come into our office have already talked about their problem with at least three other people, and they heard 14 different stories. I can understand why some people are angry.' Occasionally, a man—'usually it's a man'—will walk into the Activity Center and he will be irate, ready to 'give [the employee] attitude': 'He will be in my face, yelling right through me, not listening to what I say. The first thing I try to do is calm him down, but if that doesn't work I try to pull him aside.'

The employees try to contain these problem customers, some do it well, some don't, and some simply avoid the irate types: 'There are some people in this office who either don't know how to deal with irate people, or just won't. They end up pissing off the customer and making the problem worse.' Those who know they can handle these difficult customers try to get to them before their 'less-skilled' co-workers exacerbate the situation.

But attitude is more than one's emotional state. The real "attitude" problems arise when the problem has been solved, or, in the least, the customer has been provided with some alternative compensation for their complaint and they continue to be rude and abusive. While, in most cases, "attitude" can be diffused with an offer of compensation, this is not always the case: 'It's the ones that think they are owed something that really get me, or worse, the homeowners who think they own the place. They are the hardest to deal with. And they don't realize that we are going out of our way to please them. They just treat us like peons.' These types of customers would be seen as "having an attitude." When customers "give [the employees] attitude" they are usually using a particular tone of voice, being rude and acting as if something is owed to them.

The snowboarder attitude is of a different type. It is usually presented by a male in his early 20s in a moderately inarticulate manner and matter-of-fact tone that leaves the unspoken question 'so what are you going to do about it?' hanging in the air: 'I have seen some of the ladies refuse to deal with snowboarders. They just say 'too bad, so sad, bye bye.' And it is too bad, cause maybe they weren't being jerks or we could solve the problem easily. They definitely discriminate against snowboarders.' The person who told me this is one of the younger employees who both skis and rides. She hates to see her co-workers respond to snowboarders this way.

'I have some sympathy for them, cause I also ride. You know, a few bad seeds ruined it for everyone. And sure, some people like the reputation, they play it up. It is too bad.' Her theory is that these ladies feel that they aren't shown enough respect and they don't like the way the young snowboarders look and speak. When asked if this was the result of a difference between generations, she said, yes but, even so, there is an issue with snowboarders. 'The thing is, they just don't like snowboarders. You could have an older man walk in here in snowboard boots, all decked out, in a ski suit, the works, he'd probably be European, snowboarding is popular there, and he wouldn't get the same treatment he would if he had walked in, in ski boots. It's crazy.'

The manager denied that there were any difference between the treatment of snowboarders and skiers. "We treat each person the same way," but later in the conversation she insisted that "each situation is unique." Still later, she mentioned that most of the employees at the Activity Center are "a little older," and they grew up in a time where people respected adults and seniors. 'I just don't see young people today showing the proper respect to adults, it is a different generation. You know, we expect to be treated a little more nicely by younger people.'

As a result, there is, she said, some age discrimination. She sees it as the outgrowth of the older employees' opinions about the younger generation. 'I hate to say it, but I think we are less likely to go out of our way to help a young person that is giving us a hard time.' The younger employee concurs. 'If a senior forgets their ID, we will usually go ahead and give them the discount, but if a college student forgets their ID, we are much more strict.' If you are a young male snowboarder with an attitude, you won't go far in the Activity Center.

Consequences

The "attitude" category evoked a number of responses; calm them down, contain them, get to them before an employee who "can't deal" gets there first, and fix their problem. If the customer is "giving [the employee] attitude" the response will be less friendly than usual and the employee might even politely hold the hard line: "I'm sorry that happened to you, better luck next time."

Attempting to calm and contain an irate customer often requires displays of empathy by an employee. This becomes particularly difficult over time when many inane complaints are heard daily. The employees grow to view their customers as children who fall, scrape their knee and scream bloody murder. Empathy, however, doesn't always work. The next step is to fix the problem. On occasion, the Activity Center Director authorizes what the staff think is far beyond 'reasonable compensation' so that the customers don't leave angry. Many employees feel that this practice perpetuates the resort's reputation as 'giving away the farm' and serves to reinforce aberrant behavior.

The idea that some employees 'can't deal' with irate customers creates the means for a power hierarchy and the definition of skill through the designation of "dealing with irate customers" as some of the hardest work. The employees that can "deal" will do so and they will be seen to be the most competent in the workplace.

Customers "giving [the employee] attitude" provide legitimate opportunities for the staffers to exercise some discretion in their work. It is in these instances where discrimination comes into play. Young "snowboarders with attitude" have three strikes against them. Often they are not compensated for the inconveniences suffered. Even in the cases where young snowboarders were not perceived as having an attitude, the outcomes remained the same.

CONCLUSIONS

By showing photographs, interviewing and observation, I elicited Lift Operators' and Activity Center employees' responses to different customers. I then looked to the evoked responses to understand the meaning of the categories driving the variation in response and assessed the consequences arising from the use of these categories.

In the case of the Lift Operators, the use of the snowboarder category and demographic categories marked identity groups. The responses engendered by these categories helped to define the substance of those groups; (i.e., Asians are "other," kids and seniors are fun to interact with, etc.). The use of identification processes to vary responses sends the signal that some customers should feel more at home than others. Also, the importance placed on smilers and flailers led to contradictory experiences for employees and customers.

For Activity Center employees, "attitude" explained the most variation in response. The consequences were far-ranging—from the organization's reputation as "giving away the farm," to the valuation of the work and means for determining competence, to the experience of the interactions as emotional work. Additionally, most Activity Center employees distanced their association with snowboarders and younger people with attitude through withholding hospitality.

Of particular interest is the finding that the two different employee groups read and responded to the same category—snowboarders—in vastly different ways. That both groups selected the snowboarder identity group above all others is a significant indication of a shared culture. Although these employees live in the same social world, their subcultures create radically different meanings. Some of the young employees identify strongly with the snowboarder group, whereas most of the Activity Center employees consider the group as a part of a generation distant from theirs in both etiquette and values. This has important implications for the possibilities of standardizing customization by customer, or even by type of customer.

The meaning of categories, or the semantic, is thus defined by a host of phenomena. It is the life context of the reader that provides the social position from which a reading takes place. It is the historical traces of the word's use as experienced by the reader that provides the initial semantic; repetition of that style of use within the same kind of interaction (an employee greeting a snowboarder), and the application and use in different situations. It is the immediate context of the interaction, with considerations of space, time, weather, mood, the audience in attendance, etc., that provides guidelines for choosing the appropriate and relevant words. It is the purpose of the interaction that directs the word use. And finally, it is the consequences of that word use that both affect the course of the immediate interaction (immediate subsequent use), the future semantic of the word, and the larger social forces at play. The meaning of words, a word such as "snowboarder," are not fixed or found. Meaning is made, it is shaped through use.

BIBLIOGRAPHY

Austin, J.L. (1962) *How to Do Things with Words, 2nd Edition,* Cambridge: Harvard University.

Benson, S.P. (1986) *Counter Cultures: Saleswomen, Managers, and Customers in American Department Stores, 1890–1940,* Urbana: University of Illinois Press.

Biggart, N.W. (1989) *Charismatic Capitalism: Direct Selling Organizations in America,* Chicago: University of Chicago Press.

Dewey, J. (1931) *Philosophy And Civilization,* New York, Minton, Balch.

Eco, U. (1990) *The Limits of Interpretation,* Bloomington, IN: University of Indiana Press.

Firth, J.R. (1957) *Papers in Linguistics, 1934–1951,* London: Oxford University Press.

Hochschild, A.R. (1983) *The Managed Heart: The Commercialization of Human Feeling,* Berkeley: University of California Press.

James, W. (1909) *Pragmatism, A New Name For Some Old Ways Of Thinking: Popular Lectures On Philosophy,* New York: Longmans, Green.

Leidner, R. (1993) *Fast Food, Fast Talk, Service Work and the Routinization of Everyday Life,* Berkeley: University of California Press.

Leidner, R. (1996) "Rethinking Questions of Control: Lessons from McDonald's" in C.L. MacDonald and C. Sirianni, eds., *Working in the Service Society,* Philadelphia: Temple University Press.

Morris, C.W. (1935, 1970) *Foundations of the Theory of Signs,* Chicago: University of Chicago Press.

Pierce, C.S. (1878, 1982) "How to Make Our Ideas Clear" in H. S. Thayer, ed., *Pragmatism: The Classic Writings,* Indianapolis: Hackett Publishing Company.

Paules, G.F. (1991) *Dishing It Out,* Philadelphia: Temple University Press.

Searle, J.R (1969) *Speech Acts: An Essay in the Philosophy of Language,* Cambridge: Cambridge University Press.

Wharton, A. (1996) "Service with a Smile: Understanding the Consequences of Emotional Labor" in C.L. MacDonald and C. Sirianni, eds., *Working in the Service Society,* Philadelphia: Temple University Press.

16

CAPTURING MEMORIES:
THE TOURIST EXPERIENCE

Julia Harrison

This chapter presents preliminary results from a study of a small group of Canadian tourists—those who can be seen to be emblematic of and trying to escape from the 'industrial subculture.' I explore elements of their 'consumption' of the tourist experience, and suggest that tourists seek to find, or reinforce, intimacy and authenticity in their travels.

INTRODUCTION

The World Tourism Organization reported that in 1991 450 million international tourism journeys were made. North Americans, Japanese and Germans represent the largest percentages of those who travel internationally. Inquiries about who or what is a tourist evokes a range of responses. MacCannell (1989) defined the tourist as someone seeking authenticity in an alienating modern world.

Social scientists have made efforts to classify different tourists according to types of travel (Cohen, 1979, a, b), and to explain motivations for travel at a psychological level (Crompton, 1979). Little work has been done on the consumption side of the tourism equation. There has been some examination of the image of the 'other' as reinforced through the tourist experience (Bruner, 1991). There have also been studies of the market for arts and crafts that has been developing in response to tourists' demands (Graburn, 1984). But, the issue upon which I chose to focus was how the tourist experience is re-created and reconstructed into memories and understandings of experience once travelers return home.

Recent writing on social memory emphasizes the dynamic and creative nature of the exercise of remembering (Terdiman, 1993; Melion and Kuchler, 1991; Connerton, 1989). As a way of examining the consumptive dimensions of the tourist experience and the re-creation of these experiences in their everyday lives, I began a study that focused on photographs/videos/slides taken, souvenirs purchased, and postcards selected by a group of Canadian tourists.

Subjects for the project were located through ads placed in *The Globe and Mail, The Toronto Star, Travel Scoop* (a travel magazine for independent travelers), and the *Peterborough Examiner.* I received 82 initial replies, mailed a general questionnaire to all 82 and received 52 completed responses—24 women, 13 men plus 15 couples whose ages ranged from 30 to 75. The majority of the respondents were professionals with income levels ranging from $C24,000 to $C80,000. These people were my target but clearly they are in no way fully representative of the generic tourist. This is obviously a self-selected group who love to travel, and who consider it an important part of their life.

QUESTIONNAIRE RESPONSES

One respondent summarized very succinctly her delight in international travel. She said:

[I travel] to see, feel, touch, smell. [To] meet people, see things one only sees in pictures, swim in warm waters and see what lies below, to renew ties with family and friends, escape the Canadian winter, have a little adventure, make new friends, talk to interesting people, see exotic flowers, birds, and animals, try different cuisines, and of course [for] the scenery, history, and wonder of it all.

Her comments reflect many of the points raised by other respondents. Travel was prompted by a desire to see and experience new things, to connect with family and friends, to meet new people, to see key markers of personal and global history, and to be amazed by it all.

This respondent, like others, kept a variety of records of her travels, including videos, photograph albums, day-by-day diaries, and expense records. Very few of the respondents purchased large numbers of souvenirs. Among the souvenirs reported most frequently were rocks, sand, shells, postcards, and T-shirts (usually to be given away). Those who did acquire souvenirs of handicrafts emphasized that items had to be locally made and small.

Many valued the experience of international travel because it taught them about the material and spiritual riches of life in Canada. Important to many was the exposure to other cultures and people and a sense of connection with history. Repeated references to meeting people, renewing friendships, making new ones and establishing personal connections (sometimes triggered by the tourist's inappropriate behavior) emphasizes the human connections that are such an important part of travel.

For some, travel simply gave them memories and experiences that contributed to a sense that one is a richer, more human creature for the experience. For many travel created a sense of a personally understood global landscape—both human and physical. For many this landscape provided a sense of being connected to the wider world. One couple openly acknowledged the creative energy that was part of that process. They said they valued the "creative aspect, being able to record what we see and later bring it into a form that pleases us." They were truly 'creating' memories with their custom-made video productions, their own personalized view of the world. And when these personalized landscapes were brutally transformed through war into a newly constructed and thus 'unknown' landscape like Yugoslavia they mourned their losses.

For many respondents the most memorable experiences varied from visits to famous places, pilgrimage experiences (visiting the grave of a favored adventurer or poet), life-threatening experiences (bus crashes, being held up by guerrillas, muggings, etc.), encounters that brought the tourist closer together with local life (dealing with local police to get a car unclamped), getting stranded (having to take local transportation instead of the tourist bus), to tests of physical endurance, missing travel connections because of acts of nature or local unrest, sunsets, and the sounds and smell of local markets.

IN-DEPTH INTERVIEWS

During phase one of the project I selected 12 respondents for in-depth interviews. In addition to selecting people who were geographically accessible and who represented a fairly broad demographic sample, I was looking for people who seemed to be articulate and reflective of their experiences as a tourist. Another key factor in the initial selection were plans to travel again in the next 12 to 14 months.

Each initial interview with the selected respondents was from four to eight hours long. The interview covered a wide range of topics about their general background and their traveling experience. A second interview focused on their most recent trip. All interviews were taped and all sessions in which photographs and/or souvenirs were examined were videotaped.

My original intention was to focus our discussions around souvenirs and photographs, but I discovered that these items were not central to the respondents' narratives. Even though some of interviewees had constructed elaborate photo albums, the narrative of their travels was only very peripherally focused on them. Souvenirs seem rarely to warrant mention, with individuals often unable to remember exactly what it was they got where and when.

Several of those I interviewed, and several of those who completed only the questionnaire lamented that nobody really wanted to look at their photographs or hear their stories. Many admitted that their photographs were really only for themselves as others only gave them a cursory glance. One young woman took great pride in her photographs and had a fairly wide audience among those with whom she worked. But in the same context she had also encountered hostility towards the viewing of her photographs and, by association, her travels.

People were most content just to tell me of their travels and to give me a wandering narrative of their experiences. It soon became obvious that I provided an engaged listener, someone who wanted to hear of their travels and experiences.

As the project progressed I began to reflect on an unexpected aspect of the interviews and began to wonder if I had fortuitously selected twelve extraordinarily gracious and hospitable individuals as subjects. Although initially I was a total stranger to them all, I had a certain legitimacy as a university professor and people had made contact with me through such reputable instruments as the *Globe and Mail* and *Travel Scoop*. I was warmly and graciously welcomed by all of those whom I interviewed. The majority of those that I selected to interview invited me to lunch or dinner in their homes without having met me before. While I did not expect to be harshly treated, the hospitality and warmth extended was well beyond what I expected would be offered a complete stranger. I realized that my experience was one dimension that many of the tourists in my study sought in their travels. They sought a personal connection and shared experience across time and space. Recounting their travel narratives facilitated another connection in the web that they sought to create with other people and places.

In thinking about the 'narrative' nature of my interviews, I realized that many of them reflected the ways in which Mary Pratt (1992) has outlined tropes for various types of early travel writing. These narratives she suggested were classificatory in the tradition of Linnaean natural history; some parallel to what she called the "poetics of science," and others to the Victorian genre she labeled the monarch-of-all-that-I-survey.

In my interviews, the classificatory Linnaean narrative was exemplified by a female tourist whose discussion of her travels focused on the structure of her itinerary and types of roads that connected places. She also spoke of wanting to 'complete Australia'—by traveling to all points accessed by a certain luxury travel company. The narrative of her travels was characterized by progression through a taxonomic order. Places were identified, accessed, collected, recognized and categorized in the same way that early explorers set out to order the world in the taxonomic structure developed by Linnaeus. She said

The pick-up was from Darwin. Then we went to Kakadu over night to the Crocodile Hotel in Kakadu . . . From there, back to Darwin, we had two nights, I think it was, in Darwin. And then, down to Katherine. And that was, uh, a one night in Katherine. Then from Katherine, we went to Kanunurra. We're now coming south and west . . . And we had an overnight in Kanunurra. From Kanunurra to Halls Creek . . . I took an optional flight there . . . The pick-up from Kanunurra that morning. The coach went on down the road . . . we had . . . a tour of the mine . . . some of us were able to fly over the Bungle Bungles and come back to meet the coach just short of the Argyle Diamond Mine. So, that was one of the side trips. A well worthwhile one, actually. Very interesting . . . We, we were mostly on . . . the tarred road. But, we did a fair amount of dirt road as well to get to some of the more interesting places . . . From Fitzroy Crossing . . . that's where we went off into the bush (on) a grit road . . . That's one of the main grit roads that . . . might at some time get some tarmac on it. But . . . it's the shortest distance between Windham and Derby.

A civil engineer and his wife provided another example of this genre by traveling to see all the major civil engineering feats in the world. This included such things as the Aswan Dam and the Panama Canal, but once this checklist was complete questions arose as to where to go next.

In the 'poetics of science' tradition, which Pratt identifies with Alexander von Humboldt's explorations of South America in the late 18th century, the experiences had a "dramatic, extraordinary nature, a spectacle capable of overwhelming human knowledge and understanding" (p. 120). As von Humboldt experienced nature in a manner which "engulfed and miniaturized" him, so did some of the tourists to whom I spoke. Their experiences had "dense and powerful" meaning. One woman spoke particularly of her recent trip to Southern Africa:

In some way I have changed for having seen it. In some way I am a different person. Kind of like people can tell you what its like to have a baby but you don't know until you do it . . . Southern Africa—I felt very comfortable . . . I know I was meant to be here . . . It just felt right. I could understand people, I could understand the allure of people who would move there.

The Victorian trope Pratt (1992:201) identifies as the 'monarch-of-all-that-I-survey' used 'verbal painting . . . to produce for the home audience the peak moments at which geographical 'discoveries' were 'won' for England.' A key part of this process was to make something real for the traveler by bringing 'it into being through texts: a name on a map, a report to the Royal Geographical Society, a diary, a lecture, a travel book' (p. 204). The following commentary reflects the same process of 'creating a text' in her description of how she sorts her photographs when she returns home and how she captures personal moments and icons in her images:

I try to do it by sort of the days that I took them. Try to make an order of them that way. It doesn't always work because sometimes—because I hate having to turn the book all the time, I try to put all the vertical ones and all the horizontal ones so that you at least have one page where everything you look at is the same direction. It doesn't always work, but, there you go. Anyway, these two are little things [referring to enlargements of two animals hanging on her wall] that I had blown up . . . I'm not sure the larger picture of either of these is in this particular album, but when you see them the animal is quite small, so I was quite pleased with these because they stayed quite crisp when they were blown up . . . This was my absolute favorite picture . . . I saw them as I was . . . looking in the viewfinder they all turned . . . when I first chose to photograph this clump of animals they weren't look-ing all one way but just as I put my eye up to the viewfinder they all did so. I just grabbed it . . . I took a lot of bird shots which the driver caught on after a couple of days that I was also interested in birds . . . because my father really liked birds so I thought I'd take lots of pictures of birds, but they were just an amazing variety of birds in these places . . .

These narrative styles frame the experiences that form the essence of what these tourists are trying to find; what I am calling at this stage the 'seeking of intimacy'. The Oxford English Dictionary defines intimacy as "essential, intrinsic and closely personal." While I can find parallels between these tourists' narratives and those of earlier times, I suggest the motives that drive tourists in the late 20th Century are quite different than those which drove von Humboldt and others. The are un-doubtedly multiple levels on which "seeking of intimacy" operates. It bonds travel partners together.

(Travel) creates something really special, and that's one of our bonds in our marriage is that we both feel like we want to do this. We enjoy the same things, and this is a life long goal for us to do more and more and to enjoy more and more. So that is one of the, I guess that's one of the intimacies of our, of our relationship. I've never really thought about it that way before, but it is. Its something that just he and I share, and that we can share with very few others, because how do you tell your friends how wonderful it is to watch the sunrise over Tikal . . . unless they've been there? How can you tell them (the sound of) a volcano rumbling . . . how loud it is . . . unless they heard it.

Unexpected linkages reflect a form of intimacy that later becomes the highlight of a travel narrative. As one of my informants said:

One of the highlights, and you talk about memories making travel (was) . . . the last morn-ing that I was in Queenstown . . . I went for a walk around the edge of the lake. And it was one of those crystal clear bright mornings . . . not overly hot. But, just a little ripple on the lake, sort of beautiful photographic weather. You know, you want reflections and all the rest of it. And, I had walked around the end of the lake . . . It's just sort of wild and with a track and joggers and people doing their dogs out, etc . . . I suppose this is about an hour and a half out or so . . . I was sort of meandering around the edge . . . I was, mind-ing my own business. And there was a little old lady with a dog . . . and we fell into step and she started talking . . . her husband had gone shopping in the local shops which were actually just by the bus stop that I was destined myself for. And he caught up. I could see the look as he came around. Oh, God, wonder who she's got talking to now. [laughter] writ-ten all over his face. But, she had already sort of said enough to (pique) further interest. Cutting a long story short, he was a retired cardiologist who had worked in Essex, in Eng-land . . . knew my late husband, knew all the people, the senior academics staff as they then were when I was at the London . . . He knew the London hospital as . . . it was during the war years and immediately afterwards because a lot of its activities had been sort of chan-neled out into Essex. He knew a lot of the people that I know at London . . . That little walk along the edge of the lake ended up in the back yard of their cottage, which was just round the corner at the end of the lake. And they had a summer residence there . . . we finished

*up with cup of coffee and . . . cookies . . . Now, if you'd told me that I would have found
a retired cardiologist who knew my late husband [laughter] from the, the end of the war
years, etc. in the backwoods of South Island, New Zealand.*

Travel bonds strangers across time and space. One individual whom I interviewed regaled me with his adventures of camping in Russia in 1960. Years before
he had been befriended by a hotel manager in Czechoslovakia one night when he
had no place to stay. The objective of his holiday in April 1996 was to find this man
again so he could say thank you. Determined to find the former manager, he used
a range of personal contacts, contacting the Red Cross and putting ads in Slovakian
newspapers to try and locate him. This was the way he described their first meeting
in 1960; a meeting which had connected them in his mind for over thirty years.

*. . . we got to this place by late afternoon, nightfall, and we went to a hotel building and
the fellow there, the manager, and he spoke English, fortunately, and he said "I don't have
room in my hotel, but I have a friend with a hotel." He'll put you up and lock your car in
a compound so that all this camping gear, everything on top plus the inside stuff is safe . . .
and he arranged that and he said, "come back and have dinner at my hotel." So, we did
that and he had been a diplomat in the Czech Foreign Service before the Communists took
over. He was a wonderful guy and spoke excellent English and he kept asking us questions
. . . It was a very closed society and country. But he was so pleasant and we didn't mind, it
was just fun talking about what his experiences were and he gave us Pilsner beer with a wonderful Czech meal because the Czech's food is good. So, I said, at the end of the meal, "how
much do I owe you." "Nothing, it's on me. I'm just so glad to talk to some foreigners first
hand from the free world." He said I will ask you one thing, "would you send me a post-
card?" So I got his address, and then we left.*

One woman traveled in search of details of the life of a distant ancestor with
whom she shared a birth date and a love of travel.

*I also have an interesting ancestor who was the governor of Russia-America in 1817. And,
because his birth date was on the same day as mine, and we had this old account in a fam-
ily-kind of armoire, so—I always was intrigued by him. And he traveled around the world
so many times. And he traveled a lot. And he did research. And so he was in Sitka and he
was in Siberia and so. So, somehow, it has developed that I'm researching his life . . . And
I have piles of things, of letters. (There is) an island in Bristol Bay in Alaska named after
him. So I've even articles about this island and I, I ordered detailed maps of the area. And
I went to Siberia and I went to Irkutz. But, of course, there it wasn't so good because I did-
n't speak Russian. It was fun but I couldn't get very specific questions answered. I found out
by strange coincidence somehow that . . . a descendant of this ancestor of mine . . . lives in
St. Petersburg so last year, no two years ago . . . I visit(ed) him. I just started writing letters
. . . He has the telescope (of) this ancestor who was the governor of Russian America.*

I tentatively offer the suggestion that it is these bonds of intimacy or connectedness rather than some sense of 'authenticity' that lure people into traveling.

These bonds confirm tourists' desire to take ownership of their experiences and to understand the human and physical landscape of their 'world'. For many of the respondents, they are at the hub of a series of networks of people and places. Through travel, the world that enters their living rooms through TV and other media on a daily basis is personalized.

The commentary offered by the tourists that I interviewed suggested more a sense of looking 'inward' rather than looking 'outward' experiences that contrasted (in McCannell's terms 'authentic') with their normal life. This pursuit however becomes ever more ironic the more that they travel. The bonds of intimacy become increasingly located in their travel experiences as few in their daily lives care to hear much of their travels and of their global 'connections' that they have made while traveling. Somehow in this context, intimacy becomes something acted out in the global arena—a concept that seems somehow implicitly paradoxical, yet profoundly real in the minds of those who call themselves 'tourists'.

BIBLIOGRAPHY

Bruner, E.M. (1991) "Transformation Of Self In Tourism" *Annals of Tourism Research* 18, 2, 238–250.

Connerton, P. (1989) *How Societies Remember,* Cambridge: Cambridge University Press.

Cohen, E. (1979a) "A Phenomenology Of Tourist Experiences" *The Journal of the British Sociological Association* 13, 2, 179–201.

Cohen, E. (1979b) "Rethinking The Sociology Of Tourism" *Annals of Tourism Research* 6, 18–35.

Crompton, J. L. (1979) "Motivations For Pleasure Vacation" *Annals of Tourism Research* 6, 408–424.

Graburn, N. (1984) "The Evolution Of Tourist Arts" *Annals of Tourism Research* 11, 393–419.

MacCannell, D. (1989) *The Tourist: A New Theory of the Leisure Class,* New York: Schocken Books.

Melion, W. and S. Kuchler (1991) *Images of Memory: On Remembering and Representation,* Washington: Smithsonian Institution Press.

Pratt, M. L. (1992) *Imperial Eyes: Travel Writing and Transculturation,* London: Routledge.

Terdiman, R. (1993) *Present Past: Modernity and the Memory Crisis,* Ithaca, NY: Cornell University Press.

17

ART AS LIFE—LIFE AS ART:
THE EMBEDEDNESS OF ART IN LIFE
AND LIFE IN ART IN POSTMODERNITY

Laurie A. Meamber

Art is one of the least understood phenomena in our culture. Few art studies have employed scientific inquiry. Philosophers and historians have staked their disciplinary claims to the subject of art and come much closer to the nature of art with their emphases on abstract concepts, fundamental questions and retrospective presentations. They discuss art products and principles but fall short of capturing art and aesthetics in a larger context. To understand art more completely it must be understood in relation its producers and consumers.

INTRODUCTION

The aesthetization of life (Debord, 1983) or transaestheticization (Baudrillard, 1995) makes it necessary to explore art and aesthetics within the context of everyday activities, of everyday production and consumption behavior, and in relation to the technology that is transforming our lives. In Western countries the primary organizing influence in our lives is the market that shapes us as consumers (Firat and Venkatesh, 1995). No exploration of art can ignore this or the power relationships involved in the circulation of art and aesthetics in daily life.

In the postmodern world, all objects have aesthetic qualities, thus, differentiating 'art' from 'non-art' is an impossible task. Some cultural/art theorists suggest (Kaye, 1994) that we are only able to delimit art in finite instances. Today's definitions of art are based on criteria that are present and operational 'in the moment'. They include a combination of personal preferences (based on prior experience, taste, etc.), market-filtered criteria (including educational and other forms of economic and cultural capital), structural forces (fields) and their manifestations/interpretations (habitus) (Bourdieu, 1984). Current definitions are always in a process of 'becoming'. But finding a definition of art is not what matters the most, rather it is the search for definitions that is the important aspect of the process.

This essay represents a Western perspective. A discussion of non-Western art(s) may lead to quite different conclusions, as the notions of art, art and the everyday, art and the market, and art and the individual mean something quite different in cultures where Modernity and Western ideology of the market is absent or only recently introduced. There is no denying that the processes of globalization have made much of the non-Western world and vice-versa (although to a lesser degree) (Appadurai, 1986). Here I focus on art in Western thought and cultures, primarily within postindustrial subcultures.

Throughout the history of Western thought, 'art' and 'life' have been juxtaposed. The philosophies of art and beauty emphasize the distinction between the terms 'art' (aligned with beauty) versus 'non-art' (life, the mundane, everyday, ordinary). These terms are usually used to highlight their differences and to privilege one term in relation to the other. For example, art is thought to reflect life according to principles of Western classical art (Plato). Art is subordinated to life as art is defined as a mirror of life. This assumes that important, distinctive aspects of life are chosen to become art, and the mundane or banal cannot or should not be represented in art.

This idea has been extended by scholars in the twentieth century who believed that art should reflect an ideal society. According to Max Weber (1958), art and religion can be defined as components of ethics that give direction to social behavior, and that therefore should be moral in its outlook. Cooley (1966) agreed that art has a moral function, and that beauty and ideal are related and appropriate subjects of art.

The corollary to privileging 'life' over 'art' is simply that life informs art. According to this line of thought, life is in the service of art. Life provides the subjects for art. However, art is also subordinate to life, as it is art that selectively chooses aspects of life as its focus. It is not merely that proper or legitimate parts of life become subjects of artwork, but that the artist's past and current life experience impact the work being produced.

A more recent pairing of these terms is found in the argument that 'art' influences 'life'. This argument is found in Pollay (1986), Marchand (1985), Lears (1994) and others in relation to advertising texts; texts that are simultaneously art and socialization instruments. Advertising offers moments of intellectual stimulation, entertainment and the pleasure of art. Art (or advertising pictorials and messages) portrays a particular view of the world (Nava and Nava, 1996). Thus art, as a consequence of its selective nature, creates a specific vision of the world. "In a manner of speaking, art is life and encodes the complexities of life" (Sherry, 1995:391). Some argue that art is distinct from advertising and other cultural products. However, as Brown (1995) and Nava and Nava (1996) argue, art and advertising are one and the same as aesthetic/artistic products.

> *. . . the very fact of excluding advertising from the sphere of 'art' forms and identifying it as 'other', as defined predominantly by its material concerns, serves not only to differenti-ate and cleanse other forms, it also obscures the material determinants which operate across all of them* (Nava and Nava, 1996:174).

Jameson (1983:124) goes even further, suggesting that all forms of consumer cul-ture are artistic.

> *For one thing, commodity production and in particular our clothing, furniture, buildings and other artifacts are now intimately tied in with styling changes which derive from artis-tic experimentation; our advertising, for example, is fed by postmodernism in the arts and inconceivable without it.*

Along the same lines, marketing and popular culture scholars, such as Borgerson and Schroeder (1997), examine the imagery (both visual and aural) found in Hawaiian popular music (i.e., both radio programs and record albums of the 1950s and 1960s) and argue that these forces helped 'construct' a Hawaii that exists even today.

Closely related is the distinction between (high) art and (low) culture. In clas-sical Greece, there were no divisions between high and low culture (Boëthius, 1995). The tragic did not exclude a comic view of the world and both co-existed. Greek tragedies were followed by satyr plays. Mikail Bakhtin writes that there was no sharp contention between official and popular culture.

> *Popular culture first acquired a non-official status during Roman antiquity. During the Middle Ages, the gap or division became a fact. Laughter and frivolity were rejected from the religious cults, and from the feudal ceremonies and from the social rules of etiquette. The official medieval culture came to be permeated by a profound seriousness* (Bakhtin, 1965/1984:13).

According to Burke (1978), there were two cultural traditions, the 'great' and the 'little.' The great was of the educated minority, nobility and priesthood and was communicated in Latin. The little was of the majority and used the local or national language. Those who belonged to the great culture also had access to and appreciated the little culture. While the official or great culture represented seri-ousness, the non-official represented play, joke, and laughter.

Popular culture developed through recurrence. Medieval people devoted three months to festivals and celebrations. During these times, order was turned upside down. The culture was anchored in youth participation and based on oral tradi-tions which women passed on to future generations (Boëthius, 1995).

In the arts, for example, for any piece of work to be recognized as arts, especially as modernity progressed, it needed to have permanence and materiality. Also important . . . was the extraction and separation or detachment of the piece of art from everyday life experiences. A piece of art . . . had to be separated from everyday common usage to command an interest in it as an investment, as art, as something that had durability beyond common, functional or utilitarian consumption. Quilting, for example, has gained in stature as art . . . as more and more quilts were made, not to be used in keeping warm, but to be 'exhibited' by hanging on the wall or otherwise. (Firat, 1996)

During the 16th century, distancing of the upper social classes from popular culture began and was complete by the 18th century. It was during this time that the market for (religious) visual art developed (Schroeder, 1997). A capitalistic economy emerged, the commodity market expanded, and greater differentiation and specialization in production and distribution ensued. Communication also expanded as people moved into cities (Chandler, 1977).

During the first phase of withdrawal of the upper classes from popular culture, Christian orthodoxy was prominent, and popular culture was deemed heathen, indecent and immoral. By the mid-16th century Europe the medieval mystery play with its blend of high and low, serious and comic (devil played by a clown) was forbidden in several European countries (Boëthius, 1995).

During the second phase, popular culture was attacked for being counter to reason, science and taste. The aristocracy began to distinguish itself through its taste (Bourdieu, 1984). Through a process of civilizing and disciplining (Elias, 1969/1978; Foucault, 1975/1979), restraint and good taste were advocated. For example, reason and self-restraint triumph in the tragedies of Racine and comedies of Moliere.

In the countryside, women came under attack, as the oral tradition was replaced by a masculine culture characterized by written works. In cities, where fertility didn't matter, the feasts and festivals lost significance. The vertical and dualistic attitudes of Christianity replaced popular belief in manifold supernatural forces and popular culture's more complex view of good and evil, heaven and hell, body and soul.

Manufacture became standardized and people bought rather than made items. Similarly, popular entertainment was centralized and commercialized, transforming festivals into circuses and public sports. Story tellers and ballad singers were replaced by printed text. Old folk culture was replaced by centrally produced mass culture that authorities tried to control and use. Dime novels, panoramas and dioramas developed, and were adapted to suit the public.

Moreover, within bourgeois culture a differentiation occurred. The arts were specialized and professionalized; the visual arts, music and literature developed independently within special, ever-more-autonomous spheres. Specialization was accompanied by a dichotomizing process: within art, music and literature, one began to distinguish between 'high' and 'low', between 'serious' and 'popular' (Boëthius, 1995).

High culture is creator-oriented and its aesthetics and principles of criticism are based on this orientation. The belief that the creator's intentions are crucial and the audience almost irrelevant functions to protect creators from the audience, making it easier for them to create, although it ignores the reality that every creator must respond to some extent to an audience. The popular arts are, on the whole, user-oriented, and exist to satisfy audience values and wishes. High culture needs an audience as much as popular culture, but it is fearful that the audience will be wooed away by a user-oriented culture or that it will demand what might be called its democratic-cultural right to be considered in the creative process of high culture. (Gans, 1974:62–63)

The same process of sacrilization has also been traced by Levine (1988:21,29,39 and 60) in the contexts of Shakespeare, opera, symphonic music, photography in eighteenth- and nineteenth-century America.

Shakespeare's popularity can be determined not only by the frequency of Shakespearean productions and the size of the audiences for them but also by the nature of the productions and the manner in which they were presented. Shakespeare was performed not merely alongside popular entertainment as an elite supplement to it; Shakespeare was performed as an integral part of it . . . The theater in the first half of the nineteenth century played the role that movies played in the first half of the twentieth: it was a kaleidoscopic, democratic institution presenting a widely varying bill of fare to all classes and socioeconomic groups.

During this time, the audience governed the stage.

These frenetic displays of approval and disapproval were signs of engagement in what was happening on the stage—an engagement that on occasion could blur the line between audience and actors.

People overflowed on the stage and participated in action. Audiences simultaneously saw drama as both reality and representation.

The place of Shakespearean drama in the nineteenth century American theater should make it clear how difficult it is to draw arbitrary lines between popular and folk culture. Here was professional entertainment containing numerous folkish elements, including a knowledgeable, participatory audience exerting important degrees of control. The integration of Shakespeare into the culture as a whole should bring into serious question our tendency to see culture on a vertical plane, neatly divided into a hierarchy of inclusive adjectival categories such as 'high,' 'low,' 'pop,' 'mass,' 'folk,' and the like. If the phenomenon of Shakespeare was not an aberration then the study of Shakespeare's relationship to the American people helps reveal the existence of a shared public culture to which we have not paid enough attention.

Why was Shakespeare transformed from a playwright for the general public into one for a specific audience?

The dramatic split in the American theater was part of more extensive bifurcations that were taking place in American culture and society.

The changes were not cataclysmic, but were gradual. They took place in stages—physical or spatial bifurcation, to stylistic separation, and finally a bifurcation of content, mirroring a growing chasm between serious and popular culture. The point then is not that there was a conspiracy to remove Shakespeare from the American people but rather that cultural development produced the same result. This was further compounded by the fact that during these years American entertainment was shaped by many of the same forces of consolidation and centralization that shaped other businesses (Levine, 1988:195).

Throughout these years the audience was being transformed . . . into a spectator rather than a witness and . . . lost a sense of itself as an active force, as a public. With important exceptions . . . sports and religion—audiences in America had become less interactive, less of a public and more of a group of mute receptors. Art was becoming a one-way process: the artist communicating and the audience receiving.

The exaggerated antithesis between art and life, between the aesthetic and the Philistine, the worthy and the unworthy, the pure and the tainted, embodied in the host of oppositional categories so firmly established at the turn of the century, has unquestionably colored our view of culture ever since (Boëthius, 1995; Levine, 1988).

As much as the "everyday" has been introduced into art in recent decades, there are still some subjects which are not found in art. If brought into the cultural space defined as art, these topics question art's very boundaries. So, for instance, bodily functions and other biologically based bodily practices, such as sexual relations, are rarely portrayed in art. Sexual relations are conceptualized as belonging to the "private" realm, or if "public," are characterized as pornography, but rarely art. "No matter how marginal, or banal, or even obscene it may be, everything is subject to aesthetization, culturation, mumification" (Baudrillard, 1995).

Today, however, we are witnessing a challenge or reversal of the idea of what constitutes a work of art. The everyday is being captured in artworks, although by its portrayal, it becomes stylized. Body art, such as that of Fakir Musifar, Ron Athey, the art of the body, its functions and practices, such as that of Sally Mann, Orlan, Valie Export, and Annie Sprinkle among others, disrupt notions of what is or is not art. The distinction between the practice of everyday life and the practice of art is blurring as many of these 'artists' live both figuratively and literally through the making of their art.

Art and life cannot be separated, but are coterminous in nature. That is, the notion that 'art' and 'life' are distinct and oppositional terms, that cannot reflect, inform, impact or influence the other is fallacious. Art is life. Life is art. Both art and life determine the other. In fact, carrying this argument to its logical end, there is no 'other,' in the sense that art and life are one in the same.

The idea that art and life construct one another can be argued from a number of perspectives, that include biological and psychological 'proof' regarding the impetus for artistic creation; philosophical writings on art, beauty and the nature of humankind; and postmodern/poststructuralist critique related to the nature of production/consumption.

BIOLOGICAL AND PSYCHOLOGICAL DISCUSSIONS OF ART

Biologists and psychologists view art and art production as a consequence of innate and learned needs. All are based on theories of motivation; the belief that art transcends culture and that objective standards of quality exist that can be discovered through cross-cultural studies based on universal principles of aesthetics such as unity, harmony, symmetry (Holbrook and Zirlin, 1985). These ideas led to studies of the relationship between the ability to judge aesthetics and adolescent patronage behavior (Bamossy, 1985). Predictably, those adolescents with greater abilities for aesthetic judgment show the greatest tendency for patronage behavior, suggesting that nurturing aesthetic judgment can impact lifelong patronage behavior.

Psychological theories of motivation, such as arousal theory, emotional experiencing and habituation have also been studied in the context of arts attendance. Specifically, Woods (1987) found that the arousal potential of works of fine arts ('masterpieces') does not provide a sufficient basis for their marketing except in the context of other benefits, such as affiliation, status, and education. However, these types of research are limited by the assumption that aesthetic judgment is constant or universal (Nava and Nava, 1996; Semenik and Bamossy, 1986).

The work of several anthropologists suggests that art-making is linked to social processes or forces. Anthropologist Franz Boas (1955) indicates that art springs from the practice of making utilitarian objects. His observation was supported by Jule-Rosette's (1984) study of tourist art in Nairobi, where carvers have begun to refine their carvings to create them according to principles of style and aesthetics. Meier (1942) theorizes that art is integral to human experience and from a study of "primitive" art argues that art allowed primitive people to externalize experience.

Read (1965) uses pre-historic cave drawings as a starting point to trace the notion that art holds a central place in the development of human consciousness, and maps their parallel development. He writes that images on cave walls were 'vital,' that is, the artists sought to capture or enhance the ritual potency of the figure. Cave drawings signified feeling. In the Neolithic period of human development, art as symbol or 'icon' came into being, anticipating the development of concepts (Deleuze and Guattari, 1994). The shift from vital image to icon was important in the development of a notion of human consciousness as the notion of icon required aptitudes and skills dependent upon human consciousness.

Read (1965) maps the development of art along with human consciousness. From vital images to the discovery of beauty and inventive images through craft-making, humans came to know geometry and discover the esthetic principle of symmetry in a coherent form. With the birth of Christianity came the art which depicted symbols of the unknown, a world beyond the senses; a transcendental, metaphysical realm. Next, the human subject became ideal, and subjectivity and humanity became intertwined in art. By the end of the Middle Ages, art became increasingly rule-bound, and subject to representation, or the illusion of the real. The final steps in the development of human consciousness through art came with the use of art to explore the frontiers of selfhood and finally to art as a constructive image.

PHILOSOPHICAL CONSIDERATION OF ART AND BEAUTY AND HUMANKIND

From Plato to Heidegger (a span of 2,200 years), art has been a recurrent topic of Western philosophy. Modern philosophers have drawn upon ideas put forth by classical philosophers and created complete philosophies of aesthetics (Hofstader and Kuhns, 1964). In the eighteenth century, the word aesthetics was derived from Greek etymological origins by the German, Alexander Gottlieb Baumgarten, meaning all kinds of sensory experience whether beautiful or not and regardless of whether the cause of the experience is natural or artistic (Strati, 1996; White, 1996).

Cassirer (1944) wrote that man is 'animal symbolicum'—a creative being in constant search of self, a creature who constantly examines the conditions of this existence through work, or systems of human activities, language, myth, religion, art, science, and history. Read (1965) took this idea further, arguing that art was the most important of human activities because of its role in the development of human consciousness. It was Cassirer (1944:22 and 25), however, who provided a basis for the separation of art from other activities, while still proving a basis for examining art as symbol.

> *Psychology, ethnology, anthropology, and history have amassed an astoundingly rich and constantly increasing body of facts . . . We appear, nonetheless, not yet to have found a method for the mastery and organization of this material . . . Unless we succeed in finding a clue of Ariadne to lead us out of this labyrinth, we can have no real insight into the general character of human culture; we shall remain lost in a mass of disconnected and disintegrated data which seem to lack all conceptual unity.*
>
> *No longer in a merely physical universe, man lives in a symbolic universe. Language, myth, art, and religion are parts of this universe. They are the varied threads which weave the symbolic net, the tangled web of human experience . . . Physical reality seems to recede in proportion as man's symbolic activity advances. Instead of dealing with the things themselves man is in a sense constantly conversing with himself.*

Although symbols vary, they are universal in humankind. Cassirer (1944) sites Helen Keller as an example of ability to transform animal-like knowledge of the world to human-like knowledge through the development of symbolic knowledge and language.

As with Deleuze and Guattari (1994), however, Cassirer (1944) views art in relation to Greek theories of beauty and thus ends up setting art apart from the everyday. Tracing views of imitative art (as distinct from the idea of art or *techne*) from Aristotle (*Metaphysics*) and Kant (*Critique of Judgment*), who linked art to the 'ideal' in the second half of the eighteenth century and Rousseau and Goethe who saw art as formative, the discovery of reality or intensification of reality. Cassirer (1944:149) argues that aesthetic experience is the experience of contemplation:

In this world all our feelings undergo a sort of transubstantiation with respect to their essence and their character . . . The calmness of the work of art is, paradoxically, a dynamic, not a static calmness. Art gives the emotions of the human soul in all their depth and variety. But the form, the measure and rhythm, of these motions is not comparable to any single state of emotion. What we feel in art is . . . the dynamic process of life itself—the continuous oscillation between opposite poles, between joy and grief, hope and fear, exaltation and despair . . . In the work of the artist the power of passion itself has been made a formative power.

For Cassirer (1944) art constructs and organizes human experience by framing the human universe. Art is *poieses* or generates what isn't there already; and contains a hidden dimension that can't be mastered (Deleuze and Guattari, 1994). Langer (1957) expands on Cassirer's work and defines art as the creation of expressive forms which set forth the nature of human feeling. Our feelings and our experience of feeling imply forms not directly accessible to our minds through language and other discursive symbol systems. Instead, feelings come from presentational symbol systems that includes art, but, that does not obey the one-to-one signifier-signified of semiotic discursive symbol systems. Sense is perceived in a Gestalt manner.

Common to all of these philosophies on art and beauty is the idea that art is central to life. However, from these perspectives art is distinguished from the "otherness" of life because of its importance in human development and metaphysics makes it privileged.

POSTMODERN/POSTSTRUCTURALIST CRITIQUE

Its [Modernity] project, Habermas writes, is one with that of Enlightenment: to develop the spheres of science, morality and art 'according to their inner logic' . . . Rich though this disciplinary project once was—and urgent given the incursions of kitsch on one side and academe on the other—it nevertheless came to rarefy culture, to reify its forms—so much that is provoked, at least in art, a counter-project in the form of an anarchic avant-garde (one thinks of Dadaism and Surrealism especially) (Foster, 1983).

The philosophical ideas about art displace art from everyday life. Art, as separate from culture, science and morality assumes a distance from the lifeworld

(Habermas, 1983, 1984) and begins to assume a special quality related closely to the sacred or civilized. Thus when art begins to change into something unrecognizable and cannot be understood in relation to the special quality of previous artistic periods, it comes under attack and is devalued and debased. Taken to the extreme, art is said not to exist (Baudrillard, 1995). However, it is with new types of art that art achieves significance and ultimate realization in the construction of our everyday existence. While art in previous periods was symbolic in nature, and thus created meaning in our lives, art today can be a true creative force in our development as human subjects. This point is highlighted in the organizational theory literature related to the constitution of organizational life.

> *The constitutive status of beauty in this regard carries important implications. For if beauty were constitutive in various elements of organization theory, then it could be argued that subsuming beauty under the rubrics of organizational 'symbolism' (e.g., Turner, 1990:1–4) or 'paradigm' (Hassard, 1993:76ff)—as if beauty were only a symbolic factor interpretively imported from the outside—is an unnecessary attempt at accommodating beauty to, perhaps, a purely functional interpretation of an organization. When examined from the constitutive perspective, beauty does not name a symbolic aspect of an organization, with the covert but nonetheless real sense that its status as symbolic somehow sets up a measure of distance between beauty and the actual reality of organizational life; rather, beauty is an essential, constitutive part of an organization, and must be recognized as such* (White, 1996:198).

An over-reliance on aesthetic philosophy to depict the function of art has its limitations. For example, in Plato's dialogues *Symposium* and *Phaedrus,* beauty and art are the clearest example of eternal and material form. However, Kant in *Critique and Judgment* (1791) characterizes beauty as something that provokes disinterest (i.e., possession is not necessary), is universal, has purposiveness without purpose, and necessary. Universalism has come under attack even in art history. Numerous scholars in the emerging field of visual culture are uncovering the historical, cultural reasons for privileging/disprivileging of art and visual experience (Jay, 1993). Along with the sacrilization process of high art over popular culture, a corresponding emphasis on distancing the subject in visual art fueled the commoditization of painting in the seventeenth century (Jay, 1993).

> *Cultural objects make visible the cultural principles and categories that form the basis of any society. Art objects are not exceptions. However, unlike other forms of material culture, they not only reflect, persuade, and convince the community of the importance of these rules* (McCracken, 1986) *but also critique and challenge the very fabric of society* (Sherry, 1995:351).

Perhaps art has now moved beyond form or, as Baudrillard (1995) suggests, is no longer distinct from a proliferation of signs *ad infinitum* and the recycling of culture. Art has moved beyond form and from foundation to critique. This is not to say that art is no longer art because it has "lost" what Baudrillard (1995) calls its "secret collusiveness" with culture so that what is left are signifiers which we decode according to more contradictory criteria. Rather, there is a realization that art is no longer distinct from life and its aesthetization.

In relation to the market, art was distanced from the lifeworld (Habermas, 1984) but made increasingly subject to the forces of the market. Art became marketized; valued in terms of market values or proxies thereof, such as attendance figures or box-office receipts. It is the market forces that devalue forms of culture that do not correspond to the market or co-opt them into a value that can be understood by the market. But, resistance abounds in the world of art, and meaning generation and diffusion seems to provide the answer.

> *In assessing the transformations of Aboriginal art . . . we conclude that even though this art means something different to its producers and consumers and even though both ends of this channel as well as the channel intermediaries have shaped and changed the nature and interpretation of Aboriginal art in response to the world boom of interest in this art, there are a number of positive aspects to be found within this imperfect exchange of meanings* (Belk and Groves, 1997: 448).
>
> *Debates . . . have always surrounded new stages in the dissemination of knowledge. Reading . . . was considered a contentious activity in the nineteenth century . . . Earlier in this century Walter Benjamin (1973) claimed that . . . film would help to develop in spectators a more acute and critical perception. Film as a cultural form was not only more popular and democratic, it was potentially revolutionary . . . Adorno and Horkheimer (1973), condemned the culture industry for what they alleged was taming both of critical art and the minds of the people.*
>
> *More recently Frederic Jameson (1983) has asked . . . to what extent can postmodern forms be considered oppositional or progressive? . . . Our answer must be that the forms alone cannot be subversive, but that the critical tools as well as the pleasures they have generated, and from which they are in any case inseparable, may indeed subvert and fragment existing networks of power-knowledge* (Nava and Nava, 1996: 183).

Indeed, as John Berger (1972:32) points out, it is no longer accurate to say that art is something distant and inaccessible to the masses. Indeed, it is the reproducibility of art in the postmodern age that allows for subversion of the market mechanisms.

> *What the modern means of reproduction have done is to destroy the authority of art and to remove it . . . from any preserve. For the first time ever, images of art have become ephemeral, ubiquitous, insubstantial, available, valueless, free. They surround us in the same way as a language surrounds us. They have entered the mainstream of life over which they no longer, in themselves, have power.*

Andy Warhol understood the relationship between reproduction in everyday life and art. He borrowed from the cultural world of images, objects and people. He consumed them on an everyday basis and created art that played on the repetitious nature of life images (Schroeder, 1997). From the 1960s to the present, artists such as Laurie Anderson, Spalding Gray, Andy Kaufman and numerous others have used notions of resistance and repetition to create their art, themselves and their audiences, increasingly aided by technologies (Auslander, 1992).

THE RELATIONSHIP BETWEEN PRODUCTION/CONSUMPTION AND TECHNOLOGY

Increasingly, the audience and artist are directly involved in both the production of the outcome, either through audience participation or by their interaction with technology that links the artist, audience and product being created. According to postmodernist critiques, products are constructed and re-constructed, infused with symbols that are linked to meanings in the production and consumption processes. The consumer is no longer at the end of the process, but is part of an ongoing process of symbol construction/consumption and meaning generation (Firat and Venkatesh, 1995). Artistic products are created and consumed through this process of symbol construction and meaning creation. Thus, mere engagement with art constitutes simultaneously an act of production and consumption. Even 'complete' artistic products are not actually complete without viewer participation.

The idea that art and life are intertwined can be taken a step further. As the world moves to an information-based global culture, arts production and arts consumption is increasingly tied to technology. Never before has technology served to alter the essence (Benjamin, 1969) of the artistic production. In the past, new technologies have been used primarily to enhance the traditional art form or to create new forms, such as film and photography (Friedberg, 1993). In the contemporary arts world, the basic nature of conventional artistic forms (i.e., dance, theater, visual art, music) is being challenged as the result of technology. Scholars have noted that traditional distinctions between genres are becoming fuzzy, creating new "mosaics" of consumption experiences for audiences, and thus, altering the arts genres themselves.

With the advent of the 'spectacle' and the instrumentalization of visual culture through the development of the panorama in 1792 and diorama in 1823, the notion of illusion became an important focus of newly formed entertainment industries (Friedberg, 1993; MacCannell, 1989; Urry, 1990). 'Spectators' were provided a spatial and temporal mobility—real mobility in the case of tourists, and 'virtual' mobility in the case of the entertainment audiences. The technology of these entertainment experiences depended on spectator immobility, but offered visual excursions away from everyday confinement in space and time.

Walter Benjamin (1969) wrote about the social changes manifested by so-called "mechanical representation" characterizing much of the entertainment world (i.e., photography, cinema, phonographic recordings). Mechanically produced entertainment experiences were no longer unique: they could be replicated over and over again. He postulated that the mystified quality of authenticity of the original was lost in mechanical reproduction.

> *Even the most perfect reproduction of a work of art is lacking in one element: its presence in time in space, its unique existence at the place where it happens to be* (Benjamin, 1969:220).

The emergence of multi-media, interactive/virtual technology is transforming previously distinct categories of artist/audience and the role of the marketer in the cultural production/diffusion process. Writers such as Rheingold (1991) link emerging technology to new artistic experiences and aesthetic/performance philosophy/theory. Quoting from Randall Walser's (1990:286) "Elements of a Cyberspace Playhouse,"

> *Whereas film is used to show a reality to an audience, cyberspace is used to give a virtual body, and a role, to everyone in the audience. Print and radio tell; stage and film show; cyberspace embodies . . . Whereas the playwright and the filmmaker both try to communicate the idea of an experience, the spacemaker sets up a world for an audience to act directly within . . . Thus the spacemaker can never hope to communicate a particular reality, but only to set up opportunities for certain kinds of realities to emerge. The filmmaker says, "Look, I'll show you." The spacemaker says, "Here, I'll help you discover."*

Multi-media, interactive/virtual artistic products are already possible. In dance, Kozel (1994a; 1994b) discusses the work of choreographers and dancers experimenting with technology and dance. Kozel herself participated in one of these dances and describes the experience in which she, as the virtual body, was behind a screen and audience members interacted with her shadow.

> *For the people in the room I was an image and they were flesh; the monitors which showed the action in both rooms transformed them into images and me into the image of a projection; from my perspective if I decided to ignore the monitors I was flesh and my dance partners simply did not exist. These varying physical states swirled and danced while we did the same* (Kozel, 1994a: p. 47).

While these experiences are far from common, the nature of art is being rapidly and frequently altered through technology. The influence of technology is not confined to the artistic product, but constructs the way in which we perceive the world. In an article on the future of performance and virtual technology, McKenzie (1994:90) writes:

> *More importantly, if we understand theatre as but one determined form of a more generalized human performance, then ritual, speech acts, everyday life, and performance art, in short the entire spectrum of performance studies, all become creative and critical avenues for addressing the human experience of computers.*

Technology is transforming the nature of the artistic production/consumption process in that artists and audience are linked; and moreover, technology and its use in the arts is transforming our conceptualization of everyday life.

CONCLUSION

Whether argued on historical, philosophical, biological, psychological, anthropological, sociological, postmodernist or technological means, the reality is that we as members of the postindustrial/postmodernist subcultures cannot escape the influence of art, and can no longer accept the distinction between art and life. Art is life and life is art. Art surrounds us, and shapes us and our lives in postmodernity.

BIBLIOGRAPHY

Appadurai, A. (1986) *The Social Life of Things: Commodities in Cultural Perspective,* New York: Cambridge University Press.

Aristotle, "Metaphysics" in A. Hofstadter and R. Kuhns, eds. *Philosophies of Art and Beauty: Selected Readings in Aesthetics from Plato to Heidegger,* (1964) Chicago: University of Chicago Press, 80–96.

Auslander, P. (1992) *Presence and Resistance: Postmodernism and Cultural Politics in Contemporary American Performance,* Ann Arbor: University of Michigan Press.

Bakhtin, M. (1965/1984) *Rabelais and His World,* Bloomington; Indiana University Press.

Bamossy, G. (1985) "Aesthetic Judgment And Arts Patronage Of Adolescents" *Advances in Nonprofit Marketing,* 1, 161–206.

Baudrillard, J. (1995) "Transaesthetics," in J. Baudrillard trans. by J. Benedict *The Transparency of Evil: Essays on Extreme Phenomena,* New York: Verso.

Belk, R.W. and R. Groves (1995/1997) "Aboriginal Art As Commodity: Meaning Modification In A Marketing Channel" *working paper and video,* Perth, Western Australia: Edith Cowan University, 56 min.

Benjamin, W. (1969) "The Work Of Art In The Age Of Mechanical Reproduction" in Hannah Arendt ed., trans. by H. Zohn *Illuminations,* New York: Schocken Books, 217–251.

Berger, J. et al. (1972) *Ways of Seeing,* London: British Broadcasting Corporation and Penguin Books.

Boas, F. (1955) *Primitive Art,* New York: Dover Press.

Boëthius, U. (1995) "The History Of High And Low Culture," in J. Forniäs and G. Bolin, eds. *Youth Culture in Late Modernity,* Newbury Park, CA: Sage Publications, 12–38.

Borgerson, J. L. and J. E. Schroeder (1997), "The Ethics of Representation: Packaging Paradise: Consuming the 50th State" presentation at the National Ethics and Popular Culture Conference, April 1997.

Bourdieu, P. (1984) *Distinction: A Social Critique of the Judgement of Taste,* Cambridge: Harvard University Press.

Brown, S. (1995) *Postmodern Marketing,* London: Routledge.

Burke, P. (1978) *Popular Culture in Early Modern Europe,* New York: Harper and Row.

Cassirer, E. (1944) *An Essay on Man: An Introduction to A Philosophy of Human Culture,* Yale University Press.

Chandler, A.D. (1977) *The Visible Hand: The Managerial Revolution in American Business,* Cambridge: Belknap Press of Harvard University Press.

Cooley, C.H. (1966) *Social Process,* Carbondale, IL: Southern Illinois University Press.

Debord, G. (1983) *Society of the Spectacle,* Detroit: Black and Red.

Deleuze, G. and F. Guattari (1994*) What is Philosophy,* New York: Verso.

Elias, N. (1969/1978) *The History of Manners,* New York: Wizen Books.

Firat, A.F. (1996) "Literacy In The Age Of New Information Technologies," in R.R. Dholakia, N. Mundorf and N. Dholakia, eds., *New Infortainment Technologies in the Home,* Mahwah, NJ: Lawrence Erlbaum Associates, 173–179.

Firat, A.F. and A. Venkatesh (1995) "Liberatory Postmodernism and the Reenchantment of Consumption" *Journal of Consumer Research,* 22, December, 239–267.

Foster, H., ed. (1983) *The Anti-Aesthetic: Essays on Postmodern Culture,* Seattle, WA: Bay Press.

Foucault, M. (1975/1979) *Discipline and Punish: The Birth of the Prison,* New York: Vintage/Random.

Friedberg, A. (1993) *Window Shopping: Cinema and the Postmodern,* Berkeley: University of California Press.

Gans, H.J. (1974) *Popular Culture and High Culture: An Analysis and Evaluation of Taste,* New York: Basic Books.

Habermas, J. (1984) *The Theory of Communicative Action,* Vol. 1, Boston: Beacon.

Habermas, J. (1983) "Modernity—An Incomplete Project," in H. Foster, ed. *The Anti-Aesthetic: Essays on Postmodern Culture,* Seattle: Bay Press.

Hofstadter, A. and R. Kuhns, eds. (1964) *Philosophies of Art and Beauty: Selected Readings in Aesthetics from Plato to Heidegger,* Chicago: University of Chicago Press.

Holbrook, M.B. and R.B. Zirlin (1985) "Artistic Creation, Artworks, And Aesthetic Appreciation: Some Philosophical Contributions to Nonprofit Marketing" *Advances in Nonprofit Marketing,* 1, 1–54.

Jameson, F. (1983) "Postmodernism and Consumer Society," in H. Foster, ed. *The Anti-Aesthetic: Essays on Postmodern Culture,* Seattle, WA: Bay Press, 111–126.

Jay, M. (1993) *Downcast Eyes: The Denigration of Vision in Twentieth-Century French Thought,* Berkeley: University of California Press.

Jules-Rosette, B. (1984) *The Messages of Tourist Art,* New York: Plenum Press.

Kant, Immanuel (1791) "Critique of Judgment," in *Philosophies of Art and Beauty: Selected Readings in Aesthetics from Plato to Heidegger,* A. Hofstadter, and R. Kuhns, eds. (1964), Chicago: University of Chicago Press, 280–343.

Kaye, N. (1994) *Postmodernism and Performance,* New York: St. Martin's Press.

Kozel, S. (1994a) "Spacemaking: Experiences of a Virtual Body," *Dance Theatre Journal,* 11, 3, Autumn, 12–47.

Kozel, S. (1994b) "Virtual Reality: Choreographing Cyberspace," *Dance Theatre Journal,* 11, 2 Spring/Summer 34–37.

Langer, S. (1957) *Philosophy in a New Key,* Cambridge, MA: Harvard University Press.

Lears, J. (1994) *Fables of Abundance: A Cultural History of Advertising in America,* New York: Basic Books.

Levine, L.W. (1988) *Highbrow/Lowbrow: The Emergence of Cultural Hierarchy in America,* Harvard University Press.

MacCannell, D. (1989) *The Tourist: A New Theory of the Leisure Class,* New York: Shocken Books.

Marchand, R. (1985) *Advertising the American Dream: Making Way for Modernity 1920–1940,* Los Angeles: University of California Press.

McKenzie, J. (1994) "Virtual Reality: Performance, Immersion, and the Thaw," *The Drama Review,* 38, 4, Winter, 83–106.

Meier, N.C. (1942) *Art in Human Affairs: An Introduction to the Psychology of Art,* New York, NY: McGraw-Hill Book Company, Inc.

Nava, M. with O. Nava (1992) "Discriminating or Duped? Young People as Consumers of Advertising/Art," in M. Nava *Changing Cultures: Feminism, Youth and Consumption,* Newbury Park, CA: Sage Publications.

Plato, "Phaedrus" (1964) in A. Hofstadter and R. Kuhns, eds. *Philosophies of Art and Beauty: Selected Readings in Aesthetics from Plato to Heidegger,* Chicago: University of Chicago Press, 53–67.

Pollay, R.W. (1986) "The Distorted Mirror: Reflections On The Unintended Consequences Of Advertising" *Journal of Marketing,* 50, April, 18–36.

Read, H. (1965) *Icon and Idea: The Function of Art in the Development of Human Consciousness,* New York, NY: Shocken Books.

Rheingold, B. (1991) *Virtual Reality,* New York: Simon and Schuster.

Schroeder, J.E. (1997) "Andy Warhol: Consumer Researcher" in D. MacGinnis and M. Brucks, eds. *Advances in Consumer Research,* 24, 476–482.

Schroeder, J.E. (1997) "Roots Of Modern Marketing In Italian Renaissance Art, *Proceedings of the Twenty-Second Macromarketing Conference,* A. Flakenberg, ed., Bergen: Norwegian School of Business and Economics.

Semenik, R.J. and G. Bamossy (1986) "The Experiential Nature Of Cultural Consumption And The Shaping Of A New 'Aesthetic'" in D.V. Shaw, W.S. Hendon, and C.R. Weits, eds., *Artists and Cultural Consumers,* Akron: Association for Cultural Economics, 147–154.

Sherry, J.F., ed. (1995) *Contemporary Marketing and Consumer Behavior: An Anthropological Sourcebook,* Newbury Park, CA: Sage Publications.

Strati, A. (1996) "Organizations Viewed Through The Lens Of Aesthetics," *Organization,* 3, 2, 209–218.

Urry, J. (1990) *The Tourist Gaze,* London: Sage.

Walser, R. (1990) "Elements Of A Cyberspace Playhouse" *Proceedings of the National Computer Graphics Association '90,* Anaheim CA.

Weber, M. (1958) *The Rational and Social Foundations of Music,* Carbondale: Southern Illinois University Press.

White, D.A. (1996) "It's Working Beautifully! Philosophical Reflections On Aesthetics And Organization Theory," *Organization,* 3, 2, 195–208.

Woods, W. A. (1987) "Classical Aesthetics And Arousal Theory: Implications for Fine Arts Marketing," *Advances in Nonprofit Marketing,* 2, 203–239.

18

SECTION SUMMARY:
SERVICE, INTIMACY, LEISURE

Richard A. Goodman

One of the fascinating issues of modern, bureaucratic life is the high variation among personnel responsible for dealing with customers. Organizations make rules to control the customer experience. Service delivery personnel then choose whether to enforce them. This challenge was clearly articulated in 1939 when Chester Barnard asserted that authority flows from the bottom to the top. In our modernist views we tend to forget Barnard and design organizations from the top down.

Many years ago, in preparing for a sabbatical year in London, I visited the British consulate. At the time there was a possibility that I might work while in the U.K. at the Tavistock Institute or the London School of Economics and so I needed to find out how to obtain a work permit. The clerk began in a traditional work-by-the-rules manner. A work permit had to be obtained in the United States prior to my departure for the U.K. and the Bank of England had to be informed so that the funds earned could be paid into an 'external' account. This was discouraging news, as the offers were still pending and would not be formalized until after face-to-face meetings that could only take place after I arrived in London. I went away disheartened, spent an hour in the consulate library, and then returned to the clerk at the counter.

Again I asked about obtaining a work permit. This time the answer was much less discouraging. "Not to worry, once you get there either LSE or the Tavistock can take care of the paperwork because these rules are really not fair. When you arrive in the UK remember that Immigration, Inland Revenue, Excise Tax and other officials are often willing to work around rules if they perceive fairness is at stake."

This time the clerk was very forthcoming helping me with the specific problem and also providing helpful advice for future encounters. During my year in London, I tested this advice on numerous occasions and in most instances the issues were resolved successfully using this technique.

Within each encounter, the initial presentation was generally a recitation of the rules. Typically, it was then followed by a relaxation of the rules. In each of these situations, modernist rules did not appear to limit pragmatic adjustment. Thus, organizational design and practice are often at odds with one another. As organizational scientists we have frequently met designers using modernist concepts of rules and control who simultaneously understand that the most subversive employee response would be to actually 'work-to-rule.' Thus, one of the organizational conundrums of the postindustrial subculture is the 'design' of service delivery that usually occurs far from management and their direct control. In most organizational designs, service is actually delivered by personnel at the lower rungs of the organizational status hierarchy. Thus, pragmatic work-arounds and other deviations from managerial intent is a common experience.

Given these experiences, I recognized that the search for illicit pleasures presented by Ian Atkin and Mike Lowe in "Dances with Shadows, Dance Clubs, Mirrored Balls and Reflected Pleasures" was a robust structuring of the same service conundrum. The chapter evokes a wonderful image of a two-pronged organizational challenge. The first is the obvious fact that customer demands are frequently at variance with management intent. Ian and Mike report that both the design and management of 'dance club culture' recognize the demands for illicit pleasures while formally denying that rules, control and conformance needs would be at risk. The second challenge derives from the need to commodify the 'dance club culture' for legitimization and/or profit thus creating a barrier between the authentic experiences being sought and the 'manufactured' experiences being offered. These responses give unofficial discretion to front-line personnel while creating an organizational design that appears legitimate to external agencies. Management's modernist rules do not delimit pragmatic adjustment within the club.

These differences were demonstrated dramatically by Atkin and Lowe, but they reflect many more common circumstances when the ideal and the actual are at odds. Sometimes the variances are rather minor. We commonly encounter clerks giving customers small discount for marred products. Sometimes, however, the pragmatic response seems more serious. For example, I was once at the Southend Airport in England en route to Rotterdam when I realized that I didn't have my passport. After initially refusing to help, the immigration officer relented a bit and assured me that exit and entrance to the UK was permissible since I had my alien registration document with me. This, of course, solved only half my problem, as I still had to be admitted into the Netherlands at the other end of the flight. Still pondering the next step, I approached the immigration officer again and this time was told to talk to the airline representative. I discovered that the airline commonly made arrangements with the Dutch immigration officials for passengers without full documentation. Surprising to me was the fact that the rules regarding cross-border travel could also be pragmatically adjusted. In this case, the issue was resolved by the airline, the only organization involved that had a financial interest in my travel plans and thus was motivated to solve the problem as to avoid losing revenue.

Wendy Guild's "Using Categories to Provide Customized Service: Meanings Created in Ski Resort Subcultures" also illustrates these issues. Here costumes were the clue to subculture identification, and subculture identification was the trigger for decisions about service variations. Once again the variations were determined by personnel on the front line rather than by the upper management. In this case, cultural mis-matches between service delivery personnel and individual customers were a more significant source of variation than individual judgment. Earlier, Anette Risberg argued that working with cultural ambiguity had significant power in crafting a more effective marriage between cultures. Wendy's chapter is an example of another kind of management challenge as the actors in her story do not use cultural mis-matches as an opportunity for improvement. Rather, each subculture remains unaffected by encounters with other subcultures.

The service industry as a whole and the front line personnel within many service organizations normally have only transitory connections with individual customers. These kinds of brief encounters don't provide a platform for much learning. On the ski slopes it actually seems to provide a platform for reinforcing stereotypes. In contrast, the cultural inter-penetration described in the first section of this volume involved long-term interactions. In these studies, the need to work together in one form or another was constant, and joint problem solving was necessity. Learning and adjustments that evolve in the course of a long-term relationship are very different than those that typically occur during short transactions.

Julia Harrison's work "Capturing Memories: The Tourist Experience" supports one of Atkin and Lowe's premises by focusing on the search for authenticity that seems to be an inimitable aspect of virtually all tourists. Even when the tourists' choice is the commodified tour, their most memorable stories are often based on experiences or encounters that fall outside the parameters of the official tour experience. Interestingly, what we find in this work is a lack of intimacy. The assemblage of the photo album and the souvenir closet are personal endeavors that typically have only limited audiences. A study of the Japanese photographic market identified similar patterns—a significant desire to take photographs and then to assemble them into albums, etc. was found but there was not a great concern with actually sharing them. This experience echoes Julia's findings. Although not explored directly, it is also similar to the phenomena of friends and colleagues who often ignore stories of friends newly returning from vacation in favor of dealing with today's business. The search for authenticity reflected in this essay isn't very different from the dance club patrons and the organizational response takes the similar form of manufactured pleasures.

Several years ago an acquaintance ran a marathon down the slopes of Mount Everest. Intrigued by an ad, he responded, hoping to participate in a truly unique experience. When he took the journey however, he discovered that there were more doctors than runners in the group and that medical evacuation helicopters had been hired and fully paid for well in advance of the run. His search for authenticity was limited to the Sherpa guides, the long trek to run's starting point, and the breathing difficulties caused by high altitudes.

The final chapter in this section conveys a dual message. It reinforces a number of issues relating to the changing nature of life in a postindustrial world. Laurie Meamber's "Art as Life—Life as Art: The Embededness of Art in Life and Life in Art in Postmodernity" focuses on postindustrial and postmodern explanations of the shifting locus and role of art. In many ways so-called high art has become commodified by the nature and structure of the art market. To some this is the ultimate effect of the Getty Foundation. Ironically, the Getty Foundation also focuses on new art, new artists and the encouragement of the avant garde in its programming if not in its collections. Industrial design and mediated art have gained more and more importance in recent times and creative talent has migrated toward this kind of outlet. Thus the commodification of art as cultural and product iconography has moved the 'value' and appreciation of art from the salons to the masses. The arbiter of art's artistic value and commercial value has passed from the putative 'critic' to the masses. For many of us, objects similar to those we discarded twenty years ago have now become collectibles adorning our homes and finding places in museums. By shifting the source of valuation and the determination of meaning, the individual has become more privileged.

While the individual is seemingly becoming more privileged through a democratization of ideas and points of view there are also some counter impacts to this process. Later sections will illuminate the tension of the individual view within a larger society.

SECTION FOUR

19

MODERN AND POSTMODERN CULTURAL THEMES AND STRUCTURES IN BRITISH RADIO DRAMA

M. L. James and B. James

This paper examines British radio drama as a distinctive art form, considering structuring techniques, symbolism and the mythic themes of the subject matter. During this study, a modern/postmodern dualism emerged at two levels, within the symbolism and construction of the plays, and within the plays' messages and the themes. In addition, the dramatists' relationships to their medium and to the British Broadcasting Corporation reflect significant changing of culture from those envisioned when the BBC was originally established in the 1920s.

INTRODUCTION

Historically, the BBC has been the dominant patron and provider of radio drama since broadcasting began. In April 1993 John Tydeman, Head of BBC Radio Drama, was quoted as saying that of the 300 original scripts received each week "around ten will have some worth" (Curtis, 1993). Typically, 200 new plays are produced each year and 600 plays are broadcast (Reynolds, 1993).

A good radio play is characterized by precision in writing and the placement of sound effects, music and silence to create qualities of mutual coherence and illumination such as those found within the construction of a poem. Ultimately, to produce a poetic construct all the elements of a play should be subordinated and integrated into an organic whole. In an effective radio play the author creates a subculture in the listener's mind and manages to involve the listener and the characters in the play. The way this is done and the purposes for which it is done appear to reflect the values and concerns of the times.

Early plays display characteristics of content and structure that are typically 'modernist', while later plays take on a more 'postmodern' character. This is not to argue that there is a sharp division between the 'modern' and a 'postmodern' era of radio plays—indeed some early plays demonstrate as much imagination and variety as many contemporary plays. We also detect a recent reversion to certain features that are reminiscent of what we have identified as 'modernism.' This is especially evident in terms of theme.

THE 'STUFF' OF RADIO AND THE CREATION OF MEANING IN RADIO DRAMA

It's confusing that we refer to radio plays, making them sound like theatrical events with large audiences. Most people listen alone. Radio isn't communal. It's closer to a novel, where the writer and the reader or listener create a world between them. (Warburton, 1986)

In 1991, Tydeman claimed an audience of over 750 million for the 1,250 hours of drama broadcast the previous year (Linklater, 1991). Martin Esslin (1971) put audience figures into perspective by relating listening figures to the size of theater audiences. According to his calculations, the audience of a Saturday Night Theatre play (repeated on a Monday afternoon) was the equivalent to between 1500 and 2000 sold-out performances in a theater holding a thousand people.

Unlike theater the radio audience is made up of individual listeners. Listening is a highly personal activity, as opposed to a communal one. To make sense out of the sounds, the listener must become involved in an act of creative collaboration with the production. As Esslin described it: "The play comes to life in the listener's own imagination, so the *stage* on which it is performed is the listener's own mind. He himself, by having to provide the visual component . . . is an active collaborator with the producer" (Esslin, 1971:5).

Both radio plays and stage plays are offered at a fixed time that cannot be adjusted by the audience. Both require a sustained imaginative engagement throughout. And both demand involvement to be quickly and dramatically secured. Like radio plays, a film is made up of individual images and performances re-assembled in the cutting room to fit the director's vision. Narrative continuity is irrelevant. The cinema director is liberated from the 'unities' that characterize stage drama (largely because of physical constraints) through the use of techniques such as cutting, juxtaposition of images and the use of multiple camera shots. Radio's equivalent of visual scene changes occurs through use of sound—fades, cuts, dissolves, wipes and fans, for example (Sieveking,1934). These liberate and permit a wide variety of structural and presentational forms that can be varied to fit the themes and messages of the particular radio play.

Of supreme importance are the use of words. Cinema audiences make meaning primarily from visual signs. Radio listeners make meaning from words and from sounds given additional significance within the context of words. The radio writer and producer have the film director's freedom of space and time and the same ability to focus on individual images. Thus the radio medium offers the unique capacity to engage directly with the individual listener's imagination, with no intermediate visual stimulus. A radio play has the freedom of film to ignore rigid rules of narrative and to concentrate on events that are significant to the visions of both the writer and producer.

As practitioners such as Martin Esslin (1971), Donald McWhinnie (1959) and Richard Imison (1965) have observed, on the basis of patterning and rhythm, a radio play can also be compared with a musical composition. Richard Imison has said that a radio play script is "like a musical score for a production." McWhinnie (1959:39) goes further: "The sound complex of radio works on the emotions in the same way as music: aside from its total meaning, it, too, exists in time, not space, it has its own rhythmic and melodic patterns, its musical shape."

The fact that the listener's mind is stimulated by a structure consisting predominantly of words to create specific images and shapes and to move in both time and space takes the radio play closer to poetry. McWhinnie, as a radio producer, has an instinctive feeling that radio drama is similar to poetry because of its nature and effect. In this he is close to a definition of what makes a play poetic, as given by T.C. Worsley: "a play is poetic when its concrete elements, plot, agency, scene, speech, gesture continuously exhibit in their internal relationships those qualities of mutual coherence and illumination required of the words of a poem" (Hinchcliffe, 1977:13).

A further definition of relevance is the description of "poetry of the theatre" by Jean Cocteau as "coarse lace, a lace of ropes, a ship at sea: the scenes are integrated like the words of a poem" (Hinchcliffe, 1977:13). Central to these two definitions of poetic drama is clear applicability of the concept of organic unity to radio drama. This was specifically elucidated by Edward Sackville-West in the Preface to Louis MacNeice's "The Rescue": "The word *artist* means *joiner*, and the artist in radio composition is . . . one who joins things together—words, music, all manner of sounds. But whatever is joined must make a ring, not a straight ribbon" (Smith, 1979:221).

Smith, a radio producer himself, really sums up: "No matter what its theme, a radio play . . . must be free of certain damning shortcomings and it must bring together in a well-constructed organic whole some or all of the technical devices available to the writer and/or director." (Smith, 1979:220). BBC's *Notes on Radio Drama*, available to aspiring writers, have made a similar point:

> *Since radio involves only one of the senses, it is important to construct each individual sequence and the play as a whole to provide a variety of sound which will hold the listener's attention. This variety can be achieved in lengths of sequences, number of people speaking, pace of dialogue, volume of sound, background acoustics and location of action.* (BBC, 1986:5)

The case can be taken further by reference to the content of radio drama which, for R.D. Smith, is inseparable from its form: "Content and form, form and content are inseparable and the critic will find that the works he is drawn to will all operate at more than one level. It is not for nothing that voyages, quests, fairy tales and parables have inspired so much of the best radio writing" (Smith, 1979:230).

This view highlights an additional argument for radio drama as a form of poetic drama, the belief that it is especially suited to the presentation of fundamental mythic themes and patterns that were the original substance of oral literature and symbolic interpretations of reality: "all myths . . . have their grounding in the actual generalised experience of ancient peoples, and represent their attempts to impose a satisfactory, graspable, human shape on it" (Hawkes, 1977:13).

From the narrative point of view, the writer must think like a newspaper reporter and provide answers to who?, what?, when?, where?, and how? questions of the listeners. Whereas in stage, film and television viewers have visual clues, radio drama listeners rely solely on narrative and sound effects for information. Andrew Crisell defines this process as a "transcodification—the replacement of one code or set of codes, in this case, visual ones, by another, in this case auditory, the code of speech" (Crisell, 1986:138).

This can be achieved partly by having a narrator to guide the listener. If the writer chooses not to use a narrator, then the narrative functions have to be incorporated into dialogue, at the same time that the dialogue fulfills other requirements. Listeners need signposts such as time and location with transitions clearly signaled. This information alone, however, is not sufficient to stimulate listeners to create a 'shared reality'. More is needed.

Jeremy Howe made this comparison: "TV has made me a firm believer in the visual mechanics of radio writing. Radio has got to put images into the dialogue, while its rhythms are different from the stage play" (Beck, 1991). Here, Howe is acknowledging the need to provide prompts to enable the reader to imagine the visual aspects of the drama such as setting, clothes, and stage business. This must be achieved through dialogue without overloading the picture, as is deliberately done in the classic parody of the radio play by Timothy West, "This Gun that I Hold in My Right Hand is Loaded" (Ash, 1987:37).

An example of this economy occurs in "Scenes from an Execution," a play by Howard Barker. In this play a Venetian renaissance painting leads to conflict between the artist, her public and the state. Listeners are only given the information that it is "a painting able to move people to tears." The painting is never described. Thus, each listener has to create a personal vision of the painting to fit his or her interpretation of the description.

The voices of the actors must also be appropriate to the image the writer wants to create in the listener's mind. This is another aspect of the way in which signification is related to words being spoken on the radio: "[Words] therefore constitute a binary code in which the words themselves are symbols of what they represent, while the voice in which they are heard is an index of the person or "character" who is speaking . . . In other words, such factors as accent and stress have semiotic functions, or at least, effects" (Crisell, 1986:46).

Aspiring radio dramatists face a particular challenge. The utter concentration on the word in its full range of connotation and denotation freed from any visual stimulus ultimately determines the uniqueness of radio drama and underscores its strong affinity with poetry. The ways that words have been used to create the organic unities, the 'subcultures' of the plays, reflect modernist and postmodernist tendencies in the history of the medium, and, in turn, reflect the way the 'culture' of the BBC has changed to reflect the times.

LINEAR NARRATIVE, SOCIAL REPRESSION AND THE RETREAT TO INNER REALITY IN EARLY RADIO PLAYS

Guthrie's "Squirrel's Cage" and "The Flowers Are Not for You to Pick" focus centrally on the repression of individual personality by social mechanisms. "Squirrel's Cage" (1929) conveys a pessimistic impression of successive generations conditioned to accept a routine, individuality-suppressing life, for which a squirrel in a cage is an apt symbol. The remorseless linear narrative framework, logical and 'modern', is an excellent vehicle for this message. The play is a series of scenes that depict Henry's life beginning just before his birth to the point where Henry has become husband and father and show restrictions on his baby son that mirror his own life. The caged squirrel is introduced in the first scene, the object of an argument between Mary, who wants to free it, and John, who disagrees, because "they get so used to captivity that freedom makes them afraid" (Guthrie, 1931:21–22). A key verbal motif is established, with reference to the futility and repetitiveness of the squirrel's life:

> *JOHN: When it's awake it runs round and around in the wire wheel.*
> *MARY: Round and round.*
> *JOHN: Yes, round and round.* (22)

Henry's conditioning is presented impressionistically through the Interludes. The first contains a verbal collage of different voices giving "Don't" commands which simulate situations in which a baby disobeys. Then "All" repeat the words of "The One" like a kind of litany which reaches a climax and then fades:

> *THE ONE: How many times have I got to tell you that (shouting) You're not to—*
> *ALL (shouting): Not to—not to—not to—*
> *ALL (quietly echo): Not to—not to—not to—* (28)

The voices are a virtual verbal battering ram. The second Interlude conveys impressionistically the conditioning of school, summed up in the Schoolmaster's "Don't argue. Your business is to obey, not argue" (41).

At this point there is a scene in which a genuine dramatic conflict takes place—the fight for Henry's future and soul as he faces a career choice. He can join a schoolfellow who is going to South Africa to grow oranges, or he can follow in his father's footsteps working in an office until he is 21 and then go to South Africa. Aunt Mary tries to save him from this: "It'll be SIX years before you're 21. Six years—up in the train, down in the train, office routine—for SIX years. By the time you're 21 you won't want to go to South Africa. You'll be— My god—you'll be a City Man! (Gong—the stroke of doom)" (57). He is offered the choice again, followed by another gong and he chooses conformity, as the gong is identified as the signal for the meal, symbol of domestic life and security.

Interlude 3 picks up the train routine foretold by Aunt Mary. The dialogue throughout is accompanied by the rhythmic puffing of a train. Again, a collage of voices reproduces snatches of conversations, building up speed and volume with the "One" voice echoed by "All", until the words "up" and "down" predominate. A note to the producer emphasizes that the chorus "up" and "down" should imitate the rhythmic motion of a speeding train.

The train sound is replaced by a typewriter for Interlude 4, which represents the unvarying routine of life at the office. Henry's secretary, Miss Nemo (Latin for 'no one') takes dictation endlessly, varying the letter only by the date, the typewriter sound intercutting the dictation.

The only music in the play is present both functionally and symbolically in scene 4. Against the background of a waltz, that echoes the "round and round" motif, Henry proposes to Ivy, who is a "clinger" like his mother, Rose. A four-second pause succeeds the final dance music, then the organ is heard playing a fragment of Mendelssohn's 'Wedding March'. This cliché in musical shorthand says all there is to be said about such a marriage.

It is no surprise, then, that in scene 5 Henry and Ivy appear as exact replicas of Henry's father and mother. In scene 1 John recalls an exchange about bacon that he once had with Henry's mother, Rose, where she was wearing a pink dress. Now Henry comments on both Ivy's pink dress and the bacon. Using almost identical words to those Rose uttered, Ivy replies:

HENRY: By Jove, all frizzly. That's how I like it.
IVY: Do you? I'll tell Lizzie to do it like that always. (74)

Interlude 5 has fragments of Interludes 3 and 4 cross-fading into each other. Guthrie says "The effect should be a composite image of the Commuter's day— trains fading into typewriters—railway lines merging into lines of print" (75).

The last scene of the play is a dramatized version of interlude 1, in which it is obvious that Henry's son will be a duplicate of his father. The baby is nagged in the way the voices in the Interlude nagged, in order to stifle exploration and independence: "Don't touch those letters, baby" (81). But there is a level of irony here that was not found earlier. Henry wishes he could cut loose from the "same old routine day after day—round and round. Like a squirrel in a cage" (80). He feels it's justified because of "the feeling that we're PROGRESSING—NOT just running round" (81). This is an example of a character retreating into an inner reality to cope with a depressing social situation, a theme explored in more depth by Sieveking.

In addition to using the voice itself as a sound effect, Guthrie also uses two immediately recognizable sounds from everyday life—the train and the typewriter—in such a manner that they, too, become defamiliarized and take on a larger-than-life dimension to symbolize the weight of conformity that oppresses the individual.

"Intimate Snapshots" (Sieveking, 1929) used radio to explore the inner reality of people a stage further. This was described in the *Radio Times* as:

> *A radio-dramatic experiment taking the form of an argument between two people in which the examples come to life. One protagonist argues that life is nothing but a series of meaningless repetitions day after day, year after year, and suggests that somehow men and women should try to escape. His opponent holds that there is no escape from the outward daily repetitions but these are merely a background which does not matter. The real experiences, he says, take place in the mind.* (280–281)

An underground lift conductor, a charwoman in a girls' school and a newspaper reporter were chosen as examples in mundane jobs. The newspaper reporter was sent to interview the other two, "To find out something about what goes on inside their heads" (297). The lift conductor establishes the existence of this 'inner reality' by talking about the difficulty of understanding other people when he reflects on a girlfriend and on the way his father used to study people. Then Mrs. Trimble, the charwoman, almost goes into a dream state to recall her inner life:

> (*The acoustic is hollow and suggestive of a dream.*)
> MRS. TRIMBLE: *Ah, it's a fearful thing when anyone gets the upper 'and of you, like Joe did of me. It all comes of beginning wrong. When we was first married . . .* (302)

She 'escapes' from her unhappy life by reliving her relationship with her dead husband over and over in her mind. Crushed by society like the individuals in Guthrie's plays, Sieveking's characters find solace only in introspection, the refuge for individual personality in the modernist's world.

WORDS AND A BOTANICAL ETHNOGRAPHY: THE DOCK PLANTS' MEANING

Don Howarth's play "On a Day in Summer in a Garden" (1975) illustrates the use of words and their narrative and dramatic functions in a play that delivers a pessimistic 'modernist' message about the relationship of individuals to their situation.

It does so by means of a 'postmodern structure' and mode of presentation—the central 'individuals' are conversational dock plants!

This is a play that could only be realized successfully through the medium of radio. Several generations of dock plants are threatened by a man using a herbicidal spray. The listener shares the suspense and fear as they watch and speculate about the man's movements, that finally leads to the gruesome death of "Uncle Jim." The other two plants, young Jack and Grandad (Dick), are saved by rain. However, in a satisfying twist of irony, spray blows back into the man's face and he dies horribly.

The narrative aspects of 'who' and 'where' are covered ingeniously in the opening section, which also uses sound effects:

> (*Birds: a dawn chorus.*)
> DICK: *Nice morning.*
> JIM: *Grand.*

Listeners may think that two old men are beginning a fairly typical conversation. This is a deliberate ploy to establish an expectation which is then challenged. Sound effects of bullocks lowing and sheep bleating establish a rural location before more information is given and 'Jack' is introduced:

> JIM: *Nippy, though.*
> DICK: *Morning mist. Morning mist and morning dew. Going to be hot today, young Jack.*
> JACK: *Is it, Grandad?*
> DICK: *When the sun strikes through on a hot day, early summer, there's no better thing to be in creation than a dock plant in this garden.*
> JIM: *Because we fear nothing.*
> DICK: *Correct.*
> JACK: *What is there to fear, Uncle Jim?*
> DICK: *Nothing.*
> JIM: *Encroachment.* (150)

This interchange immediately forces listeners to transform their images from a person to a plant. Listeners are immediately swept on by creating suspense (*i.e.,* suggesting Dick's rosy picture is false) and dramatic conflict (by having Jim contradict Dick). The identification of the characters and their relationships has been established quickly by the way they address each other—young Jack, Grandad, Uncle Jim. This is reinforced by the actors' voices. The two older characters are further identified as dock plants by the images that emerge in a humorous dispute about their appearance:

> DICK: *You're dusty, Jim, from towering against that wall. You're asymmetric.*
> JACK (*Making the peace*): *But he's quite tall, Grandad.*
> JIM: *Considerably taller than your grandad.*
> DICK: *He's got next to no leaf.*

JIM (ironically): And your grandad, Jack, has some lovely broad fronds.
DICK: I do at least look like a dock plant, not crawling up the wallside like the nettles. (109)

Because the dock plants don't understand human language, they hear the conversation of the play's other characters, Man and Woman, as gibberish:

(Country sounds. Fade. The voices of the man and woman are at a distance.)
WOMAN (asking a question): Hebble trebble babble settle?
MAN (replying): Base trough rough rass.
WOMAN: Hebble trebble ten.
MAN: Base trough.
JIM: He's going to the field. (110)

To the dock plants, who think they hold intelligent conversations, the exchanges between people are about as meaningful as the other sounds they hear in nature:

JACK: And the persons, grandad?
DICK: Much the same, I suppose.
JIM: Communicating.
DICK: But nothing precise. The bullocks low and the sheep bleat and the persons, one of them babbles and the other burbles. (110)

The dock plants see human behavior as strange. They theorize about human movement. So for instance, after observing an incident, they decide that humans move about to get out of the way of falling cowpats:

JACK: I was asking about the persons moving.
JIM: That's the explanation. They move so they don't get bogged on by the bullocks.
JACK: Perhaps that's why he closes the gate.
JIM: How?
JACK: So the bullocks can't follow him into the house and bog on him there.
(Distant lowing of bullocks. Sheep. Birds.)
JIM (suddenly and alarmed): Now that was the tank, that was his tank. Listen. (119)

Within seconds the plants' speculation changes into fear and suspense as sounds the older plants associate with the deadly spray tank are heard. This sequence marks the transition to tragedy and pathos as the dock plants watch other plants being destroyed and anticipate their own deaths. Accompanied by sound effects, the plants share a running commentary on what happens:

JIM: They're rising up into the sky like contorted worms, they're swelling like melons . . . Look at that, that chap writhing up, his head purple and orange and—oh, it's burst open. (125–6)

Through the plants' commentary and raised hopes listeners realize that the man gets spray blown all over him and that it is having an effect:

> DICK: *He's stopped. He's leaning against the house wall. His ears have gone purple.*
> JACK: *Ears?*
> DICK: *Those two fronds beside his head.*
> JIM: *They're always that colour.*
> DICK: *Not that deep tint, Jim. Not quite that hue. Look, his head's drooping, he's sagging.*
> (128)

Nevertheless, the man resumes his attack on the plants. They respond heroically, especially Grandad, who tries to encourage the others:

> DICK (*angrily at man*): *The bullocks will bog on you. We finished the old one off. Get back in your cold frame where you belong . . . Hold on, Jim. Keep your roots tight around the limestone.*
> JACK (*weakly and fading*): *The autumn, grandad, I've never seen an autumn, nor known a winter in the soil.*
> DICK (*Hoarsely and urgently*): *Jack. Jack..Jack. Rouse, lad, fight, hold on.* (129–30)

The 'when' aspect of this play is conveyed through the dialogue and deserves some comment. Unlike most radio plays, there are no flashbacks. The sense of the past life is created through the memories that the two older plants share with young Jack as they educate him. For example, a catalogue of plants that have encroached and been defeated conveys a sense of the intrepidity of the dock plants.

> JIM: *And when was the groundsel?*
> DICK: *And the tares and the dandelions.*
> JIM: *And the thistles and the treacle mustard.*
> DICK: *It's hard to remember what came in what year. We've choked them all in our time.*
> (106)

The plot moves in a linear fashion, even though the perspective is novel. It covers the space of a day, from early morning as the play opens to evening as the vehicle takes away the man's body:

> JACK: *So that's what's meant by taking him away in the vehicle, grandad.*
> DICK (*restored but tired*): *Honour's even at the end of the day.*
> JACK: *Quite a nice evening, grandad.* (134)

It is within this traditional time of reflection that young Jack tries to come to terms with the experiences of the day:

> JACK: *It's a pity then, isn't it, grandad—encroachment and the spray, Uncle Jim rotting there with his broken roots in the air and the person taken away in the vehicle.* (135)

Grandad doesn't have any answers, beyond something about it being "natural, inevitable." Nonetheless, the listener is drawn into their sense that something has been resolved and that it is, as Dick says, a "Nice calm evening."

Finally, it is night, signaled by the replacement of bird song by the hoot of an owl.

(Separate distant bird notes)
DICK: *Grand night.*
(*Owl Hoots.*)
DICK: *Grand night beneath the stars.* (135)

DAVID CREGAN: CONTEMPORARY SOCIAL ISSUES AND THE IMAGINATIVE USE OF THE MEDIUM

Most of David Cregan's protagonists are motivated by a quest that causes conflict in their own lives and threatens their families or challenges institutions. Individuals conflict with and within social structures, succeed as well as fail, and have more complex relationships with their social surroundings than is normally the case in 'modern' plays. Dramatically, the plays are strong on theme and characterization, but serious themes are often accompanied by comic treatment. What gives Cregan's plays their unique 'radio' dimension is their construction and use of language. His plays are postmodern in structure as well as in content and presentation.

Cregan's particular skill is to present plays that deal with contemporary social concerns. Their language, structure and imaginative use of the medium itself provide poetic dimensions. He began radio writing in the 1970s as an established playwright, after having had five plays produced at the Royal Court during the 1960s. Since then he has continued writing for the stage, television, and radio.

Two of Cregan's radio plays, "The Awful Insulation of Rage" (Sony Drama Script award, 1987) and "A Butler Did It" (Giles Cooper award winner, 1990), were directed by John Tydeman. The protagonist of "The Awful Insulation of Rage," Douglas Poole, is an artist at odds with society. His tension arises from being a successful church organist who is an atheist. His rage is directed against institutionalized art, religion and music and against mismanaged relationships with family and friends. The play provides insights into diverse perceptions about how the artist is regarded in contemporary society and uses music to provide a 'concrete' form of art that listeners can 'see'.

The overall structure pivots on an opening incident in which Douglas admits to Harold, Dean of the Cathedral, that he needs spiritual help. The succeeding scene in Harold's office, an equivalent of the confessional, takes up most of the rest of the play, as the present is interspersed with flashbacks to Douglas' schooldays. Harold serves as a Dante-esque guide through the often comic hell of Douglas' life as it is re-enacted and commented on throughout the course of the play. It proceeds beyond the end of Douglas's stint at the cathedral to the point where he is rumored to have been offered a similar post at Westminster Abbey—an ironic career 'success' given his antipathy and rage toward the Church.

The play has the satisfying circularity of starting in the present, going back in time and eventually coming forward again to the same point, plus a postscript regarding the protagonist's future. There is a similar sense of shape present in the internal structure of the play, which the author describes as a series of cocoons or brackets. These are related to the intricate way the narrative function is shared between the characters.

Structurally, the play moves from an outer bracket or cocoon (Harold's knowledge of Douglas from direct experience) to an inner bracket (Douglas's perception of himself and events affecting his family and career). Subsequently, Douglas's 'narrative control' is subtly handed over in flashback to his wife, Rosa, and to his son, Tom, who form the innermost bracket or core of the play. Then control returns to Douglas narrating more recent events up to the afternoon of the present crisis. This closes the inner bracket before Harold resumes the narration of what became of Douglas after that day. This technique provides a skillful form of suspense as characters refer, sometimes almost accidentally, to incidents that are fully explained later in the play.

The moment of exact return to the present is accompanied by a reprise of the Widor piece with which the play began:

(*THE DEAN'S ROOM*)
DOUGLAS: *And then I screamed, and you came by, and now—I'm going to resign.*

What has changed is Douglas' attitude. Calm decisiveness has replaced confused and frustrated anger. This can be seen as the equivalent of the spiritual calm following confession, penance and absolution.

Observations made by David Cregan about the creation and production of "Rage" add considerably to our insights. The protagonist was originally a German schoolmaster who lived on the Rhine. After hearing a public rehearsal of Tippett's "A Child in our Time" in St. Albans Abbey, where a former school associate of Cregan's was then Dean, the protagonist became an organist. The radio production involved a close collaboration with John Tydeman. Tydeman participated in the decision to have one of the characters shoot himself rather than commit suicide by an overdose. He was also involved in the decision to add the implication that Douglas got the job at Westminster Abbey. With these modifications the play had a tighter dramatic focus and enriched impact.

Both in script and on tape, "The Awful Insulation of Rage" has a riveting effect on its audience. Its language encompasses the range from crude realism to complex theological metaphor, often with devastating comic effect. Sound effects function naturalistically for the most part, only occasionally becoming subjectivized. Narration is used like a scalpel peeling away the layers of Douglas's personality and relationships. At the same time, however, the play's construction demonstrates that while his experiences are all interconnected, they may appear differently depending on the perspective of the character involved. Besides serving to advance the story, the music becomes an extension of characterization and frequently takes on a symbolic role. Because of its construction, characterization, use of language, music and sound, "The Awful Insulation of Rage" offers vivid commentary on the complex dilemmas and paradoxes faced by talented artists in late twentieth-century life.

A BUTLER TRIES SOME SOCIAL RESTRUCTURING

"A Butler Did It" was first broadcast on Radio Three on Tuesday, 31st July, 1990. It utilizes the murder mystery cliché to examine the motives and characterization of the Butler and explores the lifestyle illusions of his wealthy employer. The play's rich audio and verbal symbolism helps convey a subculture of family and social relations based on newly made wealth and highlights contemporary environmental and social concerns. They highlight the Butler's perceptions and motivations and help to create a complex and paradoxical relationship between him, his employment situation, and his employer. Unlike the complex narrative structure of "The Awful Insulation of Rage," Honeyman, the butler, provides the sole narrative perspective. Narrative tautness is provided through a concentrated, largely linear, time span, but repetition and variation are integral to the play's action. Honeyman's narration, an extended act of confession, demonstrates the director's control when Honeyman speaks directly to the audience and then makes explicit transitions between scenes to scenes at which he could not have been present.

Honeyman occupies an interesting place in David Cregan's gallery of artist-idealists. He has a profound admiration for those who can create music (56) and in a modest way, is a painter of miniatures himself (46). Yet he has chosen to live his life at second-hand, playing the role of a butler. This enables him to resolve two incompatible impulses. On the one hand, he is "deeply in love with the life of the very, very rich because it purchased so much culture." On the other hand, he feels "scorn and loathing for the way huge wealth was acquired, depressing humanity in general for the benefit of the few." Being a butler, "living well and taking no responsibility for it" (9), is the answer. It also meant having no sense of loyalty: "I felt no duty to my master and was prepared always, when the time came, to ditch him" (8).

This emerges in the course of flashback conversations with his brother Harry, a bank manager. Honeyman confides his potential power to expose huge financial corruption by killing his employer. Harry's shocked reaction—"Human life is sacred" (14)—is dismissed by Honeyman as evidence of loyalty being shown to the human race.

Honeyman's employer, Sir Desmond Lisle, is a very wealthy self-made industrialist. As head of a global business empire he is very wealthy but lacks security or confidence. Having a butler is one way in which he tries to bolster this image: "You can't be rich and powerful unless there's someone to be rich and powerful over" (6).

In a "confessional" scene where Honeyman is running a bath for him, Sir Desmond reveals that his life is a constant battle to keep his early origins in industrially polluted Stockport at bay. This is expressed in repulsive nature imagery: "Stockport was a mud pie of trolley trucks, and cobblestones, and greasy black sludge. It was as if a huge slug had crawled across the banks of the river and stopped, coughed and died" (24–25). Sir Desmond's revulsion at this background turns out to be ironic. After his death, Honeyman finds out that the Desmond business empire controls "half the world's agri-chemical businesses, chopping down the rain forests and doing naughties in the Thames" (54).

In retrospect, Sir Desmond's preoccupation with taking baths and with watering geraniums and begonias in his conservatory seems deeply ironic. The physical manifestations of wealth provide a bulwark against all that Stockport represents. These are summed up by his possessions: a country house in the south of England, "and the gardens in Salisbury, flowery cushioned ramparts against the oozing north of England" (25). The two central symbols of nature and of the family are seen throughout the play. Sir Desmond has a son, Alfred, a daughter, Samantha, who is married to Alastair, and a grand-daughter, Paula. Sir Desmond's family occupies a role in his world that is akin to his material possessions: "For me, money is the power that keeps Stockport at bay. And on Sunday I shall have my family about me for lunch in the country. That, Honeyman, is achievement—a big house in the southern counties and all my family about me" (25).

There is something of the grandiose naiveté of King Lear about Sir Desmond. He has been deluded into thinking that his family will play the roles he desires because of his material hold on them. The illusory nature of this view is first exposed when Sir Desmond and members of the family gather for a family tea. His daughter, Samantha, articulates it through parody and direct statement:

SAM: Our father, which art in the conservatory—
SIR DESMOND: Welcome to the simple pleasures, the country—
SAM: We're all so locked into your daydreams, father, that we almost don't exist. (8)

In trying to control the lives of his children and grand-daughter he has almost suppressed their individuality. Each is on the point of rebelling and none will attend lunch. But Honeyman does not tell Sir Desmond about this, and continues to prepare as director "the scenery for Sir Desmond's game of happy families" (16).

The irony of Sir Desmond's expectations is enhanced by the subject of a sermon he hears in Salisbury Cathedral and the disappointment he feels when immediately afterwards he returns home to realize that his illusion of a happy family is a total sham:

CLERICAL VOICE: The family, of course, is the centre of all Christian imagery and the image of the father bears the central weight of that great metaphor. As we all sit together

round our family dinner tables today, we should recall that we are part of one of the greatest and weightiest poems of social and religious significance . . .
SIR DESMOND: So where the bloody hell are they? (29–30)

Honeyman's comfortable pretense that he is part of the family is then put to the test. As compensation for failing to secure his employer's wishes, he is asked to attend lunch as a surrogate:

SIR DESMOND: You're part of the family, paid not to let me down.
HONEYMAN: But I'd be out of place!
SIR DESMOND: You'll be out of place if you don't do what I say. Sacked without a reference. (32)

For Honeyman this creates panic. He feels that his ambivalent relationship to his employer is being threatened:

Had I accepted my position as a parasite more completely than I thought? Was I truly part of the family now? (32)

Sir Desmond is so angry with his family for abandoning him that he confides to Honeyman and to Alastair, "I'm going to screw them" (43). Honeyman infers that this means the creation of a new will that will tie Sir Desmond's heirs to his business enterprises and prevent the exposure of corruption. He sees the removal of Sir Desmond as the only way to prevent this, a step that he can morally justify: "There's a certain saintliness in sacrificing a loved one, especially when it is so obviously done for the good of mankind" (46). In a scene that is initially reassuring, Honeyman cossets his employer. The listener begins to share Sir Desmond's curiosity as it becomes apparent that he is to be killed:

SIR DESMOND: What's that?
HONEYMAN: It's a very large, very powerful electric element from the hot water system of an expensive suite in a hotel I once worked in as a lad. Claridges, in fact.
SIR DESMOND: Is it plugged in?
HONEYMAN: Yes.
SIR DESMOND: What are you going to do with it?
HONEYMAN: I'm going to put it in the bath, like this.
(Suitable cries, then silence.)
HONEYMAN (VOICE-OVER) Not a mark on him. Such a simple pleasure for both of us: he, warm in his bath, I, warm in the sanctity of acting for mankind. (49)

Unfortunately, Honeyman's satisfaction doesn't last long. What he didn't know was that Sir Desmond has made a new will that was to be signed shortly. Had the will been signed, Sir Desmond's fortune would have gone to the Tate Gallery. The income from his family's shares would go to the National Theatre, and Honeyman would have been in charge of managing these operations on a salary of £60,000 a year.

The final irony for Honeyman is that his actions have failed to change anything. Honeyman becomes butler to Sir Desmond's son and draws a bath for him just as he did for his father. Before the heating element is introduced, Alfred comments on the vastness of the Lisle empire and its remoteness from its Stockport origins. He talks about the fact that it will "go on and on, controlling the status quo from no one quite knows where" (54).

> ALFRED: *What's that, Honeyman?*
> HONEYMAN: *It's a very large heating element from Claridges, Mr. Alfred. Would you just move your legs? Thank you.*
> (*DEATH SOUNDS AGAIN.*)
> HONEYMAN: *This could go on and on.* (55)

Honeyman's comment at the end of the scene illustrates his ironic awareness of his entrapment in a futile mission to destroy the Desmond empire by killing the surviving directors.

The irrelevance of who actually controls the business empire is borne out by the BBC announcement of Alfred's death. It stated that "shares in the Stockport and Eccles Building Society and Allied Southampton Construction remain unchanged" (55). What Honeyman has yet to learn is that there is no place for him in the family of which he saw himself a part. The new heir, Samantha, asks directly if he killed her father and brother and he replies by using the cliché as a way of deflecting the question: "I am the butler, and (*Laughing*), you know what they say about butlers" (56).

Honeyman is rejected by both Lisle women. Thus, his humiliation is complete: "Old-fashioned executioner of a modern monster that wouldn't, couldn't die . . . Oh dear, how small I was" (57). Seeking refuge with Alastair, Honeyman finds that this move has been anticipated by Harry, his one "real" family member. Consistent with his belief in the sanctity of human life, Harry has put this above loyalty to his brother and has called the police to arrest Honeyman for the murders.

At the end of the play, Honeyman is left reflecting on his inadequacy:

> *The empire born from Sir Desmond's simple fear of Stockport grows and grows, and floats above the globe, gobbling the ozone layer, killing Indians . . . It sheds compound interest on those who bow to it . . . Some other way than mine is needed to be rid of it* (60) . . . *I still don't quite understand about being out of date . . . such a patronising criticism . . . The monster cannot be allowed to become the master, can it?* (*end of radio version, 1990*)

If the play has ironic outcomes for Honeyman, the same can be said for Sir Desmond. His personal "fortress" against Stockport grows into a monster beyond any one individual's control. Whoever is at the top, in reality, is of as little consequence as a butler.

CONCLUSION

Early BBC radio plays reflected concerns typical of the modern period. In 1924, the harshness of industry was described in the first acknowledged radio play "Danger," which depicted a disaster in a Welsh coal mine (Hughes, 1924). The scourge of war, another vivid concern of the time, is the main theme of Captain Richard Berkeley's "The White Chateau," produced the following year. The helplessness of the individual in the face of social mechanisms, a classic concern of modernist literature, was featured in a variety of themes and contexts. Sieveking (1929) used the frustration of people doing mundane jobs as the pretext for exploring people's inner reality. Various works of Guthrie between 1929 and 1931, such as "Squirrel's Cage", "The Flowers Are not for You to Pick," and "Matrimonial News" symbolize this sense of individual inadequacy within a variety of social structures.

The plays by Guthrie and Sieveking that depict the repression of the individual by social mechanisms use a linear narrative structure well-suited to such a pessimistically determinist message. An extract from Howarth's 1976 play "On a Day in a Summer Garden" illustrates a world in which perspective is provided by several generations of dock plants in a garden—a postmodern method of presentation with a basically modernist, pessimistic message contained within a linear narrative structure.

The move to the postmodern approach is evidenced by the plays of the 1970s and 1980s. Examples that echo the concerns of more recent times are seen in David Cregan's "From a Second Home in Picardy" (1990), which is concerned with privacy and ecology, and "The Awful Insulation of Rage," (1987) which focuses on the return to religion, the role of the church, terrorism, the search for individual fulfillment, and redemption and suicide. These themes contrast with the modernist plays where values, other than the crushing of individual personality by society, are relatively trivial.

The theme change is matched by imaginative presentation and structuring. Cregan uses quest themes to explore the situation of the creative individual, and enriches his work with heightened language and poetic illusions. An especially vivid example of the blending of postmodern themes, (corruption, wealth and insecurity, ecology, concern with symbolism, building of personal relationships) with a postmodern presentational style is found in his "A Butler Did It" (1990). In this play a distinctive postmodern combination of individual optimism and global pessimism is found in the butler who, in an extreme act, kills his industrialist employer to effect what proves to be extensive but illusory change.

The complexity of the structure of Cregan's plays mirrors a greater degree of complexity in the relations between the individual and society than that found in earlier plays. Cregan's protagonists criticize, even tilt at, society, and may achieve a degree of satisfaction and even success. However, the ambiguity of the relationship between the individual and society, the apparent ability of the individual to effect unpredictable and often undesirable change, sometimes leads the dramatists back to a neo-modern subordination of the individual to the social context. For example, Cregan himself, in "The Monument," explores the eventual helplessness of the museum curator caught between the forces of the political right and the left. Perhaps most significant of all, Kavanagh's radio and TV play "The Spot FX Man," broadcast simultaneously in both media on the night of 18 December 1993, chronicles the suicide of the creative FX man faced with new technology and the pressures of the market that now infuse his organization. This play raises questions whether market-driven neo-modernism will stifle the creativity that has been emerging in radio drama during the last twenty years and lead to a return to plays with less creative structures and forms of presentation, and more easily accessible themes. We end with a caution about the future as 'market forces' to which the BBC is now exposed and which threatens to drive the medium back towards more pessimistic, neo-modernist, messages and forms.

BIBLIOGRAPHY

Ash, W. (1987) *The Way to Write Radio Drama,* London: Elm Tree Books.

BBC (1986) *Notes on Radio Drama,* British Broadcasting Corporation: Unpublished.

Beck, A. (1991) "Spot Effects", *Radio Quarterly,* June.

Berkeley, R. (1925) *The White Chateau,* Script in BBC Drama Script Library, Broadcasting House.

Cregan, D. (1975) *The Monument,* Author's audiotape of broadcast of 2/4/85.

Cregan, D. (1983) *Events in a Museum,* Author's television script and videotape.

Cregan, D. (1987) *The Awful Insulation of Rage,* BBC publication of script for the play's entry in the 1987 Prix Italia competition, and author's audiotape.

Cregan, D. (1990) *A Second Home in Picardy,* Author's typescript.

Cregan, D. (1990) *A Butler Did It,* Author's typescript and audiotape.

Cregan, D. (1988, 1993) Interviews with the author on 23 March 1988, 11 January 1993, 15 July 1993.

Crisell, A. (1986) *Understanding Radio,* London: Methuen.

Curtis, N. (1993) "Acting up a Storm on Air", *Media Guardian,* 26 April.

Eckersley, P. (1941) *The Power behind the Microphone,* London: Jonathan Cape.

Esslin, M. (1971) "The Mind as a Stage", *Theatre Quarterly,* 1, 3.

Guthrie, T. (1931) *"Squirrel's Cage" and other Microphone Plays,* London: Cobden and Sanderson.

Hawkes, T. (1977) *Structuralism and Semiotics,* London: Methuen and Co.

Hinchcliffe, A.P. (1977) *Modern Verse Drama,* London: Methuen and Co.

Howarth, D. (1976) "On a Day in Summer in a Garden", in J. Redmond and H. Tennyson, eds. *Contemporary One Act Plays,* London: Heinemann.

Hughes, R. (1924) *Danger,* Script in BBC Radio Drama Script Library, Broadcasting House.

Imison, R. (1965) "Drama at the BBC", *Plays and Players,* December.

Kavanagh, P. (1993) *The Spot FX Man* , BBC Radio and Television simultaneous transmission for "Arena Radio Night", 18 December.

Linklater, A. (1991) "Death in the Afternoon", *The Daily Telegraph Magazine,* 25 January.

McWhinnie, D. (1959) *The Art of Radio,* London: Faber and Faber.

Reynolds, G. (1993) "How Radio Puts TV to Shame", *The Daily Telegraph,* 24 July.

Reynolds, G. (1993) "How the Airwaves Are Making Waves", *The Daily Telegraph,* 20 September.

Reynolds, G. (1993) "The Night Radio Showed Its Face", *The Daily Telegraph,* 21 December.

Sieveking, L. (1934) *The Stuff of Radio,* London: Cassell and Co.

Smith, R.D. (1979) "One Grain of Truth", in P. Lewis, ed. *Papers of the Durham Radio Literature Conference, 1977* Durham University Printing Unit.

Warburton, N . (1986) "Hear This!" *Radio Times,* 5–11 July.

20

EYE OF THE CAMERA: AN EXPLORATION OF ORGANIZATIONAL LIFE AS PORTRAYED ON TELEVISION

Michèle A. Bowring

I examine two popular television shows, *The Mary Tyler Moore Show* and *Murphy Brown,* studying how issues such as gender, race, authority relations, leadership and sexuality are portrayed. By selecting programs set in different eras I could draw some parallels between both the portrayal of organizational life on television and the way in which it may (or may not) mirror changes in society.

INTRODUCTION

In May 1992, Murphy Brown, a character on a television comedy of the same name, gave birth to a son, and decided to keep the child, keep her highly demanding job as newscaster, and remain unmarried. The day after the episode was aired, Dan Quayle, then Vice President of the United States, spoke about the deterioration of family values, bemoaning the fate of an America where highly successful professional women were portrayed on television as 'mocking the importance of fathers by bearing a child alone and calling it another lifestyle choice' (Brooks, 1995).

The ensuing discourse involved additional comments on the subject by politicians making cameo appearances on the show as well as a riposte by the producer and by other members of the television community. Some focused on Murphy's actions and their potential effect on people who watched the program. Issues of free speech were countered by admonitions regarding the dire consequences of the 'liberal agenda' of some Hollywood filmmakers.

In contemporary America, popular culture, especially television, has become a vehicle for communication and connection, not only between producers and consumers of television shows, but between all members of that society. Mr. Quayle was speaking about a fictional character, and yet his speech engaged that character in debate about values he felt were important for America. While many ridiculed his speech, it was not discounted. And even though everyone knew that speech focused on a fictional character, it led to continued discussion and debate.

Television is a powerful medium. It connects millions of people, reaching a large proportion of the world population. Television is eclectic in its choice of subject matter, and, as the Murphy Brown episode illustrates, depictions of organizations and organizational life are watched by huge numbers of people on a regular basis. Television and its characters and programs have become a part of our cultural vocabulary.

This study represents one attempt at understanding the television portrayals of organizations and life within them, and what that means for the millions who watch every night and then go off to their individual workplaces the next morning. First, I look at the development of structuralism and the development of semiotics. Then, I examine how semiotics, in various incarnations, has been used to study texts. Wright (1975) and Barthes (1972) provide two examples of what Craib (1992) calls a structuralist method of inquiry. Barthes (1972) used semiotics to look at modern myths, and Wright (1975) used semiotics to analyze the structure of the Western movie. My use of semiotics attempts to separate the semiotic method from the structuralist metaphysical assumptions that underlie that method and then to integrate it with a more interpretive form of discourse analysis. This integration makes possible the analysis of television programs as texts mediated by a discourse grounded within the context of late-twentieth-century North American society.

SEMIOTICS

Semiotics is the study of signs with roots in the structuralist school of sociology—itself derived from functionalism (Maryanski and Turner, 1991). *Sign* is used to identify not only language but other forms of communication as well. Ferdinand de Saussure, one of the founders of linguistics, was interested in the way language develops over time. Semiotics then studies signs using methods that are analogous to the study of language (Craib, 1992). It is important distinguish between *parole,* or speech, and *langue,* or language as de Saussure did when he explained that language is the underlying structure that determines how we use speech. The object in semiotics is to discover the underlying structure that governs the use of these signs.

Functionalism uses an organismic metaphor to understand social structures. Specifically, 'sociocultural structures are analyzed with respect to their effects on the need states or requisites of the more inclusive system' (Maryanski and Turner, 1991:106). Durkheim emphasizes the problem of social integration and the mechanisms that meet this requisite. He proposes four types of such mechanisms: cultural, structural, interpersonal and cognitive. Durkheim's work falls into a social facts paradigm (Ritzer, 1992), and it describes ways of classifying social facts in terms of "their number, nature and their mode of combination" (Maryanski and Turner, 1991:107). He viewed structure as social morphology, and it is this concept that was used by both British and French structuralists in the development of their theories.

Of special interest to this study, however, is the development of the French structuralist school. In *Primitive Classification* (1903) Durkheim and Mauss emphasized the importance of mythology as an important source for decoding the structure of thought. Mental structures 'are composed of logical connections that reflect how material and cultural 'facts' are juxtaposed, merged, distinguished, and most important, opposed' (Maryanski and Turner, 1991:109). These structures enable us to see phenomena as part of a coherent, systematic whole.

Levi-Strauss pursued the notion of mythology making three important contributions (Silverstone, 1988): first, he identified myths as a basic element of culture; second, he pursued inquiries into the conditions that make myths possible, their significance, and their significance in and for the societies in which they are generated; and third, he suggested that myths are coherent and logical, even though they may at times seem implausible, and that they represent a culture thinking about itself.

This idea was taken up by Roland Barthes. According to Barthes, a text can be analyzed at three levels. First is the denotative level, which consists of signifier and signified. Second is the connotative level, which looks at what the text says *about* the matter to which it refers. Third is the way the text draws on complex cultural understandings or myths to support statements about the matter to which it refers (Phillips and Brown, 1993). In his *Mythologies* (1972), Barthes uses semiotics to analyze social phenomena of everyday French life, e.g., films, toys, striptease, cars, etc. Barthes ties each phenomenon to its history, reveals its structural components, and in the process creates a modern mythology of everyday life. In the second part of his book he reiterates Levi-Strauss' assertion that myth is "a system of communication, a message" (109). He further explains that myth cannot be an object, a concept or an idea, but must instead be a *form* of signification.

While Barthes' work is very important in semiotics, Will Wright's *Six Guns and Society* (1975) is more germane to my purpose. Wright uses Levi-Strauss's ideas regarding myths in a completely different way. He states: 'Levi-Strauss wants to discover the meaning of a myth in order to exhibit its mental structure, *while I want to exhibit the structure of a myth in order to discover its social meaning*' (1972:17, italics mine). In this he returns to Durkheim's conception of mythology, which saw the structure of the material world as influencing the development of its cognitive classifications.

For Wright, myths create a conceptual model of important social types of people that are located in a particular and complete social situation. The mythic action relates to the everyday social lives and actions of individuals. The members of a society interpret the narrative actions of their myths and their narrative structure (ibid.: 124). Such explanations help to explain how characters' actions are interpreted and how they create social situations that are desirable in everyday life of society.

Wright points out that the structure of a social myth must 'symbolically reflect the structure of social actions *as those actions are patterned and constrained* by the central institutions of society' (Wright, 1992:131, italics mine). To support this idea, he shows how the two major expressions of the Western myth correspond in time and structure to the periods of economic organizations present in pre- and post-World War II America. Thus, Wright says "the narrative form is maximumly meaningful" providing a far greater context of understanding than is possible in life itself.

There are both advantages and disadvantages to the structuralist method. According to Craib (1992:144–145), the advantages of this method include its ability to allow us to classify not just categories, but the relationships between them as well. By uncovering the rules we can identify stories that are similar even though on the surface they may seem quite different. By discovering the underlying structure of the Western, Wright is able to group together films that on the surface seem to have vastly different plots. Structure exists at several levels, and the analysis of underlying levels can yield insight into more then surface levels of structure. This contrasts markedly with the *functionalist* conception of structure, which only acknowledges one 'true' level of reality or structure. It gives us a way to analyze diverse elements of culture in the same way.

It is useful to be able to compare different elements of a culture, (e.g., books, stories, movies, ballet, etc.) in a similar fashion, to try to uncover they way they reflect the organizing principles of the culture within which they operate.

Craib points out that structural analysis cannot account for variations and change in the myth. The only way that Wright was able to account for the variation in the Westerns he studied was to go outside the Westerns to society itself although in a very limited way. Wright (1972:152) discusses the relationship between weak and strong in the Western, suggesting that if one were to substitute 'women' and 'men' for 'weak' and 'strong' we would have 'a fairly accurate account of the relations between men and women in American society, at least until the mid-fifties, when the classical Western began to disappear.' The actual landscape of the West was populated not only with white men, but also with women, black people, Native people, Hispanic people, etc. The absence of these other groups from the Western in itself bears investigation, since presumably they were as present in Western societies as they are today. This is what structuralist semiotics as a method 'on its own' does not provide.

When attempting to analyze a text from multiple perspectives, we turn to methods such as deconstruction, discourse analysis or semiotic discourse analysis (Manning and Cullum-Swan, 1994:470) as a way to interject history and context into semiotic analysis:

Meaning is derived from an understanding of social and cultural norms rather than from personal knowledge gained through reflexive communication with others. The purpose of such an analysis is to place signs in context with the relevant interpretants over time. This permits analysis of differential meaning by demographic features, such as gender, race and class, and by personal elements such as self, role relations and group membership.

In keeping with Wright's ideas that structure exists at many levels, my approach to 'semiotic discourse analysis' looks at both the surface and underlying levels of each television series. The unit of analysis is neither the individual scene nor the individual episode, but rather the whole body of work represented by each series. Television series develop over time. This important element of the series format gives the viewer an opportunity to become familiar with characters' personalities and their worlds. Further, this repetitive character allows producers freedom to deal with a multiplicity of issues or with a relatively small set of issues in different guises.

The purpose of the analysis is to understand the myths about organizational life that each series created or perpetuated at the time in which they were produced. This is driven by the assumption that these myths become part of the way that people make sense and give meaning to their own organizational lives.

AN EXAMPLE OF SEMIOTIC DISCOURSE ANALYSIS

Silverstone's (1988:20) work centers on the "character of television as text, as process, as mediator of reality." He begins by pointing out three ways in which television is like myth. First, television presents the content of myths. Second, it presents a communication that maintains a form of "familiar and formulaic storytelling that are the product of a significantly oral culture." Third, it uses its technology to create a distinct temporal-spatial environment which viewers are invited to enter and experience.

Like previous myth-producers, television is a source of popular entertainment available to most members of society and which reflects multiple facets of the society. Since the Enlightenment, Western culture has privileged the literary form. Nevertheless, both television and the movies are oral forms that have developed and gained great importance overtime. As McLuhan said, 'In television there occurs an extension of the sense of active, exploratory touch which involves all the senses simultaneously, rather than that of sight alone . . . Television demands participation and involvement in depth of the whole being' (McLuhan and Fiore, 1967:125). This is a most compelling reason for paying attention to what it says about organizational life.

Why compare two shows about newsrooms set in different times? Like Wright's westerns, these two shows are the *products* of two different time periods. Massive changes have occurred within the workplace between 1977 when *The Mary Tyler*

Moore Show (MTM) ended, and the time of *Murphy Brown* (MB). In 1977, downsizing, cutbacks, telecommuting, etc. were either nonexistent or had different connotations. Now, there are debates regarding the effectiveness, efficiency and even desirability of such programs as affirmative action, employment equity, and on-site day care to name a few.

If we accept the fact that television, as a producer of myth, presents us with a conceptual model of important social facts that are located in a particular and complete social situation (Wright, 1975), then we should also believe that the programs people watch on television must affect the way they feel and the way they make sense of what is happening around them. Zynda (1988:126) argues that MTM (along with *All in the Family* and *MASH*) represents "the watershed in American television." He explains that after the 'Golden Age' of the 1950s, when high-quality drama, variety and comedy shows appeared on the small screen, television production was taken over by the major studios. Production 'was rationalized in the form of the series, which, as the fundamental unit of television, gave programming the consistency and uniformity of any mass-market product.' (ibid.). He describes the effect on the product in this way: 'By the end of the 1950's, television had become an economic and organizational combine of the networks, the major studios, and the major advertisers, for whom ideal television was ideologically somewhere between Ozzie and Harriet (1952–1966) and the Donna Reed Show (1958–1966)' (126–127). From the 1950s to the early 1970s, television was intended to deliver consumers to advertisers and in large measure to avoid controversy. Between 1970 and 1972, the industry was transformed (Zynda, 1988). A series of small, independent producers bypassed the major studios and succeeded in establishing a presence on the air. They brought on board scriptwriters, actors, directors who were part of the first generation to have grown up with television, and who brought with them the social concern and independent spirit that had characterized that generation since their young adulthood in the 1960s. These people turned their television series, especially situation comedy, into arenas for the representation and discussion of the salient issues of that turbulent time.

MTM dealt with key issues of the time, chief among them the difficulty of being a young single woman brought up in the 1950s negotiating her way through the 1970s. MTM's pivotal role is demonstrated by the large number of papers and books devoted to an analysis of the show, its style and quality, its effect on subsequent situation comedies and dramatic series (Feuer, 1984).

In some way Murphy Brown is MTM of the 1980s. In both shows the workplace is central to the life of the main character and to the stories that they tell. MB, like MTM, generated critique as well as discussion in the press and other public arenas. In both shows the women are trying to negotiate life in uncertain times. Mary and Murphy were both brought up in worlds vastly different from the ones in which they find themselves, and each is constantly struggling with issues surrounding their work identity, their personal identity, their conflicting commitments, and most importantly, what it means to be a single working woman in contemporary Western society. This seemed eminently suitable to the task of deepening an understanding of how people make sense of their work lives.

SERIES SYNOPSES

MTM ran from September 1970 until September 1977. The main character, Mary Richards, had just arrived in Minneapolis after breaking up with her long-time live-in boyfriend, a medical student who reneged on his promise to marry her at the end of his studies.[1] She obtains a job at WJM, a local television station. Her title is 'Associate Producer', although it is a long time before she actually gets to produce anything.

The series centers around Mary's life with an ensemble of characters that include her co-workers Murray Slaughter, the station newswriter, and Ted Baxter, the anchorman for the six o'clock news. Murray is happily married and a very experienced competent newswriter. Ted is a pompous, ineffectual newscaster who can barely get through each show without mispronouncing or misstating something. Mary's boss, Lou Grant, is a 'gruff but lovable' experienced newsman. During the first few seasons Lou is married to Edie but they later divorce. Lou is called 'Lou' by everyone who works at WJM except Mary. She can never bring herself to call him anything but 'Mr. Grant'.

Mary lives in a bachelor apartment in an old house where the landlady Phyllis, happily married wife of dermatologist Lars Lindstrom, visits frequently, as does Mary's best friend Rhoda Morgenstern who lives upstairs. Other occasional cast members include Sue-Ann Nivens, the sex-starved single host of "The Happy Homemaker" show at WJM, and Georgette Baxter, Ted's wife in later episodes.

Some of the recurring themes include Ted's ineptness as a broadcaster, Rhoda's obsession with being overweight and finding a boyfriend, and Mary's inability to find a 'nice guy' to date.

MB has been running since November, 1988. Its main character, Murphy Brown, is the star reporter of FYI, a successful weekly TV newsmagazine series. When the series starts, FYI had been running for twelve years, and Murphy had just returned from a stint at the Betty Ford Clinic, where she had undergone treatment for alcoholism. In contrast to Mary Richards, who was very sweet and pleasant, Murphy is opinionated, sarcastic, egotistical and overbearing. She is also dedicated, hard-working, and has a strong sense of ethical obligations as a newscaster.

---

[1] Interestingly, in the initial script, Mary was supposed to be recently divorced. However, CBS decided that the actress, Mary Tyler Moore, was so strongly identified with Laura Petrie, the role that she had played opposite Dick van Dyke on *The Dick van Dyke Show,* that people might mix the two of them together. They were afraid that the show would be ill-received if people thought that Mary Richards had divorced Rob Petrie, an unthinkable occurrence in that particular television world. However, in order to explain the fact that Mary was thirty and yet unmarried, they agreed to the live-in boyfriend, even though that was considered risqué for television at the time.

Murphy lives in an attractive townhouse in Washington, and drives a Porsche. She shares the FYI spotlight with Jim Dial, Frank Fontana, and Corky Sherwood. Jim is a veteran newsman, who takes his work seriously and is fond of quoting Edward R. Murrow. He is seen as humorless, and he is the 'adult' of the anchor team. Jim and his wife Doris are very happily married, the only long-term couple in the cast. Frank is FYI's investigative reporter, known for the perilous ordeals he has endured in pursuit of stories. Corky Sherwood is an ex-Miss America, invited to join FYI on the strength of her looks and perkiness, but with very little knowledge of reporting. She married writer Will Sherwood (becoming Corky Sherwood-Forrest, much to Murphy's amusement), although they divorced after Will's first novel became a best-seller and he was invited to Hollywood to write the screenplay for the screen adaptation.

Murphy's boss is FYI's executive producer Miles Silverberg. At the start of the series Miles is a 25-year old Harvard MBA who knows nothing about the news or television business. Miles is younger and less experienced than the rest, and his neuroses keep the manufacturers of stomach remedies in business. A regular character who left the series in 1994 was Eldin Bernecky, who started out as Murphy's house painter, and stayed on as painter, confidante and best friend outside of FYI. When Murphy's son Avery was born in 1992, she despaired of finding a suitable nanny, until Eldin agreed accept the job. Eldin is as comfortable on a motorcycle as in a nursery, a real 90's man.

Who Do We See In These Two Shows?

Mary Richards is every-working-woman. She is middle class, works in a middle-class job with middle-class people and friends. Mary is representative of a large group of women who were faced with her choices and her situation in the 1970s. As such she is a familiar figure, and her apartment, clothes, and lifestyle signify normalcy and everyday life. She is always stylishly dressed albeit in very sensible and everyday clothes. None of the characters are glamorous, and most of them are of medium or heavy build. Almost the entirety of Mary's apartment is visible to the audience. She sleeps on a pull-out couch and cooks in a galley kitchen. Her identity is emphasized by a large 'M' hanging on the wall.

In contrast, Murphy Brown is the exceptional woman. MTM may have given us the promise that every woman could be successful,[2] and that the workplace could be a better place. But MB shows us that success comes at a price, and is reserved for the selfish, the pushy and the relentlessly driven. Murphy is a star anchor, Corky is a former beauty queen, and Frank jumps out of helicopters under gunfire to get his stories. The MB characters are sleek and svelte, they live and dress expensively. Murphy lives in a large townhouse, wears designer clothes and drives

---

[2]The theme song is titled "Love is All Around", and ends with the line "You're gonna make it after all."

an expensive car. She can afford a nanny and gets invited to White House balls. Her identity is proclaimed in her office, where the walls are covered with pictures and magazine covers of Murphy on assignment or receiving awards.

It would be easy to explain the differences by pointing out that the two characters work for radically different kinds of news shows. It is important to understand, however, that the producers of these shows *chose* these vehicles for their characters. Taylor (1989) has argued that during the 1970s the television family was not immune from outside conflict. She contends that the television family moved from the home to the workplace in response to the perceptions that the family home was being attacked by outside forces and torn with inner turmoil. This is certainly borne out in the relationships that Mary and the rest of the characters have on MTM.

MTM reflects many of the societal values that existed during the 1970s. Concern for others, a belief that "we're gonna make it after all" permeated both the political and social landscape *and* television shows such as MTM. But, the political environment of 1988 was more conservative than that of 1972 and the promises of the 1970s seemed unfulfilled. Stories about making money through real-estate flipping, junk-bond trading and other dubious practices filled the news. MBA enrollment reached unprecedented heights and the boom was in full swing as people looked to business and business practices for a better way of life. The ensuing economic downturn, and the effect of downsizing, cutbacks and rationalization on employees doesn't seem to be reflected in shows such as MB, which continue to portray the lives of the exceptional.

Gender and Race Roles in the Series

In comparing roles that each character plays in MTM and MB, we can see that the bosses are men. Although Lou and Miles are different types of leaders, they are clearly in charge. In one episode of MB there was a female vice-president, but she didn't last very long.

This is not to say that the types of women depicted in the two series are the same. In MTM, Mary's expertise is initially limited and Mary's work, although important, is not portrayed as central to her existence in the same way that Murphy's is. At first Mary is really a secretary, and she eventually becomes a producer only through her persistence in learning the business and finally by persuading Lou to give her a chance to prove herself. Murphy on the other hand is portrayed as a seasoned professional journalist from the very start.

Almost all the regular players in both series are white although MTM's weatherman (recurring, not regular, role) was black. The same can be said of MB, which, although it is accused of being part of a 'liberal Hollywood agenda' rarely tackles the issue. The sole exception is an episode that dealt with the FYI team's reaction to a new station owner who wanted to effect some changes. The episode recounts Murphy's horror at discovering that she treats him differently because he is black and she is most surprised of all when the new owner eventually points out that his being black is affecting her behavior towards him. While in Murphy's case this means that she is nice to him rather than nasty, she had always believed she was prejudice-free, and is appalled at her differential behavior.

Sexuality in the Series

At the time of the show's first run, sexuality and Mary Richards seemed almost incompatible. Mary was the girl next door, attractive, funny, and a host of other wonderful things, but she rarely kissed anyone on the show, much less had any sexual liaisons. She has a sexual history, but it is background noise that disappears over the course of time. Although Mary is still looking for Mr. Right, she doesn't participate in the sexual discourse of her time. Interestingly, Sue-Ann Nivens, the middle-aged hostess of the Happy Homemaker Show, exemplifies the opposite end of the sexual spectrum. In constant pursuit of sexual adventures, she is at the forefront of the sexual revolution. She's not looking for Mr. Right, just Mr. Sexually Available. But her interest in sex and pursuit of men are ridiculed by the WJM employees. Lou, who is her contemporary, has several liaisons after his divorce from Edie, while Ted, close to Lou in age, marries a younger woman and has a child, yet these are presented as legitimate occurrences. Sue-Ann however, as a middle-aged woman, is not supposed to have sexual feelings or relationships.

At the start of MB, Murphy is nearing her fortieth birthday. There is no question that her sexuality is part of her personality. During the course of the series she has several liaisons and yet she is close to Sue-Ann Nivens' age. Although she's had sexual adventures in the past, within her new-found sobriety sexuality is usually contained within relationships. The notable exception is a brief fling with her ex-husband, the result of which is a pregnancy at the age of forty-one. Clearly, there are consequences to having sex incautiously.

The Leadership Discourse

Both news teams have very effective leaders. Mary's boss, Lou, is a parental figure who rules through authority. He and Mary have a father/daughter relationship, extending the family in the workplace metaphor. Lou's authority and credibility are based on his experience as a newspaperman. It is his long career in newspapers that provides him with a great deal of legitimacy. In an episode when Mary has problems falling asleep, it is Lou who stays up with her until she falls asleep without using sleeping pills. When Murray needs advice or when Ted gets out of hand, Lou is there to put things right.

In contrast, Miles's effectiveness comes from his ability to negotiate his stars' egos, and to threaten, cajole and bribe them into doing his bidding. Given the absence of experience, his authority comes from his Harvard MBA. Murphy comes to grudgingly respect Miles for his ability to get things done, but the news team's acceptance of his authority is constantly negotiated and at risk of dissolving.

These divergent views of leadership are consistent with perceptions of the usefulness of experience and management education respectively, in middle-management positions. Lou is part of the existing generation in which experience is the proof of eligibility for advancement. During the 1970s a record number of baby boomers had gone to college but had yet to make their mark on organizational management practices. By the time MB started, however, these same people were beginning to face plateaus in their advancement up the corporate ladder. Experience gave way to professional management education as the ticket to the upper-management ranks, coinciding with an increased turn to professionalism in the work arena. In MTM's time, experience alone could open doors. Managing employees was seen as skill that was developed over time. Today, it is most often seen as an expert skill, acquired through MBAs, management training seminars and other educational avenues. It is also seen as a portable skill needed to navigate today's uncertain and unstable career paths.

The Teamwork Discourse

One of the most interesting contrasts between the two shows comes from the teamwork discourse. During the time that MB has been on the air, teams and teamwork have become increasingly important in organizational life. FYI's organization as a news *team* is an example of that concept. Yet, a deeper examination of the series reveals that the FYI anchors are a team in name only. Each is willing to go to some lengths to get a story, even if it means taking it away from one of the others. They are unable to share airtime and credit without Miles's sometimes heavy-handed intervention. In one episode they were invited to receive a team-based broadcasting award at a public function. When they attended the awards ceremony and were asked to answer questions from the audience, they began fighting over who would answer, until Murphy simply grabbed the microphone and started speaking. The inability to share and the desire to get a story at any cost are recurring themes in this series.

In contrast, even though MTM was produced before the teamwork discourse had become part of organizational life, the WJM news people work as a team, even though they don't formally identify themselves as one. When Ted makes a mistake, as he often does, the rest of the crew cover for him. When Murray works at a second job so that he can buy his wife a new car, Mary covers for him by proof-reading his copy. Murray helps Mary to develop her skills as a newswriter, and helps her produce her first show.

The Management Relations Discourse

One of the things that MTM and MB do share is the opposition that exists between upper management and the rest of the employees within their respective organizations. The network owners in MB are seen as money-grubbing and indifferent to journalistic principles if they cost too much. In one episode, FYI was preparing to do an exposé on tobacco companies. After the legal department told Stan Lansing, the owner, that the network could be sued for millions if the story airs, he cancels it. The news anchors and Miles are unanimous in their disgust, and Jim eventually resigns over this issue, after persuading Murphy not to do the same. This is just one example of the disregard in which upper management is held. In another episode seven vice-presidents show up to examine the office as part of an attempt to increase profits by recommending the elimination of some positions. They (and most other upper managers) were portrayed as bumbling fools, who knew nothing about the news business. Their plan was thwarted when the FYI group pointed out to them how much more money could be saved by cutting highly paid vice-presidents rather than lower-paid employees.

The same kind of relationships between the station owners and the news staff was portrayed on MTM. When writers and other production staff go on strike, Lou and Mary, as management, must come in to ensure that the news will be broadcast. The episode deals with Mary's unhappiness at having to cross a picket line, and with the difficulty that she and Lou experience in putting on a show without the professionals who normally do the work. It is clear, however, that Lou and Mary are understanding of the strikers' position, and that they feel a solidarity that goes beyond their management/non-management classifications. The ultimate expression of the absurdity of upper management is demonstrated in the show's final episode. The station is bought by new owners, who fire everyone except Ted, the most inept of them all.

The Family/Work Balance Discourse

By the end of MTM's run, every one in the ensemble was married except for Mary. The married people were seen as being happy in their roles as spouses, parents and employees. As much as Mary's inability to find a suitable partner may have been part of the show's formula, it was problematic for her. She wonders why, and so do the viewers, for she has no faults so obvious that they preclude her finding a suitable spouse.

In contrast, Jim Dial is MB's only happily married character. Key here, however, is the fact that Jim is also the only person on the show who is content. Murphy was once married briefly and has several opportunities to marry again, but she decides that she is happier remaining single. Frank is terrified at the prospect of commitment of any kind, and Corky's first marriage to Will falls victim to their competing careers. Her second marriage, to Miles, is highly unconventional. After dating for a while they marry and regret it instantly, feeling that they are not ready for such a commitment. Although they remain married, they continue to live separately without consummating their marriage, all the while working on getting to know each other well enough to assume the trappings of 'authentic' marriage conventions such as living in the same house, having sex, and sharing their lives.

DISCUSSION AND IMPLICATIONS FOR ORGANIZATIONAL STUDIES

On a theoretical level, we have seen that discourse analysis can enrich a semiotic analysis. By looking at these series, both set in the workplace, we have been able to counterpose the ways in which certain issues were addressed. By exploring the social and cultural context of the programs we have gained greater insights into the myths offered by television. Further, we have seen how some of these portrayals of organizational life mirror changes in society and in organizations over time, while others do not.

We can compare some of the significant issues as follows in Table 20.1. Are these recipes for success in the workplace, or are they merely reflections of the status quo? The purpose of this chapter is not to make value judgments, but rather to illuminate key issues. I am not arguing that these are the only interpretations of the two series in question. Rather, I am suggesting that these series, at the height of their popularity, attracted millions of viewers over long periods of time. They continue to do so, both in prime-time and in syndication. People watch them, and then go off to work. Surely they must draw some parallels and have some expectations of work based on what they see on television.

The important difference between the two series is that MTM was about ordinary people, and could thus provide the "social situations that are desirable in the

Table 20.1. Comparative Myths

Myths Articulated in the *Mary Tyler Moore Show*	Myths Articulated in *Murphy Brown*
If you work hard and get along, you'll "make it after all."	To get ahead you must be driven, pushy, and egotistic.
Coworkers are like family, they cover for and help other coworkers.	Coworkers are friends, but don't let that get in the way of getting ahead.
Marriage and work are not necessarily mutually exclusive.	Marriage and work don't usually mix.
Go home at the end of the day.	Work is always a priority.
Everyday people are worth your attention.	The only people who really count are the exceptional ones.
Experience is the best teacher.	Experience is not as important as education and innovation.
Upper management doesn't understand the important things about this organization.	Upper management doesn't understand the important things about this organization.

everyday life of the members of society" that Wright discussed, while MB is about the exceptional and the extraordinary. While it can be said that watching MTM could help viewers make sense of their working lives, what does MB help them make sense of? Is it an accurate portrayal of organizational life today, a cynical exposé of its warts, or a cleverly crafted parody of a work culture that has come to value the professional over the personal, individual gain over collaboration, and success at almost any price? Whichever it is, it is clear that the representations of organizations that we see on television become part of our work vocabulary, and part of our own expectations about working life.

BIBLIOGRAPHY

Barthes, R. (1957) *Mythologies,* trans. A. Lavers. London: Jonathan Cape.

Brooks, T. (1995) *The Complete Directory to Prime-time TV Shows: 1946 to Present,* New York: Ballantine Books.

Craib, I. ed. (1992) *Modern Social Theory: From Parsons to Habermas,* 2nd ed., New York: St. Martin's Press.

Feuer, J. (1984) "The MTM Style" in J. Feyer, P. Kerr and T. Vahimagi. eds., *MTM: Quality Television,* London: British Film Institute.

Durkheim, E. and M. Mauss (1903) *Primitive Classification,* London: Cohen and West.

Maryanski, A. and J.H. Turner (1991) "The Offspring of Functionalism: French and British Structuralism" *Sociological Theory* 9, 1, Spring, 106–115.

McLuhan, M. and Q. Fiore (1967) *The Medium is the Message,* Toronto: Random House.

Phillips, N. and J. Brown. (1993) "Analyzing Communication in and Around Organizations: A Critical Hermeneutics Approach" *The Academy of Management Journal,* 36, 6, 1547–1576.

Ritzer, G. ed. (1992) *Contemporary Sociological Theory,* 3rd ed., New York: McGraw-Hill.

Silverstone, R. (1988) "Television Myth and Culture" in J.W. Carey, ed., *Media, Myths, and Narratives: Television and the Press.* Newbury Park, CA: Sage.

Smith, D.E. (1992) "Sociology from Women's Experience: A Reaffirmation" *Sociological Theory,* 10, 1, Spring, 88–98.

Taylor, E. (1989) *Prime-time Families: Television Culture in Post-war America,* Berkeley: University of California Press.

Wright, W. (1975) *Six Guns and Society: A Structural Study of the Western,* Berkeley: University of California Press.

Zynda, T.H. (1988) "*The Mary Tyler Moore Show* and The Transformation of Situation Comedy" in J.W. Carey, ed., *Media, Myths, and Narratives: Television and the Press.* Newbury Park, CA: Sage.

21

EURO DISNEY: A CROSS-CULTURAL COMMUNICATIONS FAILURE?

Janet L. Hamnett

Euro Disney provides an excellent opportunity to analyze the export of a 'produced' culture—an iconized American theme park—into a European culture. In this chapter, the history of amusement parks, the phenomenon of culture and its production, and the physical environment in relation to managed landscapes and spectacles are explored. While cultural, historical and geographical arguments are supported, other criteria such as competition, organizational change, global uncertainty and market chaos also have affected Euro Disney's viability. In the final analysis, the issue of landscape used as spectacle—theme park development—may prove the most important issue raised.

> "Everything in the world has turned to show business."
> Felix Rohatyn

> "There is no public spectacle without violence to the spirit."
> Tertullian

INTRODUCTION

Cross-cultural communication varies in form from simple face-to-face encounters between members of different cultures to more mediated forms of encounter via television or the Internet. Cultural artifacts have been circulated and exchanged, first locally and now internationally. One form of cultural encounter, only recently explored in detail, is the 'theme park' (Richards, 1990, Wilson, 1991, Weinstein, 1992). King (1991:24) has noted, "theme parks serve as modern museums and history parks, doing even better than museums at spreading knowledge, inciting pleasure, and stimulating curiosity."

The best known of today's theme parks are those developed by the Disney Corporation. With the exception of Euro Disney, their theme parks have been unqualified successes.

The common assumption is that a serious judgment error in cross-cultural communications was a primary reason for Euro Disney's failure. This assumption is based, in part, on well-documented anti-American sentiment throughout Europe and especially in France.

To look deeper into this question I examined three issues: the history of fairs, amusement parks and exhibitions; the physical environment in relation to managed landscapes and spectacles; and the phenomenon of cultural production and exportation. While others have examined each of these issues separately, few have attempted to incorporate all perspectives in their studies of Disney.

Beginning with early mobile European fairs and markets, and becoming increasingly sophisticated over the past three hundred years, simple fairs and pleasure gardens evolved into the extravagant theme parks of the late twentieth century. Within its own unique history, Euro Disney is a complex entity operating within a number of contexts that include the physical, economic, ethical and aesthetic. Here I take the view that social phenomenon, human dilemmas, and the nature of specific cases are situational and thus influenced by happenings of many kinds (Denzin and Lincoln, 1994). That is, the events affecting Euro Disney are neither simply nor singly caused.

The Issue of Temporary vs. Permanent

Land use for the purpose of spectacle or event is the subject of ongoing environmental and philosophical debates which argue their legitimacy (Wilson, 1991). The evolution of the modern theme park from the temporary carnival or fair site in medieval times, which could be set up in a small plot of land, to the construction of huge and elaborate permanent structures like the Crystal Palace in the latter part of the nineteenth century, and finally, the modern theme park which may encompass hundreds of landscaped acres, is also a study of the increasing demand for space.

These issues have become particularly important in the wake of global efforts on the part of environmentalists and preservationists alike to educate the world about the fragility of our planet, the reasons it has become so, and how we can ensure its survival.

EURO DISNEY IN CONTEXT

Fairs where people gathered to trade, sell animals, and watch traveling entertainers can be traced to Roman times. Over the centuries, as roads and technology improved, the combination of commerce and entertainment grew into larger-scaled traveling shows with side shows, menageries and elaborate rides. The discovery of electricity literally lit up the skies and revolutionized the rides (Ware, 1977). During the Victorian Age in Britain, the Industrial Revolution and an aura of optimism culminated into the Great Exhibition of 1851. The mere existence of the Crystal Palace where the exhibits were housed was reassuring. Those who entered were filled with a sense of wonder at its unparalleled size and mystery as they gazed upon the awe-inspiring exhibits representative of modern technology within its glass and iron structure. In their minds there was no doubt that material progress would continue forever (Bird, 1976). The Palace enshrined the era's technological progress amid its slums, poverty and social indifference.

Although public exhibitions were not new, the Great Exhibition of 1851 was done on a scale previously unknown and was the first to be profitable. For the most part the public's main attraction was the Crystal Palace. But, once the Exhibition was over, interest waned as the structure became less fashionable and shabby over time. The Tivoli Gardens in Copenhagen, Denmark, on the other hand, was also created during the same period, yet it was designed from its inception as a permanent place of leisure. It is as popular today as in the 1850s and provides an attractive place of entertainment, recreation and relaxation for residents and visitors alike.

By the twentieth century, amusement parks like Coney Island in the United States had evolved into big businesses even though the entertainment was termed 'vulgar' by high culture critics. Along with this development, the public's taste has shifted more dramatically in the last two decades than in the entire century. We consume ever-repetitive and imitative images at a previously unknown rate (Twitchell, 1992).

Spectacles: Articulating Culture

Pred (1991:45) discusses articulation of culture in the form of modern spectacles as "a space designed to manufacture all consuming desires, ideologically melting together messages of nationalism, progress and consumption." He emphasizes that to create articulation either culturally, linguistically or physically, elements that are otherwise discrete and separate must be united by physically connecting them. In other words, the physical landscape utilized for a structural fantasy like Disneyland becomes the catalyst that assists the imported icon to become a permanent reality over time.

On the other hand, Ley and Olds (1988) argue that these kinds of spectacles impose hegemonic meaning and are instruments of hegemonic power used to foist the values of an elite on mass publics within a "domain of the spectacle" (Ley and Olds, 1988:191). They contend, however, that consumers of spectacle have the capacity to resist such domination. Debord (1992) discusses spectacle as society itself where all attention and consciousness converges into a locus of illusion and false consciousness, or as "a social relationship between people that is mediated by images" (Debord, 1992:2).

Barrett (1979) refers to culture as a socially and historically situated process for the production of meanings. Thus the relationship between the material conditions of existence and the process of producing meanings within it is the production of culture. Bourdieu (1993) first turned his attention to the field of cultural production in the 1960s. Since then, he has developed a theory that analyzes produced culture, such as Euro Disney, within the space of available possibilities and historical context. This is also related to the producers', critics' and consumers' individual biases and expectations.

Smoodin (1994) refers to Louis Marin's 1977 analysis of Disneyland as 'degenerate utopia,' yet at the same time, discusses Disney's importance in relation to its film, television and theme park connections to urban planning, ecological politics, technological innovation, and the construction of national character.

Twitchell (1992) claims that global organizations like Disney repetitively produce and exhibit that which they don't understand until they saturate the market and the point is reached when nobody wants to participate in them any more. He also cites modern American popular culture as a global culture of the free market. In other words, Disney along with other American television programs, Levis, hamburgers and verbal slang can be seen and heard from Moscow to Paris.

The Dawn of a New Era for Euro Disney, or its Demise?

Given the history of amusement parks, culture production and exportation, and the physical environment, the notion that Euro Disney is a cross-cultural communications failure is extremely puzzling. In Paris, in 1989, cynics dubbed the planned Euro Disney a "cultural Chernobyl" and pelted Michael Eisner with eggs (Jenshell, 1994). By 1992 the French were still asking "what's the point?" Perhaps Disney has been overly optimistic in its belief that the Disney concept can be successfully exported anywhere in the world.

In 1992, George Will used the opening of Euro Disney to criticize unnamed European left wing intellectuals who rail against cultural homogenization. He emphasized the stabilizing effects of the Disney product on an unreliable continent, stating that "for modern Europe, with its history of pogroms, national socialism and Nuremberg rallies, Mickey Mouse is a giant step up" (Smoodin, 1994:5).

A French President, Phillippe Bourguinon, now presides over Euro Disney. A Saudi Prince has injected $500 million into the ailing Magic Kingdom, and a new marketing campaign has been implemented to build the re-named Disneyland Paris into a predominantly European rather than American experience. Attendance is up, expenses are down, and management remains optimistic about Euro Disney's long term viability.

The most interesting critique of Euro Disney may not be to lament an international popular culture controlled by the United States. The Disney company is not simply inflicting American mythology upon the unwitting masses. In this case,

French management is using Disney to re-create its own nationalistic fantasy re-calling a glorious era of France's imperialist past.

INTERPRETATIONS

"All generalizations are false."
Victor Hugo

Walt Disney was determined to create more than just a conventional amuse-ment park and he extended his vision to create a unique entertainment experience in which guests would be both spectators and participants. Over one billion peo-ple have visited a Disney park since the first one opened in Anaheim, California. From his apartment above Main Street in the Anaheim Disneyland park, Walt Dis-ney said: "I don't want the public to see the world they live in while they're in the park. I want them to feel they're in another world" (Wilson, 1991:158). As such, the Disney parks idealize American culture as pure, clean, economically superior, historically romanticized and always progressive.

Disney himself carried on and expanded the legacies of those who, in the nine-teenth century, combined business with spectacle. Disneyland pays homage to the possibility of the future as an extension of the gigantic public spectacles of the last century like the Chicago Columbian Exposition of 1893. These spectacles cele-brated, and continue to celebrate, the apparently endless possibilities of technol-ogy, which invoke awe and create amazement and even horror.

In the past few years, however, the amusement park business has become a mat-ter of spills and thrills. As Michael Eisner has proclaimed the 1990s the Disney decade, it may become a decade of crisis as the enterprise attempts to adapt and profit from the uncertainties of a cultural and economic situation that not even Walt Dis-ney could have predicted: "If there's one thing Disney has learned about the theme park business, it's that tomorrow doesn't look like it used to" (*Newsweek,* 1994:43).

The Disneyland Parks harken back to simpler times. From an ideal perspective, park 'guests' are transported to a clean and safe environment where entire families can be amazed, excited, and have fun together. In this sense, the Disney Parks ap-pear to be innocuous, isolated, harmless pleasure havens for those who have the inclination and the price of admission.

The history of amusement parks supports the notion of constant evolution dic-tated by changes in technology, the environment, and consumer taste. We are ex-periencing a technological explosion which shows signs of continuously accelerat-ing. As consumers we are bombarded by the rapid introduction of new choices, gizmos and spectacular experiences. To further this end, the theme park industry at large has adopted and replicated Disney prototypes throughout the world. They exist everywhere with many more in the planning stages.

The element of proliferation alone is a serious problem for Euro Disney. And it is not so much a cross-cultural issue, but rather, one of saturation and competition. How many of these forms of leisure can be supported by the public? And can they continue to re-create themselves as the public becomes bored with them?

It may be that American culture is already a world culture. Its infiltration and pervasiveness through the world's mass media communications channels transcend global boundaries and Disney, much like Coca Cola, is now a fixture of everyday international life.

Much of the initial coolness directed at the Euro Disney theme park has dissipated. Attendance is up, and in fact, is the highest for theme parks across Europe. Euro Disney management credits its French management team for innovations such as lower prices, and European, especially French, traditions like the availability of alcoholic beverages as reasons for the turnaround. The Park is also becoming a visible sponsor and host to many high-profile French community projects, from serving underprivileged children to community bicycle marathons.

CONCLUSIONS

At the outset of this research project, we assumed that, in the context of well-documented and historical anti-American sentiments which exist in France, the major problems associated with Euro Disney's struggle for survival were related to cross-cultural communications rather than financial disasters. Upon closer investigation, however, Disney as popular culture has been successful with the masses, in spite of negative media reports and the loud lambastes from France's intellectual elite, over the past nine years. Thus, these assumptions were not wholly supported within the confines of this exploration. While cultural, historical and geographical arguments are realized, other environmental criteria such as competition, organizational change, global uncertainty and market chaos certainly impact Euro Disney's viability as well.

In fact, Disney has influenced the theme park industry throughout Europe. It appears that the theme parks are throwbacks to the early fairs and carnivals from which they emanated. Theme park attendees across Europe, and, in fact the world at large, are as enamored of this form of leisure as their American counterparts.

It appears that Disney may have created a Frankenstein monster. The issue of Euro Disney is not solely a cross-cultural problem. Although cross-cultural issues do exist there are broader and more important aspects which should be addressed in relation to the ballooning numbers of global theme parks in place now, and those that are in the planning stages.

The issue of land use as spectacle was explored, from both environmental and philosophical perspectives, as it relates to the permanency of theme park structures. Globally, the trend in theme park development has been towards 'bigger and yet bigger.' In turn, the physical space they occupy and utilize have expanded dramatically and are accompanied by the mounting pollution and other associated problems. As permanent structures, there are far more environmental and philosophical questions that can be raised. The traveling fairs of earlier times were short-lived, temporary events. Residents of nearby towns and villages enjoyed themselves for the duration of their stay. When they were gone, it was as if they had never been there at all.

Theme parks like Euro Disney are situated on vast expanses of land which is massively developed and then 're-naturalized'. From a geographical perspective, little attention has been paid towards the scale of these massive theme park developments. In addition, the kind of land that is used and its sustainability are critical issues warranting further study. Of all forms of American popular entertainment, only the outdoor amusement industry and the circus have managed to survive changing times, tastes, and the proliferation of leisure alternatives.

It seems as if the Disney enterprise has always been with us. What began as "Walt's Folly" now transcends cultural borders. Culture, as such, is not a fixed condition. It is a process or flow of shifting ideas and things. Products and meanings we attach to these ideas and events change in relation to our interaction with the past and the present, the familiar and the strange. These interactions, however, are intensifying and the results are less predictable than ever. In turn, people handle stimulus and chaos in different ways.

There are social and cultural forces that continually shape and affect individual behavior within the global environment. Throughout the world, individuals reflect the interaction of their unique personalities with the collective forces of the culture and milieu within which they have developed and experienced life. This includes the influences of other cultures and popular cultures that are mass produced, mass distributed, and mass consumed. According to Twitchell (1992:48), popular culture is "the last gasp of capitalism—the stuff produced before the revolution."

Anthropologist Victor Turner (Schudsen, 1987) discussed the centrality of performances in social life as 'social dramas' that do not mirror underlying social structures, but act as society's 'subjunctive' mood. They are rituals, carnivals, festivals, and theater, and these vehicles express desire and possibilities rather than fact or even reality.

While the need to be entertained and to escape will probably endure, consumer preferences are continually changing. From the 1920s to the 1940s, we wanted to be titillated. From the 1950s, through the 80s, we desired protection, comfort, luxury, and passive entertainment. In the 1990s, we want to be actively engaged, and frequently amazed.

Disney worlds are simulations or creations of idealized urban space that are created on large tracts of rural land, and articulate sensory, emotional, cognitive and spatial positioning activities. As human beings, our innate connection to the earth is not often taken into consideration when new parks are created and developed. We come from the earth and we ultimately become part of the earth again. We must take care of our natural world and be thoughtful when we are creating things to put on it to ensure that we do not incur nature's wrath.

BIBLIOGRAPHY

Barrett, M. et al. (1979) *Ideology and Cultural Production,* New York: St. Martins Press.

Bird, A. (1976) *Paxton's Palace,* London: Cassell and Company.

Bourdieu, P. (1993) *The Field of Cultural Production,* New York: Columbia University Press.

Debord, G. (1992) *The Society of the Spectacle,* New York: Zone Books.

Denzin, N. and Y. Lincoln (1994) *Handbook of Qualitative Research,* London: Sage.

Jenshell, L. (1994) "Disney's Dilemma" *Newsweek,* September 17, 40–59.

King, M. (1991) "The New American Muse: Notes on the Amusement/Theme Park" *Journal of Popular Culture,* 15, 1, 56–62.

Ley, D. and K. Olds (1988) "Landscape as Spectacle: World's Fairs and The Culture of Heroic Consumption" *Environment and Planning: Society and Space,* 6, 191–212.

Pred, A. (1991) "Spectacular Articulations of Modernity: The Stockholm Exhibition of 1897" *Geografiska Annaler,* 73B, 45–84.

Smoodin, E. (1994) *Disney Discourse,* New York: Routledge.

Twitchell, J. (1992) *Carnival Culture,* New York: Columbia University Press.

Ware, M. (1977) *Historic Fairground Scenes,* Buxton: Moorland Publishing.

Wilson, A. (1991) *The Culture of Nature,* Toronto: Between The Lines.

22

SYMBOL-INTENSIVE ORGANIZATIONS: MANAGEMENT IN THE AGE OF METAPHOR AND RHETORIC

Virpi Leikola and Thomaz Wood Jr.

This chapter introduces the Symbol-Intensive Organization (SIO). SIOs are environments where: symbolic leadership is predominant as a managerial style; both leaders and those led, consciously or unconsciously, apply impression-management techniques; managerial innovation is treated as a dramaturgical event; and symbolic analysts are prevalent within the work-force. In the post- (or late-) modern era, organizations have become magical kingdoms of fantasy, rhetoric and symbol manipulation. Within universities, Positivistic and Rationalist discourse shares the stage with new approaches encompassing Organizational Symbolism and Culture Studies.

PRACTITIONERS AND RESEARCHERS IN THE ERA OF ORGANIZATIONAL SYMBOLISM

A few years ago, while conducting field research, we noticed that workers were using 'Scheinian' terms to rationalize the change processes. While surprised, we realized that appropriation of managerial rhetoric was not the only peculiar phenomenon. Within the new managerial discourse, "authoritarian leadership gave place to 'democratic' management and traditional forms of control were substituted by mission statements and shared visions" (Wood, Curado and Campos, 1994). The success of this change process, based on commitment and participa-

248

tion, was linked to a new social contract between the managerial team and the workers. To assure these conditions, a complete set of rituals, impression-management techniques, and image manipulation were implemented. The firm had become a Symbol-Intensive Organization (SIO).

After years of Positivistic and Rationalistic discourse, Organization Interpretation, encompassing Organizational Symbolism and Organizational Culture, has become mainstream within Organization Studies (see *Administrative Science Quarterly*, 1983; Alvesson and Berg, 1992; Calas and MacGuire, 1990; Dandridge, 1983; Dandridge, Mitroff and Joyce, 1980; Gagliardi, 1990; *Journal of Management*, 1985; Sievers, 1990; Turner, 1990).

SPIRIT, IMAGE AND VIRTUAL TOMATOES

As the spirit of the present establishes itself as the predominant mood, 'imaginization' takes place and organizational stages turn into virtual settings. As a result, the distance between substance and image on organizational stages is growing.

Spirit: Mr. Taylor Goes Hollywood

The spirit of Frederick Taylor is still omnipresent. When we talk about organizations, we instinctively think in "a state of orderly relations between clearly defined parts that have some determinate order . . . we are talking about a set of mechanical relations" (Morgan, 1986:22). Machine-like behaviors are part of everyday life. We see it in car factories and fast food restaurants; in the way films are produced, papers are written, and classes are prepared.

Most recently the Walt Disney spirit—a magical kingdom of fantasy and intensive exploration of happiness—has captured our imagination. Evidence of the 'theme-park' rage is everywhere, it has even permeated organizational settings. According to Boje (1995:1000), the Disney company now is an example of a:

> collective storytelling system in which the performance of stories is a key part of members' sense-making and a means to allow them to supplement individual memories with institutional memories . . . at one extreme, the storytelling organization can oppress by subordinating everyone and collapsing everything to one 'grand narrative' or 'grand story'. At the other extreme, the storytelling organization can be a pluralistic construction of a multiplicity of stories, storytellers and story performance events.

Struggles between dominant discourses and peripheral voices occur frequently when apostles of the 'grand-narrative' apply their privileged positions to conduct sense-making processes through symbolic manipulation.

Image: Running Away from Substance

'We live in a visual era and everything is image'. This theme is now the focus of attention in multiple disciplines, from philosophy to literature and from cinema to culture studies (see Harvey, 1989; Denzin, 1991, 1995).

Alvesson (1990) relates recent interest in organizational culture and symbolism to wider tendencies in society. According to him (1990:373): "a broad trend in modern corporate life is portrayed and conceptualized as a development from a strong focus on 'substantive issues' to an increased emphasis on dealing with images as a critical aspect of organizational functioning and management." Today's social reality is fragmented and mutable. Individual identity is weak, more vulnerable and more flexible. The centrality, distinctiveness and continuity of identity is questionable (Berger, 1984). Such openness of borders at individual, organizational and national levels creates a receptiveness for images, symbols, and possibilities for changing symbolic repertoires. Image becomes prevalent. Identity becomes a matter of image.

Another important trend is the expansion of the mass media. The increasing presence of the media in everyday life is transforming events in news and creating pseudo-events.

The idea that we live in a dramaturgical society is not new. Debord's 1995 book *The Society of the Spectacle* was first published, in French, in 1967. According to him, "The whole life of those societies in which modern conditions of production prevail presents itself as an immense accumulation of 'spectacles'." That which was once directly lived has become mere representation. Consequently, it is quantity, not quality, that differentiates the '80s and the '90s from earlier decades. The combination of these tendencies creates a framework for understanding the SIO phenomenon.

Virtual Tomatoes: The Symbolization of the Workplace

The use of 'organizational change' processes reached its peak in the '80s and continues essentially unabated. Buzzwords and fads like downsizing, TQM, and reengineering continue to follow each other with cyclical constancy. The '80s marked the period of fascination with organizational culture (see Deal and Kennedy, 1982; Schein, 1985; Kilmann, 1984). Managers began to think about the subjective side of organizing and organizations. In seminars and workshops they listened to consultants and theorists tell them that culture as well as structure, strategy and technology could be managed, and that socially constructed meanings could be shaped through symbolic actions to enhance organizational performance (Wood and Caldas, 1995).

The change processes used by companies during the last decade have some commonalties concerning work organization, structure, technology, symbolic manipulation and culture control. Nine major trends have been identified. They are:

- *Elements of organizational culture are used for control and coordination.* Culture institutionalizes norms and shared meanings, provides solutions for known problems, and creates guidelines for decision-making priorities.
- *Rituals are used to celebrate commitment to change processes and leaders.* Meetings and public presentations help managers guide the construction of new shared meanings.
- *Retrospective sense-making or the collective 'reorganization of the past' occurs.* These might be characterized by dignifying everything related to the change and defaming the past and those representative of the old way.
- *Success stories are constructed and used.* The 'war stories' of significant events work as control systems by transmitting the new managerial ideology.
- *Reality is over-simplified.* Turn-around agents and radical change leaders usually adopt discourses characterized by objectivity and simplicity. To deal with complexity and ambiguity, they employ rhetoric and slogans.
- *Pop-management buzzwords are popularized.* Expressions like "we had the wrong culture," "we must change our basic values," or "we need to implement a new managerial paradigm" become clichés among managers and workers involved in changing processes.
- *Deviant voices are excluded.* Culture manipulation entails the search for uniformity and, thus, criticism is seldom accepted. When employees point out problems, they do it very carefully so as to not stain the process image.
- *The discourse of participation is used.* Control through culture is heavily based on participation and commitment. To foster these conditions, decision-making processes are usually turned into participative practices.
- *Official heroes and champions of the change process are celebrated.* In a cultural intervention there is no place for rebels. A few rebels might be transformed in heroes, 'a so-called good rebel,' but most would be eliminated from the 'narrative'.

There is, of course, much ambivalence about culture control and symbolic manipulation. A few employees choose the new life, some adopt the grand-narrative by fear, others embrace the discourse to feel that they belong, and many use the new values cynically to protect themselves (see Van Maanen and Kunda, 1989).

A strong need for conformity is noticeable. As observed by Rouanet (1993:53):

In certain conditions, the collective psychology annuls individual psychology, the individuals' intelligence declines, he/she exaggerates his/her effectiveness, and language becomes a instrument for mobilization. All these conditions: thoughts and emotions uniformity, affection and unconscious preponderance correspond to archaic mental activities, as the ones that might have been predominant in the primitive horde.

UNFOLDING SYMBOL-INTENSIVE ORGANIZATIONS

The SIO concept focuses on the complex texture of organizing and managing. Management may therefore be understood as the process of assuring minimal convergence and consistency in a chaotic, complex and ambiguous environment.

Here we illustrate the SIO using three analytical categories of leadership, innovation, and work-force. In a postmodern perspective, these three categories may be considered as rhetorical devices, root-metaphors or 'narrative providers'. They allow users to illustrate or describe concepts without fixing borders or eliminating alternative discourses.

By using these narrative providers, SIOs can be defined as environments where the predominant management style is symbolic leadership, leaders consciously or unconsciously manage impressions, managerial innovation is treated as a dramaturgical event, and symbolic analysts are prevalent within the work-force.

Symbolic Leadership: Managers as Meaning-Generators

Leadership is by far the most popular topic on the business bookshelves. Managers' willingness to buy exotic titles like *Jesus CEO: Using Ancient Wisdom for Visionary Leadership* (Jones, 1995) or *Make It So: Leadership Lessons from Star Trek: The Next Generation* (Roberts, 1995) is rooted in the popular myth of leadership. Books like these capture managers' attention, using popular figures and common sense to provide quick-fix solutions to complex problems. By using the fairy-tale mode, the authors disable readers' critical sense. According to Sievers (1994:159):

> *The way in which social theory and practice in contemporary organizations tend to deal with the notion of leadership resembles to some extent the way we have come to deal with sexuality: leadership and sex have both been continuously reified into scientific objects, making them products which, because of their broad appeal, can be marketed with endless variations in approach, model and position.*

Leadership can be understood as an interactional process of influencing and seducing that permeates power games in organizations. Within SIOs, leadership is essentially an exercise to control meaning through symbolic manipulation.

Czarniawska-Jorges and Wolf (1991:529) see leadership as "a symbolic performance, expressing the hope of control over destiny." The same authors look at management as "the activity of introducing order by coordinating flows of things and people towards collective action."

Leaders frame and define reality for others (Smircich and Morgan, 1982). Leaders succeed when they enact existent shared meanings and structure experience in acceptable ways. This process is more pervasive in unstructured environments than in more formalized settings.

In formalized settings, roles and norms are already institutionalized and provide the framework for leaders and followers interactions. Formalized settings are seen as 'safe' and stagnant environments. They are usually characterized by conflicts and tensions between institutionalized patterns of leadership and the 'natural', less formal process of leadership through which individuals can react and modify meanings and patterns.

Conversely, SIOs could be associated with unstructured settings. In such environments people are usually more eager to change the patterns and 'old dogmas' frequently give place to 'new dogmas'. In SIOs leadership is a symbolic activity, encompassing socially constructed creation of images and meanings. Leadership is also a process through which "individuals surrender their power to interpret and create reality to others" (Smircich and Morgan 1982:259).

Through the symbolic process of leadership, leaders' actions and rhetoric transform complexity and ambiguous situations into manageable questions. Leaders create points of reference and interpretative schemes to direct decision making and conduct future actions. They use other managerial artifacts such as information systems, plans and budgets, and apply rhetoric, images, metaphors, and symbolic actions. "At the end of reasons comes persuasion," pointed out Wittgenstein (Lampel, 1995:3).

Managerial Innovation: There's No Show Like Businesses' Show

Visitors to Disneyland pay a few dollars for a tour. But managers interested in 'Disney secrets' pay more than $2,000 for a complete tour of the Disney corporate domain. After years of studying world-class Japanese firms like Toyota, Honda and Sony, American managers are now focusing on local 'excellent' firms such as Motorola, Federal Express and AT&T (see Byrne, 1995). After frequent mention of their managerial innovations in popular management best-sellers, these companies became "businesses' show."

Since the 1980s, innovation studies have focused on managerial innovation. Managerial innovation can be defined as "any program, product or technique which represents a significant departure from the state of the art of management at the time it first appears and which affects the nature, location, quality, or quantity of information that is available in the decision making process" (Kimberly, 1981:86). Gill and Whittle (1992) employ a life cycle metaphor and suggest that administrative innovation follow a cyclical path from enthusiasm and adoption, to disillusionment and decline. Most of these innovations are designed and sold as management panaceas and their transitory nature lies in cultural and psychodynamic phenomena occurring within the organization.

In SIOs, managerial innovation has a strong theatrical component. Dramaturgical events and rhetoric help convince people to adopt new ideas, facilitate implementation, and affect evaluation and legitimization. Symbols thus serve as triggers for change, and, once change takes place, serve to legitimize new systems (Armenakis et al, 1995).

The process of innovation begins with leaders and change agents. Its implementation, legitimization and evaluation is characterized by actors enacting roles in support of the new idea. People not involved in the beginning of the change may present resistance, but perhaps can be convinced by later dramaturgical acts.

Staging performances are elements of persuasion used by innovators. Lampel (1995) studied major events in the history of technological innovations like Edison's unveiling of his illumination system and Steven Jobs' presentation of the Next computer. He argues that the success of major innovations depends on breaking down the resistance of market and financial supporters through dramaturgical staging of technological performance. Innovators used dramaturgical events to shape cognition and to influence future action, and, therefore, to succeed.

To compare technological innovations and managerial innovations may provide some useful insights. Consultants and managers normally face a double challenge when trying to implement new systems or ideas. They have to face internal resistance to the adoption of novelties by institutionalized groups. Additionally, they experience pressures to conform to a business environment saturated by myths and fads, where a number of concurrent programs compete for attention. Within this context it is often hard to obtain support for new ideas.

Unlike technological innovation, where benefits are often tangible and measurable, the impact of managerial innovations is far more subtle. To overcome barriers to adoption innovators use dramatic communication, images, metaphors and symbols. Dramatic communication includes daily interactions among leaders and subordinates as well as major events or public happenings.

Objective communication strategies, focused on detailed, rational analysis, often generate uncertainty and decrease potential support. People engaged in this kind of discourse seldom understand the 'subjective' nature of managerial innovation.

Dramatic communication, on the other hand, distances itself from objectivity, induces empathy and generates support and enthusiasm. Managers using dramatic communication tend to be more effective than those using objective communication.

Why adopt a managerial innovation? Will the innovation pay? There is no easy answer for these questions. Although innovators normally provide data, they usually rely on optimistic visions and wishful thinking. Adoption is often an act of faith. Faith also influences the way results are measured and interpreted and conditions the evaluation of the innovation. In SIOs, innovation is frequent, faith is high and drama pays.

Impression Management: Using Rhetoric and Metaphors

Impression management can be broadly described as the strategies used by actors to guide the audience's perceptions and interpretations. Impression management as a methodology, or set of techniques, relies on the assumption that image-making affects people's perception and thus their decision making processes. According to Morgan, Frost and Pondy (1983:20), "organizations are pre-eminently involved with the business of impression management, in relation to the general public, other corporations, consumers, employees, government, and other significant actors capable of influencing their well being." SIOs are social environments where impression management strategies are widely applied. SIOs are ambiguous settings in which conformity behaviors are especially common. Conformity behaviors are largely influenced by the cultural milieu: values, basic assumptions and shared meanings.

In situations of ambiguity, actors look around for guidance. In SIOs, managers apply rhetoric and metaphorical reasoning as strategies to influence behaviors and to achieve an adequate level of conformity. According to Russ (1991:222), "a major role of the top management is to enact the environment; that is, to create a shared understanding of the events that occur and the environment in which the organization operates." Rhetoric, or artificial eloquence, is a fundamental device in impression management. Linstead (1995:231) defines rhetoric as "the means by which discursive fields are linked in specific texts to concrete social forms, with the persuasive aim of naturalizing particular preferred arrangements." For Aristotle, rhetoric was the art of persuasion. For Plato, rhetoric was the capacity to argue for or against any position whatsoever, often with a destructive effect. Employing rhetoric in communication is using language that is showy and elaborate but largely empty of clear ideas or sincere emotions.

The use of rhetoric encourages the audience to gloss over ambiguities and contradictions through a process of mystification that usually supports the official version—the grand narrative. An eloquent speaker, using rhetorical skills, embodies emotions and shows somebody else's feelings as if they were his or hers. The discourse takes precedence over the actors' reality (see Hopfl, 1995).

While using rhetoric, SIO managers also apply metaphorical language. Like bridges, metaphors conduct mental connections of high level between entities (Beck, 1987). Metaphors express meanings that are impossible to translate into literary language (Gibbs and Hall, 1987).

Italian philosopher Gianbatista Vico (1668–1744) was probably the first to point out cognitive function of metaphors. He analyzed fables, myths and epic poetry, demonstrating the relationship between metaphorical reasoning and the transformation of states of abstraction and consciousness (Haskell, 1987).

Sometimes considered merely a hazardous speech mechanism, metaphors have been rehabilitated as a manifestation of fundamental cognitive processes (e.g. Morgan, 1980, 1986).

As with the use of rhetoric, metaphorical language is related to the process of mystification. Using metaphorical language, SIO managers hide ambiguities and contradictions. In SIOs, both forms of symbolic communications are widely used as impression management techniques.

From Mondrian to the Symbolic Analysts

Piet Mondrian pursued the quest for pure abstraction with greater consistency than any of his contemporaries. According to Frankel (1995:48), "Piet Mondrian . . . spent a lifetime straining to strip the art of painting to its starkest essence, purifying shapes and colors and training our eyes to acquire a whole new sensibility. Like all great artists in every medium, he progressively created his own language, which most of us can only gradually learn to understand."

In complex environments, work is characterized by abstraction. Mondrian was a precursor of the symbolic analysts, symbolic artists and scholars who identify and solve problems by manipulating symbols. Their skills entail a wide range of tools from mathematical algorithms to psychological concepts. According to Reich (1991:178), "Their primary task is to simplify reality into abstract images that can be rearranged and experimented with, communicated to other specialists and, then, eventually, transformed back into reality." The products of their work vary widely from new molecules to movies, from reengineered technologies to strategic plans, from inter-firm networks to industrial process improvements.

Reich (1991) argues that the contemporary corporation is only superficially similar to its mid-century counterpart. The contemporary corporation may be a national, regional or international web. Research and development, engineering, production and distribution activities, once concentrated in a few sites under centralized control, may now be spread worldwide. Furthermore, strategic alliances and outsourcing practices are transforming management practices. In the new corporate world, flows of capital, products, services, people, and knowledge cross organizational and national borders.

Reich holds that existent job classifications don't accurately reflect this reality. Jobs are usually classified according to prestige and income. Classification should mirror the social-economic status and particular conditions of each society in time. Existing schemes classify occupational groups using categories such as service works, professional specialty, technical and administrative support, etc. Categories that are becoming increasingly unfitting to current business realities.

Reich proposes (1991:174–177) three new categories: The first is 'routine product services', which includes production and services activities characterized by repetitive tasks. The second category is 'in-person services', which also entails routines and repetitive tasks, but are usually provided in a person-to-person basis. The third is 'symbolic-analytic services', which entails problem identifying, problem solving, and strategic-brokering activities.

The new category of symbolic analysts may include professional categories like designers, research scientists, cultural workers, artists, consultants and strategists. Symbolic analysts, working in complex environments, cannot rely on existing knowledge. The knowledge they apply is neither institutionalized nor formalized. Information is fragmented and existing solutions often obsolete. Symbolic analysts need the ability to creatively use current knowledge. They cross discipline and paradigm borders to create new knowledge. Their work is comprised primarily of complex, abstract and ambiguous activities. Results are seldom tangible and almost never directly measurable.

Symbolic analysts are becoming increasingly prevalent as strategic alliances, worldwide webs, virtual companies and other network forms proliferate. Symbolic analysts are SIOs' predominant work force.

REORGANIZING THE PAST

Imaginization, or (re)symbolization, is an irreversible process occurring in all sectors of society. Mass media and pop culture play a major role in defining our symbolic repertoire.

SIOs are representative of this process. SIOs may be firms, departments, teams or human arrangements where symbolism is a central element in the management game. SIOs' managers and employees make extensive use of rhetoric and metaphors. In so doing, they try to manipulate symbols fluidly, thus modifying the 'organizational texture'.

SIOs are therefore theatrical arenas, where many plays are taking place simultaneously. Furthermore, SIOs are cinematic settings, where reality is continuously reinterpreted, 'edited' and exhibited.

PROPOSING THE FUTURE

Organizational theorists have been demonstrating increased concern with postmodern theory (e. g. Cooper and Burrel, 1988; Burrel, 1988, 1994; Cooper, 1989; Clegg, 1990; Hassard, 1993; Hassard and Parker, 1993; Chia, 1995). According to Cooper and Burrel (1988:91), under a postmodern perspective, "organization is less the expression of planned thought . . . and a more defensive reaction to forces intrinsic to the social body which constantly threaten the stability of organizational life." The SIO concept should be further developed by framing the idea in postmodern terms. Future research could also explore alternative narrative providers to those presented here. A different field of research could evolve from the idea of the virtual corporation (Davidow and Malone, 1993; Clancy, 1994). In Hal Salwen's 1995 low-budget movie *Denise Calls Up*, the characters never meet. There is absolutely no physical contact. They only communicate through phones, facsimile machines and computers. Friendship, work, and (even) sex are media events; virtual reality substitutes for reality.

In the new virtual—or imaginary—workplaces, management becomes metamanagement. Virtual organizations constitute a half life between the real and the non-real. These settings are characterized by the massive use of information technology, boundary spanning, telecommuting practices, frequent participation of customers in the value-chain creating process and location of important functions and activities outside their physical frontiers. The locus of management is imaginary, hence, coordination and control turn into media phenomena. Virtual organizations may also be distinguished by high symbol intensity. Future research might therefore focus on commonalties and contrasts between virtual organizations and SIOs.

CINEMATIC ORGANIZATIONS?

In his book *The Cinematic Society: The Voyeur's Gaze,* Denzin (1995:1) advocates that "The postmodern is a visual, cinematic age; it knows itself in a part through the reflections that flow from the camera's eye. The voyeur is the iconic, postmodern self. Adrift in a sea of symbols, we find ourselves, voyeurs all, products of the cinematic gaze." Instead of audience or supporting actors in a 'dramaturgical, theatrical existence' (Goffman, 1959), we became voyeurs in a 'cinematic (un)reality'. This put to the SIO spirit: Mr. Taylor and Mr. Disney together, visiting Mondrian's exhibition.

BIBLIOGRAPHY

Administrative Science Quarterly (1983). Special Issue on Organizational Symbolism, 28.

Alvesson, M. (1990) "Organization: From Substance to Image?" *Organization Studies* 11, 3, 373–394.

Alvesson, M. and P. O. Berg (1992) *Corporate Culture and Organizational Symbolism: An Overview,* Berlin: de Gruyter.

Armenakis et al. (1995) "Symbolic Actions Used by Business Turnaround Change Agents" *Academy of Management Best Papers Proceedings.* Vancouver.

Baudrillard, J. (1995) "The Virtual Illusion: Or The Automatic Writing Of The World." *Theory, Culture and Society* 12, 97–107.

Beck, B. E. F. (1987) "Metaphors, Cognition And Artificial Intelligence" in R. E. Haskell, ed., *Cognition and Symbolic Structures: The Psychology of Metaphoric Transformation,* Ablex: Norwood.

Berger, P. (1984) "Musil And The Salvage Of The Self" *Partisan Review,* V, LI, 638–650.

Boje, D. M. (1995) "Stories Of The Storytelling Organization: A Postmodern Analysis Of Disney As 'Tamara-land'" *Academy of Management Journal* 38, 4, 997–1035.

Burrel, G. (1988) "Modernism, Postmodernism and Organizational Analysis: The Contribution of Michel Foucault" *Organization Studies* 9, 2, 221–235.

Burrel, G. (1994) "Modernism, Postmodernism and Organizational Analysis: The Contribution of Jurgen Habermas" *Organization Studies* 15, 1, 1–45.

Byrne, J. A. (1995) "Management Meccas" *Business Week* September 18, 122–133.

Calas, M. B. and J. B. Macguire (1990) "Organizations As Networks Of Power And Symbolism" in B. A. Turner *Organizational Symbolism,* Berlin: de Gruyter

Chia, R. (1995) "From Modern To Postmodern Organizational Analysis" *Organization Studies* 16, 4, 579–604.

Clancy, T. (1994) "The Virtual Corporation, Telecommuting And The Concept Of Team" *Academy of Management Executive* 8, 2, 7–10.

Clegg, S. R. (1990) *Modern Organizations: Organization Studies in the Postmodern World,* London: Sage.

Cooper, R. (1989) "Modernism, Postmodernism and Organizational Analysis: The Contribution Of Jacques Derrida" *Organization Studies* 10, 4, 479–500.

Cooper, R. and G. Burrel (1988) "Modernism, Postmodernism and Organizational Analysis: An Introduction" *Organization Studies* 9, 1, 91–112.

Czarniawska-Jorges, B. and R. Wolff (1991) "Leaders, Managers, Entrepreneurs On And Off The Organizational Stage" *Organization Studies* 12, 4, 529–546.

Dandridge, T.C. (1983) "Symbol's Function And Use" in L.R. Pondy, et al., *Organizational Symbolism* Greenwich: CT: JAI Press.

Dandridge, T. C., I. Mitroff and W. F. Joyce (1980) "Organizational Symbolism: A Topic To Expand Organizational Analysis" *Academy of Management Review,* 5, 1, 77–82.

Davidow, W. H. and M. S. Malone (1993) *The Virtual Corporation* New York: Harper-Business.

Deal, T. E. and A. A. Kennedy (1982) *Corporate Cultures,* Reading, MA: Addison-Wesley.

Debord, G. (1995) *The Society of Spectacle,* New York: Zone Books.

Denzin, N. K. (1991) *Images of Postmodern Society: Social Theory and Contemporary Cinema,* London: Sage.

Denzin, N. K. (1995) *The Cinematic Society: The Voyeur's Gaze,* London: Sage.

Frankel, Max (1995) "Museum Magic" *The New York Times Magazine,* December 3.

Gagliardi, P., ed. (1990) *Symbols and Artifacts: Views of the Corporate Landscape,* Berlin: de Gruyter.

Gibbs Jr, R. W. and C. K. Hall (1987) "What Does it Mean to Say that a Metaphor has been Understood?" in R.E. Haskell, ed., *Cognition and Symbolic Structures: The Psychology of Metaphoric Transformation,* Ablex: Norwood.

Gill, J. and S. Whittle (1992) "Management by Panacea: Accounting for Transience" *Journal of Management Studies,* 30, 2, 281–295.

Goffman, E. (1959) *The Presentation of Self in Everyday Life,* New York: Anchor Books.

Harvey, D. (1989) *The Condition of Postmodernity: An Inquiry into the Origins of Cultural Change,* Oxford: Basil Blackwell.

Haskell, R. E. (1987) "Gianbatista and the Discovery of Metaphoric Cognition" in Haskell, R. E., ed., *Cognition and Symbolic Structures: The Psychology of Metaphoric Transformation,* Ablex: Norwood.

Hassard, J. (1993) *Sociology and Organization Theory: Positivism, Paradigms and Postmodernity,* New York: Cambridge University Press.

Hassard, J. and M. Parker, eds. (1993) *Postmodernism and Organizations,* London: Sage.

Hopfl, H. (1995) "Organizational Rhetoric and The Threat of Ambivalence" *Studies in Culture, Organization and Society* 1, 2, 175–187.

Jones, L. B. (1995) *Jesus CEO: Ancient Wisdon for Visionary Leadership.* New York: Hyperion.

Journal of Management (1985) Special Issue—Organizational Symbolism 11, 2.

Kilmann, R. H. (1984) *Beyond the Quick Fix: Managing Five Tracks to Organizational Success,* San Francisco: Jossey-Bass.

Kimberly, J. R. (1981) "Managerial Innovation" in P. C. Nystron and W. H. Starbuck, *Handbook of Organizational Design—Volume 1,* Oxford: Oxford University Press.

Lampel, J. (1995) "Innovation As Spectacle: Dramaturgical Construction Of Technological Change" *Paper presented at Conference on The Social Construction of Industries and Markets,* Chicago.

Linstead, S. (1995) "After The Autumn Harvest: Rhetoric And Representation In An Asian Industrial Dispute" *Studies in Culture, Organization and Society* 1, 2, 231–252.

Morgan, G. (1980) "Paradigms, Metaphors, And Puzzle Solving In Organization Theory" *Administrative Science Quarterly* 25, 605–622.

Morgan, G. (1986) *Images of Organization,* Newbury Park: Sage.

Morgan, G., P. J. Frost, and L. R. Pondy (1983) "Organizational Symbolism" in Pondy, L. R. et al., eds., *Organizational Symbolism* Greenwich, CT: JAI Press.

Reich, R. (1991) *The Work of Nations,* New York: Vintage Books.

Roberts, W. (1995) *Make It So: Leadership Lessons of Star Trek: The Next Generation,* New York: Pocket Books.

Rouanet, P. S. (1993) "O mal estar na modernidade ('modern times' nausea')" *IDE* 23, 40–53.

Russ, G. S. "Symbolic Communication And Image Management In Organizations" in Giacalone, R. A. and Rosenfeld, P. (eds.) (1991).

Schein, E. H. (1985) *Organizational Culture and Leadership: A Dynamic View,* San Francisco: Jossey-Bass.

Sievers, B. (1994) *Work, Death and Life Itself: Essays on Management and Organization,* Berlin: de Gruyter.

Smircich, L. and G. Morgan, (1982) "Leadership: The Management of Meaning," *The Journal of Applied Behavioral Science* 18, 3, 257–273.

Turner, B. A. (1990) *Organizational Symbolism,* Berlin: de Gruyter.

Van Maanen, J. and G. Kunda (1989) "Real Feelings: Emotional Expressions And Organizational Culture" *Research in Organization Behavior* 11, 43–103.

Wood Jr, T. and M. P. Caldas (1995) "Who's Afraid of Electrofads? Change, Identity and Convulsive Organization Therapies" *Paper presented at 13th. SCOS.* Turku, Finland.

Wood Jr., T. and I. B. Curado, and H. M. Campos, (1994) "Managers Symbolic Action And The Transformation Of Culture" *Paper presented at 12th SCOS,* Calgary, Canada.

23

THE BUSINESS OF MEDIA: ORGANIZING CARNIVAL BY THE NEW ENTREPRENEURS

Ken Khoury and Dick Raspa

Madonna, Donald Trump, and Ted Turner are three well-known examples of the new entrepreneurs in the postindustrial society. They conduct business enterprises as media events and use media to create their wealth; in the process they themselves have become defined as media events. They are not only show-people but the show itself. They seem to be "on stage" all the time and this performance even intrudes into their personal lives. When away from the adoring crowds they are isolated and lonely, a state associated with anger and rejection. The stage, the camera, and the microphone have become the foundation, vision, and articulation of their lives.

INTRODUCTION

Not long ago, Ted Turner and his wife, actress Jane Fonda, entered a gathering where celebrities were being entertained by a comedian. After realizing that no one had noticed them, they exited quickly and made their triumphant re-entry after the comedian had finished his act (Bibb, 1995). The show must go on.

This paper explores the ways that three entrepreneurial business people—Madonna, Donald Trump, and Ted Turner—exploit the media and its power to create reality. All three inhabit a postindustrial subculture—the media industry. They create a distinctive yet shared set of meanings by blurring traditional boundaries between self and other, propriety and decadence, order and chaos, private and public, between what remains in their subculture and what emerges in the dominant culture. Within their work transactions, they have challenged notions about the proper sphere of business, raised questions about what constitutes the province of the personal. They push the limits of self as commodity, and in doing so they reveal that what has traditionally been labeled 'the personal and the private' is not only exposed but also for sale. The self has become the medium of transaction.

THE BUSINESS OF MEDIA

We chose these three people because they have emerged as cultural icons of post-industrial media culture. Many others in business, politics, and other fields are affected by the significant media-oriented cultural changes in Western societies. The royal family of Britain, once clothed in traditional pageantry, is now unclothed in the texts and photographs of sensational journalism. Princess Di and Prince Charles became media obsessions not because of royal affairs but through personal affairs. American newsmen like Pat Buchanan and Steve Forbes are no longer content to report on presidential politics but are now candidates themselves. Media has redefined the boundaries of 'information' for public consumption and 'challenges' to established systems of power and politics.

The business of media is the art of parlaying news into profit. Words, images, sounds are marketed for mass consumption. On a late night talk show, Madonna offends the host by whimsically referring to urine as a cure for athlete's foot. Her discussion of peeing is a public act that ultimately drenches the offended host in insults. Everything—even private bodily fluids—is subject to commodification. Madonna uses media to entertain and to titillate by revealing the private parts of her life and body. Donald Trump uses the media to build his reputation as the world's greatest entrepreneur and to create credit lines for future acquisitions. And Ted Turner uses media to create a virtual universe that parallels and, at times, even subverts the established power and political universe. In directing and organizing their business empires, these entrepreneurs transgress the boundaries that traditionally separate private lives and public displays of the self. The result is the creation of carnival in Bakhtin's sense—an inversion of the social order and its systems of meaning and power (Bakhtin, 1968).

Work is a theatrical enactment divorced from its industrial roots in labor, discipline, and stoicism. For these postindustrial entrepreneurs work has become an Epicurean spectacle—a parade of obsession, sensationalism, and excess. Their public lives have become forms of popular entertainment, as the secret dimensions of the self—the intimate details of family, sex, and work life—are commodified and displayed in tabloid journals and mass media for public consumption.

ORGANIZING CARNIVAL

Postindustrial media business is carnival. It is a spectacle of inversions. In its mythic expression carnivals, such as Mardi Gras, exist in the domain of liminality where cultural norms and practices are juxtaposed and contested. In liminal space what is ordinarily hidden and within the shadows appears under the three-ring tent as well as in the side-shows. Nonsense prevails over common sense, pushing and even breaking boundaries. New realities emerge. Carnival is a shadow world brought to light, dramatizing those dark forces in the human psyche, in institutions, and in communities, simultaneously fascinating and frightening the audience. Animal trainers reveal the extraordinary courage shown by the tamers of big cats. The world's strongest man demonstrates the Herculean strength of the human animal. An exotic world invades predictable space for a time and then packs up and goes. After Carnival, life returns to normal.

The essence of Carnival is the possibility of having one's system of beliefs and constructions of the world challenged and possibly changed. The ordinary common sense way of knowing and perceiving is questioned. The seduction of Carnival is its power to test the taken-for-granted, naturalized world. What is normal, human, real, true, and possible is pushed into the foreground. The experience is both exciting and dangerous. It is the stuff of fantasy and nightmare.

During Carnival, systems of hierarchy are reversed. Clowns, fools, even beggars assume positions of authority, mocking the limitations of everyday social mores and promoting order and denial of gratification. Madonna, Trump, and Turner are Carnival figures as they mock the moral and aesthetic traditions of American business life.

THE NEW ENTREPRENEURS

In the industrial age, intense pragmatism and rationality infused conventional American business life. Old-time businessmen, people like Henry Ford and John D. Rockefeller, were behind-the-scenes organizers, producers and directors whose public images were conservative and cautious. Madonna, Trump, and Turner, on the other hand, live their psycho-social lives on a public stage, and as entrepreneurs who are both entertaining and reckless. They work and live on a planet of electronic, virtual reality. They are willing to have their lives publicly dissected in the media, and offer biography as the ultimate form of engagement and entertainment to be eagerly devoured by the insatiable appetite of mass consumers. In so doing, all three break down the boundaries of their industries.

Madonna pushes the edge of entertainment, Trump expands the borders of real estate, and Turner breaks down the boundaries of news. Characteristic metaphors richly evoke the ways each of these three media figures make their business enterprises carnivalesque.

Madonna: The Stripper—Posing Is the Show

Madonna, from Bay City, Michigan, lost her mother at the age of five. The burden of that loss lies in not having a model from whom to base a developing sense of identity. The opportunity that loss provides is the freedom to be whatever she wanted to be:

> *As a celebrity or unbelievably famous person, you are, in this country, allowed to operate with everyone's approval for a certain amount of time. People do live vicariously through you and have fantasies about being you and wanting to do what you do. But it can never last; . . . you need to disappear, run out of steam, run out of ideas. You need to get married, have a lot of children, get fat or something. You need to have a drinking or drug problem. You need to go in and out of rehab so people can feel sorry for you. Or you need to kill yourself, basically.* (Mailer, 1994)

Though schooled by Roman Catholic nuns, Madonna rejected identification with the sisters. Instead of becoming the 'Holy Madonna,' she leads a crusade to provoke and challenge the societal norms. Her poses are paradoxes. She becomes the material girl while rejecting the accouterments of wealth. *Sex,* her presumed autobiography, sells through the allurement of eroticism. Even in transgressing every aesthetic and moral boundary in its representation of sexual exhibitionism with men, women, animals, and inanimate objects, the book deflects the erotic. Readers are frustrated because the metal cover does not reveal all when it is removed. It is the pornographic impulse that is the exploited, not the exploiter. It is voyeurism that is prostituted but the author gets the money: "My whole thing is that you use all you have—all you have—your sexuality, your femininity, your—any testosterone you have inside you—your intellect—use whatever you have and use bits and pieces wherever it's good" (Mailer, 1994).

When she sings, dances, acts, directs, writes, talks, dates, Madonna is the show. In her *Truth Or Dare* video, the autobiographical Blond Ambition tour attempts to tell the truth by daring convention. Madonna uses the body in a postindustrial sense to breakdown normal gender boundaries—challenging the audience to see the person rather than the woman: "This revolution is in the name of human beings relating to human beings and relating to each other with compassion . . . This is not about me being a woman but about me being a human being" (Mailer, 1994).

Madonna's main theme is not the sensual but the politics of sex, power, and dominance. A dance, such as *Like a Virgin* in the *Truth Or Dare* video, emphasizes a postindustrial relocation of sexual organs, gender, and the texture of breasts converted from soft to hard:

> *I reversed the role playboy bunny thing . . . Just two playboys in some costume that pushes their bodies in some unnatural shape . . . But now it's the men . . . The idea is to take something meant for one part of the body and place it on another part . . . The idea behind it is that breasts are these soft things that men rely on to some extent, so it's a way of saying:*

'Come on, Fuck off.' Not, fuck on forever and ever. Just think of my breasts in another way. That's all. Not something soft you can fall into. (Mailer, 1994)

Madonna's presentation of the body is clinical, not erotic, as if examining a specimen sample or performing surgery or endoscopy. Her dance is not a strip of tease but strip of war. Aggression and anger emote rather than sensuality and love. Her dance is sensate but not sensual.

In a birthday poem, Madonna comments on the care of her dirty underwear and the warming value of bedtime flatulence. She carnivalesques her body, using every part and function and violates limits to emphasize her point. In her autobiography *Sex*, she resists going all the away and spreading her legs. Instead, she violates propriety by putting her mouth between the buttocks of a man. Like swallowing fire in a carnival side show, Madonna symbolically swallows the forbidden and the rejected. She figuratively turns the anger of 'kiss my ass' bottoms up.

She is both the creator and the creation and what she produces, directs, and enacts are portraits of the narcissistic self. Mailer (1994) says to Madonna: "You are trapped in the cruelest pit of the narcissist—you are not only more interested in yourself than anyone else alive, but suffer from the likely suspicion that this may be justified." In all her performances, she is propelled by the recurring theme of striking a pose against conventional morality, against social boundaries, against systems of hierarchy and control, against stereotypes of people.

Her energy is highest when her provocations are challenged, especially by conventional authority, as when the Italian and Canadian police threatened to close down her show for obscene gesturing. As she challenges the authority of her childhood Catholicism by dancing and thrusting in the garb of a priest, she incites both herself and her audience: "I do believe religion and eroticism are very related" (Mailer, 1994). She challenges the conventional authority of self concept, of who she is as a person. Private self can't be separated from public invention. Private life and public exposure blend in the carnival of the body. Her work exposes the self by angrily tearing away at conventional mores.

She beckons us into the carnival, but once inside we enter an inverted world. The audience becomes the play. Through her own narcissism, she brings out the narcissism of the audience. It becomes interactive and she doesn't let the audience remain passive owners of the performance. "You want to be with me, then come along for the fucking cure" (Mailer, 1994).

Donald Trump: The Barker—Making a Deal, Being a Big Wheel

I have the largest living room in New York City and I have the most incredible view. (Hurt, 1993)

I've been America's most successful business man. I've done things nobody thought could be done, and I've got big plans. (Hurt, 1993)

I believe I've added show business to the real estate business, and that's been a positive for my properties and my life. (Hurt, 1993)

Donald Trump, referred to as *The Donald* in gossip columns, creates his own carnavalesque persona. He challenges the traditional real estate business by using the media. He believes his name alone virtually doubles the value of any deal. He has created an empire that is the 'most successful business of America.' He parlays his persona in the media into credit lines that allow him to acquire the Manhattan real estate trophies. His signature provides him with capital and influence that is built into the skylines of New York City and Atlantic City—both symbolically and literally.

Like the traditional American myth, the Trump family grew from rags to riches. Trump's father created a real estate fortune from circumspect roots in Queens and Donald carries on the family tradition of empire building. He quotes from one of his heroes, the late 19th century American President Teddy Roosevelt, whose optimism reflects Trump's own vision of life: "The credit belongs to the man who's actually in the arena; whose face is marred by dust and sweat; who strives valiantly, who errs and fails again and again. But there's no effort without error or shortcoming; but who does actually strive to do the deeds, who does know the great enthusiasm, the great devotion" (Trump, 1990).

Trump entered his father's successful real-estate business and learned the tricks of the trade, including his father's sometimes shady deal-making. After attending the University of Pennsylvania's Wharton School of Business, Donald's visions grew. He wanted to acquire Manhattan properties, such as the Empire State Building and the Chrysler Building, that were icons of the real estate world. He targeted Penn Central's bankrupt Commodore Hotel and an abandoned rail yard on 34th Street. In 1974, at the age of twenty-eight, Donald was able to purchase the Penn Central property for 100 million dollars.

Donald added manipulation of media and public opinion to the tools he used to pursue his goals and maneuver his competitors out of the way. As Donald says, "Good publicity is preferable to bad, but from a bottom line perspective bad publicity is better than none. Bad publicity is sometimes better than no publicity at all" (Hurt,1993). Trump prides himself on this manipulation. He once told his publicist: "I want you to leak to the gossip columns that [actress] Catherine Oxenberg is chasing me." The rumors then circulate in New York and Los Angeles, exemplifying Trump's consistent use of the media to advantage. Donald's view of publicity drew admiration from his father who expressed the belief that his son was the smartest business man of all (Hurt, 1993).

Donald Trump fantasized about stamping the New York skyline with the Trump name and putting up a building that would rival the Taj Mahal. He purchased a much-desired property on 5th Avenue and 57th Street, and next to the world's most expensive clothes and jewelry shops he erected the seventy-one story Trump Towers. With the Trump Towers completed, he turned his attention to the flow-ing cash of the gaming industry in Atlantic City. This step, unfortunately, proved to be a financial disaster.

In the midst of the potential collapse of his real-estate dynasty, Trump's exalted relationship with his wife, Ivana, also fell apart. In his desire for young beautiful women, he began focusing his attention on Marla Maples, a model and aspiring actress, an involvement that led to the dissolution of his marriage and partnership with Ivana. With financial and marital difficulties, the biographies became more critical—*Trumped, the Inside Story, of the Real Donald Trump, His Cunning Rise and Spectacular Fall* and *Lost Tycoon: The Many Lives of Donald J. Trump.*

But jumping on Trump when he is down misses much of the point of who he is and what he represents in the media. Donald Trump is the ultimate promoter of himself and his name, then of his properties and businesses, and, finally, of his trophy women: "I've made Ivana a very popular woman." He was a baseball star in college, the star of his family, the star of his father's dictum to be a success at all costs. He attracts and promotes other stars, entertainers, professional athletes, beautiful women. Choosing to play the game is the essential dictum. "Come and try your luck, let it all roll," he seems to beckon. "I have and I've won big. So can you." For Trump, it is the transaction that counts: selling the ticket, making the deal. What happens once you're in isn't so important.

Though Donald Trump's name is on the buildings, in some ways it is all of our names. After all he is just "The Donald." He is a Walt Disney figure, a child with passions naively open and out of control. His life is a Monopoly game in which greed runs wild and acquisitions are victories that taunt opponents gleefully, and failures that incite anger and the urge to kick the game board and topple the pieces. Prancing, gloating, screaming, and cursing are part of Trump's game etiquette.

Divorce and financial over-leveraging combined to endanger his empire. But such risk was always a necessary part of the wager, the price of a ticket into the ring. He seeks the thrill of hitting the long shot, of overcoming the odds. He is compelled to lay it all on the line, again and again and again. But what attracts the audience, what brings us all into the big show is his carnivalesque audacity. Trump's narcissism reflects our own.

But why do the wives or partners, or investors, or bankers, or bondholders participate? As P.T. Barnum put it, "There's a sucker born every minute." For Trump, that means enticing people into his real-estate game, including quite literally the Atlantic City gaming enterprises of his multi-casino construct, where gambling thrives and where boxing tournaments are held. So what if a girl gets raped by the World's Heavy Weight Champion? Trump's sportsmen are modern gladiators brought into the ring to entertain. They may play a bit rough but so did he, when he pushed a recently purchased race horse lame and then refused to pay for it.

Donald Trump, himself, was engaged in the three-ringed circus as he shuttled between Ivana, his wife, and Marla Maples, his mistress. They threw the rings both diamond and interpersonal back and forth like flying trapeze performers. The personal ring, an unbroken circle symbolizing commitment, is transformed into the media ring, circling the world. The media records every thrust and withdrawal of his affair with Monroe-like model Maples, until she is almost publicly impregnated and wed. The blood-stained sheets are hung for all to see outside his penthouse windows at the Trump Towers, New York's Taj Majal.

Trump's first wife, Ivana, the old world spouse of tradition, observes from the vantage of embarrassed rejection. Refusing to be shed painlessly, the traditional bride exacts her price legally and financially, and goes on to promote her own personal lines of glamour consumption. Donald still manages to promote her, even by rejection. He is *The Donald Juan,* whose potency can neither be contained nor constrained either by the vows of traditional society or the old world. He is the media of potency, of making the public deal, of making it happen. He is an emperor without clothing but he has a palace in spite of it all and he lets us peek in to see ourselves, perhaps not big wheels, but deal makers all.

Ted Turner: The Ringmaster—Casting the News

Ted Turner is the modern showman supreme, the electronic ringmaster of television. His satellite broadcast empire includes CNN (Cable Network News—the first twenty-four hour news channel), TNT (Turner Network Television), and TBS (Turner Broadcast System). He has built an enterprise that reaches over 150 countries. At any given moment, fifty million people might be watching CNN (Bibb, 1993). He reaches heads of state as well as ordinary citizens of the world. Ex-President George Bush has said he learned more from CNN than he did from the CIA (Bibb, 1993).

Turner enterprises have changed the definition of information and influenced the way we see, live, and understand the world. Turner's round-the-clock broadcasts have far-reaching implications for the postindustrial era. In the past, the news was represented as historical fact, something that had happened. Reporters could get to the "bottom of it," as if the story was physically configured like a barrel and contained all the facts of any given situation. Good reporters could arrive at the objective truth, ferreting out the hidden facts and disguised motives that were present in the story.

CNN changed that. The news is no longer in the past. It is in the present and it is brought to television audiences during the act of reporting. Reporters have become newscasters looking for stories that are happening or about to happen. The very presence of newscasters can frame a story a certain way so that those on the periphery may become central, and vice-versa. Such inversions have allowed CNN to carnavalesque the news.

The power of world-wide instant access to significant events is incredible, turning the world topsy-turvey. Geo-political borders separating countries, governments, cultures, people, even our conceptions of those realities, have been blurred irrevocably by CNN news. Not long ago, President Bill Clinton was in a CNN studio participating in an international press conference, taking questions from journalists in Seoul, Johannesburg, and Jerusalem. Suddenly, Clinton turned to the camera and spoke with great emotion: "I believe we may have North Koreans watching us tonight. I say to you, the United States wishes to have friendly and open relationships with you. We wish to have a constructive relationship" (Bibb, 1993). President Clinton made this address because he learned that the North Korean leadership watched CNN. Thus, North Korea's Kim Il Sung is connected to CNN, which communicates to Clinton, who talks to Kim Il Sung while speaking on CNN.

What is emerging is a shadow or virtual diplomacy, originating not in Washington, the traditional center of American political power, but on the periphery, in a television news room in Atlanta, Georgia. It is diplomacy that no longer is conducted secretly by professional diplomats and elected government officials in smoke-filled back rooms, but on television, and it is happening as millions of people watch. It is a form of diplomacy produced and directed by Ted Turner.

Like great theater impresarios, Turner is the premier caster—selecting the information to be cast as news, deciding who will be the cast for the show, and, through the power of electronic communication, even casting the participants in roles. He brings each community to the ringside, and in doing so, brings the leaders into the ring. CNN News has electronically created the global village. Heads of state, prime ministers, presidents, ambassadors, diplomatic personalities, senators, and congressmen, are all part of the show. This media of virtual diplomacy has subverted the regular, established channels of international political exchange. Politicians cannot avoid responding to a wide variety of happenings occurring almost simultaneously throughout the globe. Indeed, their responses become news, requiring new dialogues of communication and exchange.

Information flows twenty-four hours a day, is available at the flick of a switch and redefines news as live coverage, as events are occurring and happening to us. It is all-consuming, as Turner says:

We're a lot like the modern chicken farmer. They grind up the feet to make the fertilizer. They grind up the intestines to make dog food. The feathers go into pillows. Even the chicken manure is made into fertilizer. They use every bit of the chicken. Well, that's what we try to do with the television product, use everything to its fullest extent. (Bibb, 1993)

Postindustrial news is not just out there, but here, in the present, in our lives and homes—here and everywhere. Ted's 'ring' is the postmodern world of information and he is its 'master'.

In 1980, when Turner put the first twenty-four-hour news channel on the air, he said to the staff: "I want to welcome you all to CNN and wish you the best of luck. See, we're going to take the news and put it on the satellite and then we're going to beam it down to Russia and we're going to bring world peace and we're all going to get rich in the process" (Applebaum, 1994). The utopian aspect in his personality permits him to juxtapose improbable outcomes, for example, getting rich by bringing about world peace. Turner founded the Better World Society in

1985, inspired by Jacques Cousteau, to educate people about environmental devastation. His efforts have been recognized by some native American populations. Today, the Paiute Indians call Ted Turner 'Wovoka' after a medicine man who introduced the ghost dance to his people and said the buffalo would return and the Indians would flourish again. The Paiute people believe Turner is the modern medicine man, the shaman, who has the power to restore aboriginal American culture to its former glory.

Turner's rise to power as the electronic ringmaster was always uncertain, always a stretch: "My father said, 'Never set goals you can achieve in your lifetime. After you accomplish them, there's nothing left'" (Bibb, 1993). Ted was raised to be hard, independent, resourceful, and self-reliant. Immediately upon arriving in a new boarding school, he challenged other boys to fight, even those bigger and stronger. It was his way of making his place, of controlling his boundaries, of forging his identity. He was a family of one. In school and in his famous racing career, he was always in the center of the ring and yet alone. He was like his father. There could only be one man, one master of the ring, one vision: "Ted always puts himself in the middle of anything he talked about. He somehow manages to make himself the focal point of any conversation. But, in all the time we've spent together, he's never once talked about his family, his father, his wife, or his marriages. It is always his ambitions, his dreams. Ted is all about dreaming" (Bibb, 1993). This would never be an institutional man. An institution? Maybe.

Turner joined his father's expanding billboard business and found that the ring was not big enough for both of them. After acquiring another large billboard business, Turner's father feared the 1960's Beautify America Campaign would threaten his business. He panicked and negotiated the sale of a significant part of his business. Ted hotly objected to the downsizing. The senior Turner refused to cancel the sale and killed himself on his 53rd birthday. Did he lack confidence in his son's ability to run the enlarged business or did he fear his son would succeed and show him up? In any event Ted took control, recanted the sale, threatened his father's former associates with legal action, and grew the business further,

Business didn't mean giving up sports. Even while dealing with the billboard business, his primary focus remained ocean sailing. Unlike his workaholic father, Ted was intent on balancing both business and sports, while winning at both. In fact, Ted Turner has won more records and titles in ocean sailing than any other single person. He moved from triumphs in the aristocracy of yachting's America Cup to championships in all-American baseball, when the team he purchased, the Atlanta Braves, won its first World Series victory, all the while showing them on TNT and making them a very successful business.

In the same way, he purchased many of the movies and TV shows he enjoyed as childhood entertainment, shows like *Leave it To Beaver* and *Lassie,* which idealize boyhood and the American Family. In owning the shows, Turner has the opportunity to rescript the ideal mother, father, and childhood he never enjoyed. Rather than merely go to the show, Turner bought it.

Turner's career reflects the power of letting go of the boundaries of the past in the face of opportunity. He married an expert sailor, Judy Nye. Three years later they divorced when he rammed her boat in a race she would have otherwise have won. She was pregnant with their second child at the time. When her new husband expressed ambivalence about the children, Turner turned to his second wife, Jane Hartman, to care for them. This marriage of twenty-two years and three children was more of a convenience than a bond. He told Jane: "Business comes first, my boat comes second, and you come third. See you later" (Bibb, 1993).

During the course of these marriages, Turner also had multiple liaisons, including one with J.J. Ebaugh who was a pilot for the family. Turner justified his affairs as a game: "The way I get it, if you don't like the way your team is going, you trade the players. If you don't like your wife, you trade her" (Bibb, 1993). J.J. guided Turner to seek therapy and start on lithium after his second marriage ended. When J.J. decided to leave him after an eight year relationship, Turner turned to show business and to Jane Fonda. Through J.J. and Fonda, Turner finally seemed to find his enormous energies consumed by his passion for one woman.

Jane Fonda shares a history that is remarkably similar to Ted's. She became a self-made success in multiple media and is one of the most famous anti-establishment figures of our time. She has also struggled with lifelong emotional conflicts, including bulimia. For years Fonda toyed with death through the addictive dance of bulimia. Her workout tapes were not only exercise for the body but exercises by a conflicted self. She became the ring mistress of women seeking the ideal body and self through plastic surgery and self-discipline of diet and aerobics. She tried to control her own fate and defeat nature, age, and genetics.

The coupling of Ted and Jane became a major media event, a blurring of distinctions between public and private lives. The rebels finally came together and became an institution themselves. People would say they were meant for each other, the ultimate power couple. But it is their vision that binds them: "Everything I do is a war between the forces of good and evil, hatred and stupidity, greed and materialism versus the forces of light," Turner says (Applebaum, 1994).

They have grown weary of the isolated inside show: "We're so busy with our lives that we miss the big picture," and are ready to share the big ring together: "I decided we had to take better care of our planet because in taking care of our planet we might even be able to save ourselves" (Applebaum, 1993). It is a life or death choice for them. It always has been. Just as it is for all of us, the whole audience, the world of destruction or peace: "He stands for the all-American idea that talking—talking by phone or by satellite link-up, or talking in person, can solve problems and wars and bring world peace" (Applebaum, 1994). Jane has been searching for peace for a long time. She tried to find it with Tom Hayden. Now she has a partner who brings the world together. Turner and Fonda have mastered personal communication and resolved their life-long isolation. Their personal ringmastery reflects their public one.

Turner and Fonda's mastery is to cast the ring of communication, the ultimate postmodern family, an international one wedded electronically through access to information. Turner has electrified the audience of consumers and created a virtual planet of communication. He is the ringmaster of the electronic carnival. Turner began as an archetypal figure in American cultural life—the rugged individual who in developing his twenty-four-hour news program challenged the big networks—NBC, CBS, and ABC—and won. In Stockholm, after a sailing victory banquet, Turner stood up and introduced himself by saying: "Well, there sure are a lot of kings in this room. But where I come from, every man is a king."

SUMMARY

Madonna, Trump, and Turner live as iconic media figures. They fascinate us by exaggerating and relishing the fundamental shifts that we, their audience, encounter in our own journeys through life. Their lives are end-of-the-century spectacles that dramatize the transitions of childhood, psychodramas which enact through the business of media the ordinary childhood conflicts we all face. Bonding and separating, attention and rejection, success and failure, meaning and futility, courage and resistance, life and death all come into public portrayal. Their main attraction is their carnavalesque temerity and willingness to resolve conflicts in open view. They draw us into the ring of narcissism, to test our own struggles against theirs, to laugh at their clowning, to fume at their effrontery, to admire and envy their victories, to grieve or relish their failures. The themes are theirs and ours. The audience becomes the show.

These media stars do not modulate their behavior for anyone. They do not defer to presidents, fans, competitors, parents, friends; they will not bow to any system of authority or power, anyplace or anytime. They are the triumphant kings and the queen of misrule and we love them or hate them for it. In fact, all three reinvent their kingdoms for the audience each time they appear in public. They bestow their gifts upon an admiring crowd. They thrive against the odds. Each is intent on becoming the greatest show on earth. How do they do it?

In their aggressive pushing, knocking, and banging on limits of social constructions, they have become models for all of us. We watch and our own narcissism is gratified by their performance. Our sense of religious and institutional oppression is evoked in Madonna's singing and dancing, as she strips away hypocrisy. Anyone who has played Monopoly can identify with Trump's acquisitional excitement. 'Real' estate is not a home, it's a deal. Turner brings out our sense of daring, the desire to confront the limits of the elements, of authorities, of the established systems of power and control and money. Through daredevil acts, they make their dreams come true.

Madonna, Trump, and Turner are new cultural icons. The subculture they inhabit shapes the dominant culture, even defines American popular culture. They are the new entrepreneurs. They model the moral and aesthetic proportions of the individual and the emerging social order of late twentieth century America. In doing so they transform business life. Their merchandise is the self. But, for sales to be culminated, they must gratify the purchaser's needs. These exhibitors tantalize the voyeuristic consumers who, in turn, strip the exhibitionists naked. The dialectic creates the postindustrial psychodrama of media carnival.

BIBLIOGRAPHY

Applebaum, A. "How to Make a Billion and Bring Peace on Earth," in *The Spectator,* 14 May 1994, 8–10.

Bakhtin, M.(1968) *Rabelais and His World,* Cambridge: MIT Press.

Bibb, P. (1993) *It Ain't as Easy as It Looks: Ted Turner's Amazing Story,* New York: Crown.

Hurt, H.(1993) *Lost Tycoon: The Many Lives of Donald J. Trump,* New York: W.W. Norton.

Mailer, Norman, (1994) "Like a Lady," in *Esquire,* August, 41–56.

Newsweek, March 23, 1996, 32–33.

O'Donnell, J. (1991) *Trumped! The Inside Story of the Real Donald Trump—His Cunning Rise and Spectacular Fall,* New York: Simon and Schuster.

Trump, D. with C. Leerhsen (1990) *Trump: Surviving at the Top,* New York: Random House.

Trump, D. with T. Schwartz (1987) *Trump: The Art of the Deal,* New York: Random House.

24

SECTION SUMMARY: MEDIA AND CARNIVAL

Richard A. Goodman

The postindustrial world is permeated by the impact of all forms of media. Print media and broadcast compete with the quickly evolving Internet medium. Radio and television programming reach millions of citizens around the world every day. Such programming contains news and entertainment in the form of drama or music. The substance of the programming may tell a surface story and a deeper one about values of the social milieu. In many areas of the world, nations' media offerings are limited and thus the offerings are consciously controlled. Sometimes the control is rigorous and other times relaxed. Increased channel capacity from satellite TV and from the effects of deregulation have begun enriching available information and entertainment world-wide. The increased availability of the Internet also makes strict control less likely. This democratization of information has begun to raise problems among the guardians of thought in various national venues. But, regardless of guardianship and control, the basic result is that more and more members of the general population are receiving images conveying messages about their own very local situation, other and larger situations within their country as well as information from foreign situations.

Since media come from a variety sources, the actual content of media is highly variable and does not necessarily lead to the projection of sensible messages. A historical look at what is considered sensible shows that it is generally built on the value system of the previous decades rather than on the present or future decades. Stories built on current values will generally seem radical when compared to the previous decade's sense of what is sensible. Thus, it is often the older generation who perform the role as guardians of thought and who believe in the power of media to affect the actual behaviors and values of all.

Debate rages about whether the images depicted by the media really impact the social milieu and/or individual behavior. The prime argument against the impact of media on culture seems to be generated by media executives and their representatives. Well known social scientists like Ruth Benedict in her cultural-at-a-distance analysis certainly believed that media provides a good lens into the character of a nation. It is reasonable to assume that organizational participants are conditioned by what they see and hear through various media. How strongly conditioned is debatable. Repeated viewing of stories that present consistent messages about the meaning of life and works certainly affect participants' expectations about appropriate behavior in organizations and of organizations.

Certain media forms such as radio have been under-analyzed because of their apparent lack of impact. Radio broadcasts much more music than news or drama but messages are carried by all three modes of expression. Because of the large musical content on radio, the enormous radio audience is often overlooked by social scientists.

In "Modern and Postmodern Cultural Themes and Structure in British Radio Drama," Louise and Bernard James provide a fascinating insight in the world of radio drama, the size of the radio audience and the potential impact of radio drama. In some ways their premise was foreshadowed by Fred Emery and Eric Trist in their 1969 article about the year 2000. They concluded that the best prognostications were articulated by writers and artists rather than by scientist or economists. In Louise and Bernard's study, though, the authors did not 'foreshadow' discontinuous events. Instead, in both the structure of their writing and the themes of their stories, they 'reflected' the evolving social milieu. Postmodern structures were matched with postmodern plots. Radio drama authors selected from basic societal trends to inform their work. And through the selection of theme and structure they demonstrated prognostic ability as they constructed dramas based upon the early phase of a trend that would prove increasingly dominant over time. 'Media leads life' might well be the theme of their work. And so, in their conclusion they ask, "will the 'market forces' to which the BBC is now exposed stifle the creativity that has been emerging in radio drama during the last twenty years and drive the medium back towards more pessimistic, neo-modernist, messages and forms."

Michèle A. Bowring in "Eye of the Camera: An Exploration of Organizational Life as Portrayed on Television" travels a similar road but draws a different conclusion. Rather than argue that 'media leads life' she maintains that media reflects the social fabric of its time. Her argument about the impact of the media is illustrated by the debate between mythical television characters and a real candidate for the vice presidency of the United States. This vignette about the use of media by a politician is a theme reflected in other papers of this section. There is certainly good evidence for the impact of various television programs on the everyday conversation of the audiences—whether it be *Sesame Street* or *Coronation Street*.

The television series *The Mary Tyler Moore Show* was produced when times were simpler and women had yet to break into the corporate mainstream in significant numbers. In contrast, *Murphy Brown,* a series currently being produced, reflects a time when women have moved up the corporate ladder but still do not occupy the upper reaches of management significantly. Thus, the two programs reflect the society at large without a conscious attempt on the part of the producers and management to make serious points about the underlying social milieu. They were successful because the shows resonated with the society at large.

Michèle's semiotic discourse analysis is strongly suggestive of a society/media co-evolution. If media had a serious impact on and is a reflection of what is commonly considered appropriate organizational behavior, then the impact conditions organizational design, as organizational depiction in the media are far outside the control of management. The impact of the media can be ignored only at some risk.

These first chapters in this section focused on the relationship between the media depiction of organizational life and its potential effects on actual organizational life. In both works organizations are passive and adaptive. In the remaining three chapters organizations take an active role in using the media for their benefit. One focuses on pro-activity in the external environment. A second pro-actively promotes an appropriate internal environment. The final chapter reinforces the tendencies for media to be manipulated in a Bahktin-esque carnival.

'Landscape used as spectacle' is the central focus of Janet L. Hamnett's "Euro Disney: A Cross-Cultural Communications Failure?" Regardless of the activities that take place within this park, it is the setting that is the dominant feature. This chapter is about a bigger-than-life use of landscape-as-spectacle in the export of "produced" culture. It parallels Laurie Meamber's "Art Is Life—Life Is Art" in its description of the migration of 'high culture' into popular culture. The product of the theme park is embedded in its physical environment. This is also true of several other remarkable structures, such as the Pompidou Center in Paris or the Getty Center in Los Angeles. Both buildings overwhelm their contents. These managed landscapes and spectacles envelope visitors with meta-symbolic messages that control the produced culture. Like the museums, the theme park presents entertainment that is subordinated to the spectacle of the landscape and physical structure in which it is contained. In the Getty, like the Pompidou, the architecture dominates the cultural experience. In Euro Disney, the cultural experience is dominated by the firm's corporate vision. Here the experience is mediated by the physical 'design.' But in terms of what is sensible, Janet argues that Disney as popular culture has been successful with the masses, in spite of negative media reports and loud protests from France's intellectual elite.

Within "Symbol-Intensive Organizations: Management in the Age of Metaphor and Rhetoric," Virpi Leikola and Thomaz Wood Jr. argue that leadership has moved from a realistic style to a symbolic one. Impression management techniques have become the main work of organizations and managerial innovation is treated as a dramaturgical event. Symbol-Intensive Organization (SIO) managers hide ambiguities and contradictions behind metaphorical language.

Mass-media and pop-culture play major roles in defining our symbolic repertoire and reinterpreting the past. SIO managers and employees make extensive use of rhetoric and metaphors. In so doing, they try to manipulate symbols fluidly, thus modifying the 'organizational texture'. Furthermore, SIOs are cinematic settings, where reality is continuously reinterpreted, 'edited' and exhibited.

The massive use of information technology, boundary spanning, telecommuting practices, frequent participation of customers in the value-chain creating process and location of important functions and activities outside their physical frontiers means that the locus of management has become imaginary. Hence, coordination and control turn into media phenomena.

The Bowring vignette about the use of popular television as a foil for a politician reflects the power of media and how it can be used to persuade and manipulate. Ken Khoury and Dick Raspa in "The Business of Media: Organizing Carnival by the New Entrepreneurs" reflect on the growing carnival-like atmosphere of many businesses. They argue that the most unlikely people are able conduct their businesses as media events and use media to create personal wealth. In some way the most unsavory acts command the most money as they become not only show-people but the show itself. They seem to be 'on stage' all the time and with increased frequency, their performances intrude into their personal lives.

Madonna, Trump, and Turner are new cultural icons. The subculture they inhabit shapes the dominant culture, even defines American popular culture. They are the new entrepreneurs. They model the moral and aesthetic proportions of the individual and the emerging social order of late 20th century America and in the process they transform business life. Their merchandise is the self. But for sales to be realized, they must gratify purchasers' needs. These exhibitors tantalize the voyeuristic consumers who, in turn, strip the exhibitionists naked. The dialectic creates the postindustrial psychodrama of media carnival.

Media conveys images rather than reality. Media can be a powerful tool for conveying appropriate organizational behavior. Media can affect what is expected of organizations. Media can be controlled by a number of different forces and 'sensibility' can be lost to carnival as currency can be lost to tradition.

SECTION FIVE

25

LOOSE LINKS AND TIGHT ATTACHMENTS: MODES OF EMPLOYMENT AND MEANING-MAKING IN A CHANGING LABOR MARKET

Christina Garsten

The transformation of labor markets, globalization, and increased use of media technologies have given rise to new relationships that are emerging between organizations and their employees. The character of 'organizational' identity and boundaries and of personal 'professional' identity is changing. New labor market conditions and more diverse organizational contexts promote looser formal links between employers and employees and create new conditions for organizational meaning-making. This paper examines the dynamics and dilemmas of cultural management in contemporary organizations using an ongoing anthropological study of professionally trained 'temporary personnel.'

INTRODUCTION: RECENT TRENDS IN ORGANIZING

Organizing, as we commonly know it, is about relationships. It concerns the structuring of relations between collectives and individuals. The character of these relations has a significant bearing upon the kind of involvement an individual may have, and should have, in an organization. Following postindustrialism, new kinds of relationships are emerging between organizations and employees. The kinds of changes that concern me here are changes in the nature of belonging in an organization, based on contractual, formal agreements, but having wider social, emotional implications. In general, the favoring of loose contracts is interlinked with strivings towards tight emotional attachments in the workplace. 'Networked' organizations of highly committed, yet mobile, individuals are gradually replacing the more stable structures and stationary employees of the individual era, it seems. These developments have stimulated change, debate and research among both social scientists and the general public. Our perception of what is obvious and desirable in terms of organization and affiliation seem to be changing.

Along with transformations in corporations and labor markets, there is a boom in descriptive rhetoric. As described elsewhere (Garsten, 1997) the choice of words in this discursive flow has associative links to a neo-liberal political discourse. According to this rhetoric, we are now all 'customers,' or 'actors on the market.' Parts of the public sector have been 'exposed to competition' and have to 'package' and 'customize' goods and services. Concepts such as 'lean-production,' 'outsourcing,' and 'just-in-time production' echo significant changes of direction and logic. As Gustafsson (1994) notes, the urge to be efficient, rational and diligent does not primarily characterize a trivial 'must' to survive. The 'morality of efficiency' is spreading to other aspects of reality, to arenas which do not easily lend themselves to the efficiency conceptual frame. He (1994:184) points out: "It becomes increasingly difficult for us, each and every one of us, to question the imperative of the efficiency moral. Even play is slowly being pulled into the sawmill" (my translation).

The character of these concepts and images derive mainly from the private sector and to conditions that apply to business-driven organizations. In broad terms, private-sector organizations have a particular kind of relation to the market and its actors, to customers and their supposed needs. Even so, the 'customization' and 'packaging' of all sorts of public-sector products and services is gaining momentum. We used to think of the market and public institutions as relatively discrete cultures but they are now becoming more complex and intertwined.

In postmodernist thought, the shift to postmodern society assumes the replacement of older modernist and intellectual notions of rationality with the reality of the marketplace as the privileged pathway (Bauman, 1988). 'Consumer freedom' has become the cognitive and moral focus of life, the integrative bond of society, and the focus of systemic management (Clegg, 1993).

In Clegg's words (1993), the use of an empowering rhetoric with utopian signature does not, however, mean that power has become forgotten or obsolete. On the contrary, it covers a new and equally significant economy and culture of power, in which a plethora of new competencies, skills, empowerments, and states of mind play the leading roles. Our failure to grasp it is because "The canvas is not fixed; the palette not given; the style not dictated. Representations can be fixed anywhere, anyhow, anyway. This is the post-modern democratic freedom of the market" (1993:275).

For individuals experiencing the effects of the down-sizing and re-structuring of organizations, the influence of the market does not stop at the organizational border. It affects them not least as a heightened awareness of one's market value, skills, competencies and experiences. Under such conditions, the continuous monitoring of competitive skills and image presented in the marketplace becomes a rational consequence of the commodification of professional identity[1,2]. For 'just-in-time personnel,' whose services are bought on temporary bases according to customers' needs, management of a professional image becomes especially important.

One significant aspect of current changes is higher flexibility and mobility in the labor market. This has allowed employers to take advantage of high levels of unemployment and weakened union power to push for more flexible work conditions and labor contracts. Even for regular employees work schedules that vary according to periods of demand are becoming more common. More important for my purposes here, however, is the move away from regular employment towards increasing reliance upon part-time, temporary or sub-contracted work arrangements. The current trend is to reduce the number of 'core' workers and to rely increasingly upon a work force that can be taken quickly on board when needed and laid off when not.

The result is a labor market structure often depicted in terms of a core and two categories of peripheral workers (Harvey, 1989). The core consists of employees with full-time, permanent status and is central to the long-term future of the organization. They enjoy greater job security, good promotion and reskilling prospects, and relatively generous pension, insurance, and other fringe benefit rights. Nevertheless, they are expected to be adaptable, flexible, and if necessary geographically mobile. According to reports from both sides of the Atlantic this is a steadily shrinking group.

The periphery encompasses two rather different sub-groups. The first consists of full-time employees hired to do clerical, secretarial, routine and lesser skilled manual work. The second group includes part-timers, casuals, fixed-term contract staff. These temps have less job security than the first group and are subject to high flexibility demands. Temporary personnel agencies have found a niche by turning the idea of flexibility into a business idea. As a temp agency manager recently told me, "We want to be an independent resource for large and medium-sized companies; their elastic band."

Of particular interest here is the fact that within the category of temporary personnel itself there is a great deal of variation. Economists, technicians, lawyers, and doctors have recently joined the ranks of professionals working through temp agencies. In the US, the number of executive-level temporary placement firms has increased five-fold in five years (*New York Times,* December 17, 1995).

Similar trends are seen in other parts of the world as well. The trend towards

---

[1] I use the term professional identity in a loose sense, referring to a socially constructed sense of control over a more or less delimited field of competence.

[2] The way in which the new market conditions are described by Clegg makes it appear as though the role of actors in shaping, altering, or opposing such things as "the black hole" of the market have been forgotten in the theoretical framework, leaving us with weak conceptual tools for actually understanding the new frameworks of power.

temporary employment is a significant aspect of the globalization of labor markets. The U.S., Great Britain, the Netherlands, France, Belgium, Sweden and Japan have seen a growing percentage of temps in the workforce. For the temp this entails both opportunity and risk. It places new demands on skills and competencies and raises a challenge for trade unions to create various types of contracts for collective action and articulation of member interests.

Large-scale international organizations produce and organize a global flow of people, ideas, and commodities. They contribute to enacting and legitimizing preferable ways of organizing, and desirable professional skills and competencies across nations. They build a strong corporate culture at their core (Garsten, 1994).

Recent interest in organizational culture and commitment can be seen as a reflection of the relatively fickle and transient character of many contemporary social formations. The reflexive bent also generates constant demands for monitoring the new organizational structures and the actions of individuals, creating continually evolving needs for cultural management (Bauman 1992:195). The increasing interest in organizational culture and the abundance of rhetoric on new types of organization and new personal and interpersonal competencies, is also a consequence of the way in which an idea is marketed. Here, organization consultants, described by Czarniawska-Joerges (1988) as 'merchants of meaning' play an influential role. Burrell (1992:87) describes them as "seeking to provide the expensive but quick fix to an industrial and commercial audience who, ever hungry for novelty, are eager to consume different ideas before turning greedily to a newer fad in the relentless pursuit of busyness" (Alvesson 1993:5). This, in turn, leads to the fundamental question of what is it like to work as a temp or 'hired consultant' in an organization that lacks important aspects of continuity, yet offers an embracing ethos and sense of belonging to its members?

The idea of an embracing organizational culture, as promoted by many organization consultants, is apparently at odds with the idea of the substantial use of temporary personnel.

My focus here is on the peripheral members of organizational communities. As part of a study of temps and their relations to temporary placement firms and client organizations, I explore modes of employment and of belonging and characterize current trends. Specifically, I show how the simultaneous existence of centrifugal and centripetal forces in the labor market influences the conditions for 'just-in-time' personnel while also changing the dynamics and dilemmas of cultural management within global firms.

LOOSE LINKS: TEMPS ON THE PERIPHERY

Reich (1992) argues that the ideal organization now resembles a spider's web. 'Strategic brokers' are found at the center but there are numerous connections in which they are not directly involved and new ones are spun all the time. The central skills are rapid problem-identification and problem-solving. Everything else can be obtained 'as needed.' Office space, factories, and warehouses can be rented; standard equipment can be leased; standard components can be bought wholesale from cheap producers; secretaries, routine data processors, bookkeepers, and routine production workers can be hired on a temporary basis. In fact, "relatively few people actually work for the high-value enterprise in the traditional sense of having steady jobs with fixed salaries" (Reich, 1992:89).

Although this imagery tells more about desired states than about actual ones, field work I did at Apple in 1988–90 (Garsten, 1994) supports these trends. There was a core of non-exempt employees on the regular payroll, and a periphery of temps or contractors. The core of non-exempt employees received regular wages and generous fringe benefits. They also had, more or less, unlimited access to company locales, meetings, and information channels. Through access to AppleLink, the electronic network, they had access to a vast amount of information crucial to successful performance and for keeping abreast of organizational changes.

On the periphery were contractors and temps who had delimited employment. Temps were generally hired for administrative positions that demanded little professional training and skill, while contractors were generally free-lance engineers or other skilled professionals. Many of them viewed their temporary assignment as an opportunity to join the Apple employment core.

In many cases temps engaged in activities that were separate, performed backstage as it were, and created a platform for core members be successful in their work (Kunda, 1992). Temps and contractors were also peripheral in the sense that they had limited access to information channels and locales, although they were often invited to participate in off-site team-building sessions and other social events. Rarely were they granted the same benefits as non-exempts.

These employment trends create a variety of pressures on firms and governments. In Sweden, for instance, temporary placement firms are a relatively recent phenomenon. Government labor market policies have traditionally strengthened the position of employees vis-à-vis employers, limiting the possibilities for using temps. A commission on working life regulation was created to evaluate regulations and to lay the groundwork for a more flexible and timely regulatory framework while at the same time ensuring individuals' needs for security and safety. Labor unions, employer associations, private corporations, state authorities and individuals all have stakes in the ongoing discussion. On a European and global level, similar discussions are being held.

A flexible workforce is generally said to offer organizations and employees financial advantages and intangible benefits. Not surprisingly, private corporations and employers favor loose formal links between employers and employees. For instance, in Sweden, a recent radio advertisement for a temp agency features a manager telephoning a vacationing employee. The employee assumes that call is an indication that he is needed at work and while initially he is flattered he is also concerned that he will have return to work sooner than planned. In fact, the manager is calling to tell him just the opposite, he does not have to come home at all! In his absence they leased some one from a temp agency who has proven to be so good that they have decided to keep him.

The message is clearly one of interchangeability, the notion that skills and experiences of one particular employee can easily be replaced by those of another (Ahrne, 1994). Even though the recognition and identification of individual employees is important for an organization, no individual can be indispensable if the organization is to last. In this particular case, years of service does not count for much. Skills and experiences may be bought, sold or leased just like any other commodity. The message, heard in numerous countries including the US, seems to be that market dynamics clearly drive organizing processes.

Advertisements for temporary personnel highlight the notion of interchangeability, adding a competitive and for some an uneasy edge to the message. In these messages the fact that knowledge and experience may easily be transferred from one context to another is underlined. One advertisement recently featured in the Stockholm area in metro-stations and on buses says, "Bank director with guarantee. Let us recruit. You pay only if you are satisfied." Another temp agency ran a similar ad more or less simultaneously: "Completely healthy collaborators, Whenever you want, With guarantee."

Conversely, a temp agency manager suggested that a high level of professional experience is required from people who seek employment as 'hired consultants.' Consequently, they are not looking for young people with eager minds, but rather for middle-aged, self-confident professionals with long-term experience. Thus, the demand for increasing specialization in skills and knowledge favors an image of temps as individuals with unique qualities and skills. The recent trend for professionals to work through placement agencies underscores this image.

Labor market conditions and the trend towards loose formal contracts lead temp agencies to look for individuals with a particular set of professional and individual skills. Especially conspicuous at present are demands for initiative and readiness for change. Such capacities have become to be highly valued in high velocity societies.

Davidow and Malone (1992) speak of 'a new breed' of employees whose core characteristics stand in opposition to those required during the industrial era. Organizations now look for 'socially competent' people, who embrace the idea of change and continuous learning, and are flexible enough to adjust rapidly to new circumstances. One temp agency manager I interviewed confirms the public image by saying that 'hired consultants' should be "lone wolves with a social talent, confident in themselves."

We may interpret this in line with Giddens (1990), who argues that the continuous need for learning characteristic of late-modernity represents a change in social conditions and in the critical relationship between abstract systems of knowledge and the individual lay agent. To be on the periphery stresses the need to stay abreast of developments within one's professional arena.

A related issue concerns the relationship of 'professional image and identity' with the 'identity of the self.' Preoccupation with individual skills, competencies and characteristics suggest distinctly new ways in which organizational subjectivity is learned and reproduced. The discourse and the projects of defining and developing 'the self' may be understood as disciplinary constructs that represent an extension of the arena of organizational control. Most likely, 'the organization man' of the industrial age will appear as a seemingly independent 'just-in-time consultant.'

TIGHT ATTACHMENTS: IMAGINED COMMUNITIES OF THE WORKPLACE

In client organizations, individuals on a temporary assignment have more restricted access to meetings and information channels than employees in general and top managers in particular. Nevertheless, temps and contractors are often expected to 'fit in' with the work environment both in terms of personality and value-orientation. Corporations vary in this respect. Human resource policies, work structures and the like contribute to defining expectations. The temps at 'Tech,' the American high-tech organization described by Kunda (1992), are exempt from membership demands and their deeper implications. At Tech temps are neither expected nor allowed to become full-fledged participants or subjects of the organization's ideology. From the managerial view, they are present in body only and the relationship is purely economic. Thus, there is no managerial attempt to encompass or penetrate the self. "What is not expected from temporary workers suggests what is expected from others: an exchange that is more than economic" (Kunda, 1992:209).

The 'Apple culture,' on the other hand, addresses everyone who is involved with the company—employees, developers, dealers and users. Apple is more expansive in its outreach. Not only is there a transnational drive, but also a transorganizational one. The firm ideologically embraces everyone through their common attraction to Apple products. Although on the periphery, temps, just like central managers and other core employees, are embraced by the same ideological message.

Organizational leaders try to counteract the lack of loyalty that may follow loose formal links by playing on inclusiveness and community-oriented strivings. As Ahrne (1994:92) notes, "Organizations are formed under tensions between centripetal and centrifugal forces that keep affiliates together or make them drift apart." While the links and dependencies between organizations and placement firms are important centrifugal forces, organizational cultures promoting ideological and affective commitment work in the opposite direction as centripetal forces. This inclusive aspect is also present in the notion of 'the virtual organization'—an artificially created community of ideas, people and products that crosses spatial and temporal boundaries. The virtual organization is rather like a network of loosely connected individuals, offices, or computers. In Davidow and Malone's (1992:5–6) view 'the virtual organization' evades a clear structural understanding:

> *What will a virtual corporation look like? There is no single answer. To the outside observer, it will appear almost edgeless, with permeable and continuously changing interfaces between company, supplier, and customers. From inside the firm the view will be no less amorphous, with traditional offices, departments, and operating divisions constantly reforming according to need. Job responsibilities will regularly shift, as will lines of authority—even the very definition of employee will change, as some customers and suppliers begin to spend more time in the company.*

Apple employs the network metaphor while downplaying the clear, formal lines of hierarchy and communication (Garsten 1994). The importance of 'networking' is an all-pervasive theme. The notion of networking as a verb occupies a central place in the organization. Having a wide network increases the possibility of obtaining information about what is going to happen. In other words, it constitutes a powerful resource, and hence a basis for power within the organization.

The discourse of networking relates closely to the rhetoric of equality and change. It is ripe with positive connotations that suggest a 'flat' model of organization that emphasizes each individual as an important node in the network, rather than as a position in a hierarchy. As Sculley said (1987:96), "The beauty of a network is that it has no center. It is a process more than a structure." Apple's technology also supports the network model of organizing. This can be seen even through its advertisements. During my fieldwork at the Swedish subsidiary in Kista, an ad was designed in the shape of a network, where each node was a tiny Apple logo with the name of a subsidiary employee printed underneath. The ad read: "Would you like to work in a network with us and tear down pyramids? The Macintosh . . . stimulates a flatter network organization where the integrated powers of individuals give the organization its strength."

It is assumed that networks have an integrating function and imply a more democratic way of organizing. Much of the allure of the term can be attributed to the hope that this form of organization would combine *Gemeinschaft* with *Gesellschaft;* a social formation characterized by organic unity, a sense of belonging, and direct, closely intertwined relations with that of a mechanistic constellation of separate individuals who have rational motives for group formation (Garsten, 1997).

It is obvious that we are dealing with the management of emotional ties between employees and the workplace as well as with mythical realities defining modes of appropriate thinking and acting. What is striking is that it is the company itself and the emotions and images it evokes that is important rather than the products. In a comment about market strategies, John Sculley (1987:55) said:

> *Consumers are not middle-class or upper-class; they're hybrids. These days someone might buy a cheap digital watch, yet drive a BMW. Or drive to a fast-food restaurant in a Mercedes. To reach these hybrid consumers, we try to attract a 'share of mind' rather than*

traditional 'share of market.' To do that, we have to position not just the product, which has an ever-shrinking shelf life, but the company—who we are, and why we are important to consumers beyond the life of the product, today and tomorrow.

Today many companies use ideologically motivated themes where the individual stands out against big bureaucracy and oppressive structures to create loyalty and mind share. Capturing a share of mind rather than a share of the market requires an appeal to values rather than to status. It calls for drama, narrative, or myth. The images need to be recognizable and touch upon aspirations and dreams. The construction of mind share requires affective identification. A temp agency advertising campaign run recently in the Stockholm area captures this idea. It said simply, "You make a difference."

Today's marketing of temporary personnel builds on a view of individuals as strong and independent, capable of tailoring their own careers and planning their own spare time. Yet they must be highly motivated to get the client's job done. A degree of emotional involvement and loyalty is therefore indispensable.

Many organizations with the number of loosely connected actors oscillating dramatically are truly 'imagined communities' (Anderson, 1983)—the community aspect being only illusory. The effort required to create mind share and community is directly related to the lack of stability and institutionalized continuity of 'imagined communities.'

Having no other (and above all no objectified, supra-individual) anchors except the affections of their "members," imagined communities exist solely through their manifestations: through occasional spectacular outbursts of togetherness (demonstrations, festivals, riots)—sudden materializations of the idea, all the more effective and convincing for blatantly violating the routine of quotidianity. (Bauman, 1992: xix–xx)

During the course of everyday work life, temps work closely with other employees, often performing similar tasks. From an outsider's perspective they could easily pass as insiders. Temps also cross organizational boundaries as their numbers increase and decrease with workload. Within particular symbolic domains, however, their status as peripheral members and trespassers of the organizational boundary appears more clearly.[3] Their presence serves as a defining contrast for others who are more fully part of the organizational community.

This raises the issue of the conditions for maintaining professional integrity in organizations where social interdependencies rely on personal attachments and a strong sense of organizational community. Professional integrity may be weakened by encroachments from others such as managers striving for control over the way

---

[3]The concept of symbolic domain here refers to the differing interpretative framework that characterize different work settings (Schultz, 1991). The concept has been used within organizational theory, closely linked, for example, to concepts of organizational "arena" and "context" (Tainio, et al., 1983, Goffman, 1959).

in which professionals work. For many, a temporary position creates an internal tension between commitments.

The concept of 'network' is commonly used instead of 'organization' as it connotes personal relations between people rather than bureaucracy and hierarchy. It is perceived as being dynamic, creative and friendly (Ahrne, 1994). Work relations resting on personal relations are more vulnerable than strictly formal ones. They are more open to gradual shifts and redefinitions. 'The network fad' and the favoring of loose formal ties illustrate the double emphasis on egalitarian teamwork and the inarticulate presence of authority and power in contemporary organizations. Personal engagement, loyalty and shared visions become powerful sources for allegiance when the formal contract between employer and employed is fickle and flexible.

'JUST-IN-TIME PERSONNEL' AND THE PREVALENCE OF ORGANIZATIONAL DOUBLE-BINDS

The increasing trend towards the use of temps brings forth a number of dynamic tensions, ambiguities and paradoxes. Centrifugal forces seem to be dominating, with sub-contracting, leasing, franchising taking on increased importance. Formal ties between employers and employees are becoming looser and can be dissolved more easily than in the past. Hence organizations must work on strengthening ties of affection and mind share as a way of promoting cohesion and loyalty. If affiliates share a sense of community, centrifugal tendencies can be overcome while the financial benefits of leasing workforce members can still be maintained.

Professionals generally have an advantage because they control a specific domain of knowledge which they maintain as a personal source of value. Experts are not as easy to replace as others, and their sense of professional integrity makes them less amenable to control. This leads us to think that professionals working for temp agencies should be able to acquire a relatively large degree of independence and status based on their particular professional training. The massive advertising for skilled secretaries, economists, assistants, and technicians supports the idea of a specialized and highly competent flexible workforce by employing glamorous and extravagant promises of 'personnel power.'

On the other hand, the condition of temps and contractors is generally described as a move towards a more generalized set of skills and professional competencies among a large number of white-collar service-sector workers. Reich (1992) even contends that former business and professional categories and entities are becoming irrelevant. In the emerging global economy, he sees "the ecumenical company" where professional categories give way to new broad categories of work that better reflects the individual's competitive position. He calls them *routine production services, in-person services,* and *symbolic-analytic services.*

The latter category, symbolic-analytic services, is of particular importance. It includes problem-solving, problem-identifying, and strategic brokering activities of researchers, management consultants, management information specialists, strategic planners, marketing strategists, journalists, to mention only a few professional categories. It is also in this category that we find a number of high-profile temps, working as accountants, computer engineers, or human-resource consultants.

In Reich's view, a job category officially classified 'professional' or 'managerial' has little bearing upon its role in the world economy. Not all professionals are symbolic analysts. Nor are all symbolic analysts professionals. Symbolic analysts are said to be able to draw on established bodies of knowledge with the touch of a computer key. What is more valuable than professional credentials is the capacity to effectively and creatively use the knowledge.

Professions have to be socially viable to be successful; they have to be *mediating* institutions; they must contain within themselves a variety of approaches to match the varying approaches of their diverse clients. Such a view speaks of the precarious balancing act of temporary staff, to whom changing conditions may entail new and enhanced opportunities for mediating between parties, as well as a loss of professional identity and a sense of wholeness and integrity in work (Schwartz and Thompson, 1990).

The rhetoric of networked organizations with temps circling in and out clearly give evidence to the double-bind of temporary work conditions. As seen in advertisements, it highlights the resourceful independence of 'hired consultants'. The other side of the equation is the market driven by the interchangeability of temps. Organizational policies show a degree of ambivalence in dealing with temps who, while they gain acceptance and admission into organizational work processes and cultural narratives, are also reminded that they are outsiders.

Temps themselves must deal with the challenge of maintaining a balance between flexibility and stability. A temp once commented that the most valuable thing to her is learning how to juggle constantly changing priorities and job assignments. They are people who challenge, oppose, question and improvise. As one said, they are 'odds and ends persons.' Their actions embody ambivalence about the optimal compromise necessary for dealing effectively with the incompatible demands of flexibility and stability (Weick 1979). Upholding professional identity and community in an environment where those very attributes are undermined by continuous change is a precarious match.

The trend for 'just-in-time' arrangements in the labor market is only one way in which the established industrial age models are being questioned, dissolved, and replaced by new ones. Corporations are no longer easily carved out of their environment; the discrete cultures of private and public are no more finite; nor is organizational membership easily determined. 'Just-in-time' personnel embody social changes that are underway within society at large and challenge existing categories in the realms of work, employment, and organization.

BIBLIOGRAPHY

Abbott, A. (1988) *The System of Professions,* Chicago: The University of Chicago Press.

Ahrne, G. (1994) *Social Organizations. Interaction Inside, Outside and Between Organizations,* London: Sage.

Alvesson, M. (1993) *Cultural Perspectives on Organizations,* Cambridge: Cambridge University Press.

Anderson, B. (1983) *Imagined Communities,* London: Verso.

Bauman, Z. (1988) "Viewpoint: Sociology And Postmodernity" *Sociological Review,* 36, 4, 790–813.

Bauman, Z. (1992) *Intimations of Postmodernity,* London: Routledge and Kegan Paul.

Burrage, M. and R. Thorstendahl (1990) *Professions in Theory and History,* London: Sage.

Burrell, G. (1992) "The Organization of Pleasure" in M. Alvesson and M. Willmott, eds., *Critical Management Studies,* London: Sage.

Clegg, S. (1993) *Frameworks of Power,* London: Sage.

Czarniawska-Joerges, B. (1988) *To Coin a Phrase. On Organizational Talk, Organizational Control and Management Consulting,* Stockholm: Stockholm School of Economics.

Davidow, W.H. and M.S. Malone (1993) *The Virtual Corporation: Structuring and Revitalizing the Corporation for the 21st Century.* New York: HarperBusiness.

Garsten, C. (1994) *Apple World: Core And Periphery In A Transnational Organizational Culture,* Stockholm: Stockholm Studies in Social Anthropology. Doctoral dissertation.

Garsten, C. (1997) "The Double-Dealing Of Rhetoric—An Anthropological Perspective On The Dynamics Of Organizing In The Swedish Public Sector" in A. Bugra and B. Usdiken, eds., *State, Market and Organizational Forms,* Berlin: Walter de Gruyter.

Giddens, A. (1990) *The Consequences of Modernity,* Stanford: Stanford University Press.

Goffman, E. (1959) *The Presentation of Self in Everyday Life,* Harmondsworth: Penguin.

Gustafsson, C. (1994) *Produktion av allvar.* Om det ekonomiska förnuftets metafysik, Stockholm: Nerenius and Santérus Förlag.

Harvey, D. (1989) *The Condition of Postmodernity. An Enquiry into the Origins of Cultural Change,* Oxford: Blackwell.

Kunda, G. (1992) *Engineering Culture: Control and Commitment in a High-Tech Corporation,* Philadelphia: Temple University Press.

New York Times, December 17, 1995.

Reich, R.B. (1992) *The Work of Nations: Preparing Ourselves for 21st-Century Capitalism,* New York: Vintage Books.

Schultz, M. (1991) "Transitions Between Symbolic Domains In Organizations" *Organization Studies,* 12,4, 489–506.

Schwartz, M. and M. Thompson (1990) *Divided We Stand. Redefining Politics, Technology and Social Choice,* New York: Harvester Wheatsheaf.

Sculley, J. with J.A. Byrne (1987) *Odyssey. Pepsi to Apple: A Journey of Adventure, Ideas, and the Future,* New York: Harper and Row.

Tainio, R, et al. (1983) "Managerial 'Arenas' Of The Firm" *Working Papers Helsinki School of Economics.* F-67, 1–38.

Weick, K.E. (1969) *The Social Psychology of Organizing,* New York: Random House.

26

COMPETITION: THE STRUCTURING OF POSTINDUSTRIAL ORGANIZATIONAL LIFE

Patricia Riley and Lisa Howard

There seem to be many contradictions in emerging postindustrial organizational forms. Organizations increase participation while restructuring. Employees are asked to form enduring relationships with customers and partner organizations while jobs are outsourced. Information systems designed to flatten and democratize organizations are transformed into advertising and sales venues. In this chapter we investigate competition as a key structuring mechanism of the postindustrial age and as a metaphor of profound difficulties and challenges. Three diverse case studies demonstrate the power of competition as a metaphor for driving organizational change. The collaborative competitive metaphor of Mondragon is explored by way of contrast.

INTRODUCTION

You know, my business isn't distributing roofing—it's principally keeping my competitors from distributing roofing. Same with you. All we do is cut each other's throats and make the public pay for it.

Babbit, by Sinclair Lewis

"Truth" is "a mobile army of metaphors."
Nietzsche

We observe daily large and rapid reconfigurations of the increasingly global economic system. Recently we witnessed a series of intriguing but sobering events: a publishing executive touting his company's superior market position one day and announcing a merger with a chief competitor the next; a retail manufacturer spending millions of dollars to train employees in 'first-time quality' practices and then deciding to subcontract a majority of its assembly work to plants in Malaysia and Korea; and managers in a large electronics corporation explaining why there will be another layoff even though the company just announced record quarterly profits. Employees, including management, reacted quite viscerally to the obvious and in some instances even ludicrous contradictions inherent in these announcements.

These events—a merger, off-shore subcontracting, and downsizing—seem familiar and ordinary. We have come to believe people are comfortable with these scenarios because they expect that such actions are a necessary part of the 'shakeout' that continues to reproduce itself during the inexorable process of globalization. Few can argue that an intensification of globalization is dramatically changing the face of American and other business concerns. As Tapscott and Caston (1993:4) note:

> *A pressing reality of the new global environment is the emergence of a new era of competition. Competition is arising not only from traditional adversaries in traditional markets, or from new entrants to a specific industry or economic sector, but also from the disintegration of barriers to previously insulated and protected markets.*

Multinational conglomerates such as Procter and Gamble, Unilever, and Matsushita Electric are shifting the competitive focus from national to global levels (Goshal and Bartlett, 1990). The Motorolas and Eastman Kodaks of the world have expanded operations into more than 50 foreign countries (Adler, 1997). Along with these expansions is a heightening of competitive pressures as well as increasing in complexity. Kirkman and Shapiro (1997:730) claim that:

> *As a result of this increased global competition, organizations have been forced to rethink how they produce and deliver products and services. To compete more directly and effectively with global rivals, some U.S. organizations have established facilities in foreign countries. . . . However, moving their operations overseas has not been sufficient in enabling companies to compete in the global marketplace. Many rival foreign firms pay their employees low wages (Hamrin, 1980), and this has also led U.S. management to "downsize" or reduce costly workforces.* (Kozlowski, Chao, Smith and Hedlund, 1993).

The inference is unmistakable—the new era of foreign competition is the driving force behind many restructuring efforts and other corporate changes. This is, of course, an over-simplification as other forces are also at work. These include phenomena such as aerospace downsizing and mergers which have followed the break-up of the Soviet Union and significant retail consolidation due in part to the introduction of powerful new information technology. The role of competition however, does not go away. It is still a story about winning, losing, and surviving.

We contend that *competition* is one of the most significant cultural stories in the structuring of organizations in the late modern times. Seemingly it pervades all institutional forms—business, government and even academia. Our university administration, for example, has a plan to improve its competitive position in the recruiting and retention of students and to market the school to prospective students worldwide, while students demand the skills and the experience that will make them competitive in the job market, etc. This competitive positioning represents a new and evolving cultural value within an institution that hitherto has expressed very different central values.

Finding evidence that competition, as a value, is endemic in a capitalist, heavily materialistic, media-saturated environment is not exactly news. What we have learned in our investigation is that this story has some unexpected twists. It is the often taken-for-granted nature of competition in its many guises that we have found to be most illuminating and concerning. This study provides one interpretation of this story as we examine the structure of competition within three diverse organizational settings and then contrast them with Mondragon—an example of an unique organization founded on collaborative norms.

It is important to acknowledge that this endeavor risks over-generalizing and could privilege majority belief-structures and 'loud' conversations. We argue, however, that one of the principal activities of organizations is finding *a story* that makes sense to all who consider themselves members. This justifies the time and energy spent clarifying the mission and vision, engaging in strategic planning and goal alignment activities, etc. Having greater insight into the role competition plays in 'story control' helps us understand the ways other voices are silenced.

COMPETITION AS A CULTURAL METAPHOR

Competition is not a simple term. It is suffused with folk taxa of everyday usage and also has several distinct research definitions. Thus the metaphor of competition appears to be best understood as tightly knit into the fabric of its host culture—in this case America. Many analysts describe the American cultural addiction to an endless series of contests or to a staggering obsession with victory (Kohn, 1992). Paul Wachtel (1983) describes competition as our "state religion." This is not to say that competition as a structuring concept does not exist in other cultures, just that "what may be merely familiar in other places has reached exaggerated, often ludicrous, proportions in this country" (Kohn, 1992:2).

The cultural 'nature' of competition has been the subject of numerous studies. It seems logical that locales with plentiful resources would be less competitive and those lacking in resources would be more so, but this hypothesis has not been borne out by anthropological research. Highly competitive societies have emerged in areas of abundant resources while places starved for resources have often produced very cooperative social structures. "To say that people naturally become competitive when there isn't enough to go around is not merely inaccurate, but a reflection of how easily we universalize our own cultural norms" (Kohn, 1992:39).

The metaphor of competition is pervasive in our society. For example, Krugman (1994) believes that the current fascination with the competitive metaphor in political discourse is due in part to its easy comprehensibility. From early childhood (e.g., the testing process in school, Little League baseball, etc.) Americans are steeped in the language and practice of competition. The competitive nature of our business practices is widely understood. Competition as a cultural metaphor is reflexively produced across a variety of contexts, each re-legitimizing its power in alternative sites and contributing to its enduring nature.

There are definitions of interfirm rivalry where companies strive for generally incompatible positions and vie for the same resources (Hannan and Freeman, 1989). In this case, each company's products or services are pitted against its competitors' products or services and inevitably one wins, or at least dominates the market or niche. It is this sense of competition upon which the organizational discourse in this study focuses.

STRUCTURING ORGANIZATIONS METAPHORICALLY

This analysis is grounded in Giddens' (1984) structuration theory. Organizational members learn routines, follow norms, make decisions and inhabit their settings by interacting with other members and drawing on stores of mutual knowledge. The organization represents a patterning of social relations across time and space; social practices that are constituted in reproduced practices taking place in interaction. "Institutions, then, are concretized systems—patterns of relations constituted in agents' practices and put into place by their chronic reproduction" (Banks and Riley, 1993:177). Thus, organizations 'exist' only in acts of communication.

Organizational members (agents in structuration theory) draw upon rules and resources in instantiating their actions. Rules are not prescriptions but generalized procedures inherent in action settings orienting what agents do and say. Resources represent the capability to generate command over material (allocative resources) and over social conditions (authoritative resources). Rules and resources are actualized in human agency and serve as important analytic tools. Thus organizational communication is mediated by the rules and resources that are 'carried' by individuals. The rules and resources imply the 'structural' properties of organizational systems as the interaction level exist in real time and space/place, but the structural properties exist only as memory traces.

In this particular analysis the concept of agency is critical. Agency means that there is a dialectic of control between the constraints of the organizational systems (patterning of activity) and the capability of agents to 'do otherwise.' This suggests that there are times when organizational members must engage in reflexive self-monitoring to give discursive accounts of their reasons and aims. Without reflexivity it is difficult for organizational members to envision or communicate alternative courses of action.

Metaphors are key features of communication. Traditionally, scholars have recognized two types of metaphors—figurative and deep structure. In a figurative metaphor A is related to B because some quality of A resembles B and the metaphor captures this resemblance succinctly or helps articulate a subject for which there is no specific language (Ortony, 1979). Thus a firm's rival becomes the 'other side' or in a sports metaphor the 'other team.' Figurative metaphors structure complex situations by naming key elements and framing relevant issues. By telling the workforce that 'you only play one team at a time and one game at a time' management simplifies a multi-competitor market by focusing on only one competitor. This highlights certain elements but masks others (Schon, 1979).

Pondy (1983) contends that figurative metaphors serve to place explanation beyond doubt and argumentation and to facilitate change. Competition is a common example of both of these points. When the boss says, "We need to change our product mix (and by implication the workforce skill mix) because of product changes made by our prime competitor," few feel the decision is arguable, or at least not publicly arguable. Competition becomes the watchword for all subsequent changes associated with the shift in product focus.

The use of metaphors also reinforces relationships. The successful use of metaphor requires that all parties recognize the concept of 'related' qualities. This means that they share certain perceptions, interests, backgrounds, and metaphorical traditions. Metaphors cultivate intimacy (Cooper, 1984) and isolate those who are not privy to the nature of the metaphor. Harragan (1977) noted that masculine metaphors in the workplace excluded women from powerful decision-making networks. Metaphors both constrain and reinforce community membership, excluding some purposefully and some thoughtlessly.

Surface-level metaphors may be vivid or novel. Both Giddens and Schon argue they are critical to innovation even though they are often viewed as insignificant. Having fallen victim to the "pathology of metaphorizing," they may evolve into stale clichés that are perceived as nothing more than 'idle chatter' (Cooper, 1984:58). Surface-level metaphors, however, can be significant as "symptoms of a particular kind of SEEING-AS, the 'metaphoring' or 'carrying over' of perspectives from one domain to another" (Schon, 1979:254). Again, competition is a good example of 'carrying perspectives over' since competitive language and practices move from country to country, from company to company and from firm to nation-state.

A deep structure metaphor is a systematic way of talking about one domain in terms of another (Cooper, 1984). Instead of A resembling B, A is SEEN AS B. 'Argument as war' is a classic example (Lakoff and Johnson, 1980). The root metaphor communicates far more than simple resemblance. Conceiving of A as B shapes the very conception of B. For example, many organizations conceive of their difficulties as "international competition" problems—*e.g.,* that imports are pushing workers out of high-wage jobs. An appropriate response would be "being tough on US-Japan trade agreements/restrictions." If the problem were seen as one of internal quality then the response might be a TQM program.

Deep structure metaphors can be characterized as two related processes: generative metaphors and root metaphors (Berg, 1985). Generative metaphors have the ability to generate meanings for human action as control devices:

> *In the organizational change contract, we may talk about business ideas or business concepts as more or less powerful metaphors to generate meaning in complex and ambiguous situations. A dead metaphor, on the other hand, has lost its capability to generate meanings. It is no longer seen as alien to the context but is taken for granted—its meaning is commonly shared and understood, with no degrees of freedom for interpretation.* (Berg, 1985: 291)

A powerful metaphor needs a certain internal 'distance' to create tension and thus understanding. Absent these qualities the metaphor is dead and it will cease to generate new meanings (Charlton, 1975). Rorty (1989:16) notes that "[Donald] Davidson lets us think of the history of language, and thus of culture, as Darwin taught us to think of the history of a coral reef. Old metaphors are constantly dying off into literalness, and then serving as a platform and foil for new metaphors." Competition serves as a generative metaphor when organizational members can find ways to freshen it. An example would be shifting the focus of competition from the threat of superior Japanese quality to the more general threat of Asian power. As Japan's bubble economy burst, growth in Korean or Chinese capability keeps the organization's level of concern high.

Root metaphors, on the other hand, are the "fundamental image of the world from which models and illustrative metaphors may be derived" (Brown, 1976: 170). From this perspective the metaphor serves as a structuring device that allows individuals to code and sort organizational experiences. A change in a root metaphor profoundly affects its members' overall frame of reference and the content and form of the organizational narrative (Berg, 1985). An example of changes that can develop from transforming a root metaphor of competition to one of collaboration is a new policy that helps organizational members re-negotiate day-to-day interactions with competitors who now are also partners.

The use of metaphors in the study of organizations is not without its detractors (Pinder and Bourgeois, 1982). Conversely, Krefting and Frost (1985) noted the unique properties of metaphorical analysis in investigation of organizations, particularly organizational cultures. The use of metaphor allows theorists to create more holistic judgments of culture. Metaphors are playful, intuitive and insightful and while they are not linear (Miller, 1982), they can embody a wide range of values including masculine or feminine values (Ferguson, 1984). Within the popular press many cultural descriptors of competition are masculine metaphors (e.g., 'customer-driven,' 'market-focused,' 'balls to the wall,' etc.). Alternatively, Kyocera's competition metaphor uses feminist values with their 'green yen' image meant to convey competitive advantage through environmental soundness.

Metaphors inform our studies of organizational symbols and theoretical sense-making through what Gergan describes as the offering of new options or alternatives. This concept is best described by the distinction that Donald Davidson draws between the literal and the metaphorical:

> *not as a distinction between two sorts of meaning, or two sorts of interpretation, but as a distinction between familiar and unfamiliar noises and marks. The literal uses of noises and marks are the uses we can handle by our old theories about what people will say under various conditions. Their metaphorical use is the sort which makes us get busy developing a new theory.* (Rorty, 1989:17)

We might find competition structuring communication in a way previously unnoticed, or unmarked in the past. Displaying it or 'recovering' it for discussion could lead to an expansion of institutional alternatives for organizational members.

COMPETITION REPRODUCES PUBLIC RATIONALES IN PRIVATE CONVERSATIONS

Each of the three cases is far more complicated than we can easily express, yet the rationales provided to employees for coming changes or decisions are simple and profoundly similar. "We had to [do it] to stay competitive" (regardless of what "it" was). Most interesting, in all three cases the ensuing lunchroom and hallway discussions and team conversations reproduced the public rationale.

As anyone who has ever been involved in mergers, outsourcing, or downsizing can attest, the employees are generally not a happy lot. These cases are not exceptions. The discourse was marked by references to the terrible circumstances in which they were trapped. In reviewing our field notes two commonalties were observed: (1) wide-spread fear about job security and (2) complaints that management was incompetent, or the decisions could have been less drastic, more humane, or more workable if those at the top were smarter, less greedy, or ahead of the power curve.

It was not until we analyzed a number of conversations that had said in essence "it could have been done better but *something had to be done,*" that we observed the emerging congruity with the public story. The decision was awful, scary, not the right idea, but "it" happened because of "competition." This was markedly different from the statements made about large-scale organizational change as recently as a decade ago, or even five years ago—that "no change was needed" and "everything would be fine if they [the management] just left people alone to do their jobs."

From the perspective of good corporate communication these cases seem exemplary. Employees appear to buy into management's description of the environment as the reason they need to change. Alternatively, it is as if employees live in the grip of the competitive specter with no escape route. In the case of the merger, there was no counter-argument about "small is beautiful," only talk about the recent mega-merger of another chief competitor that compelled them to "find a partner or die."

In the off-shore assembly case, the fact that their chief competitor only does design work was probably helpful in preparing the workforce for the change to outsourcing. But the key explanation floating across the lunch tables was that competitor's new manufacturing supplier could produce the same products in *half* the time and using only *half* as many people. Thus, although some employees thought the differences were probably the bosses' fault, they rationalized that only more sophisticated designs and equipment could account for the fact that the other company needed only half as many people as they did. Some sat in stunned silence when told about these competitive statistics. Others decided it was impossible to compete against robots (an assumption based purely on speculation and the fact that 'the competition' outsourced its assembly work to Japan). Most employees affected by the change were offered jobs with other subsidiaries of the parent company but this announcement made several employees pause. Having lost this 'competition' made other positions with the same company less attractive, In some sense, the company was now perceived as 'damaged goods.'

In the layoff case, comments about 'corporate greed' were heard. The fact that their competition's earnings were 'much higher' made the competition's performance the standard—not their own previous 'pitiful' performance (the alliteration even got laughs in the 'all hands meeting' and was mimicked in team meetings later that afternoon). This is a highly professional organization where many employees own stock. They, along with other shareholders, would rather have earnings more like the competition. It was surprising that no one asked if options such as everyone reducing hours, job sharing, other cost control measures had been considered as alternatives to layoffs. Two individuals voiced private concerns about the steepness of the earnings curve and wondered if the company was "killing its long-term chances by not spending money on R&D." Our assessment is that previous layoffs—followed by higher earnings—legitimized this strategy and quieted many voices. At the same time, in an atmosphere of repeated layoffs, few are likely to risk complaints even within the boundaries of their own team lest they end up on the next layoff list.

COMPETITION AS EXCUSE

Competition as a generative metaphor appears to still criticism through the ghost of TINA (There Is No Alternative). It is as if the unceasing reconfiguration of large and small firms and corporations in the juggernaut we call global competition has convinced many organizational members that the only viable questions are *what* changes should be made and *when* to make them, not *why* is change necessary at all. Apparently, most organization members apparently think they know why.

The danger of course, is that "competition" becomes a catch-all excuse and can quickly systematize bad management practices. One of the managers in the electronics company was a 'competition watcher'—whatever new strategy, or new service, or management practice was in use by the competition was good enough for him. Another manager was the 'competition haranguer' rationalizing all of his actions by saying that they "had to be done to stay competitive." Because no one wanted to be seen as hurting competitiveness, he could get away with it. His technique worked better than a gag order. One day he announced that his part of the corporation would not be participating in the company's voluntary flex-time plan "because it would hurt our competitiveness." He had no data and no reasons other than he didn't want to. At that point we began to comprehend the power of the metaphor since no one questioned him, and yet we knew from an employee survey that a lot of people had been in favor of the change.

COMPETITION AS MEDIATED EXPERIENCE

We need to look beyond the confines of each organization to understand the pervasiveness of the metaphor. The discussion of business competition is a minute-by-minute media drama. Regardless of the industry being described, statements like the following abound in the business press:

> *We're in an extremely competitive industry, says Quinlan, 52 [McDonald's CEO]. To grow sales in the U.S., you have to take progress away from the competition.* (Branch, 1997:123)

> *As more and more of the world's phone companies add "competition" to their vocabularies, the economic edifice built on Bell's magnificent invention is beginning to crack . . . In most places, it [telecommunications] is still a monopolistic, fat, inefficient business. But to hasten investment, governments are slowly beginning to let competition into this cloistered kingdom.* (Kupfer, 1997:105)

Or the lead article in a recent issue of the *Academy of Management Executive*, "Establishing A Standard: Competitive Strategy And Technological Standards In Winner-Take-All Industries" (Hill, 1997). We could go on but the point is clear. From every newspaper, business magazine, and newsletter, the specter of competition commands focus and structures a love-hate relationship with the stories of victory and the fear of defeat.

We are all used to reading and hearing comments like "competition will make better business decisions happen or else!" "It will create better business people by focusing their attention on those few things that matter." Competition is too big and powerful to ignore. Structuring competition in the media is likewise too big and powerful to ignore and this generative metaphor provides a great deal of power. As Turner (1990:58) once noted: "and, even in conversation with members of organizations, we have to recognize that they themselves may well be living out their own media-acquired images of the organization that they imagine themselves to be in. As Phillip Dick and Baudrillard have both observed, it's just a very large version of Disneyland."

STRUCTURING COOPERATION AND COMPETITION

How do we find alternatives to this constant reproduction of competition? Giddens (1981) argues that the overarching tension created in an environment of competition emanates from the dialectical nature of competition and cooperation. From this perspective, competition can be understood as an oppositional force to cooperation; a dialectical relationship in which the operation of the one presumes the other and tends to undermine it (Giddens, 1981). Illuminating this tension provides evidence that we are moving beyond the assumption that competition is a good thing. At individual, organizational and societal levels, the tension between competition and cooperation is manifested in a dilemma that forces a conciliation between the poles of the dialectic.

Both of these seeming contradictory processes emerge from the generative nature of the competition metaphor. Operating at both ends of the dialectic at the same time poses a dilemma to the employees. Cooperative competition requires decidedly different skills than either cooperation or competition alone, and successful managers are, as Charles Handy (1994) suggests, the masters of this paradox. These 'agile' organizational members are the cornerstone of the postindustrial flexible organization—people who are the embodiment of yet another generative metaphor.

In the postindustrial context, individual goals intersect with corporate, national, and global ones. Within organizations, individuals are expected to cooperate, but must also compete for diminishing job opportunities, shrinking organizational resources, and even for such illustrious titles as "Friendliest Employee" (Kohn, 1992:1).

Probably the most pronounced arena of newly cooperative behavior revolves around company-wide teams (Pinto, Pinto, and Prescott, 1993). This growing trend is attributed to the effectiveness of cooperation between individuals in different functional areas (Wind, 1981). Many argue that competing interests are inevitable given the structure of US businesses. For one functional area to achieve its goals, it is frequently necessary for another area to make sacrifices (Pinto, Pinto, and Prescott, 1993).

Many of the employees in our electronics case work in self-directed work teams. Prior to their team placement these employees spent a week learning the benefits of cooperation and the dysfunctions associated with individual competitive behavior. Although some teams cooperate better than others, none of them seemed to have any trouble understanding that it is all right to compete against the other teams (e.g., for awards, fewest errors, lunch-time basketball games). Less perspicacious were the cross-functional teams where internal turf competitions were common problems. During our on-site investigation, this ineffective communication tool remained a consistent irritant.

In the few effective cross functional teams that we observed, several of the team members would invoke one the CEO's favorite generative metaphors—"for the good of the enterprise." This legitimized cooperative practices that might offer other teams a competitive edge or a resource 'win.' Such metaphors may be drawn upon frequently as employees balance the enhancing and inhibiting practices generated by the competition/cooperation paradox. Where this paradox is managed successfully, the organization may be able to benefit from the increased efficiency offered by cross-functional teams. Where it is managed ineffectively the benefits may be diminished and it could even have negative impacts on effectiveness. Thus, while the competitive dominance of their market remains the final goal for many organizations attaining it requires internal cooperation.

On the inter-organizational level, pressure to cooperate with traditional competitors under conditions of heightened competition is one manifestation of this paradox. "Individual firms cannot afford the enormous costs nor bear the high risks of remaining at the cutting edge of all the technologies that are integrated in new products" (Golden, 1993:102).

Golden uses yet another metaphor to describe the situation: the "technological revolution" has catalyzed the move toward global organizational networks and in turn changed the face of competition. As information and communication technologies become more sophisticated, organizations are more able to function across temporal and spatial boundaries. Information becomes a commodity that may be most valuable when shared with conventionally competitive others. Examples in aerospace and high technology are among the most visible of these new alliances.

Strategic alliances have blurred the boundaries between customers, suppliers, and competitors (Norhia and Berkley, 1994). As boundaries become more fluid and it becomes increasingly difficult to decide how to act the competition metaphor must be recast.

In the merger case, it soon became politically incorrect to refer to their new partner by any of the pejorative nicknames it had acquired over the years. The members of the soon-to-be-gigantic firm did not let their penchant for renaming rivals die, however. They began referring to their next largest competitors as the "pips"—"'cuz they're so small," and the CEOs (all men) as "Gladys 1," "Gladys 2" (from the American music group Gladys Knight and the Pips). We are sure there is something to be said about male members of a primarily male firm 'dissing' competitors by giving them women's names, and obsessing about size metaphors, but just in case it was a simply a botched attempt at cleverness, we're not going to say it.

We also recognize that it may not be only the employees who feel uncomfortable with the new partnerships. Since competition is tightly regulated, exactly how much 'cooperation' will be allowed in any given industry is unclear. One person's 'aligned network' is another judge's 'cartel.' Although many Western organizations are prepared to go to almost any lengths to be aggressive competitors, it has yet to be determined that such a state is necessarily desirable even from a capitalist perspective. In some markets where there are many similar businesses, competitive practices assure that none can make a reasonable profit. Steel companies, deregulated electric utilities, and some airlines are examples of this situation (Moore, 1996). There is evidence that in many situations where we might expect intense competition, there is instead a tempering of aggressive behavior known as mutual forbearance that has emerged from the possibility of multimarket retaliation. The consequence of system level integration structures a different genre of competition. "Thus firms that are close competitors may not be intense rivals" (Baum and Korn, 1996:257).

While organizations struggle to find their place in these newly cooperative networks and alliances, it remains to be seen whether or not highly refined competition will result in net gains. Norman Fieleke, Vice President and Economist for the Federal Reserve Bank of Boston, has suggested that the correlation between rising income inequality and corporate globalization may indicate that globalization has depressed wages and exacerbated inequality, "making the poor even poorer" (1994:4). If that is the case, then more radical approaches to the competition dilemma need to be examined.

STRUCTURING WORKPLACE DEMOCRACY

With respect to community, family and other areas better served by cooperation than competition, it seems clear that the global, corporate brand of private enterprise/capitalism is problematic. Particularly in the United States, corporate domination in public life is so deeply embedded that it is often no longer visible. Deetz (1992:2) observed: "The modern corporation has emerged as the central form of working relations and as the dominant institution in society. In achieving dominance, the commercial corporation has eclipsed the state, family, residential community, and moral community." As Kohn argues (1992:125),

> We are product oriented. Our work is governed by the demands of the " bottom line" and often is justified as an onerous necessity in life. The time we spend in school similarly is construed as valuable only insofar as it contributes to later employment, with the pleas of relevance in our universities having evolved into a demand for marketable skills. Even leisure activities have come to resemble work: results are what matter.

There are alternatives to corporate colonization. Two related organizational forms are worker cooperatives and employee stock ownership plans (ESOPs). There are other related organizational forms grounded in the concept of workplace cooperation/democracy. Workplace democracy in this sense means more than just practices that encourage democracy in the workplace, it refers to specific models of organizations.

Since the turn of the century, worker buy-outs have become a fairly common practice, primarily as a method of saving jobs in factory shut-downs. Since the 1980s, worker cooperatives have grown explosively especially within the United States and Europe. Doubling since the 1970s, they now number in the thousands. Similarly, ESOP structures increased dramatically in the 1980s (Whyte and Whyte, 1988).

The major tenets of these organizational alternatives to private industry are fairly simple. When the enterprise is profitable, those who work for it make profits for themselves; the workforce has no external masters (e.g., shareholders); and within the enterprise a more or less democratic regime—one person, one vote—prevails when the need to vote arises. (In larger organizations there are management functions that operate with wide discretion, so that voting on every decision is not required.) These tenets provide a structural motivation that emulate community concern in public life (Oakeshott, 1978:187).

The most stinging argument against restructuring enterprises on the lines of democratic control and worker ownership has always been based on their high failure rate. Several studies of the large and highly successful federation of cooperatives known as Mondragon in the Basque region of Spain, however, are instructive. While space limitations prohibit a complete description of the many industries, services, the bank, and the rest of the entities that constitute Mondragon, it is important to identify several features that are critical to its viability absent from others that have failed.

> *Mondragon is unique. It has a network of horizontally related industries much like the Koreans and Japanese, it has technical expertise combined with social vision, and it has not made the structural mistakes of other workplace democracy enterprises (e.g., the consensus of experts is that giving workers shares is not the optimal approach). The most critical differences, however, are that it balances democratic control with efficient management and that the values of solidarity and community are paramount.* (Riley, Klumpp and Hollihan, 1995:230)

Globalization appears to be catching up with Mondragon. Right now, the key difficulty appears to be information overload. Because everyone can vote on the cooperative's business plan and also approve or disapprove management performance, members of larger cooperatives are required to absorb increasingly larger and more complex volumes of information in a limited amount of time prior to the annual meetings (Whyte and Whyte, 1988).

What Mondragon does through its generative metaphor of democracy is give voice to its members to accept or reject the model and to better balance its productivity goals with its community concerns (Cheney, 1995). What is does not do is ignore either EU or global competition. The cooperative members who compete in international markets are very focused and concerned about their competition. This suggests that the cooperative has been successful in managing a cooperative organizational form within the larger competitive economic system. One of the clear differences between Mondragon and the three organizations used in earlier examples is the degree of reflexivity displayed by their members. Unlike those organizational members who do not ask about alternatives, workers in Mondragon are constantly involved in exploring alternate solutions that will provide management efficiency and technical advancement without violating either the structure of cooperative solidarity or the nature of community life.

The deeply sedimented practices, the high level of involvement by members, their relative geographic isolation, strongly held values, and close community ties, encompass a culture unlike any other. The odds of this culture continuing to provide members with the strength they need to manage the tension between competition and cooperation appear stellar.

We think that one of the reasons they are successful is that the members of Mondragon display a culturally based difference in the way they manage competition. Most strong cultures are overly rational and somewhat nasty. As Turner (1990:95) argued:

> *A corporate culture, intended to engender company loyalty, must have a belligerent element, since its aim is to embrace everything which it can see . . . [T]his kind of "finite" cage has an arena, winners and losers. Competitors are necessary to sustain a bounded corporate culture, to keep it clear and distinct and to enable it to pursue its destiny. The inevitable conflict and competition is engaging with those beyond the boundaries, and people are far more attentive to their organizations and to its interests when there is danger from such sources.*

Unlike many other companies, including the anonymous ones in this study, Mondragon structures competition from cooperation, not the other way around. Add the high degree of reflexivity displayed by organizational members to the generative metaphors of community and solidarity, and our confidence in their ability to continue to reproduce a culture that does not see competition as a zero sum game increases. The problem, of course, is that their boundaries become more permeable by the day as new alliances and partnerships emerge.

CONCLUSION

It has become increasingly obvious that when discussing organizational change, survival, strategy, or any other top level account that requires justification, the answer relates invariably to competition. The discussion might focus on ways of communicating the cost of the new information system, the rationale for business process reengineering, the motivation for the downsizing, the need for a morale committee, why a company is investigating global expansion or even the necessity for capital improvements. Today, at least within the US, competition seems to explain all situations.

As we struggle to comprehend organizational contexts in the postindustrial age, our own complicity becomes apparent as we participate in and legitimize these competitive behaviors—particularly when we take for granted the fact that plant closings, or mergers, or any other changes were the only reasonable alternatives. The people at Mondragon convinced us that there is a postmodern (actually pre-modern) competition story after all; one that balances competition through cooperation and never reduces life to wins and losses. In structuration theory, agency is the capability to do 'otherwise'. But first we have to see what we can do about the story of competition.

BIBLIOGRAPHY

Adler, N.J. (1997) *International Dimensions Of Organizational Behavior,* 3rd ed., Cincinnati: South-Western College Publishing.

Banks, S. and P. Riley (1993) "Structuration Theory As An Ontology For Communication Research" in S. Deetz, ed., *Communication Yearbook/16,* Newbury Park, CA: Sage.

Baum, J.A. and H.J. Korn, (1996) "Competitive Dynamics Of Interfirm Rivalry" *Academy of Management Journal,* 39, 255–291.

Berg, P. (1985) "Organization Change As A Symbolic Transformation Process" in P.J. Frost, L. F. Moore, M.R. Louis, C.C. Lundberg and J. Martin, eds. *Organizational Culture.* Beverly Hills, CA: Sage.

Brown, R.H. (1976) "Social Theory As Metaphor" *Theory and Society,* 3, 196–197.

Branch, S. (1997) "What's Eating McDonald's?" *Fortune,* 136, October 13, 122–125.

Charlton, W. (1975) "Living And Dead Metaphors" *British Journal of Aesthetics,* 15, 172–178.

Cheney, G. (1995) "Democracy In The Workplace: Theory And Practice From The Perspective Of Communication" *Applied Communication Research,* 23, 167–200.

Cooper, D.E. (1984) "Metaphors We Live By" *Philosophy,* Supp. 18, 43–58.

Deetz, S.A. (1992) *Democracy In An Age Of Corporate Colonization: Developments In Communication And The Politics Of Everyday Life.* Albany: SUNY.

Ferguson, K. (1984) *The Feminist Case Against Bureaucracy,* Philadelphia: Temple University Press.

Fieleke, N.S. (1994) "Is Global Competition Making The Poor Even Poorer?" *New England Economic Review,* November/December, 4–16.

Giddens, A. (1981) *A Contemporary Critique Of Historical Materialism, Vol. 1, Power, Property And The State.* Berkeley: University of California Press.

Giddens, A. (1984) *The Constitution Of Society,* Berkeley: University of California Press.

Golden, J.R. (1993) "Economics And National Strategy: Convergence, Global Networked, And Cooperative Competition" *The Washington Quarterly,* Summer, 91–113.

Goshal, S. and C. Bartlett (1990) "The Multinational Corporation As An Interorganizational Network" *Academy of Management Review,* 15, 603–625.

Hamrin, R.D. (1980) *Managing Growth in the 1980s,* New York: Praeger.

Handy, C. (1994) *The Age of Paradox,* Boston: Harvard Business School Press.

Hannan, M.T. and J. Freeman (1989) *Organizational Ecology,* Cambridge, MA: Harvard University Press.

Harragan, B.L. (1977) *Games Mother Never Taught You,* New York: Warner Books.

Hill, C.W.L. (1997) "Establishing A Standard: Competitive Strategy And Technological Standards In Winner-Take-All Industries" *Academy of Management Executive,* 11, 2, May, 7–25.

Kirkman, B.L. and D.L. Shapiro (1997) "The Impact Of Cultural Values On Employee Resistance To Teams: Toward A Model Of Globalized Self-Managing Work Team Effectiveness" *Academy of Management Review,* 22, 730–757.

Kohn, A. (1992) *No Contest* rev. ed., Boston: Houghton-Mifflin.

Kozlowski, S.W.J., G.T. Chao, E.M. Smith, and J. Hedlund (1993) "Organizational Downsizing: Strategies, Interventions, And Research Implications" in C.L. Cooper and I.T. Robertson, eds. *International Review of Industrial and Organizational Psychology, 8,* New York: Wiley.

Krefting, L.A. and P. Frost (1985) "Untangling Webs, Surfing Waves, And Wildcatting" in P.J. Frost, L. F. Moore, M.R. Louis, C.C. Lundberg and J. Martin, eds. *Organizational Culture,* Beverly Hills, CA: Sage.

Kupfer, A. (1997) "Transforming Telecom: The Big Switch" *Fortune,* 136, Oct. 13, 105–116.

Miller, D.F. (1982) "Metaphor, Thinking and Thought" *Et cetera,* 39, 134–150.

Moore, J.F. (1996) *The Death Of Competition,* New York: HarperBusiness.

Norhia, N. and J. Berkeley (1994) "An Action Perspective: The Crux Of The New Management" *California Management Review,* 36, 4, Summer 1994, 70–92.

Oakeshott, R. (1978) *The Case For Workers' Co-Ops,* London: Routledge and Kegan Paul.

Ortony, A. (1979) "Metaphor: A Multidimensional Problem" in A. Ortony, ed., *Metaphor And Thought,* Cambridge: Cambridge University Press.

Pinder, C.C. and V.M. Bourgeois (1982) "Controlling Tropes In Administrative Science" *Administrative Science Quarterly,* 27, 641–652.

Pinto, M.B., J. Pinto, and J.E. Prescott (1993) "Antecedents And Consequences Of Project Team Cross-Functional Cooperation" *Management Science,* 39, 1281–1297.

Pondy, L.R. (1983) "The Role Of Metaphors And Myths In Organization And The Facilitation Of Change" in L.R. Pondy, P.J. Frost, G. Morgan and T.C. Dandridge, eds., *Organizational Symbolism,* Greenwich, CT: JAI Press, Inc.

Rorty, R. (1989) *Contingency, Irony, And Solidarity,* Cambridge: Cambridge University Press.

Schon, D.A. (1979) "Generative Metaphor: A Perspective On Problem-Setting In Social Policy" in A. Ortony, ed., *Metaphor And Thought,* Cambridge: Cambridge University Press.

Tapscott, D. and A. Caston (1993) *Paradigm Shift,* New York: McGraw Hill.

Turner, B, (1990) "The Rise Of Organizational Symbolism" in J. Hassard and D. Pym, eds., *The Theory And Philosophy Of Organizations: Critical Issues And New Perspectives,* London: Routledge.

Wachtel, P. (1983) *The Poverty Of Affluence,* New York: Free Press.

Whyte, W.F. and K.K. Whyte (1988) *Making Mondragon: The Growth And Dynamics Of The Worker Cooperative Complex,* Ithaca, NY: ILR Press.

Wind, Y. (1981) "Marketing And The Other Business Functions" in J.N. Seth, ed., *Research Marketing,* 5, Greenwich, CT: JAI Press.

27

TOO SCATTERED TO PROVIDE A CRITICAL MASS?: WOMEN AND MANAGERIALISM IN TWO UK UNIVERSITIES[1]

Heather Clark, John Chandler, and Jim Barry

This chapter considers gender and management in British Higher Education by focusing specifically on issues that affect women adversely. The literature on public sector 'managerialism' is reviewed and then the issue of 'masculinities' is explored. Identity and social movement theory is used to explain the findings that reveal widespread concern with working practices and evidence of collective opposition and mobilization.

INTRODUCTORY COMMENTS

If there is anywhere that women professionals should be successful, it is in the universities. We think of teaching as a woman's forte and universities as meritocratic institutions. (Acker, 1994:125)

---

[1]This is an amended version of a paper presented to the 14th International Labour Process Conference, Aston University, England, 27–29 March 1996 and The Dilemmas of Men's Higher Education International Conference, Staffordshire University, England 10–12 April 1996. We would like to thank the participants of both Conferences for their helpful comments.

> *Academic life is a sphere where in theory, women should find few barriers to equal opportunity.* (Mansard Society, 1990:64)

> *The participation of women in higher education is patchy, passionate and peculiar because we are living through a period in which vigorous reforms are taking place with a view to establishing fair or equal chances in what remains, despite many slights and denials, one of the most attractive careers for women in paid employment in modern society.* (Halsey 1995:216)

In 1980, Sandra Acker set out to consider the question of women's prospects in academe. Given that little "research [had] been done on the everyday experiences of women academics" her account was "necessarily speculative" though she did identify three likely complicating factors for women: "conflicting demands of family and careers," the "relative powerlessness of minorities," and "male domination of knowledge and practice" (Acker, 1994:125–6). In 1993, she documented the position of women in the lower ranks of British universities, noting that the "literature on academic women in Britain [was] rather sparse, probably reflecting a tendency to consider them members of an elite rather than a disadvantaged group worthy of feminist concern" (Acker, 1994:135–7).

Existing accounts of women's experiences dwelt on role conflict and discrimination, depicted women as a reserve army or as subjects of patriarchal control reflecting Liberal Socialist and Radical Feminist concerns respectively. Women seemed unlikely to do very much about this, however, as: "women academics were too scattered to provide a critical mass" (Acker, 1994).

This chapter focuses on women's accommodation, resistance and opposition to these pressures in Britain's universities. The introduction of managerialism into UK university life provides the context of our exploration.

Managerialism has assumed importance since publication of the Jarratt Report (Committee of Vice-Chancellors and Principals, 1985), which reflects concerns for economic stringency and restructuring. Perhaps the most significant aspects of Jarratt's proposals concerned managerialism which involved: "the centralization of executive control, the linkage between budgetary and academic considerations and the decentralization of accountable budgets to the lowest level" (Parker and Jary, 1995:324).

WOMEN IN HIGHER EDUCATION

We selected women lecturers and senior administrators in British universities, a predominantly middle-class population, professionally well qualified, largely 'white', with some degree of positional power, as the least favorable case for women's effectiveness. Women have traditionally been under-represented in higher education in Britain, although over time the gap has been narrowing. It is smaller in the 'new' universities than in the 'old' (Halsey, 1995; West and Lyon, 1995).

Women in universities are more likely than men to be employed in vulnerable fixed-term contract positions (Morley, 1994; Aziz, 1990). Positions such as part-time lecturer, teaching associate or assistant and contract researcher, are *usually* "low paid [and] very often female" (Davies and Holloway, 1995; West and Lyon, 1995). Davies and Holloway (1995) note that the new-found obsession with research, along with intensified levels of work, leave "weekends and evenings as the only time when personal research can be realistically carried out." They contend that this can only be detrimental to women with domestic responsibilities.

Jarratt's (1985:12) observation that "[the] crucial issue is how a university achieves the maximum value for money consonant with its objectives" certainly underlines an economic agenda of a vice-chancellor who is not only an 'academic leader but also chief executive', ensuring that 'strategic plans' link 'academic, financial and physical aspects' into 'one corporate process'. Jarratt makes it quite clear that "in our view universities are first and foremost corporate enterprises." In a discussion of the Head of Department, Jarratt makes a telling comment that almost paraphrases Machiavelli's observations on whether it is better to be feared or to be loved:

> *Ideally the individual should be both a manager and an academic leader. However the most eminent and able academic, as judged by the standards of research or teaching, is not always the person most fitted to manage a department. We take the view that it is preferable to retain the two functions in one person. In circumstances where this is impracticable, we believe the head of department must possess the requisite managerial capabilities and that he [sic] should be encouraged to delegate some part of the responsibility for academic leadership to others.*

Davies and Holloway (1995:10–11) explain:

> *the Jarratt proposals were received with enthusiasm by a senior management coming to grips with the new funding demands, realizing the need for streamlined decision making and an altogether quicker response. In their eyes, efficiency was becoming not a suspect business term, but a necessity for their survival in the new climate.*

MANAGERIALISM IN THE PUBLIC SECTOR

There seems little doubt that an overtly political agenda is linked to an underlying economic one in a period of deepening global recession and a New Right obsession with efficiency, market mechanisms, business cultures and 'value for money' (Cochrane, 1993). This is the context in which ideas about managerialism in the public sector gained currency.

Cutler and Maine (1994:x) see public sector managerialism as "characterized by the belief that the objectives of social services such as health, education, personal social services or social security can be promoted at a lower cost when the appropriate management techniques are applied." They see it appearing in four manifestations: performance management, quasi markets, compulsory competitive tendering and pay determination. It also embraces private sector 'values' leading one commentator to suggest that "managerialism [had] become the evangelism of the new age, linking private and public sectors" (Cochrane, 1993), adopting the language of the public sector in the process (e.g. substituting consumers for client, etc.), using managerial techniques and business values, supporting entrepreneurial strategies of privatization, marketization, flexibility, delayering of 'superfluous' levels of supervision and management in the precipitate scramble for efficiency.

'Culture management' (Pollitt, 1993), associated with management gurus like Tom Peters, heralds the arrival of a 'new managerialism' (Clarke and Newman, 1994; Newman, 1994), although students of management recognize features of earlier schools such as Human Relations and Organization Development (Axtell, 1986; Wood, 1989; Thompson and McHugh, 1990) lurking in the background, operating alongside and integrated with 'continuing elements of neo-Taylorism' (Pollitt, 1993).

The emphasis on cultural change in the recent attempts to control public sector organizations may well represent a significant difference in the style of management (Newman 1995).

The new management prophets (Hopfl, 1992) call not only for obedience but also expect that the restorative properties of their remedies will be believed. Yet, some argue that management gurus who recommend strong corporate cultures are merely offering new variations on old themes of control. As one respondent commented: "I send the papers and it is as if they disappear into a black hole, I never get a response . . . [theirs is an] autocratic approach . . . It's not the way I like to work." Another put it this way,

> *The changes to jobs (in organizations generally) count against women . . . It's all about quantity, there's no more quality . . . Women put a lot into communicating and more effort into helping others . . . So women will suffer trying to maintain overall standards. Women do an all-round job and will continue to try and do this . . . They find it hard to have a single minded goal, unlike men.*

Their comments, which seem to sense an iron fist in the velvet glove, suggest more than a managerial style—new or otherwise. They point to perceived differences in terms of gender.

MANAGERIALISM AND MASCULINITY?

The connection between a managerial mindset and masculinity is made specifically by Clarke and Newman (1993) and Nichols (1993:431), who argue that "Historically . . . management has been archetypically masculine, associated with both behaviour and predispositions which resembled loosely packaged testosterone."

White (1995) also notes the association of traditional leadership style with 'military hierarchies' and masculinity. Whether this remains true when managers espouse doctrines of culture-speak is an interesting question, especially as the new language is peppered with terms such as participation, empowerment and teamwork. On the face of it this seems at least one step removed from the aggressive orientation being suggested.

Indeed, at least on a superficial level, the pre-occupation with culture-management seems congruent with expectations about women's preferred styles of management—an explicit link made by Lunneborg (1990) in her discussion of Tom Peters' work. It is also in line with Rosener's (1990 and Ozga, 1993) research on women managers in non-traditional, medium-sized organizations. They develop 'interactive leadership' styles that encourage participation, share power and influence, enhance other people's self-worth and excite them in their work.

There are, nonetheless, two difficulties in linking managerialism and masculinity. First, the notion that women's preferred style of leadership is somehow participative, relational, and concerned with helping others draws upon a stereotype. Literature on the psycho-social moral development of young women sees an 'ethic of care', against a male 'logic of justice' (Gilligan, 1982), but women are equally capable of being purposeful, competitive and ambitious (Lunneborg, 1990; White, 1995). They are equally as prepared to 'succeed in business by being hard-nosed over ethical niceties' (Burke et al, 1993). This may be related to the imperatives of the organizational position and go some way to supporting a post-structuralist interpretation (Ferguson, 1984; Acker, 1990) or may simply be indicative of the acceptance that conformity is the price to be paid for success in—or even retention of—employment.

Second, there seem to be many 'masculinities' and 'patriarchies'. Hearn's (1992:3) comment that "there are effectively lots of types of men, operating simultaneously, overlapping, interrelating, contradicting" is instructive (Collinson and Hearn, 1994,1996; Court, 1994). The equation of managerialism with masculinity is problematic at best. Apparent from our own research and in other organizational studies of women in senior positions (Coe, 1992, and Faludi, 1992) is the fact that the existence of male predominance in senior organizational public sector positions seems to have led to the experience of marginalization by women.

The growing preoccupation with managerialism and control in higher education is manifested in both subtle and dictatorial ways. It has been accompanied by financial restructuring intended to render universities more responsive to the market. As West and Lyon (1995:63) put it: "as pressures mount on the university system and resources shrink, responses are increasingly couched in the pervasively masculine language of management." While women seem more adversely affected than men it is fair to say that universities are presently "not comfortable places for academics of either sex" (Davies and Holloway, 1995; Parker and Jary, 1995). The same holds for senior educational administrators.

Our respondents saw very senior male academics and administrators as part of a male club (Coe, 1992), benefiting from a new managerialism that valued aggression and individualism over the common good despise the rhetoric of participation, empowerment and vision. One woman commented on the way senior male academics took turns being 'top management' competing with each other in the hope of advancing their careers.

There is also a reference to a 'male world of committees' in higher education where men play 'boys games' scoring points endlessly to 'massage their egos'. Women, we were told, were made to feel outsiders, quite literally, marginalized by word of mouth and deed. They were bewildered at the sheer amount of time 'wasted' in what they saw as pointless posturing and tilting at windmills engaged in for its own sake and creating considerable levels of both anomie and alienation for the women concerned. As Herman (1995:39), herself the only female member in attendance at academic and other meetings, comments:

> *I was accustomed to being made to feel out of place. I recognized as exclusion devices, the opening lewd joke, made with an eye cast in my direction, the detailed discussion of football tactics before we got down to business the chairman (sic) who began with his feet on the table. They were tiresome, but they did not really bother me as they appeared to confirm that the meeting was changed because of my presence. Certain things could not be said because of my being there, certain other things could be said.*

This may be evidence of a new patriarchal managerialism. It may also be indicative of a historically sustained process of marginalization exercised over women by powerful men (Rich, 1979). From our interviews there is certainly evidence that women are presently suffering discrimination and disadvantage and feel they are outside the culture of the male-dominated organizations in both new and traditional universities.

Whether or not there is a new managerialism in higher education, the women in our research are responding to patterns of male behavior that operate through managerial control processes. In line with research conducted by Lunneborg (1990) and White (1995), the women may feel that they can exercise a range of styles in their work. But if there is a distinctive women's leadership style, there is also a question about the way that 'good leadership' (White, 1995) is exercised by the relatively few women in senior positions. This might have the effect of further enhancing the control of others; it may or may not bring positive benefits to workers (including professionals), their organizations, their public and women generally.

INDIVIDUAL ACCOMMODATION AND RESISTANCE

Accommodation and resistance often represent different sides of the same coin (Anyon, 1983). Members of subordinate groups respond to control and domination in a variety of ways that are often very subtle (Baker, 1983). Individualization of a problem makes it personal, both in experience and response, but it also puts pressure on the individual to conform. This pressure lies behind the encouragement of independence and exhortation to self-reliance found in the 'Managing Diversity' and 'Human Resource Management' literature (Liff and Wajcman, 1996; Rajvinder et al., 1995) that can be interpreted as an invitation to aspiring managers to try a variation on the old theme of 'divide and rule'.

Accommodation and resistance can be innovative and meaningful coping mechanisms, for keeping hope alive and demonstrating spirit and dignity. Our interviewees displayed such qualities and, in many respects, mirrored the behavior of female lawyers studied by Jack and Jack (1988). In drawing on Gilligan's work (1982), Jack and Jack explored ways in which women dealt with demands of the legal profession. Practicing law required the women to operate in a world regulated by principles, abstract reasoning, case law and precedent. The full apprehension of a client's often tragic personal circumstances had to be suspended for the duration of a case.

Women lawyers coped by employing one of three strategies: emulating the traditional male role, splitting the self, or attempting to reshape the role. Our respondents behaved in similar ways. When emulating the male role they denied the relational parts and suffered as a result. One lost a partner along the way and exhibited 'classic' signs of stress. Another of our interviewees 'split' her 'self' in response to the pressures from colleagues who saw the expression of care as evidence of weakness. She found it very difficult to cope at work, indicating that she felt she was not really being 'herself', though she recharged her batteries 'off duty' at home. There was also evidence of attempts to reshape expectations of the job to encompass both reason and emotion as requirements of the role. Here again respondents encountered problems: One of them reported that her career chances were fading as a result of her attempts to achieve balance in this 'way'.

The experience of an issue as private trouble (Mills, 1959) individualizes a problem and is invariably accompanied by guilt and self-doubt. Above all, it tends to disempower, until recognized as a public issue. Anyon (1983:34) makes the point well: "daily accommodation and resistance does not seek to remove the structural causes of . . . contradictions. For such transformation women need collective action." This may nonetheless overstate the argument. Individual and collective action can be seen as complementary and their combination can be a potent force for change.

COLLECTIVE RESISTANCE

Earlier we noted that women academics were too scattered to provide a critical mass, yet our research in one new British university, backed up by published research on another (Butler and Landells, 1994), suggests that this may not be entirely true. Our research revealed concern from women academics and administrators over issues that affected them as women (e.g., lighting in car parks and corridors and campus security provision, etc.). What was perhaps most interesting about this was that consciousness about these issues and the collective mobilization around them cut across conventional categories of administrator and academic as well as identities based on ethnicity and age. As a group the concerned women refused to recognize formal hierarchies or name 'leaders' to inquiring male managers whom they suspected would then target women individually so as to 'pick them off'.

The group took different forms in different circumstances. The composition of the groups changed from issue to issue. Clearly not all the women in the university were involved nor did the male hierarchy which opposed them comprise all the men. Some male colleagues did express their concern and support. Yet when the women confronted the males who held very senior positions in the institutional hierarchy on issues which they argued affected them as women, they were met with incomprehension and bewilderment. Eventually demands for improved lighting and security were met, but not until a long and bitter struggle had been played out. For the men arguments turned on issues of resources and priorities; for the women on personal safety. The emotional cost to the women involved was considerable and, as far as we know, the group has become dormant and may or may not reappear in the forms previously taken.

Powell (1990 and Brueghel and Kean, 1995) notes that the development of a network is based on trust, reciprocity, mutuality and co-operation. In academe the 'invisible college' dates back to the 17th century where it operated as a kind of old-boy network (O'Leary and Mitchell, 1990). Research shows that women may use networks to further their careers but they are more likely to use them to foster relationships, support one another and share concerns about women's disadvantage (Pringle, 1994; Greenglass, 1993; and Lie and Malik 1994).

This means that women's under-representation and professional autonomy in universities need not, in and of themselves, act as disincentives to network in order to share experiences and a sense of collective power (Morley, 1994). Networks may even develop in (or through) the research process itself (White, 1995). Butler and Landell's (1994) work on the sexual harassment of women academics seems to have enabled women to talk and raise consciousness. It freed them to break 'their silence and the taboo'. It also encouraged the researchers to share their work 'as part of a network of people, struggling to effect change in Higher Education.' This was not, however, without cost to the individuals concerned. Butler and Landells (1994) comment that their research 'both empowered and intimidated us', identifying them as 'feminists working in a University'. This experience was paralleled by women in our research. The term 'feminist' may carry a negative connotation for women so categorized by men and once you are labeled a troublemaker you are vulnerable. Even with support (Lie and O'Leary, 1990), even in collective action, the consequences are experienced individually and alone. As suggested earlier, collective and individual responses may not be as separable as they initially appear.

A REAPPRAISAL

What are we to make of these findings and their relationship to published work? One of our arguments has been that the literature has tended to conflate and generalize that which we see as a diverse, complex and contingent. This does not mean that there is no coherence to our findings. The diversity and difference encountered here are to be expected. The women in our research negotiated their lives as people with a number of different identities, any one or combination of which may be salient at particular moments in time. Where women coalesced as a cohesive group they do so around policy issues—security and lighting—which reflected their concerns over personal safety and drew on their experiences as women. This is why the men, by and large, failed to grasp the meaning for those adversely affected. Similarly, the study by Butler and Landells focused on the policy issue of sexual harassment, which affected women as women.

This does not mean that the women will not mobilize around other issues. Indeed they may well feel an affinity with certain men and draw on the experience of other identities in dealing with racial discrimination. This need not entail a drift into some variant or other of post-structuralism or postmodernism. In attempting to retain the category 'woman' in her use of a politics of identity to meet the challenge of deconstruction, Alcoff (1988) offers the insight that agency may be conceptualized through the affirmation of a collective self that is historically and socially constituted. It is these ideas that Alcoff shares with Bondi (1993) and de Lauretis (1990) who see difference and disagreement as indicative not of post-feminism, but of a flourishing, dynamic, social movement. They do not necessarily lead to a withering competition for resources with other 'pressure groups' seeking recognition. Social movement networks are dynamic and fluid, not fixed and formally organized.

There is no guarantee that consciousness will develop in any particular way. As Marshall (1995:193) puts it, in her study of women managers, several of her "research participants commented that—contrary to popular belief—other women were not necessarily instant allies or people with whom they had an affinity." This should not surprise us. Our research has shown simply that women came together around particular policy issues which affected them as women, affirmed their identity as women who shared common disadvantage, and came to a collective appreciation of their situation, taking action to seize and even create opportunities for themselves. It may be that this is what a social movement is, operating, as Melucci (1988) puts it, through the submerged networks of civil society, rendering power visible and thereby negotiable, or at least contestable, whatever the cost.

Moreover, retention (or recovery) of the notion of a women's movement, based on a shared consciousness of both differing and similar identities in creative tension, may be the most helpful way of keeping in view the broader picture of structured disadvantage that characterizes social, economic and political life in a climate currently hostile to women (Liff and Wajcman, 1996).

The 'decline of donnish dominion' (Halsey, 1995) and the proletarianization of academe, recognized some eighty years ago by Max Weber, is an important context in which to situate our concerns. The complex articulation of gender and class, along with other identities based on such factors as ethnicity and age, seem likely to continue to characterize the currently turbulent organizational life of universities. We also concur with Ware (1992) that an awareness of the nature of domination may come from drawing parallels between different subordinated groups. We know that many women involved in the recent phase of women's movement activity gained valuable experience from their participation in the civil rights movement (Freeman, 1975; Evans, 1979).

We are not 'starry-eyed' about this. Networks are fragile and vulnerable and they represent social movements in action. The potential for mobilization and unity, of the kind recounted here, offers no guarantee (Ware, 1992), but then there is no reason why it should. The women in our research reacted to the circumstances in which they found themselves: They were part of a new university and were represented in relatively large numbers. It would seem as if they were challenging forms of masculinity exercised through managerial control mechanisms.

We have, nonetheless, gone some way to addressing the issue with which we started the chapter, Acker's question about the prospects for women professionals in universities. We have also, contrary to expectation, uncovered informal networks of resistance even though women may seem on the surface too scattered to achieve a 'critical mass'. All in all this may be a good starting point for further research.

BIBLIOGRAPHY

Acker, J.(1990) "Hierarchies, Jobs, Bodies: A Theory of Gendered Organizations" *Gender and Society*, 4, 2, 139–158.

Acker, S. (1994) *Gendered Education*, Buckingham: Open University Press.

Alcoff, L. (1988) "Cultural Feminism Versus Post-Structuralism: The Identity Crisis in Feminist Theory" *Signs* 13, 405–436.

Anyon, J. (1983) "Intersections Of Gender-and Class: Accommodation And Affluent Females To Contradictory Sex-Role Ideologies" in S. Walker, and L. Barton (eds.) (1993) *Gender, Class and Education*, Lewis: Falmer Press.

Axtell, R. C. (1986) "Corporate Culture: The Last Frontier of Control?" *Journal of Management Studies*, 23, 287–297.

Aziz, A. (1990) "Women in UK Universities—the Road to 'Causalization?'" in S. Lie and V. O'Leary, *Storming the Tower*, London: Kogan Page.

Baker, M. J. (1983) *Toward a Psychology of Women*, Harmondsworth: Penguin.

Bondi, L. (1993) "Locating Identity Politics" in M. Keith, S. Pile, eds., *Place and The Politics of Identity*, London: Routledge.

Bruegel, I. and R. Bean (1995) "The Moment of Municipal Feminism: Gender And Class In 1980s Local Governments" *Critical Social Policy*, 44/45, Autumn, 147–169.

Burke, T. and S. Maddocks, A. Rose (1993) "How Ethical is British Business?: An Analysis

Of The Sensitivity Of Senior Managers And Other Professionals To Ethical Issues In Business" *University of Westminster Research Working Paper,* Series 2, No. 1.

Butler, A. and M. Landells (1994) "Telling Tales Out Of School: Research Into Sexual Harassment Of Women Academics" *University of Plymouth Equality Research Group Working Paper,* No. 1.

Clarke, J. and J. Newman (1994) "'Going About Our Business?' The Managerialization Of Public Services" in J. Clarke, et al. eds., *Managing Social Policy,* London: Sage.

Cochrane, A. (1993) *Whatever Happened to Local Government?,* Buckingham: Open University Press.

Coe, T. (1992) *The Key to the Men's Club: Opening the Doors to Women in Management,* Corby: The Institute of Management.

Collinson, D. and J. Hearn (1994) "Naming Men As Men: Implications For Work, Organization And Management" *Gender, Work and Organization,* 1, 1, 2–22.

Collinson, D. and J. Hearn (1996) "'Men' At Work: Multiple Masculinities / Multiple Work Places" in M. Mac An Ghail, ed. *Understanding Masculinities,* Buckingham: Open University Press.

Court, M. (1994) "Removing Macho Management: Lessons From The Field Of Education" *Gender, Work and Organization,* 1, 1, 33–49.

Cutler, T. and B. Waine (1994) *Managing the Welfare State,* Oxford: Berg.

Davies, C. and P. Holloway (1995) "Troubling Transformations: Gender Regimes And Organizational Culture In The Academy" in L. Morley and V. Walsh (1995) *Feminist Academics: Creative Agents for Change,* London: Taylor and Francis.

De Lauretis, T. (1990) " Upping The Anti (sic) In Feminist Theory," *Feminism,* London: Routeledge.

Evans, S. (1979) *Personal Politics,* New York: Vintage Books.

Faludi, S. (1992) *Backlash—The Undeclared War Against Women,* London: Chatto and Windus.

Ferguson, K.E. (1984) *The Feminist Case Against Bureaucracy,* Philadelphia: Temple University Press.

Freeman, J. (1975) *The Politics of Women's Liberation,* London: Longman.

Gilligan, C. (1982) *In a Different Voice: Psychological Theory and Women's Development,* Cambridge, MA: Harvard University Press.

Greenglass, E. R. (1993) "The Contribution Of Social Support To Coping Strategies" *Applied Psychology: An International Review,* 42, October, 323–340.

Halsey, A.H. (1995) *Decline of Donnish Dominion,* Oxford: Clarendon Press.

Hansard Society (1990) *The Report of The Hansard Society Commission on Women at the Top,* London: The Hansard Society.

Hearn, J. {1992) *Men in The Public Eye,* London: Routledge.

Hopfl, H. (1992) "The Making Of The Corporate Acolyte: Some Thoughts On Charismatic Leadership And The Reality of Organizational Commitment" *Journal of Management Studies* 29, 1, 23–33.

Jack D., and R. Jack (1988) "Women Lawyers: Archetype And Alternatives" in C. Gilligan et al., *Mapping the Moral Domain,* Cambridge, MA: Harvard University Press.

Jarratt Report (1985) *Report of the Steering Committee for Efficiency Studies in Universities,* CVCP.

Kerman, L. (1995) "The Good Witch: Advice To Women In Management" in L. Morley and V. Walsh (1995) *Feminist Academics: Creative Agents for Change,* London: Taylor and Francis.

Lie S. and L. Malik (1994) "Trends in the Gender Gap in Higher Education" *World Year of Education,* London: Kogan Page.

Lie S. and V. O'Leary (1990) *Storming the Tower,* London: Kogan Page.

Liff, S. and J. Wajcman (1996) "'Sameness' And 'Difference' Revisited: Which Way Forward For Equal Opportunity Initiatives?" *Journal of Management Studies,* 33, 1, 79–94.

Lunneborg, P. (1990) *Women Changing Work,* New York: Bergin and Garvey.

Marshall, J. (1995) *Woman Managers Moving On,* London: Routledge.

Melucci, A. (1988) "Social Movements And The Democratization Of Everyday Life" in J. Deane, ed. *Civil Society and the State: New European Perspectives,* London: Verso.

Mills, C. W. (1959) *The Sociological Imagination,* Harmondsworth: Penguin.

Morley, L. (1994) "Glass Ceiling Or Iron Cage: Women In UK Academia" *Gender, Work and Organization,* 1, 4, 194–204.

Newman, J. (1994) "The Limits Of Management: Gender And The Politics of Change" in J. Clarke et al., eds., *Managing Social Policy,* London: Sage.

Newman, J. (1995) "Gender And Cultural Change" in C. Ilzin, ed., *Gender, Culture and Organizational Change,* London: Routledge.

Nichols, N. (1993) "Whatever Happened to Rosie the Riveter?" *Harvard Business Review,* July–August, 54–62.

O'Leary, V. and J. Mitchell (1990) "Women Connecting With Women: Networks And Mentors" in S. Lie and V. O'Leary, *Storming the Tower,* London: Kogan Page.

Ozga, J. ed. (1993) *Women in Educational Management,* Buckingham: Open University Press.

Parker, M. and D. Jary (1995) "The McUniversity: Organization, Management And Academic Subjectivity" *Organization,* 2, 2, 319–338.

Pollitt, C. (1993) *Managerialism and the Public Services: Cuts or Cultural Change in the 1990's,* 2nd ed., Oxford: Basil Blackwell.

Powell, W.W. (1990) "Neither Market Not Hierarchy: Network Forms Of Organization" reprinted in G. Thompson et al. eds. (1991) *Markets Hierarchies, Networks: The Coordination of Social Life,* London: Sage.

Pringle, J. (1994) "Survival or Success? Ways Of 'Being' For Women In Organizations" in S. Olsson, ed., *The Gender Factor: Women in New Zealand Organizations,* New Zealand: Dunsmore Press, 193–212.

Rajvinder, K., J. Fullerton and Y. Aimed (1995) "Managing Diversity: Succeeding Where Equal Opportunities Has Failed" *Equal Opportunities Review,* 59, January/February, 31–36.

Rich, A. (1979) *On Lies, Secrets and Silence,* London: Virago.

Rosener J.G., (1990) "Ways Women Lead" *Harvard Business Review,* 90, Nov–Dec, 119–125.

Thompson, P. and D. McHugh (1990) *Work Organizations,* London: Macmillan.

Ware, V. (1992) *Beyond the Pale: White Women, Racism and History,* London: Verso.

Weber, M. (1918) "Science As A Vocation" in H.H. Gerth and C. W. Mills (1948) *From Max Meter: Essays in Sociology,* London: Routledge and Kegan Paul.

West, J. and K. Lyon (1995) "The Trouble With Equal Opportunities: The Case Of Women In Academics" *Gender and Education,* 7, 1, 51–68.

White, J. (1995) "Leading In Their Own Ways: Women Chief Executives In Local Government" in C. Itzin and J. Newman (1995) *Gender, Culture and Organizational Change,* London: Routledge.

28

THE ROAD AND THE STREAM: ON THE METHOD OF CROSSING OVER TO A "WET" CULTURE

Bruce Hanson

First there is the stream, then there is the road, and then there is the stream. The central metaphor of this chapter is a Zen koan. The road is the world of our intentions and concepts, and the stream is that which lies beyond our conceptualization and intention. The koan has many possible interpretations, but I use it to describe the western journey from pre-modern to modern to postmodern forms and experience. This study is based on the method of 'crossing over' to another culture, drawing on visceral experience that link seemingly different cultural and organizational contexts.

BACKGROUND AND CHALLENGE

While conducting a socio-technically based action research project for an American paper products company, I encountered unanticipated difficulties. The organization was successful, but it was suspicious of its own success and fearful of its ability to succeed in a turbulent environment. The instrumental rationality of its management systems had broken down and could no longer serve as a predictable monitoring tool. The 'organization' became entangled in interdependency and collapsed. Managers feared that the organization would be overcome by chaos. The source of the difficulty permeated much deeper and broader than their immediate situation.

Gadamer's definition of symbolism offers insights into deeper level needs. In Gadamer's view the term 'symbol' represents something, "in and through which we recognize someone already known to us," so that the symbol is "that other fragment which has always been sought in order to complete and make whole our own fragmentary life" (Gadamer 1986:32). We search for a 'holy grail' of corporate life to create significance and wholeness within fragmentary lives.

The firm, AMPAP, was on such a quest searching for the 'subtle concept' that would ensure success for their new product and within their organization. Since symbols operates at many levels (e.g. individual, group, organizational, etc.), they can facilitate the integration of many aspects of experience through a metaphorical influence that applies to many situations.

The socio-technical framework, based on an open systems model, allowed AMPAP to study the relationship between its system and its environment. While this conceptualization was an advance over closed system thinking, more theoretical development was needed for fuller understanding of the turbulent relationship between a system and its environment.

WHEN THE ROAD MEETS THE STREAM

AMPAP managers realized that they had reached the limits of explicit cognitive theory and found themselves in a place that exceeded the boundaries of previously explored territory. In the search for a root metaphor to understand the situation, I encountered a koan in a Dharma talk by a Zen priest, "First there is the stream, then there is the road, and then there is the stream" (Anderson, 1994). I came to understand the stream to be that which lies outside our intentions and concepts. The contrast of language between the wetness of the stream and the dryness of the road struck me.

A 'dry' culture sought definitions and explanations, directions and destinations. A 'wet' culture, such as Japan, simply experiences and moves with the environment. Greater reliance was put on lived experience than on explicit explanation. When I asked the sensei, "when is the road the stream?" He responded, "When you sit." It is in the utterly simple processes of life that unity can come.

The progression from wet stream, to dry road, to wet stream, parallels the discussion of postmodern culture in the west. According to David Boje (1995) we can find clues to postmodernity from life in pre-modern cultures. Postmodern theorists Baudrillard (1988), Deleuze and Guattari (1987) suggested returning to some tribal practices to live in greater harmony with the natural environments. To a large extent Clegg (1989) based his postmodern theories of power on Machiavelli's pre-modern discourses. Toulmin (1990) sees the modernist period as a detour between the continuity of nomadic, pre-modern and postmodern societies.

Boje (1995) suggests that the relationship between the pre-modern, modern and postmodern are not simply sequential but a concurrent conversation or discourse.

Cultures are simultaneously pre-modern, modern and postmodern. This simultaneity and sequentially underscores the breakup of monolithic and transcendental desire for progress as recursive issues continually reappear (Hans, 1989).

In Japan, the voices of the ancient pre-modern, the modern and postmodern are all present, perhaps more self-consciously because of their historical ambivalence toward technology. Within Japanese society, ancient traditions still have much influence over modern practices with which they co-exist. In pre-modern culture, individuals are not differentiated from their social or religious roles; the basic ontological concept of self and roles are unified. One of the greatest challenges of postmodernity is the issue of identity. The struggle to achieve modernity has created a split in our personae as we take on partitioned roles (Gergen, 1990).

In a remarkable integration of philosophy and psychology, James Hans (1989) contrasted the discursive method of modernity with the recursive method of pre- and post-modern cultures. In pre-modern cultures, there is an expectation of recurrent activities. What is remarkable, in the modern period, is the expectation of transcendence or progress. We expect to change the world. As Hans points out, we still have not addressed the recurrent issues of human life due largely to our fascination with technology, instrumental power, and instrumental rationality (Heidegger, 1977).

In seeing the world-as-object, we have achieved an incredible capability to change the landscape of the earth. At the same time the human condition has not changed dramatically. We know there are limits to discursive, instrumental rationality; objectification leads to the "saturation of selves" in which our identity is populated by many discrete and partitioned roles (Gergen, 1990).

The 'return to the stream' is a return with the 'knowledge of the road', but with an ability to function simply in a complex and dynamic environment. In returning to the stream there is an appreciation of 'wet', recursive processes that incorporate the progression of technology and pluralism. The primary challenge is to locate clues that illuminate ways of living in the 'wetness' of this turbulent environment. In this metaphor there is a suggestion of return with a difference. The desire for simplicity and wholeness is not the same one would experience before setting off on the road of knowledge and action and intentions and encountering turbulence. This return occurs as a surprise. It is not a calm enlightenment, but a fundamental realization and incorporation of experience.

This chapter presents several Japanese vignettes that help understand life in AM-PAP under postmodern conditions. AMPAP is an extremely resourceful and *smart* organization at a loss for words or concepts to adequately describe how it implicitly organize its life—regressing to *modern* (e.g., individualistic and mechanistic) concepts when pressure was too great. Its preferred terms were profession, project and program—each denoting a clear path toward a goal. These modern concepts only highlighted the gap between the conceptual expressions and the reality of the organizational experience.

THE METHOD OF CROSSING OVER

This study is based on the method of "crossing over" to another culture; drawing on visceral experiences that link two seemingly different cultural and organizational contexts. As a Japanese research manager said, "Our greatest discoveries occur when a researcher travels over to another culture and returns. It has little to do with the technical aspects of the project, but everything to do with his change of perspective."

An explanation for the lack of cogent cross-cultural comparison is that the basic assumptions of the cultures are often dramatically *and* subtly different. Qualitative approaches appear to be more initially fruitful. Van Maanen (1982) and others note that perhaps the best approach in this instance is the use of self-as-instrument. The associations and connections that occur between situations and episodes in life experience become the source of generative inquiry into assumptions.

Morgan (1986) and Sackmann (1989) wonderfully and creatively explored metaphor and imagination as primary vehicles for understanding organizations. It often takes a journey to shift perspective and to understand that which is right under our noses. New life and vision often came from extraordinary, 'nonproductive' trips. New products come from the gaps and cracks of the organizational process through 'under the bench' projects promoted by 'product champions.' I studied a program that took a very circuitous route before discovering its core concept. This journey, often supported with linear rationales of productivity, discovered a simplicity that tempted the organization to kick itself. "Why hadn't we thought of that before? It is so obvious!"

THE JOURNEY OF CROSSING OVER:
THE CHALLENGE AT AMPAP

At AMPAP, my primary task was to understand new product development. The mission was to improve decision-making and coordination between product development, product engineering, and manufacturing. To achieve this, I used a sociotechnical systems approach (Pava, 1989) to follow organizational deliberations.

The challenge at AMPAP was immense. It was a huge, intelligent, and successful company with a matrix structure in which functional departments interfaced product/project drivers. I followed organizational conversations over a period of about a year, living within the company for three of those months. AMPAP staff were a smart and resourceful group of people, but constantly changing. Nothing worked the way it was planned, requiring constant adaptation.

The team I followed was responsible for creating a new disposable diaper. This started with handmade versions of new designs. The handmade diapers were tested and feedback received from focus groups. Successful designs were reproduced on single machines and used by families who kept diaries concerning their use and performance. Next, the successful design was manufactured on limited production lines that duplicated the planned assembly lines. These thousands of diapers could be test-marketed in a specific city, and general market acceptance could be evaluated. Finally, the successful design was sent to plants which could produce billions of diapers.

At each step of the process, the monetary and reputation risk increased geometrically, eventually amounting to billions of dollars. The pressure on this process was immense, and as the program team members declared, "the bar is constantly raising." Toxic shock syndrome cost AMPAP billions of dollars within a week when the press associated the syndrome with their products. This forever created anxiety and focused attention on environmental anomalies. Management also wanted the product development cycle cut in half, to be assured of continual consumer preference in the market place, and to decrease the cost of the product. These forces in combination with stiff competition created tremendous pressures on the program.

One response was the implementation of an "Initiative Delivery Model"—a series of scale-up stages with decision gates. At each test point, the company wanted hard numbers before proceeding to the next stage. In the midst of these pressures for impeccable performance, the program team experienced a profound sense of loss. I would call this a postmodern experience. Their hierarchical and program structures did not work. In a 'program' where certainty was required, the program director observed, "We need several breakthroughs if we are to finish the project on time, and I don't know how we are going to do it." They were operating beyond their knowledge base. A scheduler-planner confided that, "All I have to show for four months of planning is on this eight-and-a-half by eleven sheet of paper." Their plans could not be used to monitor progress because internal and external developments changed most of the assumptions the day after the plans were finished.

Standard AMPAP organizational concepts did not fit the innovations required for the project. The management team did not have the required organizational concepts in their repertoire. Their dictionary (literally) of over 650 special terms were mostly technical acronyms that proved to be of limited use in social and organizational conceptualization. In moving forward they identified five key challenges:

- *loss of structural isolation:* New product development traditionally required the isolation of a 'skunk works'. Research and development is best accomplished in isolation but the team is constantly barraged by intrusions and meetings.
- *loss of sequence:* A well-run modern organization follows a planned and predictable sequence. To meet the time constraints, however, they needed to have multiple and concurrent processes.

- *loss of slack:* The organization is becoming 'lean.' Perhaps the greatest loss is *time.* New product introductions cannot wait until technology is ready but are often rushed to market, creating a great deal of risk and time pressure.
- *loss of differentiation:* The hallmark of a well-ordered organization is clear differentiation of functions and tasks, with career development in increasingly well-developed specialties. However, this had shifted to multi-functional teams and highly integrated efforts, and everything seemed to be bundled together.
- *loss of identity:* They wanted an executive patron to assist them in securing necessary resources, but when the hierarchy and functional distinctions started to break down they found it difficult to align personal career success with organizational success. Individualism was precarious, particularly if one began to equate one's identity with the results of one's work (often failures or changing) or products (disposable diapers, and other consumer products).

Overall, AMPAP worked extremely well by any criteria. They were still profitable and top in this product category. The key question was not whether they were going to be profitable but rather how much the category was going to earn. Many aspects of AMPAP appeared to work, although not in the intended manner. When self is separated from role and task, integration cannot occur. The individuals in the company were worried and frustrated, yet somehow it always worked out in the end.

In the desire to create a streamlined organizational system, AMPAP found itself deconstructing its explicit structure. In seeking to explicate the model and create an extremely detailed road map, it found that the model's requirements could not be made explicit. It was often forced to make expert judgments and distinctions between similar but different situations. The organizational intent to make 'empirical, data-based decisions' was short-circuited by the rush to bring new products to market. AMPAP was left with only tacit knowledge to make financially huge decisions. Because each person felt individually responsible, they wanted a *system* to assume the responsibility. Tacit knowledge presented to an organization dependent on rational discourse and empirical basis for decision-making was distressing.

The organizational *system* did work, but not because it was an explicit predictive system. It succeeded because breakthroughs or miracles happened, because seemingly unrelated thoughts came together into subtle realizations, that could neither be predicted nor anticipated. Positive results required each person to make their own sense of the organization, for the answers were far from clear in the espoused structure. The imagination required to explore and create corporate culture came from outside their local systems.

REMEMBERING NIHONEL

The greatest realization from my experiences in the US and Japan was an acute awareness of context. In a central paradox of organizational life, one can see directly only through peripheral vision. The goals and plans themselves are frequently illusory and it often takes an exotic distinction to see what is right under your nose. My work at Nihonel conducting research on basic research provided me with the exotic distinctions to illuminate my work at AMPAP.

Japan is very beautiful, a young volcanic island chain with great natural beauty, surrounded by water. Not surprisingly water is a root metaphor in Japan. My Nihonel host described Nihonel as a 'wet culture.' In a 'wet' culture, identity of self is intermingled, malleable and generally "quite large" (Devos, 1985). Learning to walk in crowded Tokyo symbolized the peripheral processes that informed one's actions in concert with the environment. In the Shinto religion (and other animist, pre-modern religions), the whole world is seen as being alive. Conduct is guided by a hope that we will not anger the gods, and people interact with respect and knowledge of the right process.

I found Nihonel not only 'wet' but much like the *pond* on the grounds of the Central laboratory. Like a pond, the water is contained and everything in the pond is related, in aesthetic balance. This geographic boundedness and socio-centric attention is a characteristic of pre-modern culture.

In the midst of my work in AMPAP, I remembered my experiences at Nihonel:

Confinement and density. At Nihonel my 'office' was a small room that I shared with 27 other people. I felt a great deal of pressure in that environment. Several times a day people would remind me to do my best, not as criticism but as general encouragement. I accomplished a great deal as norms of respect and consideration permitted individuals to do their own work. I was a company employee, limiting my freedom to wander around and work at home.

I came to appreciate the power of being on the inside of the company. I had to follow the established protocols of *nemiwashi* (using our gatekeeper for introductions to others in the organization) and *ringi* (making sure that decisions occurred in the proper sequence). While being a company employee is very restrictive, it provided a strong sense of belonging and place.

Aesthetic awareness and collegiality. Concern for the aesthetic environment in Japan was very great. It was in many ways like a bonsai culture—the nurture of miniaturization. On most desks, my fellow workers had the tools of their trade, carefully held in pencil boxes. I was encouraged to become a member of a club at Nihonel and learned to play the Shakuhachi (bamboo flute). This was an amazing experience. Emphasis was not that I learn to play a lot of notes, but *how* I played the notes. This was also true in drinking, and introductions; most aspects of life had established rituals that encouraged their sociability.

Themes versus projects. As I sought to do research on research, I discovered that they chose to use the term *theme* rather than *project* for their work. This allowed the dynamic evolution of ideas to follow discovery and the resulting change of interests and possibilities. Another visiting senior researcher sought to measure the 'stop and go' criteria (established in U.S. firms) for projects, yet few themes started or stopped. Instead they split, merged, and transformed. In a marked contrast to American corporate culture, concepts of 'concrete' were generally relational and often linguistically ambiguous.

Amorphous product visions. The role of a senior researcher is somewhat like the notion of an elder. Their visions for new products were often quite amorphous such as the "optical computer" or the "considerator." The latter was a computer that functioned more like the heuristic brain, learning and adapting, capable of discovery. These amorphous images serve as a galvanizing force in which new functionality of materials, processes and devices might discover a use. In this way, themes develop a central focus that is not overly specified and can lead to fundamentally new product creations. For example, I picked 'Success Factors in Independent Research' and worked with it until I figured out what it meant.

Never saying no. I had been trying to focus my research for several weeks and seemed to get little guidance from my manager, who was head of the Research Administration Office. He never told me directly when I was off-target. He rarely said no. Instead, he would just change the subject. Finally, I hit on an idea that was on-target and he simply gave me his lunch—a large maki roll sitting on his desk. It is very difficult to critique a work in progress; however, when it aligns, you know it. The synthesis occurs, and cannot be predicted by measurement.

The strongest personal experience was perhaps the simple experience of walking in Tokyo. People did not bump into each other in spite of the thousands of people in public places. Every aspect of life felt connected, and relationship and harmony was valued above all. Living in Japan and working at Nihonel provided few opportunities to be alone or isolated. My experience in Japan proved dramatically different from that which I anticipated from a distance. When I returned to the States I found that my perceptions had changed and I relished the closeness that I first experienced as claustrophobic.

RETURN WITH A DIFFERENCE: REMEMBRANCE AND REALIZATION AT AMPAP

Upon returning to AMPAP, I was struck by the lack of daily interaction compared to life at Nihonel. There were many more meetings but we lived apart, in silent, air-conditioned offices, often interacting over the computer network. Rituals such as introductions and acts of collegiality were far less common. At AMPAP we relied heavily on explicit, verbal communication.

I realized the nature of project funding was *time*-oriented at AMPAP. 'Short-cycle management' placed all projects into the same funding pool for immediate commercialization. Therefore, the primary impact of my consultancy was introduction of a long or deep-cycle project reference. Without my experience in Japan I would not have seen this simple distinction. Time was more often a 'deadline' at AMPAP, rather than a boundary to guide appropriateness.

Iterative nature of projects. Japanese craft tradition emphasizes thoughtfully executed repetition. When I was learning to play the shakuhachi, I was told that apprentice potters had to make a thousand pots and destroy them. I needed to practice my craft repeatedly, listening each time to the resulting sound in the air. The expectations at AMPAP were for grand movements in which the projects could be completed *once and for all.* The idea was to 'hit a home run' the first time.

Reliance on micro-environments. Creation normally occurs in small places and requires intimacy to incorporate aesthetic awareness of environmental implications. Paradoxically, containment of creation is important for fluidity. At AMPAP, containment or micro-environments were the stages in the project cycle. Their creative processes focused on the problems of the phase and these problems changed throughout scale-up. The evolution of the eventual solution was not derived from some 'grand scheme.'

Subtlety of concept. AMPAP longed for a clear concept at the inception of the product development process. By contrast, the product visions of Nihonel were not directly obtainable, but they pointed in the direction of fundamental functional transformation.

Beyond the goal framework. The linguistic distinction of *theme vs. project* was very intriguing. Projects are 'goal' oriented rather than 'direction' oriented. The organizational framing of projects and programs is not sufficiently fluid to be stable. Nihonel explicitly chose the term "theme" so to retain social and task fluidity. There was a role for projects, but a project-based organization was not sufficient (Reese, 1967).

Shift of identity. The nature of the relationship of individuals to the collective whole shifted for me. *Middle-out management* is a viable concept in the US as well as in Japan (Nonaka, 1988). *You are the company.* This represents a holographic conceptualization of identity. The notion of "group mind" has been resisted in the US because of individualism.

The qualities I saw in Nihonel were also present in AMPAP but it was the contrast that permitted me to see them. The development of the organization has more to do with poetic awareness and recognition than with implicit process. We do not have the same words for aesthetic appreciation at AMPAP. We often take the literal situation too seriously and do not appreciate the underlying continuity. At AMPAP fundamental insight occurred when a project manager connected with the Initiative Delivery Model said, "Hell, that model's no different than the engineering process we all learned in school." He was remembering something that created wholeness in his experience of fragmentation. The iterative approach integrated his thinking and feeling in the organization.

DISCUSSION

Limitations. The primary limitation is that the contexts of these two cultures are very different. However, 'remembering wet culture' suggests interesting notions of transferability. To the extent that my experience in Nihonel represents crossing over to a 'pre-modern' culture, it is limited by the boundaries of the context that are prescribed in Japan and open in the US. The integration of wet and dry cultures suggested by either eastern or western approaches, means we return from our journey (both physically and symbolically) changed with an appreciation of both the road and the stream.

Within the Nihonel culture is a very strong sense of implicit assumptions. Whereas in AMPAP 'conformance of non-conformity' is the basic value. The implied isolation is breaking down. The fortress of the organization has been fast eroding as each person nurtures connections with the environment, no longer the sole purview of a few select gatekeepers. In pre-modern times this vessel was locality, but modern science and technology has broken down traditional barriers and brought many different localities together in the challenge of 'open field synthesis.'

Postmodern cultures learn a sense of coherence from the experiences of pre-modern cultures. In Japan it is a broad base of tacit agreement and implicit assumption. The assumption basis at AMPAP is based on the professional paradigm of project cycle and time-oriented events. The basic assumptions of the culture were fewer and less palpable at AMPAP. The 'fragmentation' of postmodern experience has not yet taken place in Japan.

The difference of difference. The planner-scheduler was strangely at peace with a planning process that couldn't smoothly project into the future. He seemed to accept that continual re-orientation was needed. What was created was a living process of connecting the organization and its imagination with unknown internal and external environment. The planning process allowed them to put a 'face' on the unknown interdependencies and relationships.

In addressing the sense of loss in organizational life there is hope for uniting the road and the stream. What we are looking for is already present in the organization. We must realize that the repetition is not merely mechanical re-production, but there is a return with a difference on the other side of our projects. Heidegger called this the difference of difference (1977). If, when we return to a phase similar to where we began, we realize how things have changed in the 'second instance,' it makes a great difference in our *being*.

The development of the organization has less to do with organizing *a single story* than it does with the development of aesthetic imagination and peripheral awareness. As I learned to walk in Tokyo—a surprisingly difficult thing to do—I learned that one is most at ease when one is aware of the periphery. The loss of integration is largely one of losing ourselves in our goals and thinking about our tasks. The whole world is alive. We cannot plan our way to a new future. Most of the activity is the art of creating environments through daily activity and sharing our poetic creations. What we discover in new product development is that ideas always come in the side door and are never what we expect.

Opening the floodgates reminds us that we encounter the environment as an internal reality, not expecting a one-to-one correspondence of literal reality and structure, but somehow trusting the ground of our subtle experience and intuition. The implicit order is present through remembering with our whole inclusive selves, letting the complexity come and go to stay centered in remembering our ancient forms, remembering the stream. We have many 'trappings' that can divert our attention and cause closure, isolation and division. The unknown territory beyond 'modernity' is vaguely familiar as we return with a difference: an open future and a return to simplicity.

The process of symbolizing is one of *remembering*. Remembering does not necessarily mean that we ever were conscious of what brings wholeness. It is 'remembering' the subtle, the invisible, the unspeakable stream beyond the road of our intentions and concepts. Remembering our 'wet' culture suggests a change in our perspective, awareness, expectations and practices. Our road is transformed by the presence of the stream.

It is helpful to understand that the world is broader than that for which we have words. An appreciation of aesthetics and poetics points to that mysterious environment that we can only vaguely see, and remember that of which we are only vaguely conscious. The result can be a respect for that which is beyond our understanding, and a faith in a process beyond simple cognition.

BIBLIOGRAPHY

Anderson, R.(1994) "The Road And The Stream." A Dharma talk by Abbot Reb Anderson at Tasajara Zen Meditation Mountain Center on July 2, 1994 in Carmel Valley, CA.

Baudrillard, J.(1988) *America,* London: Verso.

Boje, D.(1995) "Stories Of The Storytelling Organization: A Postmodern Analysis Of Disney As 'Tamara-Land.'" *Academy of Management Journal* 38, 997–1035.

Clegg, S.(1989) *Frameworks Of Power,* London: Sage.

Deleuze, G., F. Guarrari(1987) *A Thousand Plateaus: Capitalism and Schizophrenia* (B. Massumi, trans.), Minneapolis: University of Minnesota Press.

Devos, G.(1985) "Dimensions Of Self In Japanese Culture" In A.J. Marsella, G. Devos, F. Hsu (Eds.), *Culture and Self,* New York: Tavistock.

Gadamer, H.(1986) *The Relevance of the Beautiful,* Cambridge: Cambridge University Press.

Gergen, K.(1990) *Saturated Selves,* San Francisco: Jossey-Bass.

Hans, J.S.(1989) *The Question of Value: Thinking Through Neitzsche, Heidegger, and Freud,* Carbondale: Southern Illinois University Press.

Hanson, B.(1995) *The Road and the Stream: Facing the Turbulent Stream of New Product Development,* Ann Arbor, MI: UMI.

Heidegger, M.(1977) *The Question Concerning Technology and Other Essays,* New York: Harper and Row.

Morgan, G.(1986) *Images of Organization,* Newbury Park, CA: Sage Publications.

Nonaka, I.(1988) "Toward Middle-up-down Management: Accelerating Information Creation" *Sloan Management Review,* Spring, 9–18.

Pava, C.(1983) *Managing New Office Technology: An Organizational Strategy,* New York: The Free Press.

Reese, C.(1969) "Some Potential Human Problems Of The Project Form Of Organization" *Academy of Management Journal,* 12(4): 459–467.

Sackmann, S.(1989) "The Role Of Metaphors In Organizational Transformation" *Human Relations,* 42, 463–485.

Toulmin, S.(1990) *Cosmopolis: The Hidden Agenda of Modernity,* New York: Free Press.

Van Maanen, J., Dabbs, J. Jr., and Faulkner, R. (1982) *Varieties of Qualitative Research.* Beverly Hills, CA: Sage.

29

SECTION SUMMARY: LOOSE CONNECTIONS, BELONGINGNESS AND COMMUNITY

Richard A. Goodman

This section heightened my own sense of belongingness and community. Much of the management literature of the 1990s has had some focus on the benefits of individual empowerment. The empowerment concept takes many forms, from the psychologically inclined, who see it as a form of maturity; to the organizationally inclined, who exhort individuals to become intrapreneurial; to the politically inclined, who exhort them to rebel and lose their chains. As more and more attention is focused upon individuals as individuals, a seemingly paradoxical phenomena arises: The focus on 'I' seems have replaced the emphasis on 'we.' The resulting focus on 'I,' although often containing positive values, is clearly symbolized by self-interest. The focus on self-interest in turn has shaped the study of organizational governance (organizational economics) by emphasizing the dark premises of human nature.

We can all recount enough examples of thoughtfulness and compassion that these negative organizational economics premises seem both puzzling and incomplete. This is reflected in a nascent intellectual thrust toward the study of citizenship behavior. Experientially we know that both good and evil are represented in our own behavior—both selfish and selfless behavior. Since both behaviors are obvious to us it is difficult to reject the various negative arguments out of hand—as they all contain some truth. The dark premises are drawn from the very basics of modernist thought. Both within this section and others are examples of modernist thinking extending into both public and private postindustrial organizations. The main issue arising from this 'dismal' extension to organizational models is the encouragement of self-interest and the discouragement of community.

Christina Garsten in "Loose Links and Tight Attachments: Modes of Employment and Meaning-Making in a Changing Labor Market" identifies this same postindustrial conundrum when she contrasts the effects of outsourcing and loyalty. The organizations she studied had bifurcated work forces with cores made up of permanent members and a large periphery of temporary members. Such organizations are clearly quasi-virtual. In this study both professional labor as well as clerical labor and manual labor are outsourced. The firm believes that certain skills need not be stockpiled and that appropriate specialists can be retained as needed. How can a firm expect a temporary worker to be loyal—'dismally' they can't—realistically they often obtain loyalty because the dismal calculative assumptions are not fully correct.

An ironic sidebar to this discussion is the current popular organizational concept of managing knowledge capital. Knowledge capital reflects a value that cannot be fully imitated. It should be made explicit and deployed to benefit the organization. We hear this from Peter Senge at MIT and from Francesco de Leo at Bocconi and even from Dick Rumelt at UCLA. They each have a different frame for the knowledge issue but willy-nilly their arguments are certainly inconsistent with the community destroying that arises from extensive outsourcing of skills.

Even while the firm believes the contract workers will be loyal to them, the contract workers need to be ready for the next job and the next, and are in a position where self-interest is mandatory. Loyalty even if it does occur is a weak form of community as it focuses on loyalty to the firm rather than the people who make up the work force. Christina argues that stronger forms cannot exist since the basic requirement of relationship cannot be met within temporary assignments.

Patricia Riley and Lisa Howard in "Competition: The Structuring of Postindustrial Organizational Life" reinforce the conundrum of individual versus community behavior. In their study this conundrum is an organizational paradox. Participation is used to reach decisions to downsize and restructure. There is a well-known paradox that separates management scholars from behavioral scholars. The basic question is, "How do a team of five members decide to select four members and exclude one using participative processes?" The behavioral scholars argue that the question is mis-specified. They want to answer a different question. Their question is, "How can we share out the work so that all five can continue being team members?" The management scholars know that four is the right answer and but they are unwilling to use a participative process. How to do both (participate and exclude) remains a conundrum. Pragmatically organizations ignore the paradox while they try to do both and, as Patti and Lisa found, employees are being asked to form enduring relationships with customers and partner organizations while jobs are outsourced.

In their chapter the power of metaphor is used to describe this two-sided behavior. They find the metaphor of competition is used to explain many actions, including those that run counter to the express intent of organizational policy. In their study, the same metaphor is used to justify self-interest as well as organizational interest. (Wray-Bliss and Willmott also report on this paradox in the next section.) As a counter example, they include the Mondragon experience—the story of a large set of interrelated firms in Spain's Basque country. The culture of the Basque region itself is a collaborative one and the Mondragon firms reflect these values well. Here we see a metaphor that blends individual self-interest with community interest. "The people at Mondragon convinced us that there is a competition story that balances competition through cooperation and never reduces life to wins and losses."

Another form of the competition metaphor is the managerialism metaphor. Within the not-for-profit world the focus is increasingly on measurement and market-related behavior. Heather Clark, John Chandler, and Jim Barry, in "Too Scattered to Provide a Critical Mass?: Women and Managerialism in Two UK Universities," provide a look into the dysfunctions the lack of community or citizenship behavior create when they are driven by a need for measurement.

I first encountered paradox as an issue in the 1970s when the Netherlands government was engaged in a cost-benefit analysis of Dutch university programs. I was somewhat at a loss to understand how one compared the benefits of philosophy with those of chemistry. While the government was pursuing modernist, managerialist initiatives, the intellectual directions of Dutch economic thought were shifting strongly toward a strong postindustrial, postmodern position. In a graduation speech that year, the Rector of the Netherlands School of Economics spoke of a new paradigm that included both economic and social issues. He specifically argued that such a paradigm did not lend itself to measurement and comparison. While this stressed the evaluation system he felt that the more robust specification of issues were certainly worthwhile. The cost-benefit fad then passed for a decade or so until the current time period when managerialism has swept back into the public purview.

This measurement-driven vision seems to be at serious odds with "citizenship" behavior and community. Most measurement qualities seem to focus on central tendencies which in traditionally male organizations are unlikely to reflect the lived experiences of female members or other minority groups. As argued earlier, if modernist or managerialist thought is really "man"agement then serious oversights can be expected. Here, Heather, John and Jim identify the potential for a unifying force among university women about women's concerns—an area in which men seem to have only minimal insights. While their focus is the issue of women and critical mass it is more broadly true that the issues of belongingness and community within many organizational subcultures is also a seriously ignored area of managerialist thought.

Bruce Hanson's story in "The Road and the Stream: On the Method of Crossing over to a 'Wet' Culture" reflects the development of community along with the abandonment of traditional hierarchy and formal planning. Within a traditional industrial setting, the developments Bruce reported represented a shift in organizational form from modernist to a postmodernist approach. Bruce's story has two elements that represent the crossing over from one culture to another. One central element is the author's own experience. He entered the work situation with specific interests and specific paradigms to apply to the issues. His envelopment by the Japanese culture forced him to change his appreciation of the situation and the ways in which he approached his tasks. In this case he was permitted to find his own way as he was welcomed into the community. The 'indirection' his colleagues provided became an opportunity to draw near and he was allowed to find his own way to their way.

Meanwhile the firm itself was engaged pursuing managerial processes that simply didn't work as expected or as they should. Thus, successfully employed experiences from the past proved to be faulty and misleading. This challenge was overcome by the development of a very different process approach that was goal seeking by indirection. The team increased its internal communication and was pleased to try various pathways simply for the increased knowledge, not for a directly instrumental goal.

The context of the Japanese and American cultures are very different. But 're-membering wet culture' suggests interesting notions of transferability. To the extent that his experience represents crossing over to a 'pre-modern' culture, it is limited by the boundaries of the context that are prescribed in Japan and open in the US. The integration of wet and dry cultures suggested by either eastern or western approaches means that when we return from our journeys—both physically and symbolically—appreciation of both the road and the stream changes us in a mixture of tangible and intangible ways.

In both examples of crossing over, it was the recollection of earlier times that heightened the learning and demonstrated the values embedded in new methods or approaches. Being at peace with a process that doesn't smoothly project into the future, accepting continual re-orientation, creating a living process of connecting the organization and its imagination with unknown internal and external environment are intertwined elements of a new process that is not based directly upon an older process. Yet the phrases used to describe the new process are in fact derived from the contrast with the old process. The new process cannot be easily conveyed *de novo* without direct reference to the previous process.

With another lens we can see this as a story that creates community and dampens individuality. Activities were selected for their enabling benefits rather than for their solution-finding benefits. Various elements of individual task were not accomplished simply to further a measurement achievement because task accomplishment did not really or symbolically represent forward progress. The robust interconnections between tasks and people, between activity and ideation, between sharing and not, all build a fluid "eddy"fying flow that touch the whole organization and everyone within it without privileging or denying the contributions of each. This situation is clearly a postmodern approach with an industrial setting.

SECTION SIX

30

SERVANTS OF GREED: POST-INDUSTRIAL SUBCULTURE(S) FROM A BUDDHIST PERSPECTIVE

David Bubna-Litic

Buddhism provides a world view that is becoming increasingly popular among postindustrial professionals looking for depth and soul in their work lives. Within this chapter Buddhist concerns are contrasted with fundamental assumptions that define ideologies of the market and private domination of the means of production. Buddhist ideologies contend that the nature of reality is extraordinarily interconnected and, as such, distinctions between private and community reflect the dominance of deluded and egoistic thinking. It is argued that the Buddhism resonates with the Romantic notions about the connection between self and nature. Buddhist reality undercuts the postmodern sensibility by placing the master narrative beyond discourse. The postindustrial era is seen as both an extension and an intensification of industrialism, in which there is a loss of deep connection with the spiritual self and a striving for mastery through technological control. This greed for control is seen as based upon illusion and ultimately results in the opposite: rather than finding freedom we become servants of greed.

INTRODUCTION

Buddhist ontology is based on the experience of Nirvana or 'enlightenment'—a deep realization of the nature of ultimate reality. Through meditation Shakyamuni Buddha discovered enlightenment some 2,500 years ago. Since then this discovery has been subjectively confirmed by generations of Buddhists. Now, the enlightenment experience is being given new expression by a growing number of Western-born Buddhist teachers whose understanding has been validated both by their Asian teachers and Western peers.

Buddhist enlightenment is ultimately beyond description. Existence is a paradoxical duality of form and emptiness, in the same way a wave is also just the ocean. According to Robert Aitken (1996:86), through Buddhist practice "we see into the nature of things and make intimate the formless, the timeless, the spiritual, the universal, the world of no-birth and no-death."

Modernist discourse has displaced *all* religion to the periphery. Thus it is not surprising that Buddhism has been virtually absent from Western 'organizational' discourse. Yet, as Burrell and Morgan (1985) point out, social theory is based on our assumptions about reality: ontological, epistemological, regarding human nature, and methodological. Arguably, the current dominant view of reality in the social sciences has drawn strongly on nineteenth-century assumptions derived largely from Newtonian physics.

As a result, the 'self' is seen as almost an epiphenomenon of an organic mechanism called the 'human being'. From the Buddhist perspective, such atomistic and ego-based views of human identity are inadequate and do not explain consciousness. Buddhist enlightenment involves a deep appreciation of the oneness of all beings. Thich Nhat Hanh (1988) coined the term "inter-being" to describe his sense of this intimacy of all things. Understanding ourselves from the perspective of the Mahayana school of Buddhism means that we recognize the paradoxical duality that permits us to be both individuals and simultaneously no other than the rocks, the stones, the sky and everything else in the universe.

The skeptical reader may ask what relevance Buddhism could have to the study of organizations. The implications of the rise of postindustrialism and its cultural partner postmodernism are twofold: the first highlights essential concerns about meaning and the second attacks the legitimacy and independence of authority, especially the implicit authority of economic rationalism that pervades the majority of management texts. The postmodern critique of basic assumptions provides an opening for other perspectives to enter the debate.

Buddhism has an unique perspective on meaning that enables it to encompass the nihilistic implications of postmodernism, *and* the failure of secular modernism and return to depth and soul in life. Zen Buddhism's stance on meaning cuts through the debate because its transcendent orientation is impossible to grasp through intellectual discourse. This is well illustrated in the famous Zen koan case (Aitken, 1990) known as the Oak Tree in the Courtyard.[1] The original question was

---

[1] A koan is a matter to be made clear through the practice of meditation and self understanding. It is a question which can only be answered through insight into Buddhist reality. It acts as a barrier or marker to the student whose teacher might also use other checking questions to test the student's insight. The answer to a koan is rarely immediately apparent and may even take the greater part of lifetime to understand.

a standard one that wandering monks asked in the hope that a teacher's answer would turn them toward some insight. The setting is a dialogue between Chaochou, the famous ninth century Chinese master of Zen, and an unknown student.

The Case

A monk asked Chao-chou, " What is the meaning of Bodhidharma's[2] *coming from the West?" Chao-chou said, " The oak tree in the courtyard."*

Commentary and Verse

If you can see intimately into the essence of Chao-chou's response, there is no Shakyamuni in the past and no Maitreya[3] in the future.

> *Words do not convey the fact;*
> *language is not an expedient.*
> *Attached to words, your life is lost;*
> *blocked by phrases, you are bewildered.*

Reality cannot be represented through discourse. Buddhism and other major Eastern religions/philosophies are based on experience that reaches beyond words. This notion is exemplified by a now famous statement made by Chao-chou's teacher Nan-ch'uan: "The Tao [reality] is not subject to knowing or not knowing" (Aitken, 1990). This view presents some formidable epistemological problems to the Western mind.

Zen Buddhism relies on direct presentation of the essential matter—as it is. Western philosophy resembles the monk who, confounded and confused, hesitates before the Master in a presentation—its life is lost in endless circles of discourse. Intuitively, many people react to the thick and heavy discourse of much postmodern writing in the same way—it is dry and misses something about life's simple fecundity.

Postmodernism is nevertheless significant because it brings us to a crossroads. Having unmasked the authoritative meta-narrative in the discourse of modernism and highlighted the ephemeral nature of absolute truth, we are left with a polyphony of voices vying for legitimacy and authority. This polyphony in organizational theory is reflected in the theoretical jungle that characterizes the field and the rise of metaphors as a basis of understanding organizing. Evidence of this can be seen through the popularity of Gareth Morgan's *Images of Organization.* This road of many voices is, however, crossed by a road of thundering silence, a road that brings back the possibility of re-enchantment into modern life. The road

---

[2]Bodhidharma is the first Indian teacher who brought meditation-based Buddhism to China.
[3]Maitreya is a mythical Buddha who is said will enlighten everyone in the far distant future.

of thundering silence is the way of Buddhist experience in which the true nature of reality, beyond concepts and judgments, issues forth in all things. It complements the postmodern, in showing the futility in attempts to find meaning through discourse and shares its skepticism of technological progress. At the same time, it opens a path for intimate spiritual connection with the here and now of everyday modern life. We can find Buddhist understanding in the silent emptiness that is the heart of all things.

The Buddhist view of inter-being muddies up the neatness of Newtonian atomism which creates a dualism that separates mind from body and humanity from nature. This separation dis-enchants the world. It is at these crossroads that the dilemma between the plurality of postmodernism and the transcendent reality of Buddhism can potentially provide new generative questions and new answers.

Bolman and Deal (1995) are responding to the growing need among professionals to integrate their feeling, human, and spiritual nature into an increasingly mechanized and seemingly meaningless world. Now for the first time a few Westerners have, through Buddhist practice, truly begun to understand the experience that has dominated Asian culture and society for centuries. It is this transmission beyond words that has finally come to the West (Batchelor, 1994).

The legacy of the East is an extremely well developed understanding of self-realization and spiritual practice, developed over generations and across national cultures. It is this wisdom and its meditative technology, rather than just the experience, that is new. Western Buddhists recognize their experience as that expressed by the poetry and writings of the Romantics, Islam, Hindu and Christian mystics. There is a growing feeling that, as the experiential knowledge of the East meets the West, Eastern technology can lead to new and different understandings.

Regardless of the changes that this new 'spiritual technology' has brought and will bring, the world is now dominated by industrial society. Intertwined with industrialization is a tendency to think of people in narrow economic and mechanistic terms. From this perspective, the self is considered a separate and bounded entity and individual rationality is seen as both possible and desirable. With post-industrialism came both an intensification of the effects of industrialism and opportunities for change.

Buddhism does not represent a return to pre-modern time. Rather it presents a different set of assumptions and requires navigating through the dilemmas of industrialism and postindustrialism using new paths that are based on integrity and compassion. Buddhism calls for a new look at the assumptions upon which social theory is based.

THE ATOMISTIC CONSTRUCTION OF SELF

The view that we are separate and disconnected individuals has long been a part of Western culture. The roots of this view can be traced to the Judeo-Christian separation between God and man. An extreme example of this view is Hobbes' concept that the natural state of humankind is one of perpetual war in which all men are pitted against all others. According to Enlightenment thinking we are saved from this brutal reality by the social structures of liberal democracy.

Although individual intellectual freedom was of paramount importance to Enlightenment scholars they had no intention of letting anarchy reign. Order and hierarchy of knowledge was established by deference to 'reason.' This view later became more sophisticated and developed into the assumption that science advanced through consensual validation, through the agency of collective reason and through peer evaluation.

Hindsight shows us that not all knowledge is equal, as the success of the physical sciences quickly led to their ascendancy in academic circles. Numerous fields of academic endeavor adopted similar approaches and methodologies in their fields of study as scholars sought to gain legitimacy in an age of reason. This was especially so in psychology with the manifesto-like writings of John Watson (1924), the great advocate of observable behavioral data. Psychology attained its scientific status by marginalizing questions of subjective experience and favoring that which was observable and replicable. As a result, the deep and interesting but complex and messy fabric of human inner life was left relatively unexplored. This trend in the social construction of knowledge resulted in self-knowledge that became mechanistic and lacked depth.

Freya Matthews (1991) argues that within the individualism of early liberal philosophers there is a strong parallel between Newtonian physics and the construction of the 'rational' person. Descartes' separation of mind and body gives primacy to the mind and hence reason. This separation is one of the fundamental platforms upon which contemporary western culture has been built. An integrated view of the nature of mind and body provides a more appropriate alternative. The repression of this integrity of mind and body is reflected in an 'out-of-touchness' with the body, leading to pathologies of denial of bodily needs and over-indulgence. Dualism with respect to the body "engenders just the same sort of controlling, exploitative and sometimes punitive attitude to the body as it does to Nature as a whole" (Matthews, 1991:36).

When this mind-body dualism is extended to Nature, nature is described by Newtonian physics as a-emotional, colorless, silent and dead. Matthews contends that this chilling aspect of Newtonian cosmology splits us off from the world. She summarizes, quoting from Randall:

Men still consider their world in terms of Newtonian science; they are still living, as White-head has put it, upon the accumulated capital of ideas laid up by the scientific pioneers of the seventeenth century. They still feel bewildered and afraid when it begins to dawn on them that it is no longer possible to live by the political and economic theory worked out for the businessmen and proprietors of the Age of Reason—and free competition . . . that earlier commercial individualism has in fact been rapidly giving way to newer forms of corporate industrial organization and welfare politics. Yet the most widely accepted theory and ideals, in America rather more than in Europe, still bear the impress of Newtonian science, with its rigid, deductive and inflexible concepts, and of the private self-interest, the irresponsible competition, the rugged individualism of that earlier commercial age. (1991:46–47)

The Newtonian view is pervasive and may be true for most areas of society. Yet freedom of public expression of ideas, so fervently sought by Enlightenment philosophers also allowed for a plurality of ideas to co-exist. This is especially true in those areas in which reason could not be the arbiter. In areas such as literature and the visual and performing arts, rationalism has had its least and most uncertain sway.

THE ROMANTICS

The atomistic view of the self of the Enlightenment was not without opposition. With the advent of the industrial revolution, the Romantic Movement grew out of an angry reaction that extended beyond the protection of jobs and the preservation of peace and safety in the work place. Romanticism objected to the dehumanizing aspects of industrialism and the view that nature was a resource to be exploited and an opponent to be conquered. As the Newtonian construction began to take force, so too did the view that animals and plants were considered to be without consciousness, soul, or rights. Blake expressed this collective sense of outrage well:

> *Now I a fourfold vision see,*
> *And a fourfold vision is given to me;*
> *'Tis fourfold in my supreme delight*
> *And threefold in soft Beulah's night*
> *And twofold always. May God us keep*
> *From Single vision and Newton's sleep!*
> William Blake, November 22, 1802.
> (Bly, 1995)

Romanticism stressed the unobservable aspects of being and nature. It emphasized the importance of humanity, depth, soul and meaning in life. While no longer respectable within many arenas of life, these romantic notions still play significant roles in contemporary culture within the arenas of personal relations and our vocabulary of moral feeling, loyalty, and inner joy. The Romantic view of the self is spiritual and interconnected.

Within academic circles, attention has been focused increasingly on making sense of the journey of scientific and technological achievements that have fueled and been fueled by societal transformation. The meaning of events has been seen as a linear progression that could be extrapolated into an ever bigger and brighter future. This vision of a brighter future persists in what can be called the postindustrial dream. Yet it is a dream in which the concept of an atomistic self has remained virtually unchanged since the Enlightenment period.

PERIODIZATION

Critical to understanding the postindustrial dream is first understanding the essence of the postindustrial world. There seem to be two general approaches in the literature, which I will call: periodization and characterization. The first is time-based and focuses on tangible linear aspects of history. Whereas the second is more fuzzy and focusing on cultural changes that are not necessarily synchronous.

Periodization type approaches track the rise of technology and seeks to identify discrete jumps that are capable of tangibly differentiating one period of history from another. From an organizational theory perspective Astley and Brahm (1989) identify 1960–1980 as a postindustrial era, albeit one of "impasse," in which "organizational forms invented in the industrial era persisted and created an impasse in organizational development." They found that this was a period in which old industrial forms in the US responded slowly to new demands and changes they had to make in order to retain competitive advantage over foreign firms.

According to Astley and Brahm, the 1980s marked the start of serious transformations within firms. Transfer of standardized technologies allowed US firms to shift their productive assets to emerging technologically dynamic areas. And developing countries competed on more favorable terms where standardized technologies could be easily transferred.

The new "high-tech" industries evolved into different organizational forms. A constantly expanding knowledge universe gave specialization higher pay-offs. Development of comprehensive expertise in all aspects of an enterprise became economically unfeasible. In combination with the potentially massive markets of a global economy, small niche specialists working together had greater potential for achieving viability than a large bureaucracy could. Cooperative relationships in the form of joint ventures and strategic alliances became increasingly prevalent. Sophisticated networks are now being heralded as the prototypes of postindustrial organization.

Daniel Bell's (1976) *The Coming of Post-Industrial Society* is another example of periodization. Bell focuses on tangible changes in the social structure of society. He identifies five major components that reflect the postindustrial era:

- Economic sector: change from goods-producing to a service economy
- Occupational distribution: pre-eminence of professional and technical class
- Axial principle: centrality of theoretical knowledge as source of innovation and of policy formulation

- Future orientation: control of technology and technological assessment
- Decision-making: creation of a new intellectual technology.

According to Margaret Rose (1991), it is impossible to make a clear distinction between industrial and postindustrial society. She argues that there are fundamental problems with Bell's landmark work, indicating, for example, that many service sectors evolved roles that women traditionally provided as individuals such as meal providers, counselors, medical care providers, educators and child care providers. This is not necessarily a fundamental change in the nature of work, but in the way it is organized. Many of the central components pre-existed the new era. Rose concludes:

> *Rather than distinguish the postindustrial from the point of view of such abstract and loosely interpretable principles, it may . . . be better to look more closely at the way in which any apparently new developments in technology and divisions of labour have marked a development of or departure from those of an industrial society.* (p. 36)

The problem lies in determining whether there has been a substantive shift in society or whether the current era is just an intensification or even peaking of what has gone before. Certainly salient factors seem to be at work in contemporary society. Change in the last twenty years has been exponential. Few would deny that almost all aspects of our lives mediated by technology have become more efficient. In relation to industry there are several forces:

- Globalization of commerce: Ethnocentric to geocentric.
- Diffusion of the skill base.
- Intelligent flexible manufacturing systems.
- Quantum leaps in technology: especially information and communication technology.

But technological changes do not occur in a vacuum. While they impact significantly on the current cultural milieu, that milieu also has an equally significant and powerful impact on the nature and character of such changes.

CHARACTERIZATION OF THE CULTURAL MILIEU

Alternatively, looking at the cultural milieu in which the postindustrial society exists provides another approach. In this way we can get a sense of postindustrial society, not by mapping particular discrete events in time, but by looking at the character of the time. Rather than focusing on the outcomes of that technology produces we can look to the beliefs and values that drive the creation of new technology. After all, technology is a means to an end. Lyotard has said (1979): "Our working hypothesis is that the status of knowledge is altered as societies enter what is known as the postindustrial age and cultures enter what is known as the postmodern age."

The dynamics by which modernity produced a new industrial and colonial world can be described as 'modernization,' a term that Docker (1995) uses to denote those processes of individualization, secularization, industrialization, cultural differentiation, commodification, urbanization, bureaucratization, and rationalization which together constitute the modern world. These processes are ultimately artifacts of our assumptions about self and the world.

The self in the modernist tradition is the subject of knowledge and scientific power. Reason is the source of progress in knowledge and society. Reason is seen as the privileged locus of truth and the foundation of systemic knowledge.

Kenneth Gergen (1991) identifies the modern vision as a grand narrative of progress. Faith in the ability of reason to solve the problems of the human condition manifests itself in architecture, psychology and even the arts. It was thought that music, dance and the visual arts could progress along with the new and better techniques. Rationality, observation, progress and essentials in the sense of rational building blocks of theory form not only the core values of the modernist leaning, they also reflect a machine metaphor.

The power of this machine metaphor is evident in all forms of human expression. It can be found in music, dance, painting, architecture and even in literature. The machine metaphor also permeated a major proportion of organizational theory. Even Morgan (1986), who makes a distinction between organic and mechanical views of organization, skims over the mechanical assumptions that support our understanding of organic phenomenon. With this distinction blurred, the breadth of influence of modernist views on organization theory is evident.

The core values of modernism were built, however, upon a platform assumption that underlying form and trappings is an intelligible truth. In the excitement of modernism the softness of Science's assumptions became obscured and Science was assumed as the only method capable of finding out *the* truth. Modern literature was also conceived as an alternative way of depicting how things really are. The unveiling of false pretensions in theater, the documentary, the exposé all reflect this modernist genre. In psychology, modernism depicted the self as capable of being intellectually understood. In this context, Romantic notions became seen as light-headed indulgences and products of undisciplined or emotional thinking.

We are entering a new phase of society called postmodern or, as Lyotard puts it, the postmodern condition. Postmodernism is extremely difficult to grasp, not only because there is substantial disagreement among scholars, but also because many postmodern writers deny that a master definition is possible. Lawrence Cahoone (1996) suggests that five general themes can be distinguished: "Postmodernism typically criticizes: presence or presentation (versus representation and construction), origin (versus phenomena), unity (versus plurality), and transcendence of norms (versus their immanence). It typically offers an analysis of phenomena through constitutive otherness."

Postmodernism challenges the assumption of the self independent of society and discourse. Not only is 'truth' dependent on context and hence perspective, but so is the construction of who we are. Hillman (1983) explores the premise that we try to make sense of our lives through stories. Our stories are the meanings we construct about the events of our lives. Anthropology has struggled to make sense of the vast differences in the way social facts are understood. Societies develop widely held interpretations of what particular facts may mean within certain contexts.

By denying a unitary and absolute perspective, a new equivocality is introduced into postindustrial society. As more voices are heard, an act that may previously have been collectively deemed immoral by society becomes a matter of choice. In the absence of an absolute position, simple acts can take on a multiplicity of meanings. An extra-marital affair may be seen as an inevitable expression of the falseness of the institution of marriage, a pre-negotiated right, a moral failing, a sin, a legitimate sign of marital dysfunction, or a sign of patriarchal domination, or something that men do naturally—the stories are endless. The truth of the matter depends on the perspective from which it is viewed.

Gergen looks to the solipsistic nature of postmodern discourse to break the binds that tie us to existing forms of social structure and morality. Relationships built on "true love" go against postmodern sensibilities that question both the validity of who is loving, who is loved and the truth of love. He (1991:7) suggests that: "all previous beliefs about the self are placed in jeopardy, and with them the patterns of action they sustain . . . The impact is more apocalyptic than that: the very concept of personal essences is thrown into doubt." The postmodern self is marked by a plurality of voices, each of which has authoritative claims to reality. According to Gergen (1991): "Under postmodern conditions, persons exist in a state of continuous construction and reconstruction; it is a world where anything goes that can be negotiated."

Neville (1995) explores the notion that we live in an *Era* dominated by the archetype of Hermes (Mercury), the divine patron of commerce. A great negotiator between the Gods, and between man and the Gods, Hermes seems most clearly manifested in those workers who are revered as movers and shakers. Paper entrepreneurs and advertising executives are typical of these postindustrial workers who although creating nothing of substance can make things happen.

Resonating with the thrust of postmodern thinking is Hillman's suggestion that the psyche is composed of a number of different archetypes. These reflect the complex and relative nature of the human psyche. One way of understanding archetypes is that they can be interpreted as constellations of meaning that dominate our lives at different times. They have no true form beyond the images that they resonate with. Hillman's conception takes an important step beyond polyphony, however; for him what underlies psyche is polytheistic. The psyche is not composed of nihilistic "constructions." For Hillman, although the nature of truth is murky there is something more. He quotes Barfield: "Truth is always in poetic form; not literal but symbolic; hiding, or veiled; light in darkness . . . The alternative to literalism is mystery" (Hillman, 1983:149).

Hillman rejects reason as the final arbiter of behavior and contends that it is our deep inner link with the divine cosmos that maintains the nexus between the archetypal perspectives of the psyche and morality. However, the postmodern world view of secular radical relativism, or solipsism of contesting personal conditions, such as Gergen (1991) suggests, betrays a profound lack of reverence for life. Something that is subjectively self-evident.

In recognizing multiple subjective perspectives of the inner archetype, Hillman suggests that it is the "Gods" alone who make radical relativism legitimate and tolerable. He suggests that what Jung meant is that the place of morality is located in authenticity of the depths of our selves not in the throne of reason, the ego. In accord with Hillman the Buddhist experience of enlightenment brings us deeply intimate with ourselves—our "real" and authentic nature. This is not subject to rational comprehension. Enlightenment is the realm of the divine cosmos. It is our deepest self that is the very essence experience that connects us with the divine. This essential nature is interconnected and links us deeply to nature. It cuts through the chaos of postindustrial society in which individuals find themselves lost in a sea of ambiguity, greedily chasing that which glitters in an endless quest for meaning and ontological security. From a Buddhist perspective one need look no further than within.

THE EMPTY MASTER NARRATIVE OF BUDDHISM

The key to Buddhist understanding involves a completely different approach to the chaos of information saturation and overload typical of the postindustrial life. According to Robert Aitken (1996) these understandings come not from analyzing life intellectually but from meditation. A common form of meditation is the dynamic process of linking a word or a question to one's breathing and when one's mind strays to return assiduously to the matter. The process is gentle and natural and over time conscious thoughts begin to drop away and insight emerges of its own accord.

According to Yamada Koun Roshi (Aitken, 1990): "When your consciousness has become ripe by true [practice]—pure like water, like a serene mountain lake, not moved by any wind—then anything may serve as a medium for enlightenment." The mysterious nature of the search for enlightenment is exemplified in the following famous case in which the student Hsiang-yen Chih-hsien gave up his Buddhist training after failing to answer the question: "What was your original face before you were born?" He left the rigorous monastery life and took a job looking after an old temple in exchange for room and board.

Some years later, Hsiang-yen was sweeping the temple garden when his broom caught a small stone, lifting it across the pavement, it struck the trunk of a bamboo with a resounding—tock! With that sound, body and mind fell away. Following this experience he composed the following verse:

One tock has made me forget all my previous knowledge.
No artificial discipline is at all needed;
In every movement I uphold the ancient way
And never fall into the rut of mere quietism;
Wherever I walk no traces are left,
And my senses are not fettered by rules of conduct;
Everywhere those who have attained to the truth
*All declare **this** to be of the highest order.*

It is this deep sense of Self, the presence that is beyond reason that motivated the Romantic movement. We can see it in the poetry of Whitman, Wordsworth, Blake and Rilke. An experience that is not unique to Buddhism, it can be encountered in any religion and is echoed in the insights of these poets and other artists.

Modernism represented a fundamental revolt against the dominance of religion in Western Society. The transformation of society in Europe had seduced several generations into believing that the sacred is either dead, old-fashioned or irrelevant. In Asia, it is associated with the humiliation of colonialism. In China the traditional cocktail of old religions led to a widespread belief in supernatural powers but failed the test of reality when confronted with the kind of power that comes out of gun barrels. To many Asians this was proof of the falseness of all sacredness and religion.

Now postindustrial society offers a new dream. The Buddhist first noble truth, that suffering is unavoidable, is being tested. The inevitable causes of death, sickness and old age are being potentially overcome by technological advances in genetic engineering and the biological and medical sciences. The long-term effects of engineered immortality will expand the potential of human life fundamentally in new and unthinkable ways. Yet from a Buddhist perspective, as long as there is desire and grasping, life will still contain suffering regardless of what technology brings. We will always be denied something, the increased efficiencies of the postindustrial economy have led to greater rather than less consumption. Since we do not live within a leisure society the result is that many have become servants of greed, working harder to maintain a position in an all-or-nothing economic system.

The change to Postmodernism from Modernism is much like the shift from Newtonian physics to theories of relativity. In a similar fashion social theory seems to have recognized that social knowledge is also related to the viewer's position. These changes in thinking may not be fundamentally new, but merely extensions of the past. They are coupled, however, with exponential changes in technology further compounded by rapid diffusion of knowledge to a growing world population. This powerful escalation of scale has resulted in what can best be described as Hypermodernism. Gergen sees the implications of postindustrialism as leading to social saturation. Saturation, however, implies some human limits.

THE ROMANTIC BACKLASH

It is because of these natural limits that a new romantic backlash is developing. Modernism's split from nature neglects the environmental costs of industrialization and this has a human parallel. The prominent American poet Robert Bly laments at the fragmentation of contemporary (postindustrial) plurality:

> *All of us, since the rise of technology, have been torn into parts so often that we can hardly grasp what an interior unity could be. High school rips body and mind apart, science rips the perceiver and the thing perceived apart, the Industrial Revolution rips man and woman apart, rips father and son apart, racism rips soul and mind apart, imperialism rips the governors and the governed apart, our firm houses separate weather and person.* (Bly, 1995:5)

In reading Bly's work, we can see that Romanticism is not dead, but has lost its naiveté. He offers some interesting insights into the way in which this return to Romanticism is manifested in contemporary American poetry. There are new developments on three fronts. The first is the introduction of shamanic themes that are connected with nature and that follow the tribal tradition of the poet as spiritual healer. The second is a meeting with the minds of eastern poets. According to Bly this is evidenced by a shift to poems that flow in different and gentler ways. The third front is movement towards poetry recitation. Oral poetry requires engagement with the listener and authenticity of feeling. The sum of these movements has resonance with the core elements of romantic poetry: "associations with Middle Ages alchemy, respect for the integrity of the natural world, respect for the night-intelligence, and careful observation of detail, is alive in recent poetry, much more alive than the average reader is aware." (Bly 1995:132)

Underpinning the rise of this *Neo*-Romantic revival movement is the vapidity of the postindustrial dream. Arguably, the postindustrial dream is rapidly turning into a nightmare that calls poets, such as Bly, back to the past. The call seems to come from all quarters and is so great that many authors perceive that societies now exhibit some sort of vague malaise. De Foore and Renesch (1995) call it "soullessness." Needleham (1994) calls it "the new poverty," where, despite a society's affluence, there is an undercurrent of fear, apprehension and loneliness. David Whyte's *The Heart Aroused: Poetry and the Preservation of the Soul in Corporate America* (1993) is an attempt to use poetry to find integration of the soul into the corporate world.

BUDDHIST INTEGRITY IN A POSTMODERN WORLD

This return to spirituality and romantic values has manifested in a new movement of Socially Engaged Buddhism which is gaining increasing popularity among professionals who seek meaning and depth in their lives. This development is facilitated by a number of Western Buddhist teachers including Jack Kornfield, Robert Aitken, Gary Snyder, Nelson Foster, Thich Nhat Hanh, and Christopher Titmus. Socially Engaged Buddhism reflects the essential evolution and transformation of Buddhism into the new culture of the West. Although strongly influenced by Asian traditions, Socially Engaged Buddhism is in large part a Western variation developed primarily in the United States. If there is a theme to what is arising it has "an emphasis on householder instead of monk, community instead of monastery, and a practice that integrates and makes use of all aspects of life, for all people, women as well as men" (Fields, 1986).

It is an attempt to redefine Buddhism and integrate it with values that are deeply embedded logistically and culturally in Western Society. This shift away from its monastic heritage means that Buddhism must find a new way to relate to the societies in which its practitioners are engaged. It is inevitable that during its metamorphosis this new branch of Buddhism will encounter the postindustrial world as this is an epoch in which Industry and Commerce hold a central place in Western societies. Buddhism must integrate into this world to survive.

The ox-herding pictures of Zen Buddhism[4] are one source which depicts Buddhist pathways to achieve this deep integration with the kaleidoscopic marketplace of the postindustrial world. In the final ox-herding picture the seeker returns to the market place disheveled, carrying a wine-gourd in hand and at ease with the muddy vicissitudes of worldly life. This last picture represents the final point in the long journey of Buddhist training. At this point in their training students are completely at home in the world; caring little for themselves they set about a life of helping others. As Jack Kornfield (1995) points out, however, Buddhism is a never-ending process; enlightenment is not something one gets and can then retire and so the practice can also begin with embodying this final ox-herding picture. In this way, Western Buddhists can enter the marketplace with compassion and non-attachment.

The Buddhist perspective suggests fundamental changes in the way we organize our postindustrial economic system. These changes derive from a deep sense of interconnectedness and compassionate action. According to Robert Aitken (1978:58), "Nirvana all alone by itself is not enough." The Buddha under the tree in his state of absolute emptiness was still not complete, he lacked karma—"The Buddha's karma, like yours and mine, is to save all beings—thus we find completion in our lives and fulfillment of the Dharma." Kenneth Kraft points out that "spiritual maturity includes the ability to actualize transcendent insight in daily life" (1993:43).

---

[4]A famous set of woodcuts with commentaries outlining the various stages on the Buddhist path from the beginning seeker searching for tracks of the ox through to enlightened Buddha returning at the completion of her training to the market-place "with bliss bestowing hands".

In Zen Buddhism, this relationship to ordinary life and the world is expressed in the archetype of the "Bodhisattva" whose work is to save all beings. The Bodhisattva, free of self-preoccupation, understands the interpenetration of all things: "if you can see that all phenomena are transparent, ephemeral, and indeed altogether void, then the thrush will sing in your heart, and you can show compassion" (Aitken, 1984).

From the Buddhist perspective work in postindustrial society takes on a different purpose. It is not about the maximization of personal or individual wealth, but an expression of our deep nature. As with the Romantic ideal it is a call for acting in integrity with our true nature. Buddhists believe that with practice we can get in touch with our connection with the sacred. Work is recognized in many spiritual traditions both as a powerful tool for insight into the depth of daily life and as an expression of deep insight. Thomas Moore drawing on the Romantic tradition recognizes this deeper function of work: "all work is a vocation, a calling from a place that is the source of meaning and identity, the roots of which lie beyond human intention and interpretation" (1992:181).

Within Zen Buddhism, work is an essential part of monastic life and considered as important as meditation, chanting sutras and other practices. Historically work in a monastic community revolved primarily around the simple life of subsistence agriculture. Although many monasteries maintain busy public schedules, most monastic work roles involve relatively simple tasks. The monastic structure that carefully selected senior positions and ritualized jobs maintained work as an extension of meditation. Work such as the mindful carrying of refuse, organizing of public funerals and cleaning of toilets is a powerful way of confronting a student's attachments and delusions. It connects us with our bodies, our feeling life, our intellect, and provides a structure for the development of community relationships. Work under these circumstances is deeply enriching.

Despite a tendency in the management literature to focus on short-term success stories,[5] a long-term view reveals that the life of most commercial organizations is generally short and deeply dependent on the ebb and flow of broad economic, natural and societal forces (Aldrich 1979). Life in organizations is often correspondingly chaotic, uncertain and full of conflict. This experience is painful for many who fall prey to the consequent restructuring. Buddhist practice is to cultivate the capacity to hold onto one's integrity in the face of such pain. According to John Kabot-Zinn, as we develop the capacity to be open to the "full catastrophe" of our working lives we learn to get a firm grip on the inner forces that drive the creation of false needs. It is these mentally fabricated needs that seduce us into greed, materialism and over-work characteristic of postindustrial society.

Integrity is the well-spring through which we can develop a sense of connectedness, coherence, wholeness, and adaptive vitality. Using this definition as a base,

---

[5]See Pettigrew (1983) for a review.

Julian Gresser (1995) has developed a methodology for negotiation that can be used to navigate in virtually any circumstance. The key to Gresser's method is the Buddhist practice of mindfulness or openness to the moment, a concept he calls presence. By entering each activity with a sense of having a 'beginner's mind', a willingness to see everything as if for the first time, people can be receptive to new possibilities and see things as they are. In negotiating their work lives people characteristically make assumptions about what is and is not possible. These assumptions and ideas get in the way of being open to the world and pre-empt the attainment of integrity within themselves and their work.

By approaching each work encounter with a stance of open awareness we can use these moments as opportunities to develop deep integrity. This stance was valued in Japan by the Samurai, who knew the subtle power of having a mind free of expectations. The true mind of "not knowing" takes this a further step. With this mind we can see our fellow workers not as opponents, but as ourselves with the compassion and freedom to respond to their actions just as they are—without expectations, prejudice or predisposing assumptions. From this position we can integrate compassionate action into our work, making decisions on the basis of what is right for each circumstance based on logic and intuition.

One of the fundamental steps in Gresser's approach to negotiation is coming to grips with what we actually need in life. This requires integrity as we live by more than bread alone and part of our soul work is understanding what is true to ourselves, what our soul life needs.

The development of Buddhist integrity begins with the understanding of our true needs, so we can begin to negotiate our work lives fully. Although the Buddhist scriptures set out a moral code as an instructive guide to integrity, moral codes alone sit uncomfortably with integrity and can become burdensome (Beebe, 1995). The spirit is quickly lost in the clouds by good and evil and rules can easily suffocate the soul. Written moral codes in the postmodern world of ambiguity and contradiction are easy prey to the solipsistic maneuvers of a clever mind which can justify acts that poison the heart. Buddhist integrity rings true the call of the thrust of the Romantic revival and demands development of all aspects of a person. Integrity, as John Tarrant (1995:5) observes, "comes from the heart, not just the head, and we have to feel our way into it." As Jack Kornfield suggests, Buddhism is a path with heart.

BIBLIOGRAPHY

Aitken, R. (1978) *A Zen Wave: Basho's Haiku and Zen,* New York: Weatherhill.

Aitken, R. (1984) *The Mind of Clover: Essays in Zen Buddhist Ethics,* San Francisco: North Point Press.

Aitken, R. (1990) *The Gateless Barrier: The Wu-men Kuan (Mumonkan),* San Francisco: North Point Press.

Aitken, R. (1996) *Original Dwelling Place: Zen Buddhist Essays,* Washington DC: Counterpoint.

Aldritch, H. (1979) *Organizations and Environments,* Englewood Cliffs, NJ: Prentice Hall.

Astley, W. G. and R.A. Brahm (1989) "Organizational Designs For Postindustrial Strategies: The Role Of Interorganizational Collaboration" *working paper.*

Batchelor, S. (1994) *The Awakening of the West: The Encounter of Buddhism and Western Culture,* Berkeley, California: Parallax Press.

Beebe, J. (1995) *Integrity in Depth,* New York: Fromm International Publishing Corporation.

Bell, D. (1976) *The Coming Of Post-Industrial Society: A Venture In Social Forecasting,* New York: Basic Books.

Blake, W. in R. Bly (1995) *News of the Universe,* San Francisco: Sierra Club Books.

Bly, R. (1995) *News of the Universe,* San Francisco: Sierra Club Books.

Bolman, L. and Deal, T. (1995) *Leading with Soul—An Uncommon Journey of Spirit,* San Francisco: Jossey-Bass.

Burrell, G. and G. Morgan (1985) *Sociological Paradigms and Organizational Analysis,* Andershot, England: Gower.

Cahoone, L. (1996) *From Modernism to Postmodernism: An Anthology,* Oxford: Blackwell.

Docker, J. (1995) "Vertigo: Postmodern And The Market" *Arena Journal,* 5, 71–87.

Fields, R. (1986) *How the Swans Came to the Lake,* Boston: Shambala.

Gergen, K., (1991) *The Saturated Self: Dilemmas of Identity in Contemporary Life,* New York: Basic Books.

Gresser, J. (1995) *Piloting Through Chaos,* Sausalito: Five Rings Press, 1995.

Hillman, J. (1983) *Healing Fiction,* Woodstock, CT: Spring Publications.

Kornfield, J. (1993) *A Path with Heart,* New York: Bantam Books.

Kraft, K. (1993) "Meditation In Action: The Emergence Of Engaged Buddhism" *Tricycle,* Spring.

Lyotard J. F. (1979) *The Postmodern Condition: A Report on Knowledge* trans. by G. Bennington and B. Massumi, Minneapolis: Minnesota University Press.

Matthews, F. (1991) *The Ecological Self,* London: Routledge.

Moore, T. (1992) *Care Of The Soul: A Guide For Cultivating Depth And Sacredness In Everyday Life,* New York: HarperCollins.

Morgan, G. (1986) *Images of Organization,* Beverly Hills: Sage.

Needleham, J. (1994) *Money And The Meaning Of Life,* New York: Currency Doubleday.

Neville, B. (1995) "Seeing Through The Postmodern Organization" *Temenos,* 2, 49–55.

Nhat Hanh, T. (1988) *The Heart of Understanding,* Berkeley: Parallax Press.

Pettigrew, A. (1983) *The Awakening Giant Continuity and Change in ICI,* Oxford: Basil Blackwell.

Rose, M. (1991) *The Postmodern And The Post-Industrial: A Critical Analysis,* Cambridge: Cambridge University Press.

Tarrant, J. (1992) "Soul" in Zen *Mind Moon Circle,* Summer, 3–19.

Tarrant, J. (1995) "Enlightenment And The Foundations of Teaching" *Blind Donkey,* 15, 2, 4–7.

Watson, J.B. (1924) *Behaviourism,* Chicago: University of Chicago Press.

Whyte, D. (1994) *The Heart Aroused: Poetry and the Preservation of the Soul in Corporate America,* New York: Currency Doubleday

Yamada, K.(1991) "Gateless Gate: Newly Translated With Commentary" in R. Aitken, *Original Dwelling Place: Zen Buddhist Essays,* Washington DC: Counterpoint.

31

YOGIC PRINCIPLES AND MANAGEMENT PRACTICE

Elisabeth M. Wilson

This chapter makes philosophical and practical comparisons between the tenets of yoga and the practice and theory of management. It discusses first the nature of yoga, and then the similarities and differences between yoga and management.

INTRODUCTION

Many believe Yoga to be a series of physical exercises with a bit of esoteric philosophy attached. In fact, yoga is a 'union'; a holistic system for life. The word yoga is derived from the Sanskrit root 'yuj' meaning to bind, join, attach. It can also mean direct or concentrate, or use and apply (Iyengar, 1966). The introduction to yoga for many students is to the physical practice of yoga, hatha yoga. Other paths of yoga are raja (control over mind), bhakti (worship or devotion), jnana (study), and karma (selfless action). Far more than just posture (asana), hatha yoga also includes gestures (mudras), energetic locks (bandhas), and breath control (pranayama). Gestures and locks strengthen posture (asana) by helping to seal and redirect energy allowing the yogi (yoga student) to become aware of vital or spiritual energy (prana) and eventually to gain control. Thus mudras, bandas, and pranayama combine with asana to aid spiritual enlightenment (Swatmarama, 1992).

Unlike many other non-competitive systems of physical exercise, hatha yoga is performed slowly and requires intense concentration. While achieving a particular refinement of an asana may be satisfying to both student and teacher, it is the 'doing' rather than the end result that is of primary importance. Hatha yoga

356

strengthens the body, makes it more supple and encourages internal balance. The physical practices, when combined with other practices such as mantra (repetition of sound) and yantra (observation of verbal images) make hatha yoga a popular approach to a spiritual path. Though commonly conceived as the physical aspect of Yoga postures, hatha yoga is 'the way towards realization through rigorous discipline' (Iyengar, 1966). Yoga encompasses mind, body, spirit and relationships with others, and is fundamentally a spiritual practice. Clearly, the practice of hatha yoga has a much deeper purpose than mere physical exercise.

Yoga originated in Hinduism, about three thousand years ago, to provide an un-dogmatic spiritual inspiration to religion. Shivapremananda (1996) noted that spiritual development can take place without adherence to specific religious beliefs, thus, without the need for dogma.

PATANJALI'S SYSTEM OF YOGA

Patanjali's *Yoga Sutras* (sayings or aphorisms) are perhaps the best known of the many yoga systems (Prabhavananda and Isherwood, 1953). Sutra means a thread or bead with which students were expected to memorize the sayings. As a verbally transmitted tradition the *Sutras* are necessarily brief. Literacy skills permit the modern student to become more deeply acquainted with the Sutras through reading commentaries on each saying (Prabhavananda and Isherwood, 1953). The *Sutras* followed earlier works such as the *Upanishads*[1] and *Bhagavad Gita*[2] that offer more poetic and contemplative thoughts. Whereas these two works are regarded as scripture, the *Yoga Sutras* are regarded as instructions.

Patanjali is believed to have lived in about the second century BC and offered the first truly comprehensive yoga system. It is described as astanga or an eight limbed system:

1. Yamas (prohibitions, restraints, abstention from evil-doing)
2. Niyamas (observances)
3. Asana (postures)
4. Pranayama (breathing techniques, control of prana or the life force)
5. Pratyahara (sense control, withdrawal of the mind from sense-objects)

---

[1] *The Upanishads* are a collection of spiritual treatises written by many different authors (Mascaro, 1965) between 800 BC and the 15th century. They are the first distinctly yogic writing. They were composed by the meditational practices of jnana yoga. They explain the relationship between Brahman, all encompassing God, and Atman, the individual soul.

[2] In addition to Patanjali's writing, prana is described and discussed in classical texts such as the *Prasna Upanishad* and the *Hatha Yoga Pradipika*. The latter is a complex book written sometime between the thirteenth and seventeenth centuries from ancient sources (Swatmarama, 1992). It was composed as an esoteric text and is a series of short instructions that require further elucidation and probably acted as an aide memoire to a much larger verbal and practical system of transmission of the yoga system.

6. Dharana (concentration)
7. Dhyana (meditation)
8. Samadhi (contentment or bliss)

The first and second limbs are a system of ethics. Asana and pranayama, the third and fourth limb, have already been discussed[3]. When Patanjali used the word prana, it meant much more than breath. Vital energy or life force might be a better translation. All senses, mental abilities and powers are subsumed under the concept, and it is described as the energetic essence of the universe (Prabhavananda and Isherwood, 1953).

Pratyahara, the fifth limb, is sense withdrawal or detachment (Prabhavananda and Isherwood, 1953), a necessary prerequisite of concentration and meditation. In some schools of meditation it is taught as a specific technique. It counteracts the aroused state and activates the parasympathetic or 'relaxation response'. The benefits of a period of concentrated relaxation extend beyond the relaxation period into everyday life. It is this extended benefit that makes yoga a popular relaxation technique in some parts of the business world.

Patanjali describes dharana (concentration) and dhyana (meditation) and their relationship to samadhi, as:

> Concentration (*dharana*) is holding the mind within a centre of spiritual consciousness in the body, or fixing it on some divine form, either within the body or outside it. Meditation (*dhyana*) is an unbroken flow of thought toward the object of concentration. When, in meditation, the true nature of the object shines forth, not distorted by the mind of the perceiver, that is absorption (*samadhi*). When these three—concentration, meditation, and absorption—are brought to bear upon one subject, they are called samyama. (Prabhavananda and Isherwood, 1953: Chapter III, 1–4)

Patanjali sees control of the mind as an essential element of Yoga. He describes different kinds of thought waves; positive ones include 'right' knowledge that involves direct perception, inference, and scriptural testimony, as opposed to the false nature of 'wrong' knowledge that is not founded upon the true nature of its object. He believes that everything has its 'essential' nature and that essential truth can be discovered.

Patanjali stresses the importance of non-attachment, the ability to avoid being weighed down by like or dislike, or material or immaterial rewards and possessions. As emphasized by Prabhavananda and Isherwood (1953), non-attachment does not mean indifference; the yogi must still be discriminating. Patanjali further describes the union of Atman (the soul) with Brahman (God). He provided guidance about ways in which one might attain this union through concentration and the

---

[3]A notable exception to this is chronicled in a special edition of *Management Education and Development* (Snell, et al, 1991).

repetition of mantra (Prabhavananda and Isherwood, 1953). Patanjali describes concentration as 'one-pointed', the total focus of one's faculties upon one object, enabling progression from concentration to meditation.

KEY FEATURES OF YOGA: A COMPARISON WITH THE PRACTICE OF MANAGEMENT

Yoga is a holistic system firmly rooted in the body. The practice of management is also embodied, although this embodiment is often denied and is less frequently studied. Both systems advocate the suppression of emotion, albeit in different ways.

In yoga, the ego is sublimated to the goal of non-attachment to the material world, however, the emotions are fully acknowledged. In the practice of management, emotions are often denied and their expression limited to prescribed forms and places.

The practices of both yoga and management could be described systemically. While both Yoga and management emphasize goals and process, this emphasis is played out in different ways. Yoga is non-competitive with an ultimate aim, the union of Atman (the individual soul) with Brahman (the collective soul). There are no sub-goals. All practice of whatever nature is a step along the way. In contrast, management is usually practiced within the context of internal and external competitiveness, has numerous sub-goals and although overriding goals such as mission statements are formulated by management, the goal posts shift frequently.

Both yoga and management use symbols and rituals. Yoga is experiential and exists only through practice. Management is also experiential but is often explained through idealized theoretical models. Both may be prescriptive, but the nature of the prescription may be radically altered in management. Yoga, even the physical practice, is contemplative, whereas management is usually not.

Yoga and management have very different underlying philosophies. The yogic philosophy is ultimately one of spiritual development and enlightenment. Many who begin yoga practice as a form of physical exercise develop unexpected spiritual awareness. On the other hand, the spirituality of organizations is seldom investigated.

The epistemology of yoga is essentialist but as new ideas have come along they are absorbed without displacing previous ideas, even when new and old conflict. Yogic teaching can thus appear contradictory and chaotic, yet all teachings are linked by a single simple purpose. Management often is described as rational and logical, also conveys chaos but without an underlying unifying purpose.

Models of management range from the essentialist to postindustrial notions of social constructivism. Yoga offers a balanced way of life. Whereas, theories of management offer ways of negotiating working life with balance supplied by non-working life.

THE APPROPRIATION OF YOGIC CONCEPTS

Of particular interest is the appropriation of terms and concepts that belong to the yogic tradition and are now applied more widely. Terms such as guru and mantra come readily to mind as ones used frequently within managerial literature.

Guru

'Management guru' is a term used almost unthinkingly by many contemporary writers to describe authoritative, usually popular, and often populist, management theorists and media experts. Jackson (1996) traces the genealogy of the term 'guru' from its Sanskrit origins to modern usage, noting that it has appeared in business journals from the 1980s onwards. Comparing Hinduism to management, he states that both have key seminal texts and sects with mantras. Both religious and management gurus recognize the importance and the esoteric nature of verbal transmission from teacher to student as well as the belief that the guru has access to absolute knowledge and truth that is otherwise unavailable.

Jackson argues that the guru's authority is derived from his charismatic qualities. Religious gurus focus on the longer term while management gurus provide instant solutions (Clark and Salaman, 1995; Jackson, 1995). Jackson discusses the authoritative and potentially authoritarian nature of the relationship, pointing out that while the original 'guru-manager' relationship is voluntary, subordinates on whom the guru's theories are subsequently imposed may experience them as authoritarian. Interestingly, there is an unrecognized but important spiritual element in the management guru's discourse. Iyengar (1966) defines a guru as a "spiritual preceptor, one who illumines the darkness of spiritual doubt."

I believe that it is important to note that the yoga guru's authority also derives from respect for knowledge acquired through study and instruction via a lineage of gurus. This lineage does not seem to form a part of the management guru experience. A further element that Jackson overlooks is the role of ego. A true follower of yoga attempts to abase the ego and does not indulge in the kind of self-publicity commonly seen in management gurus. In Yoga the aim is to abase the ego, while management gurus seek quite the opposite—self aggrandizement.

A guru in the yogic tradition is a teacher, one who waits for the student to appear with the question rather than actively proselytizing. Yoga gurus do not need to indulge in propaganda. There is a saying: when the student is ready the teacher appears. On the other hand, management gurus both proselytize and evangelize (Chapman, 1973). Jackson does not distinguish between religion and spirituality. As stated earlier, spiritual enlightenment and development can take place without specific religious beliefs and many followers of yoga are sincere adherents of faiths other than Hinduism.

For the yoga student, the guru represents a personal, long-term relationship.

Within the realm of management the guru relationship appears to be relatively transitory and one-way, although heavily invested with emotion (Clark and Salaman, 1995). Huczynski (1993) sees management "gurudom" as the identification of particular ideas with a particular individual, whereas the yoga guru engages in the transfer of esoteric knowledge that is not exclusive.

In both relationships, embodiment, or being in the presence of a guru, has special significance. The yogic or religious guru offers Darshan, an audience, although he or she may also have many followers who are unable to come into the presence (Chapman, 1973). For the manager, there is a similar benefit from attending a live seminar, rather than just learning from the guru's books or videos, though many have to content themselves with the latter.

Management gurus are dogmatic and advocate the one true way, whereas yoga gurus may be authoritative but rely on a willing surrender by the follower (Jackson, 1996). Yoga emphasizes students finding their own paths, although guidance on method is provided. Many yogis and gurus acknowledge that there are multiple paths to the same end. Thus in the common usage of the phrase 'management guru' there is a perversion of meaning.

Mantra

The word 'Mantra' is derived from the Sanskrit roots 'man' meaning mind, and 'tra' meaning to free. It was described in the first written tantras in the 4th century AD, as 'sounds of power'. A mantra encompasses words, syllables and sounds, and may also be described as 'words of power', 'influencing chants or mutterings', 'sacred syllables, words or phrases', or a sacred thought (Iyengar, 1966). In the *Hatha Yoga Pradipika* mantra is described as expressing divinity (Swatmarama, 1992).

Mantra helps concentration through the repetition of sound, as does yantra through the observation of a picture or symbol. Both mantra and yantra can be practiced physically, or can be purely mental, an overlap between hatha yoga (physical practice) and raja yoga (control of mind). The use of a rosary (mala) with repetition of the mantra may also help. The repetition or chanting of mantra, called japa (Iyengar, 1966), can be performed aloud or silently.

Parenthetically, use of mantras together with malas are seen within organized religion as well as within the practice of yoga. One notable example is the 'Hail Mary' used commonly within the Roman Catholic church. Repetition of sounds are found to have beneficial physiological and psychological effects (Wood, 1962). As with all yoga practices, the mantra's purpose is to guide the student towards the infinite and, thus, it is an aid to spiritual enlightenment.

Until the 1990s the word mantra was generally used in a traditional sense. In ABI/Inform, a popular business-journal index, all listed articles between 1973 and 1980 used the term entirely in its original meaning, usually referring to programs of yoga or meditation for the alleviation of stress (e.g. Clutterbuck, 1973). As late as 1988 the Chambers dictionary defined mantra entirely in religious and yogic terms, omitting any modern usage. Looking at recent writing, however, Wilson (1996) found that mantra was widely employed in metaphoric usage both in general discourse and more specifically in management discourse.

First, mantra is sometimes used as a synonym for belief, or theme; or philosophy, mission, and vision. In a more pejorative sense it is used in place of 'slogan,' perhaps even implying cliché (Wilson, 1996). As Jackson (1996) notes in relation to the word 'guru', the word mantra sometimes appears to be selected by the writer to imply, if not something pejorative, then at least something about which the writer is suspending judgment (Wilson, 1996).

Second, mantra is also used to mean guidance or advice. A third use relates directly to action; as committed cause, avowed intention, objective or standard, formula or blueprint for action, or program or initiative (Wilson, 1996). Mantra is used as simile as well as metaphor and sometimes combined with other ideas in extended imagery. Many passages have overlays of magic, mysticism and religion, a comparison Wilson (forthcoming) discusses and which is explored in Clark and Salaman (1995) who write about management gurus as witch doctors.

In common parlance some mantras are said aloud whereas some are for mental absorption alone. In most modern usage the mantra is conveyed in normal speech and although there are some references to chanting (e.g. Furnham and Pendleton, 1993), there is no literature indicating that this is a melodic pursuit. The word 'mantra' is sometimes used because of the concept of repetition. In the yoga tradition internal direction is the aim, although singing mantras with others as an activity may aid the process. Modern use of the word mantra indicates both internal and external direction, particularly when mantras are used in the sense of advice or mission. This would never occur within yogic practice, as a mantra is used for the edification of the person saying it rather than to benefit others. Although all mantras have meanings, the words as sounds alone produce effects. Every mantric word has four levels: the sound, the meaning that is the ground for concentration, the idea that is the ground for meditation and the spirit which is its root (Wood, 1962).

In analyzing the role of sound, there are two dimensions: whether the mantra is said or sung out loud; and whether the actual sound is part of its effectiveness. The first element, sound, is an optional extra in modern usage. As previously stated, the modern 'mantra' may be repeated silently or spoken aloud.

Meaning and idea, the second and third elements of mantra, are those most emphasized within current usage. The cognitive, intellectual, and, to a lesser extent, emotional meanings are often emphasized to the detriment of other aspects. As to the last dimension, spirit, this is perhaps something the modern mantra is trying to capture, but with varying degrees of success. In the final analysis it appears that there are significant differences in resonance between classical and modern uses of the word.

THE APPROPRIATION OF YOGIC PRACTICES

The realm of technique is another area in which appropriation has taken place. Breathing, relaxation, pre-meditative and meditative practices are all being used as methods for counteracting the stress of modern working life.

There are two stages of breathing that can be undertaken. Before specific techniques can be taught, students must become aware of habitual breathing patterns and focus on the breath so that they can breath more deeply and slowly. Pranayama (control of breath or the life force) is a series of practices that can be used for different purposes. Ujjayi (fire breath), for instance, can be used to heat up the body and give energy, whereas kapal abhati (shining skull) helps cleanse the upper respiratory tract, and nadi sodona (alternate nostril breathing) calms the nervous system. There are many types of relaxation techniques, yogic and non-yogic. The former include yoga nidra, a supine practice that encourages deep but fully conscious relaxation. Of all yoga practices, pre-meditative and meditative practices are followed most closely when transferred into the working or business environment.

Although techniques such as these have become popular to alleviate the stress of working life, it is important to recognize that a stressful environment is a holistic problem that should be tackled holistically. Relaxation exercises cannot wholly alleviate problems caused by downsizing or unsympathetic management styles. And, although in many ways the extension of any aspect of yoga into the workplace should be welcomed, it may be merely the instrumental abstraction of technique, cut off from its roots.

DISCUSSION

At this juncture a number of questions come to mind. What is happening at the level of language? Is this is just another example of one language borrowing, appropriating and amending words from another language? We tend to assume that words are borrowed to be helpful in expressing concepts not available in the borrower's language. It could be, however, that this usage does not elucidate, but rather conceals or misleads, or as discussed above, indicates uncertainty by the writer, or is even disparaging.

A related issue is the question of whether something is happening on a deeper level. Management may be seeking some apparently timeless certainties offered by older more manifestly spiritual belief systems, but dressing them up in new clothes. Yoga is essentialist and therefore offers a certainty lacking in many other fields of human endeavor. In borrowing yogic words and practices, managers and management writers may be looking for deeper authority than the transitory practice of management, a process oriented activity recreated on a daily basis. Perhaps this represents a search for missing balance and holism.

How can yoga illuminate the spirituality of organizations? I reiterate that there is a distinction between religion and spirituality, a difference I have only understood experientially (Shivapremananda, 1996). Hawkins (1991) writes about thinking and understanding with the heart in order to understand the spiritual dimension. My experience of yoga is that it has an inner aspect that sooner or later manifests itself. This inner aspect is sustaining, challenging and inspires commitment. It is above all this inner aspect which is integrative, regardless of the path by which yoga is practiced.

Is it possible to build a management system upon the specific ethical principles, acknowledgment of embodiment, self-aware control of emotion, concentration and meditation as routes to decision-making, and the embrace of spirituality that characterize yogic practice? Beyond the scope of this chapter is a question about what yoga can tell us about ethics in organizations. However, the guiding principle would be one of karma yoga (selfless or non-attached action), and for reasons discussed above, I think current organizational aims and cultures are antipathetic to this. Management in the private sector is about the free market, acquisition, and growth at the expense of other companies. This is certainly distant from a view of karma yoga with its emphasis on non-attachment. The philosophy of the not-for-profit and mutual sectors is one of service and mutual aid, and at first sight this appears to be more compatible with karma yoga. However, even if they were not being advised to adopt the practices of the private sector, the not-for-profit and mutual sectors are still attached to tasks. In whatever sector, management is about the accomplishment of tasks, predominantly in a competitive environment. Everything else ultimately is regarded as subsumed to this purpose, including the furtherance of relationships. Paramount attachment is placed on doing, and the fruits of doing.

This leads to the question of whether management can be holistic and balanced. I return to the use of yogic techniques for relaxation as an example. A yogic approach to stress would be holistic, encompassing aspects of personal life such as diet, and elements of organizational life conducive to stress. The use of relaxation and meditation techniques alone is a denial of a holistic approach, and the instrumental abstraction of technique.

On a personal level I find that I have two contradictory belief systems. Intellectually I act on the hypothesis that much of what passes for normality in organizations is socially constructed but on an experiential level I believe that there is an inner essence that may be revealed to me.

One shortcoming of a presentation such as this is that it is a purely intellectual exercise. I am writing, in part, about something experiential. But readers engage only the cognitive aspects of their brains. People engaged in the practice of management often seek to impose order through intellectual solutions. This works for critiques of management and business, but is too limited for an understanding of yoga.

Chapman (1973) writes that in the West we assume that knowledge and understanding are equivalent, and therefore that if there is a problem we have to acquire more information. To seek to understand yoga intellectually will not work. This is an intuitive and spiritual journey compared with an intellectual journey.

Since the meaning of a word or an activity is slowly unveiled by use and experience and the selection of words used are not 'accidental' but 'fit' at a deeper level perhaps we can see from this analysis an underside to management that wishes for a deeper meaning to its activities.

BIBLIOGRAPHY

Clark, T.A.R. and G. Salaman (1995) "The Management Guru As Organizational Witch-doctor" *The Open University Business School, Working Paper Series,* Milton Keynes, UK.

Clutterbuck, D. (1973) "How I Stopped Worrying" *International Management* 28, 8, August, 27–29.

Furnham, A. and D. Pendleton (1993) "Management: Seduced By The Customer Cult" *Financial Times,* June, 7, 9.

Hawkins, P. (1991) "The Spiritual Dimension Of The Learning Organisation" in R. Snell, J. Davies, T, Boydell, and M. Leary, eds. *Joining Forces: Working with Spirituality in Organisations, Management Education and Development Special Edition,* Autumn, 172–187.

Iyengar, B.K.S. (1966) *Light on Yoga,* London: George Allen and Unwin.

Jackson, B. (1995) "Re-Engineering The Sense Of Self: The Manager And The Management Guru" paper given at the Standing Conference on Organizational Symbolism 13th International conference, Turku, Finland, 29 June–1 July.

Jackson, B. (1996) "Guru's Line Is It Anyway?: An Exploratory Genealogy" *Notework,* 14, 1.

Mascaro, J. (1962) *The Bhagavad Gita,* Harmondsworth: Penguin.

Mascaro, J. (1965) *The Upanishads,* Harmondsworth: Penguin.

Snell, R., et. al., eds.,(1991) *Joining Forces: Working with Spirituality in Organisations, Management Education and Development Special Edition,* Autumn.

Prabhavananda, S. and C. Isherwood, (1953) *The Yoga Aphorisms of Patanjali,* Mentor Books: New American Library.

Shivapremananda, S. (1996) "Ruminations: Sivananda's Definition of Yoga" *Yoga and Health* July, 21, 7, 6–9.

Swatmarama, Y. S. (1992) *Hatha Yoga Pradipika,* London: George Allen and Unwin.

Wilson, E. (1996): "The Yoga of Management" paper presented at the 14th International Conference of the Standing Conference on Organizational Symbolism, University of California at Los Angeles, 3–6 July.

Wilson, E. (forthcoming) "Mantra and Meanings" *Journal of Managerial Psychology.*

Wood, E. (1962) *Yoga,* Harmondsworth: Pelican.

32

THE RETURN OF "THE INVISIBLE HAND"

Omid Nodoushani

Despite its tremendous potential, Georges Bataille's contributions to political economy and business ethics remain unknown to many advocates of postmodern business throughout the US, Canada and Europe. This essay reflects on the implications of postmodernism for business ethics by examining his contributions.[1]

INTRODUCTION

Over the past two decades, postmodern discourse in social theory and art has been a highly contested terrain in the intellectual life of Western societies. An emerging body of literature on postmodern business management extends the discourse into the business disciplines (Nodoushani, 1996). And, since this postmodern discourse calls the traditional philosophical enterprise into question, some business ethicists feel obliged to expand on "the leading edge of contemporary intellectual thinking."

This challenge to ethical theory can be translated into a challenge to all branches of applied ethics, and has potential for radically redefining the mission of business ethics. Moreover, if business ethics are to develop and have meaning for the twenty-first century, it must respond to challenges posed by the postmodern discourse or embed postmodern themes into its enterprise.

Lyotard, the pioneer of postmodernism, categorically rejects capitalism and the world of business. Thus, the notion of a postmodern business ethics discourse is

---

[1]The author would like to thank Patricia Nodoushani for her comments and help on an earlier draft of this paper.

alien. In *Postmodernism Explained to Children,* Lyotard (1986) views capitalism as a system that stimulates inordinate desires for commodities, therefore perverting human nature and reducing interpersonal relationships to a vast void exploited by mass advertising in mass markets (Walton, 1993).

Despite such opposition, some business ethicists push strongly for a merger between business ethics and postmodern discourse. Postmodern thought, we are told, yields ideas that foster a better understanding of the dynamics of markets by emphasizing the interplay between firms and the environment on which this dynamic is based (Nooteboom, 1992).

This essay reflects on the question of postmodernism and business ethics by examining the work of Georges Bataille (1879–1962). Bataille's "Copernican transformation" of capitalism redefines the postmodern business ethics discourse. Surprisingly, his contributions to political economy and business ethics still remain unknown to many of the advocates of postmodern business ethics in the US, Canada and Europe (Bataille, 1985, 1989, 1991a; 1991b). However, a reexamination of his effort to overturn the moral foundations of business disciplines as formulated by the *laissez-faire* world view should be a high priority for the postmodern business ethics discourse.

THE POSTMODERN ECONOMY

Placing Bataille's contributions in perspective requires our understanding of the structure of the postmodern economy and changes that the postmodern condition has imposed on business. Moreover, comprehending what kind of social systems have emerged in the most highly developed societies necessitates understanding of the economic implications of postmodernism. According to Lyotard (1984), "the most highly developed societies" are those for which the use of the word postmodern is the most proper. Within these highly developed societies the postmodern condition occurs concurrently with the postindustrial age.

There is general consensus that postmodernism is the cultural logic of late capitalism. It not only obeys the laws of classical capitalism—the primacy of industrial production and the omnipresence of class struggle—but also manifests another stage in the evolution of capital, highlighting the transition from market to monopoly capitalism and then to consumer capitalism (Jameson, 1984). Since the 1973–75 recession, the capital accumulation process has undergone a sea change. After a period of difficult readjustment sparked by low growth rates, high unemployment, inflation, and the demise of US hegemony, capitalist restructuring resulted in technological change, reorganization of production techniques, financial shake-ups, product innovation, and massive expansion into cultural and image production (Harvey, 1991).

Contemporary social systems have been transformed into "disorganized capitalism" through three simultaneous processes: globalization, decentralization, and disintegration of the corporation. Together they have created broad sets of changes within Western Europe and North America (Urry, 1988). The high-tech revolution, time-space compression, and the effects of globalization have not only caused great instability, but have also created a social condition in which the ability and means for people to define themselves (differently from one another) have dramatically increased (Brown, 1992). In this respect, postmodern capitalism has created both the fears of greater divisiveness, fragmentation, insecurity, and turmoil, and, paradoxically, the opportunity for mobilizing greater democratic decision-making. This marks significant change within the parameters of consumerism, profit-oriented growth, and wage-labor tension (Brown, 1991).

The notion that business activities can be unified around a single logic of organizational rationality devoted to industrial progress through the medium of 'big business' (Daly, 1991) has declined. Postmodern capitalism is transitioning from 'fordism' to 'postfordism.' That is, culminating in a shift from mass production to flexible specialization. Fordism, the prevailing model of industrial efficiency for most of the 20th century, is characterized by mass production of homogeneous products, using the rigid technology of the assembly line with dedicated machines and standardized work routines. In a period of fragmenting and differentiated markets where firms must respond to rapidly changing global demands and competitor's product innovations, mass production is usually a liability (Hirst and Zeitlin, 1989).

In contrast, under flexible specialization or 'postfordism', a combination of universal equipment and versatile workers can produce a wide and changing range of semi-customized goods, using economies of scope to reduce the cost of differentiated products. Reiterating the call for the model of a flexible firm, 'postfordism' is linked to a new form of artisan production easily adapted to the changing needs of the market (Hirst and Zeitlin, 1991).

Big corporations constitute the central institution of modern economy. Thus, the disintegration of big corporations brings fundamental societal changes. Prior to the development of big business in the late 19th century, the economy was primarily dependent upon a price system that coordinated the market and maintained macroeconomic balance. With the rise of big business, the market has been controlled increasingly by the direct efforts of large enterprises as the central institution of modern capitalism (Piore, 1987). Embracing changes in the areas of consumption, work, and technology, the postmodern drift in capitalism reverses the role of big business by invigorating the market. Thus, the worldwide move toward privatization within the era of disorganized capitalism reaffirms the premise that postmodern methods of allocating scarce resources are based on the 'laws' of laissez-faire rather than the organizational rationality of big business (Ogilvy, 1989).

In an era of disorganized capitalism, the visible hand of managerial capitalism is replaced by the invisible hand of the market. Disorganized capitalism also points primarily to an easily visible crisis marked by the realization that giant corporations can no longer secure a workable match between the production and the consumption of goods. This turbulence is neither a temporary situation nor an aberration. The big corporation, as a solution to the organizational problems created by mass production, is being dismantled in favor of the strategy of craft production (Piore and Sable, 1984).

Most notably, the strategy of craft production opens great opportunities for small and 'dynamic' firms. The role of small firms is changing drastically as they are no longer typically subordinated to big companies and/or operated primarily at the direction of the large firms (Piore and Sable, 1985). This leads to a reversal of the logic of economic modernity. The price for industrial progress is reliance upon the economies of size and scale. Instead, the strategy of craft production depends on an intimacy between the small firm and the market forces (Sable and Zeitlin, 1985). The postmodern condition, however, is still loyal to the marketplace as it is the most efficient means yet devised for real-time optimizing of an incredibly complex array of different preferences and diverse interests (Oglivy, 1989).

POSTMODERNISM AND BUSINESS ETHICS

Traditionally, an inquiry into business methods and the structure of the economy goes hand in hand with Adam Smith's theory of moral sentiment. Smith, the greatest spokesman for *laissez-faire* economics, believed that economic rationalism rests on an ethical point of view that identifies the market with society as a whole. He recognized clearly the moral character of the marketplace. According to Smith, the marketplace provides one of the few arenas in modern society in which people have an opportunity to participate directly in public life (Wuthnow, 1982).

This view of the institution of the market as an engine for shaping moral character has motivated "the business ethics revolution" since it began in the early 1980s. In the United States, for example, over 500 business ethics courses are taught on university campuses and fully 90 percent of the nation's business schools provide some kind of training in the area. There are more than 25 textbooks and three widely read academic journals dedicated to the field. At least 16 business ethics research centers are now in operation alone and a number of endowed chairs exist as well (Stark, 1993).

The business ethics revolution has surprised many practitioners in the field. The sudden growth of business ethics concerns is profoundly a postmodern phenomenon (Green, 1993). Can the enterprise of business ethics participate in 'the postmodern spirit'? Since all efforts to construct morality on the foundation of a rational justification are out of fashion, postmodern business ethics could pave the way for a multiplicity of ethical viewpoints, creating a kind of ethical pluralism based on a commitment to diversity (Green, 1993).

ETHICAL RELATIVISM

Cast under the banner of postmodernism, the rising tide of ethical relativism is becoming a major concern to a number of business ethicists. Since the traditional theories of ethics have always pledged allegiance to universal values, the celebration of diversity in moral judgment raises a question of whether or not postmodernism can be construed as an ethic after all (Rasmussen, 1993). Moreover, when moral judgments become necessary, a mode of analysis that simply juxtaposes different values can easily be intimidated by the currently fashionable political pedagogy in academe (Trundle, 1991).

In the early 1980s, business ethics was defined as a disciplined and normative reflection on the nature, meaning and context of business activity (Hoffman and Mills Moore, 1982). The business ethics revolution expanded with the question of whether people in business ought to recognize moral obligations beyond the requirements of law (Goldman, 1980). Today, among many business ethicists there is growing sentiment toward the importance of contractual relationships in organizations, thereby confirming that moral behavior is a behavior consistent with legitimate contracts (Hartman, 1994).

It is against such a background that some business ethicists should be looking into postmodernism. Yet the few attempts to merge the field of business ethics with postmodernism (Green 1993; Duska 1993; Schmidt 1993) have fallen victim to ideological manifestations of the politics of postmodernity. These scholars completely ignore the fact that a truly postmodern approach requires an overturning of utilitarianism as the moral foundation of capitalism by acting as if postmodern business ethics is merely an extension of the diversity debate.

THE OVERTURNING OF *LAISSEZ-FAIRE* ETHICS

Guidance from Georges Bataille, however, provides another vehicle for facing the challenges of the business ethics revolution. According to Bataille, a postmodern understanding of business ethics requires a transition from the utilitarian principles of modern business disciplines. Throughout the nineteenth century all industrialized societies' business values have been based upon the fallacies of a utilitarian or *laissez-faire* mind-set that raises the following principles. First, as individuals, we are made to accept the view that our motives can be described as either 'material' or 'ideal.' The incentives of everyday life are necessarily derived from 'material' incentives. Utilitarian doctrine also propounds that social institutions are determined by the economic system (Polanyi, 1947).

Utilitarianism reinforces its own rationality with two concepts regarding 'ends' and 'means.' A utilitarian value scale is postulated as the rational way of determining 'ends.' Then science is employed to determine the rational 'means' to the ends. This approach to the selection of an 'ends' scale implies that rationality is based on esthetics, and that ethics, or philosophy, is not correct. Similarly this approach to 'means' implies that rationality based on magic, myth, or metaphysics is incorrect (Polanyi, 1977).

The antecedent of such a utilitarian value-system is Smith's *The Theory of Moral*

Sentiment. His primary concern is with the interrelationships of individuals living in society. The moral sentiments (i.e., the passions, affections, and feelings) act as guides to these interrelationships and serve as intermediaries between the 'basic instincts' shared with animals and the 'calculation' of rigorous and rational people.

For Smith, the external world operated within natural laws that were discoverable by accurately observing systemic regularities in nature through "the camera theory of knowledge" or "spectatorship" (Purser, Park, and Montuori, 1995). Like his intellectual mentors, the physiocrats in France, he believed in the doctrine of natural rights and felt that the interplay between the natural efforts of all individuals for making their own condition better provided a perpetual stimulus to the economic progress of society. The constancy of human nature was testimony to the impact of moral sentiments. No wonder that the whole complex mechanism of behavior was dependent upon the wisdom of God or of nature—"the final cause" or "the invisible hand" (Smith, 1969).

Bataille argued that, despite its rational facade, such a morality system merely generalized about *homo economicus* in isolation while not taking into consideration *homo ecologicus*—that is, man/woman as a living organism (Habermas, 1984). Bataille called for a reversal of thinking in economics—a Copernican transformation—and the overturn of the grounded ethics of business disciplines (Bataille, 1991a). Bataille began by postulating three principles: the notion of expenditure; the concept of 'the gift' or as he put it 'the accursed share'; and a theory of religion culminating in an ecological value-system that fosters truly postmodern business ethics.

BATAILLE'S EXPENDITURE-BASED POSTMODERN ETHICAL THESIS

According to Bataille, the center piece of business motive is not 'utility' but rather 'loss.' Human activity consists of two distinct parts, the 'minimum necessary' for the conservation of life and 'unproductive expenditures' such as luxury, mourning, war, cults, spectacles, arts, and perverse sexual activity. Both serve as a means to the end of economic production (Bataille, 1985a).

Starting with the biological assumption that all living organisms collect more energy than they use to reproduce life, Bataille argued that surplus energy could be consumed in many different ways (e.g., through religious rituals, wars, or 'the gift'). Similarly, since society produces more than is necessary for its subsistence, the 'mode of expenditure of surplus' is the key to the further development of general economics.

Bataille then considered the relationship between the role of expenditure and the utility-based role of production and acquisition. He concluded that no matter how important production and acquisition based on utility may be within historical processes, they still remain secondary in relation to the role of 'expenditure' (Bataille, 1985a). Relying upon Marcel Mauss' thesis about the origin of capitalism as a more elaborate form of *potlatch*—a feast where the 'obligation to give' is the essence of social behavior (Mauss, 1990), Bataille argued that the 'hatred of expenditure' was the raison d'être and the justification for the utilitarian ethics (Bataille, 1985a). Potlatch as a form of agnostic expenditure determines a collective experience antithetical to the goals of utilitarian ethics because it provides a return to old and elemental business motives (Richman, 1982).

Conducting a comparative historical analysis of different forms of consumption, he found the role of expenditure as "the dialectic of economy or the accursed share" existed within various types of social systems even before the birth of modern bourgeois society in the 18th century. Bataille insisted that expenditure or consumption of wealth, rather than production, was clearly both the goal and the primary rationale for economic behavior (Bataille, 1991a).

FROM EXPENDITURE TO AN ECOLOGY-CENTERED THESIS

Bataille approached an ecologically oriented ethical theory, placing his claim on an organic style of thought, similar to the general systems approach in which the central principle lies in an emphasis upon the whole rather than the sum of its elements. If one considers the earth as an organic system, business and economic efforts are only 'aspects' of terrestrial activity. As living organisms, human beings receive more energy than is necessary for maintaining life. The excess energy often cannot be completely absorbed. Thus it must either be lost without profit or spent (Bataille, 1991a).

Human beings are the accursed ones. The introduction of labor into the world replaced an original intimacy between human beings and nature and as a result humanity is cursed by the gradual separation from the 'order of things in nature' through the fruits of human labor. Since human activity is basically conditioned by this general movement in life, labor opens up new possibilities in which the increased reproduction of human beings leads to the creation of an immense quantity of energy.

Human beings use only a part of an immense quantity of energy in achieving the necessities of life. The rest is excess. In humankind's strange myths and cruel rites, they are in search of a lost intimacy linked to the alienation caused by the growth of labor and human know-how. Contrary to labor, which limits intimacy between individuals and the ecology of nature, consumption or expenditure facilitate communication with nature and one another through consumption of the excess energy (Bataille, 1991a).

Because we assume that people consume goods for restricted purposes (e.g., material welfare, psychic welfare, and display) consumerism is sometimes castigated as greed. Bataille's theory advocates that the very idea of consumption has to be recognized as an integral part of the same social system that accounts for the drive to work, the need for relating to other people, and to establishment of mediating materials for relating people to nature (Douglas, 1979).

The Marcel Mauss theory of the gift posits a connection between religious and economic behavior (Bataille, 1991). Only in religion can humanity find their lost intimacy with nature. To restore the divine order, humanity uses animals and plants through sacred communications whose essence is consumption without profit of whatever remains in the progression of useful works (Bataille, 1989).

Within our civilization, this generous and exuberant loss of energy opens the realm of the sacred to the role of festival. The initial movement of festival is an attempt to reverse the necessities of the profane world since festival brings possibilities of consumption together. Mauss argued that the prevailing rationalism of Western societies that has turned mankind into an economic animal is a recent phenomenon. Before the rise of *homo economicus,* there was another and quite different type of human being whose ethos did not adhere to the calculating reason of Adam Smith. Mauss claimed that the desultory conditions of the present-day social life and its value system constitutes only a historic aberration, reflected throughout the current economic and juridical history (Mauss, 1990).

In searching for a collective experience that is antithetical to the ideals of utilitarian ethics, Mauss' 'theory of gift' represents an archaic form of contract, truthful to the idea of total service in which the obligation to give, to receive, and to reciprocate constitute the foundations upon which our own systems of law and economics once rested.

As romantic as Mauss's ideas may sound, it is important to remember that there are some truths in his theory. Indeed, George Gilder's theory of metaphysical forces operating within the institution of the marketplace also asserts that throughout its entire history, capitalism begins with giving. Feasting and potlatching illustrate a capitalist tendency to assemble and distribute wealth since the essence of a free-enterprise system is in supplying first, and acquiring later. Like gifts, capitalist investments are made without prior expectations of return, while the source of the gifts of capitalism is in the supply side of the economy. The unending offerings of entrepreneurs, investing in jobs and accumulating inventories, all occur long before any return is received. They constitute the fabric of capitalist economy based on a foundation of metaphysical uncertainty about the object of human desire (Gilder, 1981).

Bataille did not wish to reverse the forces of historical progress to overturn the utilitarian ethics inherited by modern capitalism. The revolutionary force which can emancipate humanity from the humiliating results of the utilitarian ethics passes through the secrets of eroticism. Yet this issue also leads to the crux of controversy that has surrounded Bataille's work. As if extending the message of the 1960s sexual revolution, Bataille argued that humanity could only approximate sovereignty by removing religious and moral taboos concerning eroticism. In this respect, eroticism is the sexual activity of humans as opposed to that of animals. Little wonder that within the coherent system of human expenditure of energy, eroticism occupies a substantial place (Bataille, 1991b).

Most importantly, however, the secrets of eroticism embrace the category of sovereignty within contemporary social consciousness and ethics. The sovereignty of which Bataille spoke has little to do with the sovereignty of states. Rather he understood an aspect in human existence that is opposed to the servile and the subordinate. Historically, sovereignty is associated with a hierarchical order that imposes freedom and slavery as well as dominance and subordination. While in modernity mankind has failed to accomplish political and economic sovereignty, it is only in eroticism that human beings can come close to being sovereign (Bataille, 1991b).

Moreover, because of a belief in the spiritual transcendence, the secrets of eroticism reveal the absence of a final cause or invisible hand through which the transgressing impacts of the dominant value-system of human sovereignty can be rendered. Instead, Bataille proposed that a critique of "dogmatic servitude" as formulated by the utilitarian ethics requires an inner experience through which we sidestep the dictum of utility in life (Bataille, 1988).

CONCLUSION

In this essay I place the merger between postmodernism and the business ethics revolution within the larger context of an emergent economy. In so doing, an overview of the conventional approach for blending postmodernism with business ethics resulted in a claim that most efforts toward such a merger confuse postmodern business ethics with the politics of postmodernity.

Instead, this paper offered the contributions of Georges Bataille. A pioneer in postmodernism, Bataille's controversial views concerning the theory of general economy represents an alternative view toward the utilitarian value-system in economic and business thoughts. Exploring various aspects of Bataille's thoughts, I conclude that in his works we are faced with an intriguing ecologically centered business ethics which begs for further examination.

BIBLIOGRAPHY

Bataille, G. (1985a) "The Notion Of Expenditure" in *Visions of Excess: Selected Writings, 1927–1939*, Minneapolis: University of Minnesota Press.
Bataille, G. (1985b) "The Critique Of The Foundations Of The Hegelian Dialectic" in *Visions of Excess: Selected Writings, 1927–1939*, Minneapolis: University of Minnesota Press.
Bataille, G. (1988) *Inner Experience*, Albany: State University of New York Press.
Bataille, G. (1989) *Theory of Religion*, New York: Zone Books.
Bataille, G. (1991a) *The Accursed Share: An Essay on General Economy, Vol. I*, New York: Zone Books.
Bataille, G. (1991b). *The Accursed Share: An Essay on General Economy, Vols. II and III*, New York: Zone Books.

Douglas, M. (1979) *The World of Goods,* New York: Basic Books.

Duska, R.F. (1993) "Aristotle: A Pre-Modern Post-Modern?: Implications for Business Ethics" *Business Ethics Quarterly,* 3, 3, 227–249.

Gilder, G. (1981) *Wealth and Poverty,* New York: Basic Books.

Goldman, A.H. (1980) "Business Ethics: Profits, Utilities, And Moral Rights" *Philosophy and Public Affairs,* 9, 3, 260–286.

Green, R.M. (1993) "Business Ethics As A Postmodern Phenomenon" *Business Ethics Quarterly,* 3, 3, 219–225.

Habermas, J. (1984) "The French Path To Postmodernity: Bataille Between Eroticism And General Economics" *New German Critique,* 33, 79–102.

Hartman, E.M. (1994) "The Status Of Business Ethics" *Business and Professional Ethics Journal,* 13, 4, 3–30.

Harvey, D. (1991) "Flexibility: Threat Or Opportunity?" *Socialist Review,* 21, 1, 65–77.

Hirst, P. and J. Zeitlin, (1989) "Flexible Specialisation And The Competitive Failure Of UK Manufacturing" *The Political Quarterly,* 60, 2, 164–178.

Hirst, P. and J. Zeitlin (1991) "Flexible Specialisation Versus Postfordism" *Economy and Society,* 20, 1, 1–56.

Hoffman, W. M., and J. Mills Moore (1982) "What Is Business Ethics?: A Reply To Peter Drucker" *Journal of Business Ethics,* 4, 1, 293–300.

Jameson, F. (1984) "Postmodernism, Or The Cultural Logic Of Late Capitalism" *New Left Review,* 146, 53–92.

Lyotard, J.-F. (1984) *The Postmodern Condition: A Report on Knowledge,* Minneapolis: University of Minnesota Press.

Mauss, M. (1990) *The Gift,* New York: W. W. Norton.

Nodoushani, O. (1996) "The Problems And Prospects Of The Postmodern Management Discourse" *Management Learning,* 27, 3, 359–381.

Nooteboom, B. (1992) "A Postmodern Philosophy Of Markets" *International Studies of Management and Organization,* 22, 2, 53–76.

Oglivy, J. (1989) "The Postmodern Business" *The Deeper News: Exploring Future Business Environment,* 1, 5, 3–23.

Piore, M.J., and C.F. Sable (1984) *The Second Industrial Divide: Possibilities for Prosperity,* New York: Basic Books.

Piore, M.J., and C.F Sable (1985) "The Second Industrial Revolution" *INC.,* 7, 9, 25–48.

Piore, M.J. (1987) "American Labor And The Industrial Crisis" *Challenge,* 30, 6, 24–30.

Polanyi, K. (1947) "Our Obsolete Market Mentality" *Commentary,* 3, 2, 109–117.

Polanyi, K. (1977) "The Economistic Fallacy" *Review,* 1, 1, 9–18.

Purser R.E., C. Park, and A. Montuori (1995) "Limits To Anthropocentrism: Toward An Ecocentric Organization Paradigm" *Academy of Management Review,* 20, 4, 1053–1089.

Rasmussen, D.M. (1993) "Business Ethics And Postmodernism: A Response" *Business Ethics Quarterly,* 3, 3, 271–277.

Richman, M.H. (1982) *Reading Georges Bataille: Beyond the Gift,* Baltimore: The Johns Hopkins Press.

Sable, C.F., and J. Zeitlin (1985) "Historical Alternatives To Mass Production: Politics, Markets and Technology in Nineteenth Century Industrialization" *Past and Present,* 108, 133–176.

Schmidt, D. P. (1993) "Postmodern Interviews In Business Ethics: A Reply To Ronald Green" *Business Ethics Quarterly,* 3, 3, 279–284.

Smith, A. (1969) *The Theory of Moral Sentiments,* New York: Arlington House.

Stark, A. (1993) "What's the Matter with Business Ethics?" *Harvard Business Review,* 71, 3, 38–48.

Trundle, R.C., Jr. (1991) "Business, Ethics, and Business Ethics: Second Thoughts On The Business-Ethics Revolution" *Thought,* 66, 298–309.

Urry, J. (1988) "Disorganized Capitalism" *Marxism Today,* 32, 10, 30–33.

Walton, C.C. (1993) "Business Ethics And Postmodernism: A Dangerous Alliance" *Business Ethics Quarterly,* 3, 3, 285–305.

Wuthnow, R. (1982) "The Moral Crisis In American Capitalism" *Harvard Business Review,* 60, 2, 76–84.

33

BATTLING WITH THE GODS: WORKERS, MANAGEMENT AND THE DEITIES OF POSTINDUSTRIAL MANAGEMENT CULTURE

Edward Wray-Bliss and Hugh Willmott

This chapter explores the influence and ethics of the twin deities of postindustrial management culture: the Customer and Information Technology. Drawing on du Gay and Salaman's (1992) exploration of the cult(ure) of the customer, we argue that postindustrial management culture is increasingly influenced by, and saturated with, the ideas and practices of 'enterprise.' Ethnographic material collected during nine months of participant observation of an 'enterprising' telephone banking department of a UK bank is used to examine bank workers' reproduction of, and resistance to, an emergent culture of enterprise. In particular, the authors show how the customer and the information technology system come to symbolize and embody quite different, and contradictory, meanings for the bank clerks. The clerks deploy (enterprising) arguments, centered around notions of 'customer needs,' to argue against the (enterprising) influence of management-controlled targets, monitored through the use of information technology. While stressing the pervasive influence of enterprise culture, and illustrating its detrimental effects on the clerks' employment conditions and quality of working life, we also focus upon the precarious and contradictory reproduction of this culture by the clerks. The chapter concludes by highlighting the possibilities for radical re-imagination/resistance by the clerks, which the culture of enterprise unwittingly promotes.

INTRODUCTION

DuGay and Salaman (1992) observe that the social and political rationality of 'enterprise' has, since the 1980s saturated postindustrial management culture. Recent restructuring of organizations and organizational life is based on management's acceptance of the normality and perceived good sense of this discourse. Political groups have long wanted to individualize our fates and free capital and individualizing social technologies have been well documented (e.g. Foucault's work on psychiatry, prisons, sexuality). In the late 1700s, the ethic of the free producer was identified as the backbone of capitalism. What is significant and unique about the discourse of enterprise in the 1980s is that it intensifies and *draws together* these ideas into a powerful and "seemingly coherent design for the radical transformation of social, cultural and economic arrangements, and a 'seductive' ethics of the self" (du Gay and Salaman 1992:630). Society, organization, and self are increasingly propelled toward the tenets of 'enterprise'—individualism, consumer sovereignty, and unrestricted capital. In this chapter, we will expose and explore some of the fractures, gaps, spaces, and contradictions in enterprise culture that open up possibilities for resistance and transformation.

The domination of enterprise is not a natural law or force of nature irresistibly imposed from above. Rather its power and truth-effects reside in the active (re)production of enterprise within practice and action. It is "always and only . . . a dimension of material practices, with material conditions of emergence and effectiveness" (du Gay and Salaman, 1992:630). By examining enterprise empirically, we attend to the *precarious and conditional (re)production of, and resistance to,* enterprise culture by workers whom otherwise may easily be regarded as passive victims.

THE POSTINDUSTRIAL MANAGEMENT CULTURE: THE DISCOURSE OF ENTERPRISE

Central to a notion of enterprise is a moral/ethical image of the sovereign, knowledgeable and empowered customer who maximizes personal freedom through the choice of goods and services. Instead of political citizens concerned with the well-being of our society, individuals are reconstituted as consumers of government services and preoccupied with the question of 'what do I get for my taxes?' People are increasingly identified as empowered individuals who have the opportunity to derive meaning as well as money from their work rather than merely being pressured and oppressed employees (Peters and Waterman, 1982). Rather than seeing such a re-imagination of citizenship and/or labor as a totalitarian attack or colonization of our identities (Willmott 1993), the discourse of enterprise presents the customer as an "empowered human being—the moral centre of the enterprising universe . . . (as) autonomous, self-regulating, and self-actualising actors, seeking to maximise the worth of their existence to themselves through personalized acts of choice in a world of goods and services" (du Gay and Salaman 1992:622).

To maximize this individualistic moral agenda our lives must be fully focused upon, and devoted to, securing self-identity as both the subject and object of market freedoms. Combined with this moral image of individualism is a political program for the progressive dismantling of institutions, agencies and ideologies that link our fates with others. The ethics of these relations are reconstituted in terms of the market provision of goods and services to customers. "(C)ommunity (and communal action in general) [is recast] from being the source of individual security into the individual's burden and bane, an extra load to carry, adding little to the individual's personal well-being" (Bauman, 1994:24).

Coupled with this image of politics as a purposeful dismantling of institutions that enshrines our commonality is the 'facilitating' role of social and information technology. Social technologies such as de-layering, quality initiatives and team work are valued because they bestow increased responsibility upon individual employees. Information and communication technologies (ICTs) are commended because they allow greater closeness to the external or internal 'customer' through instantaneous communication/monitoring, etc. Thus employees are empowered to actualize the ethical imperative of the enterprising self[1] by taking initiatives and exercising more autonomy.

In this chapter we build upon du Gay and Salaman's conceptual identification of enterprise through an ethnographic study of the telephone banking department at TeleBank (pseudonym). The combination of a major re-organization based on the constructed needs of the sovereign consumer, with sophisticated social, and especially information and communication, technologies of a telephone banking operation, made this department a particularly rich site for the study of enterprising culture in action.

This study concentrates upon the contradictions between the technological and ethical dimensions of enterprise. These contradictions are articulated *inter alia* as conflicts between the symbolic meanings ascribed to ICT and those ascribed to the customers by workers.

An analysis of the ethnographic materials suggests that the clerks' relationship with the culture of enterprise is far from simple or one-dimensional. Though enterprise dominates postindustrial culture, the culture is itself contradictory, and pregnant with possibility.

ETHNOGRAPHY: TELEBANK

This chapter is taken from data gathered during nine months of participant-observation ethnography of a medium size UK bank, which one of the authors conducted during 1995/1996. The bank has been given the pseudonym TeleBank, and the identity of all clerks similarly anonymized. It has a fairly stable foundation of

---

[1] du Gay and Salaman (1992) look exclusively at the role of social technologies in enterprise; for a discussion of the role of ICTs in enterprise, and in enterprise's latest prodigy, Business Process Reengineering, see Willmott and Wray-Bliss (1995).

traditional (especially corporate) customers, but is increasingly competing on the basis of innovative customer services, including, for instance, the telephone banking service studied in this ethnography.

Since the mid-1980s, when the UK banking industry deregulated, traditional bank-only service providers have begun experiencing competition from other financial institutions. This 'enterprising' deregulation helped TeleBank by providing a competitive stimulus for developing non-traditional innovative services targeted at affluent, discerning, 'sovereign consumers.' At the same time TeleBank began to face intensified competition from building societies that had lower costs.

The establishment of a centralized telephone banking service for both personal and corporate customers represents one crucial strategic response. The service enabled TeleBank customers to conduct most of their transactions from home or work and allowed the bank to reduce costs via large-scale ('voluntary') redundancies.

The Telephone Banking Department

The telephone banking department is now the primary contact for business customers as local branches have been phased out in favor of regional business centers who process specific authorizations (e.g. agreeing to overdrafts, loans, etc.) and non-standard arrangements (e.g. changing charging arrangements). The centralized telephone banking service handles all routine, normal banking issues such as opening accounts, administration, dealing with account problems, and closing accounts. Thus, the telephone banking department has become the customer's primary contact.

The department is open from eight to eight, Monday through Saturday and, depending on time of day and other workload factors, is staffed by as few as four and as many as fourteen people. The staff are split into two *teams* each with a '*senior team member*' who are equivalent to supervisors. They are overseen by a '*team leader*' (Garry) who is comparable to a departmental manager. The staff are positioned in front of computer screens and are connected to the telephone lines via headsets. Incoming customer telephone calls are automatically fed to the staff by a central computer that generates a beep approximately half a second before a customers voice is heard.

The department is laid out in an open plan with low partitions separating different sections. Everybody can see everyone else. There are two wall-mounted LCD displays showing the number of calls waiting and the length of time they have been waiting. The central computer also lists each clerk and their performance measures for Garry, the 'team leader.'

Customer response time is enhanced through social technologies, such as teams, and information and communication technologies which mediate customer-clerk interactions and permit supervisory and self-discipline. The technologies perversely facilitate intensification of enterprise as clerks exercise individual discretion and autonomy in their relations with the customers. Garry promotes this approach by suggesting that it is empowering for the staff and by encouraging them to "be the best they can."

Life in an Enterprising Workplace

Life in the department is frantic. Clerks answer a minimum of 95–115 calls a day. A range of 95 to 200+ calls a day is typical. To achieve this volume, clerks must be logged onto the central processing computer for the maximum amount of time possible each day.

Clerks manage their own work in a combination of ways. Calls taken must be finished quickly; customers must be 'controlled' by the clerks to assure that unproductive chat is minimized, and the essential information (*e.g.*, branch, account number, pass number, information wanted) is provided as speedily as possible.

There is a considerable amount of work to be done after each call—money has to be transferred between accounts, queries passed to other departments, notes made on the screen about customers' accounts, or letters dictated to send out forms and information. Some clerks save this work until quieter periods, when they can key in information without temporarily removing themselves from the phone queue. Others key it in hurriedly while racing to finish before the 'beep' signals that the next customer is on the phone. The result is fragmentation of work.

The pace of work, its highly fragmented nature, the concern with targets and with time are a constant source of pressure as notes taken after observing one of the clerks work shows:

> *The sheer pace of work was staggering, calls lasted 20 secs to 2 mins (average 1 min) with time in between keying in other work on screen. 'Wrap-up' button on phone not used (this appears on Garry's computer stats) between calls, as a rule. Instead Pam preferred to race to finish item before, or even during, taking next call . . . I had to stop recording times between jobs in minutes and move to seconds. Even then I often couldn't record very accurately because of the sheer speed and I am of course trying to learn the job as well! The shift between talking to me/working on another job and talking to a customer was instantaneous, giving the impression of split personality more than anything else. Professional Schizophrenia. Time takes on a completely different dimension. A 1 min 20 secs call seems like ages, a 30 secs period without a customer on the phone seems like an eternity—but not a rest. The possibility of that 'beep' and then customers voice is ever present—all work etc. is done speedily, one is always anticipating that voice/that beep . . . My recurring impression of this work is one continuous, fast paced, instantaneous, reactive NIGHTMARE!!!*

A sample of Pam's calls shows the pressures of this work:

> *12.12–30secs transfer*
> *12.13–25secs transfer (carried straight on with transfers from pile in between calls)*
> *12.15–35secs gave out business centre number (keying in other stuff while talking to customer)*

12.16–10secs transfer
12.17–65secs gave number of business centre (back to keying in)
12.19–60secs balance (keying in checks)
12.21–90secs transfer
12.24–30secs order check books
12.24–30secs transfer call
12.27–40secs transfer
12.28–60secs query, call transferred to a/c maintenance
12.32–2mins stop check (went on wrap-up)

Within 20 minutes Pam accomplished at least 13 separate processes for 12 different customers while keying in checks, other work, and talking to me in between calls. This is quite remarkable when the simplest and shortest calls require a greeting ('good afternoon/morning, TeleBank, how may I help you?'), elicitation of at least four pieces of information (branch, account number, password, customers requirements), movement through a minimum of four computer screens, reading account details, preemption of the obvious next question ('what has gone through my account today?'), by already entering another screen and being prepared to read this information out, and a polite and friendly goodbye. All of this in 30 and 60 seconds and often accomplished while finishing the details of the last customer's request. It is this type of activity, typical for normal busy periods on the department, that prompted comments: "it's like more or less working in a factory . . . and most people didn't come here to work in a factory. They could get paid more by going and working for Kellogs putting plastic toys in a box." Steve, one of the supervisors, said in interview, "How can you be into taking 100 balances a day? How can you enjoy that?"

SELF-DISCIPLINE, INFORMATION TECHNOLOGY AND THE ENTERPRISING EMPLOYEE

To produce and maintain the often frantic activity which constitutes the working day of a corporate line customer service clerk requires a large amount of self-management, and self-discipline. The pace of the work requires that clerks juggle many tasks and functions. To reach their targets consistently, clerks will often have to finish typing notes about a customer on the screen simultaneously while greeting another customer, asking for account number, branch, pass number, remembering these to input later, finish off the last task, input the new customer's details, and make all of this seem like a seamless whole for the new customer, and not like they have been delayed, or listened to with half concentration because the clerk is still working on another customer's account.

It is doubtful that the comparatively blunt tool of managerial surveillance and discipline actually can stimulate the crucial skills of shaving seconds from each of the multiple tasks. As du Gay and Salaman (1992:621) observe, *traditional methods of control (i.e. bureaucratic control) are too overtly oppressive, too alienating and too inflexible to encourage employees to behave in the subtle ways which customers define as indicating quality of service, many of which—subtleties of facial expression, nuances of verbal tone, or type of eye contact—are difficult to enforce through rules, particularly when the employee is out of sight of any supervisor.*

Faced with this challenge of providing an *embodied* service, managers sought, using the team leader's words, to 'ingrain' an identity based on successfully meeting quantified and monitored 'customer service' targets. Technologies of self surveillance allowed clerks to receive continuous feedback about their performance. This, in turn, '*facilitated*' clerks' preoccupation with performance as defined by the numbers of calls. It also '*enabled*' clerks to scrutinize and evaluate their own performance and that of others.

Information and communication technologies generated the *potential* for continuous self-surveillance, but it would be wrong to think that the ICT hardware *determined* such behavior. As Pam recalled

when the figures (performance targets) were first given out there was a lot of animosity about it because I mean for the first ten months we worked here we didn't have a target, you just came in, did your work, so there wasn't any pressure on to do a certain amount any day . . . When I first started here, it was just a case of looking in the morning to see it had logged you on and looking at the end of the day to see how many you'd done . . . just out of curiosity, whereas now it's a constant 'every time you walk past the machine how many have I done', you know it's that type of thing now.

Pam's story illustrates clearly the way in which the clerks' relationship to the ICT system changed from seeing it as an interesting curiosity to surveillance bordering on obsession. This can be attributed to the symbolic importance of targets as 'defined' by management and 'accepted' by the clerks.

Management presented ICT and targets both as an empowering device enabling clerks to achieve their potential and as a powerful surveillance and disciplinary device for management. Somewhat contradictory in nature, both views were eloquently, and publicly, expressed on separate occasions by Garry:

My management style is simply that staff should come to work to enjoy themselves . . . er . . . and that in enjoying themselves will have . . . will be fulfilled . . . I also strongly believe that staff should be empowered . . . I do believe that staff should be encouraged to develop themselves.

this machine is wonderful, it tells me when you're breathing, eating, sleeping . . . some people look on this as a version of 1984 and Big Brother . . . if you think this is bad, wait till the future, stuff is being developed that will make this seem like heaven.

This contradiction in management's representation of targets and ICT was mirrored in clerks' attitudes: "I don't believe in any of this Big Brother stuff, *If you're good at your job you've got nothing to worry about*" (Terry, emphasis added). Terry's comments demonstrate an ambivalence that lies at the heart of management's attempts to control employee's subjectivities. Clerks adopt these self-disciplining practices to secure for themselves a positive identity as competent. Here self-discipline is closely associated to the way 'enterprise' and Garry would like clerks to be. As another clerk put it: "I think the responsibility is on yourself, cause if you don't work properly, I mean for me personally it's like letting yourself down. In all the years that I've worked, in all the jobs that I've been in I've always done the best I can do."

However, rather than signifying a full-embracing of the importance of targets for clerks' identities—clerks' 'acceptance' of targets was also informed by recognition of the disciplinary power of management. Pam's comments indicate this ambivalence (emphasis added):

> *you come in with the attitude "do the best you can" then no way can you let anybody down, so in a sense sort of like me coming into work, knowing that when I go home at the end of the day I've done everything I can do that day, so I think sort of . . . if you're responsible for your actions then you can't let anybody else down. No one can come back to me any day and say like 'you've not pulled your weight today', cause I know when I come in in the morning that's purely what I've come in to do.*

For the clerks, self-management is geared toward being 'the best they can'; competent in their job. No one wants to be seen as incompetent—even an unpaid researcher working in the department wants to reach the target! However, doing 'the best you can' is also a *tactic to avoid management discipline,* a response aimed at achieving *freedom from* sanctions and discipline. The defensive aspect of the clerks self-management is geared toward ensuring their performance figures fall at or slightly above management's criteria. Meeting the targets was a means of 'avoiding' managerial discipline rather than a full acceptance of the discourse of empowerment and enterprise.

However, this response did not overtly challenge discipline, nor was it likely to provide lasting security from future discipline. As one of the supervisors commented: "They will widen target bands when people like Tracy over-achieve, so they don't have to pay people for over-achieving on PMA (performance appraisal) . . . but you didn't hear that from me." In the short term, the goal of reaching targets is problematic as the energy one has to expend, the pace, and stress, all take their toll. As this section from field notes indicates:

> *[It is v]ery draining trying to work at target pace. Work is totally fragmented. I feel hassled, I'm sure I'm making errors somewhere, lots of pressure to keep speed up, not to press wrap-up. Taking a break I'm worried all my hard work will be undone by the 15 mins off—maybe I should go back early? . . . Lunch time I just feel drained and wasted, my head won't switch off. The first half hour I'm in a kind of daze—shell-shocked literally— I feel like I walk to the sandwich shop on auto-pilot. Once back in the lunchroom feel in-*

secure, I'm sure this is from the morning's work—have I made mistakes in my haste? I made
60 calls this morning—so I should reach my target at least.

It was not only the field worker who found the work stressful, pressurized and exhausting. The daily reality of work on the department made such feelings all but unavoidable. And similarly, it was not just the researcher who resisted the effects of this work on his life (*e.g.,* by not turning up one day, by deliberately taking full breaks when encouraged not to, by talking to other clerks about the problems of this sort of work, etc.). Resistance to the effects of targets/IT was an inseparable part of the clerks' days, and took many forms, from internal telephone calls, to chatting, joking, playing computer games, day dreaming, arguing with the team leader, and more. In the next section we concentrate upon one form of opposition to targets. A discourse of customer sovereignty was used by all clerks with varying degrees of conviction and success. It was an argument that served simultaneously to highlight the precariousness and tenaciousness of enterprise.

DISCOURSE OF CUSTOMER SOVEREIGNTY

Understanding the workings of the telephone banking department is a lesson in seeing the invisible. The customer is unseen, yet defines much of clerks' work. While you might expect the customer's physical distance would produce an indifferent and impersonal attitudes, the headset communications made the clerks feel intimately, almost incestuously, close. "I find myself rubbing my hands and adopting a quiet, confidential? tone—no not confidential—close—almost agony aunt like but with less 'gush'. Other people's voices; Pam has a 'soft' voice too—'caring'."

Because the voices are automatically piped through a headset, the customer seems to become reality, rather than an interruption of reality. Time *not* on call often seemed unreal, tea breaks or lunch breaks were spent in a kind of daze and were perceived as wasted time. "No customers—no reason to be here, chatting, yawning etc., no purpose without customers however. e.g. Mat 'Oh come on!' (i.e. come on customers). people looking around bored, yawning, chatting."

Given the pressure, competition, and stress of their work it is perhaps not surprising that clerks often looked beyond their immediate environment to find meaning for their work and ultimately for themselves. More specifically, clerks looked to customers for this meaning. Customers seemed real, immediate, and close. Defining one's work around images of 'customer service', 'quality to the customer', 'customer care' etc., offered a more appealing vocabulary than the managerial discourse of targets. The idea of helping the customer, of performing a 'useful activity,' gave the meaning to the job.

The instantaneous switch from talking with colleagues to talking with customers reinforced the sense of customer time being 'real' time. Customers took absolute precedence over colleagues. 'Conversations' with customers were always finished, whereas conversations with colleagues were normally interrupted. Thus colleagues conversations were often limited to trivia, sport, TV, etc. Occasionally, deeper and sometimes highly critical conversations between clerks did take place. These conversations included discussions about the nature of the work and the contradictory demands for *quantity* of calls taken and *quality* of service provided.

Customer service and helping customers formed the predominant counter-argument to the pressures of meeting targets. In some cases, appeals to 'the customer' were successful in reducing the targets. However, as a basis for questioning and resisting managerial control, the 'customer care' discourse was somewhat ambivalent.

> (*before the targets*) *I must admit I enjoyed* (*it*) *more because the quality of service you can give is a lot better when you've not got the pressure on that today you've got to do 81 and you've only done 50 and you've got 1 hour to go, you know its a case of getting everybody off the phone, and I think that side of it . . . you're then taking away the quality issue, erm, so that was like my argument not, I mean, Garry would come back and say 'yeah but you can do that' and I would say 'I don't dispute I can do it, I know I can do it, but what quality am I going to be giving?'* (Pam)

Here the clerk argued that the service provided to customers prior to the introduction of targets was superior in quality. She claimed that the targets created pressure to get customers off the phone, not to ensure higher quality service. Another clerk drew attention to the inconsistency and ultimate absurdity of the emphasis placed upon meeting targets:

> *If you pick up the phone 100 times a day and cut them off that's okay with Garry . . . I'm at odds with Garry over targets . . . it's not good customer service . . . I've got a target of 40 calls but I don't care—I do the job as I think it should be done . . . we're here to help people* (Christine).

Meeting the targets *per se* provided little sense of meaning or fulfillment for the clerks. The perceived quality of service and help provided an important source of meaning and value to the clerks. For the majority of them, arguments about customer care and quality remained at the level of discussion among themselves. These conversations provided them with an alternative metric of value and created 'psychic' space away from the pressure of targets. Personal contact with customers made it self-evident to the clerks that the customer wanted more time, better quality service, more care, etc. Field notes demonstrate this practice:

> *Today, stressed, can't remember lots of screens/procedures, sure I'm messing things up—it's the pressure—got to keep off wrap-up for the calls. Funny how I feel responsible to meet targets even though I'm not paid! It's a case of not letting targets be better than you, however I know my customers are suffering because of this pressure.*

Ideas about customer sovereignty helped protect clerks from an uncritical identification with targets. However, the belief that targets aren't everything, and that customers matter, did little to change the clerks' behavior, or to challenge management's focus upon speed and quantity. The idea of the sovereign customer helped clerks maintain a distance from management's targets, but its effectiveness as a more general challenge to managerial control or to the culture of enterprise is open to question.

ICT, CUSTOMER CARE, AND FRACTURES IN THE DISCOURSE OF ENTERPRISE

Clerks' identification with customers presented a decidedly double-edged challenge to management. At the same time serving as an alternative to management's emphasis upon targets, it tied clerks more fully to the ethical image of the sovereign customer: the image at the heart of enterprise. Customers' "needs" were privileged over the "needs" of the clerks as the image of the sovereign customer as the highest ethical ideal of life was reinforced. High targets were deemed to be bad not because they reduce the clerks' quality of life but because they are not what customers wanted (except perhaps insofar as they reduce the *immediate* cost of service).

By looking outside of themselves and their collective powers as suppliers of labor, processors of business and creators of wealth, clerks run the risk of further individualizing themselves and reproducing their weakness vis-à-vis management. An appeal to the customer is unlikely to improve the terms and conditions of employment for clerks not least because customers' "needs" are arguably only of instrumental and secondary concern to the managers of the telephone banking department whose performance is measured primarily in terms of a crude, calls-per-clerk, measure of productivity. This led him to use an enterprising and empowering discourse to increase the work-rate of clerks.

Clerks in other words are ostensibly appealing to a managerial rhetoric as an end in itself which management regards as a means to an end—a calculative rationality that is likely to ascribe an equivalent instrumentalism to the appeals of the clerks, and thereby interpret such appeals as self-interested pleas to relieve the pressures upon them.

To leave our analysis on this pessimistic point however would be mistaken. There are far more radical possibilities from clerks' resistance to management and identification with customers than a mere extrapolation from the current situation would suggest. Economic and sociological analysis often naturalizes the present and limits itself to seeing the future as 'more of the same' (Bauman 1994). Yet, the most cursory glance at history shows this understanding to be woefully unimaginative. In the clerks' assessments of 'enterprise,' we can see far more imaginative possibilities, particularly concerning the potential for clerks to realize the limitations, and make moves toward rejecting, the ethical ideal of individualism lying at the heart of enterprise, and capitalism more generally.

In their (successful) challenges and resistance to higher targets, clerks can reduce the capital that organizations can accrue and subsequently range against them. For instance, when clerks successfully reduce their targets, managers have to employ more staff to cover the calls, thus reducing their revenue and making it more difficult to introduce more advanced information systems with which to control staff. Furthermore, by counterposing managerial rhetoric of targets and quantitative measures of work with alternative images of quality and care, clerks maintain a cognitive distance from managers, and a conscious and deliberate difference between their own identifications and what they perceive management to stand for. This deliberate maintenance of difference between clerks and management identifications may be usefully understood as clerks' perceptions of their respective class distinctions. And although the discourse clerks use to maintain this distinction is (currently) centered around ideas of customer needs and customer sovereignty, which is itself part of the ethical/political rationality of enterprise, it is still fair to say that notions of care, and providing for people's needs, still sit uneasily with the underlying profit motive of capitalist institutions. As Berger (1972:184) writes, values of care and compassion are by no means politically ineffective, on the contrary in specific conditions "compassion can become the starting point of revolution against systems of inhumanity sustained by myth."

CONCLUSION

Drawing upon the work of du Gay and Salaman, we have highlighted the culture of enterprise as *the* dominant texture of postindustrial management culture. From organizational structures, to ideas about the role of the state, to images of personal ethics and modes of being, discourses and practices of enterprise are reconstructing our institutions and identities in ways which are more favorable for the reproduction and freedom of capital.

Although pervasive, we have stressed the fact that the culture of enterprise is not irresistibly imposed *upon us* from above, but is actively reproduced *by us,* through our practices and actions as well as by our silence and inaction. This gives rise to two issues: enterprise's reproduction and enterprise's resistance. Studying clerks' responses to the technologies and ethics of enterprise, we have attempted to show that enterprise's "seemingly coherent design for the radical transformation of social, cultural and economic arrangements" (du Gay and Salaman 1992:60) is in practice essentially contradictory and precarious. For example, by *meeting* targets set by management and enshrined in complex information and communication technologies, clerks acceded to and reproduced managerial control and management's definition of acceptable behavior. But by not 'believing in' targets as the (only or best) measure of their work and value, and by preferring identities constructed around helping the customer, clerks resisted identifying with management's conceptualization of work and their "seductive ethics of the self" (ibid), and thereby opened up the space to resist its claims upon them. The successes, and limitations of such tactics could well lead clerks not to simply reject the narrowness of commercially constructed boundaries of "customers' needs," but to reject much of the ideology and ethos of individualism and separation from colleagues that underpins their existing work identities, and upon which management fundamentally rely to manage their labor.

BIBLIOGRAPHY

Bauman, Z. (1994) *Alone Again: Ethics After Certainty,* London: Demos.

Berger, P. (1963,1972) *Invitation to Sociology: A Humanist Perspective,* Middlesex: Penguin Books.

du Gay, P. and G. Salaman (1992) "The Culture Of The Customer" *Journal of Management Studies* 29, 5, 615–633.

Peters, T. and R. Waterman (1982) *In Search of Excellence; Lessons from America's Best-Run Companies,* New York: Free Press.

Willmott, H. (1993) "Strength Is Ignorance Slavery Is Freedom: Managing Culture In Modern Organisations" *Journal of Management Studies,* 30, 4, 515–552.

Willmott, H. and E. Wray-Bliss (1995) "Process Reengineering, Information Technology And The Transformation Of Accountability: The Remaindering Of The Human Resource?" in Orlikowski, Walsham, Jones and DeGross, eds., *Information Technology and Changes in Organisational Work,* London: Chapman and Hall.

34

PERSONAL MEANING AND EXPLOITATION

Richard A. Goodman

In the last section, I wrote about the conundrum of the selfish and selfless and of the paradoxes between empowerment and community. This section faces in the opposite direction and focuses upon the individual and the individual's search for meaning. While this search is often an essential part of the discourse about exploitation, it is also a part of the discourse that privileges the individual. The search can be viewed either as one of direct conflict between the individual and the organization or it can be seen as soft-edged discomfort with organizational processes. It is highly personal in its origin but may very well be driven by organizational systems.

The work reported in earlier sections on Mondragon by Patricia Riley and Lisa Howard describes organizational settings in which personal meaning and organizational intent are aligned. This is a rather unusual occurrence but nevertheless it is the subject of frequent newspaper articles and even stimulates students to frame job-hunting as searches for meaningful opportunities. The work reported by Bruce Hanson in his "Road and Stream" chapter reports a radically different type of organizational setting, albeit one in which personal meaning and organizational processes are also aligned.

Within this section there are four papers that focus on personal meaning and exploitation. They vary considerably in their perspectives, as they should. Three are essentially philosophically based, while one is empirically based. They engage at the organizational level of study as well as at the individual level.

David Bubna-Litic in "Servants of Greed: Postindustrial SubCulture(s) from a Buddhist Perspective" describes the essential postmodern nature of Buddhism and argues that postindustrial professionals looking for depth and soul in their work lives could and do embrace many of the fundamentals of Buddhism. Here I focus on the Buddhist fundamental that all of the world is deeply interconnected. Martin Fuglsang also described this in his chapter about the biotechnology industry, which he found was true to postmodern phenomenology in that the interconnectedness of the industry could not be analyzed. Bruce Hanson's study of a Japanese electronics firm also found that reality is intensely interconnected; a reality that made planning or linear processes ineffective. When this was understood and the work processes adapted to the robust reality, effectiveness improved in both settings.

Extraordinarily interconnected reality is a fundamental feature of Buddhist thought. Thus it is probably not surprising to find that a Japanese firm would embrace an organizational design grounded in this Buddhist conceptualization. After all, there is a significant Buddhist presence in Japan. David Bubna-Litic argues that egoistic thinking is the source of the complement to this fundamental of interconnected reality, separation and control, and serves to separate private benefit from organizational or community benefit.

Accepting the premise that all things are connected implies that work can be as meaningful as non-work and that personal meaning should be obtainable within the activities that constitute work. Because of admitted interconnections it further follows that work derived personal meaning must also be connected to community. Work in many traditions, Buddhist and others, is a powerful tool for gaining and expressing deep insights into daily life.

Since it places the master narrative beyond discourse, the Buddhist fundamental of high interconnectedness also undercuts the entire basis of (modernist and postmodernist) analysis. (Also a conclusion of Fuglsang's work.) We might understand this with a metaphor of a parallel universe. Modernists act as if they believe in separation rather than connection. Thus they subscribe to the dual tenets of measurement and control rather than evolutionary adjustment while in parallel subscribers to Buddhist thought act from the opposite fundamental understanding of nature. Within the metaphor of a parallel universe both processes or activities are occurring at the same time and in an intertwined fashion.

What is the opposite of plans and measurement, of modernist concerns? There are several concepts that partially fit into the opposition camp. Nate Grunstein argues, for example, that 'progress' or 'movement' only needs direction and intent. Thus one can point in a particular direction and then employ efforts to move in that direction. The complexities of reality will prevent straight-line movement but since linearity is not expected, the 'measure' of progress needs to be a non-measure. This approach may not bring us all the way to the Buddhist answer but it does soften the sense of target and measurement.

In my interpretation of the Hanson article, this movement toward Buddhist fundamentals is reflected in an organizational design that created enabling conditions for fruitful evolution. The 'beginner's mind' permitted openness and attainment of integrity from work. In Buddhist thought the beginner's mind displays a willingness to see everything as if for the first time, rather than starting with prior assumptions. From this position, work with compassionate action is possible and community can become more fully integrated into work life.

In "Yogic Principles and Management Practice" Elisabeth Wilson begins with a fundamental question that mirrors the same Buddhist question that David framed in his paper. Is it possible to build a management system based upon specific ethical principles, acknowledgment of embodiment, self-aware control of emotion, concentration and meditation as routes to decision-making, and embrace the spirituality that characterizes yogic practice? The central ethical stance of her question is one of selflessness. This ethic heightens the potential for community by strengthening the sense of personal meaning.

We might well expect to find critical differences between the profit and not-for-profit sectors since the not-for-profit organizations usually embrace missions focused on compassion and community. Unfortunately however, even these organizations are being pushed by tenets of managerialism to focus on achievement and measurement. Ultimately, everything else including the furtherance of relationships is subordinated to this purpose.

Elisabeth's description of yoga is also one of a highly interconnected system—a holistic system. One shortcoming inherent in engaging a holistic system is that it is neither linear nor solely intellectual. 'Knowledge' and 'understanding' are similar but at a deeper level understanding develops slowly even with knowledge. Thus, understanding must be developed both intuitively and spiritually. This speaks to the individual focus of understanding and refocuses attention on the conflict between 'measurement and control' and individual understanding.

Interesting is the number of yogic words found in current management use. Since the meaning of a word or an activity is slowly unveiled by use and experience, and the selection of words used are not 'accidental' but 'fit' at a deeper level, Elisabeth's analysis suggests an underside to management that is searching for deeper meaning to its own activities.

Georges Bataille's contribution to this section is an interesting argument involving capitalism, business ethics, and potlatch. Omid Nodoushani in "The Return of 'The Invisible Hand'" reminds us of the reality behind capitalism. This reality involves significant examples of citizenship behavior and derives from organizational members being themselves members of multiple cultures and multiple referent groups. Thus in the best of times, individual loyalties are fragmented. Pure capitalism does not really exist except as it is often used in critical discourse. We can find too many examples of behavior that are not consonant with conventional notions of capitalism. This can be seen at a very pragmatic level. Many years ago after a fire struck my family's business, several local competitors both large and small provided production facilities and other assistance so that we could stay in business. The theme of this story is reciprocity among rivals and it implies an ethic of citizenship behavior not directly found in capitalism. It is clearly not a logical extension of Adam Smith.

Bataille argues that capitalism begins with giving. Feasting and potlatching illustrate a capitalist tendency to assemble and distribute wealth since the essence of a free-enterprise system is in supplying first and acquiring later. The capitalist must acquire inventory and pay staff before receiving revenue from customers. This period of investment is a difficult one that actually extends throughout the life of the firm. By investing, buying, manufacturing and stocking finish goods, the firm has created a gift which may or may not be of further value. In a Barnardian sense, it is the customers that determine the value of the firm.

Within this argument, the business ethic is one of community. The potlatch phenomena though has an individual focus as individuals are encouraged to gather resources primarily so they can give them away later. Within this structure, personal meaning is derived from the rite of giving and efforts are directed toward accumulation to facilitate largess. Within this setting, personal meaning is the antithesis of exploitation.

Edward Wray-Bliss and Hugh Willmott in "Battling with the Gods: Workers, Management and the Deities of Postindustrial Management Culture" describe the interaction of managerialism and information technology to isolate individuals employees within a competition-driven management discourse. They explore both the ethics and the influence of the Customer and Information Technology in an inherently exploitive system. They use the term 'enterprising' to refer to the firms themselves and to the management discourse about individual employee work behavior.

Based on their field work they describe the workers' reproduction of, and resistance to, an emergent culture of enterprise where the organizational design aligned the employee with the customer and rather than with their colleagues or with the firm as a whole. This permitted the clerks to deploy customer needs as arguments to fight off the influence of management measurement and control. Here the only meaning permitted to the employee was customer satisfaction. The organizational design created a high-stress environment and a situation where there was no opportunity for collaboration.

Unlike Bataille, Wray-Bliss and Willmott focus on the negative aspects of capitalism in much the same way that Clark, Chandler and Barry focused on the dysfunctions of managerialism. Edward and Hugh emphasize that all too often through action and inaction, employees actively reproduce the very system that is imposed on them. When the organization is logically examined from the fundamentals of Buddhist or even yogic thought, the essential complexities give rise to an understanding of the organization's managerial intent as existentially contradictory and precarious. Organizational design efforts cannot be expected to create a coherent holistic result when the real situation is so complex and interconnected. This provides room for employee resistance through the direct use of discourses about both the customer and enterprise. Clerks can and do resist the dysfunction of the ideology and the ethos of individualism and separation from colleagues that underpins their existing work identities.

This counter argument based upon exploitation suggests that the search for personal meaning remains a central concern for employees. It also reinforces the notions that the counter-initiatives of individualism and managerialism pose a serious conundrum for the next millennium.

ABOUT THE CONTRIBUTORS

Iiris Aaltio-Marjosola, Lappeenranta Technical University, FINLAND
Ian Atkin, Bolton Institute, UNITED KINGDOM
Jim Barry, University of East London, UNITED KINGDOM
Michèle A. Bowring, University of Alberta, CANADA
David Bubna-Litic, University of Technology, Sydney, AUSTRALIA
John Chandler, University of East London, UNITED KINGDOM
Sylvie Chevrier, ESSEC, FRANCE
Heather Clark, University of East London, UNITED KINGDOM
Martin Fuglsang, Copenhagen Business School, DENMARK
Christina Garsten, Stockholm University, SWEDEN
Richard A. Goodman, UCLA, UNITED STATES
Wendy Guild, Massachusetts Institute of Technology, UNITED STATES
Janet L. Hamnett, University of Calgary, CANADA
Bruce Hanson, Pepperdine University, UNITED STATES
Julia Harrison, Trent University, CANADA
Lisa Howard, University of Southern California, UNITED STATES
Sarah Williams Jacobson, North Dakota State University, UNITED STATES
B. James, University of Hertfordshire, UNITED KINGDOM
M. L. James, Mill Hill County High School, UNITED KINGDOM
Ulla Johansson, Lund University, SWEDEN
Ken Khoury, University of California, San Diego, UNITED STATES
Gro Kvåle, Bodø College, NORWAY
Monica Lee, Lancaster University, UNITED KINGDOM
Virpi Leikola, University of Art and Design, FINLAND
Mike Lowe, Bolton Institute, UNITED KINGDOM
Laurie A. Meamber, Loyola Marymount University, UNITED STATES
Omid Nodoushani, University of New Haven, UNITED STATES
Elisabeth Pettersen, Bodø College, NORWAY
Margaret E. Phillips, Pepperdine University, UNITED STATES
Dick Raspa, Wayne State University, UNITED STATES
Patricia Riley, University of Southern California, UNITED STATES

Anette Risberg, Lund University, SWEDEN
Kathryn S. Rogers, Pitzer College, UNITED STATES
Sonja A. Sackmann, University BW, GERMANY
Burkard Sievers, Bergische Universität Wuppertal, GERMANY
Hugh Willmott, University of Manchester Institute of Science and Technology,
   UNITED KINGDOM
Elisabeth M. Wilson, Manchester University, UNITED KINGDOM
Thomaz Wood Jr., Escola de Administracao de Empresas de Sao Paulo, BRAZIL
Edward Wray-Bliss, University of Manchester Institute of Science and Technology,
   UNITED KINGDOM